VICTOR HUGO'S
Conversations with
THE SPIRIT WORLD

VICTOR HUGO'S
Conversations with
THE SPIRIT WORLD

A LITERARY GENIUS'S
HIDDEN LIFE

JOHN CHAMBERS

Introduction by Martin Ebon
Illustrations by Peri Poloni-Gabriel

DESTINY
BOOKS

Destiny Books
Rochester, Vermont

Destiny Books
One Park Street
Rochester, Vermont 05767
www.DestinyBooks.com

Destiny Books is a division of Inner Traditions International

Library of Congress Cataloging-in-Publication Data
Hugo, Victor, 1802–1885.
   Victor Hugo's conversations with the spirit world : a literary genius's hidden life / John Chambers ; introduction by Martin Ebon ; illustrations by Peri Poloni-Gabriel.
   — Rev. and expanded 2nd ed.
       p. cm.
   Rev. ed. of: Conversations with eternity. 1998.
   Summary: "First English translation of Victor Hugo's writings on his experiments in spiritualism"—Provided by publisher.
   Includes bibliographical references and index.
   ISBN-13: 978-1-59477-182-8
   ISBN-10: 1-59477-182-0
   1. Table-moving (Spiritualism) 2. Channeling (Spiritualism) 3. Spiritualism.
I. Chambers, John, 1939– II. Hugo, Victor, 1802–1885. Conversations with eternity.
III. Title.
   BF1375.H84 2008
   133.9'1—dc22
                                                                    2007038463

Printed and bound in the United States by Lake Book Manufacturing

10   9   8   7   6   5   4   3   2   1

Text design and layout by Priscilla Baker
This book was typeset in Sabon, with Cezanne and Gill Sans as display typefaces

TO MY MOTHER AND FATHER
AND TO JUDY

※※

CONTENTS

❧❦

❧❦

ACKNOWLEDGMENTS

I would like, once again, to express my profound gratitude to Martin Ebon (1917–2006), who wrote the introduction to this book, and without whose generous help, as mentor, as benefactor, and especially as friend, there would be no book. I've seen people's eyes fill with tears when they tried to tell me of the wonderful things Martin Ebon did for them; I am one of those people.

I am also indebted to Diana Neutze, Julia Jones, Marilyn Raphael, Patricia Pereira, Doug Kenyon (editor of *Atlantis Rising*), Patrick Huyghe (editor of *The Anomalist*), Guyon Neutze (Professor of Philosophy, Wellington Polytechnic, Wellington, New Zealand), Dr. Istvan Deak (Seth Low Professor Emeritus of Central and East Central European Studies, Columbia University, New York) and, of course, Judy, my wife, who every day made every bit of it possible.

Finally, I would like to bow deeply, respectfully, and gratefully in the direction of the very distinguished British author who, through the years, has given me priceless guidance, though on condition of anonymity.

The Non-living Dramatis Personae (Historical and Abstract) of *Victor Hugo's Conversations with the Spirit World*

These are the names of the spirits who spoke through the turning tables, in alphabetical order and with the number of appearances. Those with asterisks after their name are the spirits who actually make an appearance, however brief, in this book.

Abel (1)
Aeschylus* (4)
Aesop (1)
Alexander (1)
Amelia (a fairy)* (1)
Amuca (Babac) (1)
Anacreon (1)
André (Pinson's
  brother)* (1)
Apuleus (1)
Archangel Love, The (1)
Aristophanes (1)
Aristotle (1)
Balaam's Ass* (1)
Batthyány, Louis* (1)
Being Speaking Latin (1)
Being, A (1)
Bonnivard (1)
Byron* (1)
Cagliostro (1)
Cain (1)
Cerpola the Shepherd (1)
Cesarion (1)
Charlet (1)
Chateaubriand (1)
Chénier, André* (7)
Cimarosa* (1)
Civilization* (1)
Comedy (1)
Comet, A* (1)
Corday, Charlotte (1)
Criticism* (2)
Damianiels (1)
Dante* (1)
Death* (7)
Delorme, Marion (1)
Diderot (1)
Diogenes (1)

Drama, The* (16)
Finger of Death, The (1)
Flamel, Nicholas* (1)
Galileo* (2)
Glory (1)
Grim Gatekeeper, The* (1)
Hannibal* (1)
Happiness (1)
Haynau* (1)
Idea, The* (6)
India (1)
Inspiration (1)
Iron Mask, The (1)
Isaac Laquedem (1)
Isaiah (1)
Jacob* (1)
Jesus Christ* (6)
Joan of Arc (1)
Joshua* (3)
Judas (1)
Lady in White, The* (3)
Lais (1)
Latude (1)
Leonidas (1)
Lion of Androcles,
  The* (18)
Lion of Florence, The (1)
Lope de Vega (1)
Louis-Philippe (1)
Luther* (2)
Machiavelli* (1)
Marat (1)
Marie-Blanche (1)
Metempsychosis* (1)
Muhammad (1)
Molière (11)
Moses (1)
Mother, Durrieu's (1)

Mozart* (3)
Napoleon I (The Great)* (1)
Napoleon III (The Little)* (1)
Novel, The (3)
Ocean, The* (2)
Plato* (1)
Poetry (1)
Prayer (1)
Racine (1)
Raphael (1)
Reverie (1)
Robespierre (1)
Roothan (1)
Rousseau, Jean-Jacques* (2)
Russia (1)
Sappho (1)
Sesostris (1)
Shadow of the Sepulcher,
  The* (9)
Shakespeare* (11)
Sister Soul (*Ame Soror*)* (1)
Socrates (2)
Spirits, Assorted* (7)
Table draws a series of
  Pictures* (2)
Tragedy (1)
Tyatafia (from Jupiter)* (1)
Tyrtius (1)
Vestra (1)
Vestris (1)
Voltaire (2)
Vulcan (1)
Vux (1)
Walter Scott, Sir* (1)
White Wing, The (1)
Sea Wind, The (1)
Z (2)
Zoile (1)

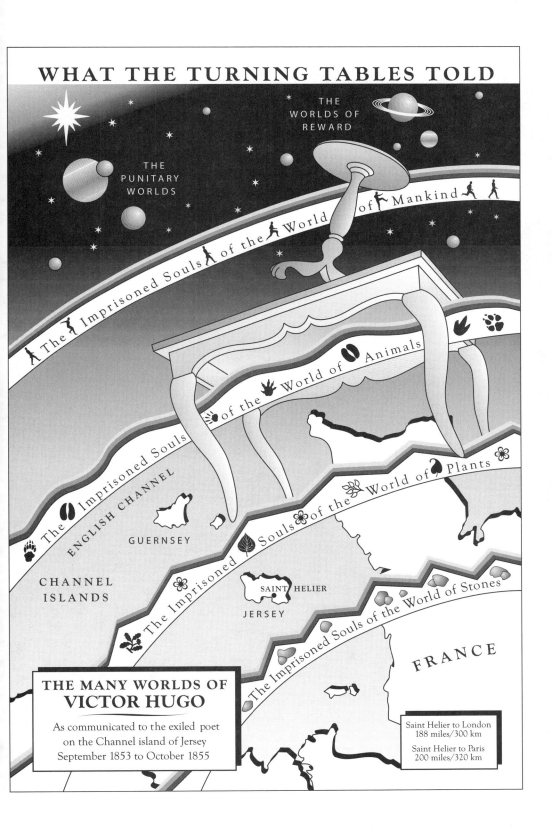

Introduction

"VICTOR THE GRANDIOSE"

By Martin Ebon

In the fall of 1950, I was sitting in a half-empty office at the Voice of America in New York surrounded by books, files, and clippings on the subject of Indochina. I had just been appointed to direct the newly established Vietnamese Unit of the United States' short-wave and medium-wave broadcasts to Vietnam, having previously served as head of the information agency's broadcasts to Indonesia. (Later, I would take over the Hindi and Urdu units, transmitting to India and Pakistan.) Now, I had to immerse myself in the political-economic and religio-cultural milieu of a new target area: Vietnam. Remember, this was years before the United States became involved in the Vietnam War; at that time, the armed struggle was for the future of Korea.

All went smoothly until I came to the religious orientations of the Vietnamese people and read that the third-largest religious movement, after Roman Catholicism and Buddhism, was a denomination known as the Cao Dai. I read that this was, broadly speaking, an amalgam of Eastern and Western faiths and that one of its three major saints was the French poet-novelist-playwright and politically volatile personage, Victor Hugo (1802–1885). I had a fairly good idea of Hugo as a commanding literary figure in Europe of the nineteenth century; but, aware of his controversial lifestyle, I had never thought of him as a saint of anything, anywhere, at any time. And what, exactly, was the Cao Dai?

Bear with me for a minute! Caodaism considers itself "the third alliance between God and man." Its actual founder was Ngô-văn-Chiêu, born in 1878, a civil servant for a short time in Saigon, who, in 1902, underwent the spiritistic experience that literally "inspired" him to found this all-encompassing religion. Thus, the movement's belief system was rooted in the region's deep spiritistic traditions; with followers numbering in excess of two million today, it represents God's third attempt to convey his ultimate truths to humanity. In November 1926, Chiêu revealed the conclusions of his four years of mediumistic contacts with the dead, many of whom were distinguished and prominent.[1]

Chiêu regarded the first attempt at conveying the divine message as coinciding with the emergence of Buddhism, Confucianism, and Taoism; the second contact was personified by Moses, and the third contact focused on the Middle Buddha, this being a much later adaptation of Buddhism (which had gone through a variety of stages and regional adaptations). These three successive waves of spiritual force were what came to make up Caodaism.[2] As an amalgam of Eastern and Western religious principles, Caodaism embraces universal ethical standards and has widely adopted vegetarianism. "Cao Dai" may be translated as "Tower of the Highest," a metaphor for God. The religion's unique characteristic lies in its combination of traditional, actually prehistoric, ancestor worship; its rituals that closely resemble such spiritistic techniques as trance mediumship; and so-called automatic writing.[3]

One Cao Dai link to Victor Hugo appears to be his own voluminous spirit communications, detailed in this volume, which took place while Hugo's family was in exile on the Channel island of Jersey. In fact, the wide-ranging messages from prominent personalities, collected by Caodaism, closely resemble the astonishing number of alleged historic spirit entities who manifested at the Jersey séances. The Hugo sittings, as far as we can tell, centered on the spiritistic rapping movements of a table leg, or actual table turning. Initially, Caodaistic spirit communications were undertaken by table turning. When participants complained that this was an extremely time-consuming technique, the entities suggested that they try instead what appears to be a very sophisticated variation of traditional spiritistic automatic writing. The central device was a wicker basket shaped like an upside-down crow. Four ropes were attached to the basket, which was known as a *corbeille à bec*. Each rope was held by a different medium, so that no single personality would, in any way, be the sole instrument of communication. The basket was positioned in such a way that the "beak" of its crow-shape made contact with flat, fine sand beneath; thus, the writings were visible in the sand.[4]

The Cao Dai spirit of Victor Hugo evolved from communications originating with an entity that initially called itself Nguyêt-Tâm-Chon-Nhon but later stated that it was, in fact, the spirit of the famous Victor Hugo. Adherents have meticulously recorded that the first, momentous encounter with this spirit took place on April 20, 1930, at 1:00 a.m., the earthly interviewer being one Hô-Pháp.[5] A bit later, the entity said that one prominent Caodaist, Trân-Quang-Vinh, was, actually, a reincarnation of the French poet's third son, François-Victor Hugo (1828–1873). Trân later became head of the Cao Dai Army, and eventually Minister of Defense (1948–1951) in the ill-fated government of Bao Dai. During a session of the Cao Dai's legislative body, the deceased Victor Hugo was appointed titular head of the movement's "foreign missions," that is, its actual ambassadorial representation abroad.[6]

One of many messages received by the Caodaists from the alleged spirit of Victor Hugo speaks eloquently of beauty, divine peace and harmony, science and wisdom, as well as of the spirit's perception that "there are . . . other universes than ours in the infinite." Moreover, "their creatures know not the word 'war'" and in these worlds "soul-power is master of human weakness." The entity also communicated that "death will be vanquished by uplifted conscience. There is no difference between living and dead."[7]

Now, back to the flesh and blood Victor Hugo, whose extraordinary prominence evolved within a very specific psycho-cultural and religio-political framework of nineteenth-century France and, specifically, within the highly politicized literary society of Paris. To say that Victor Hugo, throughout his life, was a man of multiple contradictions comes close to understatement.

Victor Hugo was the third son of a brash, self-centered father who served in the army of Napoleon Bonaparte, or Emperor Napoleon I (1769–1821), as a general: General Joseph-Léopold-Sigisbert Hugo (1773–1828). General Hugo was intermittently stationed abroad in Italy and Spain, and his family accompanied him on occasion. While Victor's father was, at least by reasons of career, a monarchist, his mother, Sophie, was, by private sentiment and conviction, republican and, therefore, anti-monarchist. Father and mother managed to get along with one another by employing a mixture of mutual disregard and opportunistic tolerance.[8]

Victor Hugo himself remained a monarchistic republican and a republicanistic monarchist, a liberal and a conservative, an elitist and a populist for most of his contradictory life. In retrospect, it is difficult to imagine the impact of a literary colossus such as Hugo during the century that his life spanned. No matter how eccentric or volatile his beliefs might have been, at any given time he was capable of expressing them in prose or poetry of such multifarious power that he could provoke the roaring cheers of the Parisian masses as well as the jealousy-tainted approval of his peers and rivals.

What was he, then?

Well, what was he not?

The term *mad genius* has pretty well gone out of fashion. But in some ways it may have applied to Victor Hugo. With due respect for exact clinical terminology, one might well generalize that he fitted, at one time or another, the categories of egomaniac, mythomaniac, and, quite possibly, manic-depressive. His hunger for admiration could never be filled. He was eager for honors and awards, such as membership in the Académie Française. He was elected to parliament, where he made long, provocative, and at times barely coherent speeches. But even if readers found it difficult to comprehend the "deeper meaning" of one of his long, metaphor-ridden poems, they might still be pulled along by the soaring rhythm of his words. Listeners, in turn, could be carried away by the fire of his passion, by his rousing, lyrical, oratorical fireworks. The fierce power behind it all was not only the fire of Hugo's genius but also the unquenchable thirst to be admired, loved, and even worshipped.

The French Empire, under Napoleon the Great, the Corsican Joseph Bonaparte (1769–1821)—who had placed the royal crown on his own head at the Cathedral of Notre Dame on December 2, 1804—spread all over Europe. One conquest demanded yet another, and still another. (And all this neo-monarchistic expansionism happened, we must remember, after the bloody, history-making, anti-monarchist French Revolution of 1789.)

Napoleon's armies swept on. Most of Europe was overrun. As the grand conquests continued, the apparently invincible emperor was hugely popular throughout France and aroused admiration, sincere or opportunistic, within much of Europe. Yet England and Russia eluded him. Eventually, grossly overextended, Napoleon had to retreat from Moscow in 1812. With this he seemed to retreat from history as well.

Victor Marie Hugo was born in Besançon on February 26, 1802.[9] So when Napoleon abdicated his throne on April 11, 1814, young Victor was twelve years old. Napoleon was exiled to the island of Elba off the west coast of Italy, and a member of the royal Bourbon family, Louis XVIII, took over the reign of the disillusioned nation. But, with surprising speed and daring, Napoleon made his stunning comeback. On March 15, 1815, he arrived on France's Mediterranean coast with an army of one thousand men. They rapidly marched up to Paris; Napoleon reconquered an unresisting France in three weeks. The masses, fickle and frightened, re-embraced the man whom they had reviled as a monster only months before. But this grand illusion was quickly followed by total disillusion: Napoleon's effort to reconquer Europe ended with his ultimate defeat on June 18 at the Battle of Waterloo. He abdicated a second time. Napoleon was taken into exile once more and died on the island of Saint Helena, five thousand miles away in the South Atlantic on May 5, 1821. He was fifty-two years old.

The end of the Napoleonic era marked the end of the profitable military career of General Hugo. Son Victor, with his older brothers Eugène and Joseph-Abel, had accompanied their mother to Italy for a brief stay with the general when the future poet was five years old.[10] When he was nine, the Hugo family settled in occupied Spain, where General Hugo had been appointed governor of the provinces of Guadalajara and Segovia. Victor was fascinated by the exotic scenery and picked up some of the Spanish language. He also mastered Latin. When Napoleon's forces retreated from Spain in early 1812, the Hugo family accompanied them, arriving back in Paris in April. Victor had spent fourteen months in France's war-torn neighbor to the south.[11]

The Hugo family, like much of the society that had allied itself with Napoleon, had fallen on relatively hard times. Victor received a rather scrappy education. From early 1815 to late 1818 he lived at a modest Parisian boarding school called the Pension Cordier, taking his lessons there and at the nearby Louis-le-Grand College. His literary fascinations burgeoned. He had always admired the work of Voltaire (1694–1778), perhaps the leading figure of the eighteenth-century Enlightenment movement. Now Hugo read voraciously. He also did quite well in philosophy, geometry, and physics.[12]

Soon his volcanic literary talents began to erupt, and he wrote a string of verses, odes, satires, acrostics, riddles, epics, and madrigals. Victor's brother Joseph-Abel edited a journal, *Le Conservateur Littéraire*.[13] Along with a great deal of quite marginal writings, Victor contributed a lengthy, highly charged short story, *Bug-Jargal,* to the short-lived periodical. It would be published in expanded form in 1826 as his second novel (his first, *Han d'Islande* [*Hans of Iceland*], would be published in 1823). The eponymous hero of *Bug-Jargal* is the black leader of a slave revolt in San Domingo. The novel is packed with fantasy and the gothic horror popular at the time. But *Bug-Jargal* is also unusual in its virtually prejudice-free depiction of the great courage and Christian virtues of Bug-Jargal.[14]

That in later years Victor Hugo achieved a wide popular readership was due in part to elements of horror and the macabre in much of his writing. These elements peek out only briefly in the Broadway musical version of Hugo's universally acclaimed *Les Misérables*—his great novel, published in 1862, of the poor, the maltreated, and the deprived. Those who have seen the Disney cartoon version of Hugo's melodramatic third novel *Notre-Dame de Paris* (*The Hunchback of Notre Dame*) are deprived of the ultimate macabre scene, which shows the skeletons of the hunchback, Quasimodo, and his much pursued lady love, Esmeralda, in a final, mortal embrace.

Victor's mother died in June 1821.[15] He asked his father for money. General Hugo refused. Secretly engaged to his childhood sweetheart Adèle Foucher, Victor Hugo spent a year sweating it out on the fringes of poverty. His observations during this period would later provide material for *Les Misérables*. Hugo could not have written in his uninhibited style had the traditional, so-called classical literary style continued to prevail. Victor Hugo, who sometimes composed full-length poems virtually in his sleep, refused to be confined to a literary straitjacket he regarded as outdated and essentially meaningless. He thus became the most prominent spokesman of a literary approach that, for much of the century, flourished under the benign label of Romanticism.

But romanticism, in that period's literary sense, does not correspond to our popular and contemporary meaning of the term. Today, romanticism is commonly identified with the purely erotic: the romance novel, romantic love, and the word *romance* as indicating a love affair. Consequently, dictionary definitions of romanticism are forced to cite disparate interpretations. One that would apply to the Hugo period describes *romanticism* as a "literary and artistic movement, originating in Europe toward the end of the eighteenth century, that sought to assert the validity of subjective experience and to escape from the prevailing subordination of content and feeling to classical forms." Of course, romanticism included, in its emphasis on "the validity of subjective experience," the specifically erotic, possibly the most subjective of all human experiences.[16]

Victor Hugo had entered the Parisian literary-political scene at ramming speed. He quickly perfected the game of sending groveling letters of thanks to his teachers and other betters, often by writing odes in their praise. Graham Robb, in his comprehensive work *Victor Hugo: A Biography,* states that his "most successful ode was the poetic begging bowl held out to 'M. le Comte François de Neufchateau, of l'Académie Française';[17] such barefaced, pandering appeals to distinguished men of letters would get Hugo far. It earned Hugo a powerful patron."

It also revealed his early understanding, and skillful manipulation, of the powerful, the rich, and the decision-makers, both in literary and political affairs. Among other deals, Hugo became Neufchateau's secret ghostwriter and his career-building-by-ingratiation accelerated as he entered his twenties. He targeted the French court, and specifically the person of Louis XVIII. Hugo's device was a volume of verses, *Odes et poésies diverses,* which contained the appropriate number of love poems for his fiancée, Adèle Foucher, but was clearly designed to attract the sentimental attention of Louis XVIII. In fact, Hugo's elegy in memory of the Duc de Berry, the king's nephew who was assassinated in 1820, is said to have brought tears to the eyes of the monarch. He gave Hugo a pension from the privy purse. This was in 1822, and Hugo was just twenty years old. The following year, the pension was doubled.[18]

With money in his pocket, Hugo heightened his courtship of Adèle. Professionally, Victor Hugo continued his output of prose and poetry. He had never been to Iceland, and his popular fantasy-and-horror novel, *Han d'Islande,* featured Hugo's first disfigured protagonist (in the vein of the hunchback Quasimodo), Han, a red-haired dwarf. Robb summarizes the plot with as much detachment as seems possible:

The novel opens promisingly in the morgue at Trondheim. Bodies have been found torn to shreds as if by a long-nailed beast. Meanwhile, among the icy crags to the north lurks a weird, red-haired dwarf, the son of a witch and the last descendant of Ingulphus the Exterminator. Abandoned in Iceland, the hideous infant–Han was taken in by a saintly bishop (a forerunner of Bishop Myriel in *Les Misérables*). Immune to Christian charity, he torches the bishop's palace and sets sail by the light of the flames on a tree-trunk, bound for Norway. There, he incinerates Trondheim cathedral, whose flying buttresses now resemble the rib cage of a mammoth's carcass. He slaughters regiments, hurls mountains down onto villages, extinguishes beacons with a single breath, carries a stone axe and rides a polar bear called "Friend." He also provides a tenuous link with the rest of the novel by stealing the casket, which contains proof of the father's innocence.[19]

Considering that not only Broadway but also Hollywood have discovered Victor Hugo's works, this horror fantasy might yet find a fresh market, either as a sex-and-violence motion picture (with earlier episodes on television), or as a musical melodrama. Robb comments that the horror novel and Hugo's letters to Adèle "spanned two years of unrequited lust, and formed a ramshackle bridge over the abyss opened by his mother's death" on June 21, 1821.[20]

In order to be able to marry Adèle, Hugo had applied to the king for yet another pension. He managed to get it, and the two were married on October 12, 1822. The great and lasting family tragedy was that Victor's brother Eugène Hugo was passionately in love with Adèle; but Eugène had shown signs of mental imbalance from time to time. If we can trust melodramatic records, he went mad on the day of the wedding and ultimately had to be committed to an asylum where he died in 1837.[21]

Meanwhile Victor's prominence was increasing, as he maintained a delicate balance between his neo-monarchist conservatism and the emerging literary revolution. He received the Legion of Honor as well as a personal invitation to the coronation of Charles X at Rheims.[22]

The next decades reinforced his position as France's outstanding progressive literary figure. Novels, poems, and plays flowed from his pen. Their content and form reflected a spirit of emotional liberation, which inevitably put him once again at odds with monarchistic paternalism. The symbol of this literary-political conflict was Hugo's play

Hernani, which he wanted to be performed at that center of French theatrical arts, the Comédie Française.

On the surface, *Hernani* was just another exotic, fanciful melodrama set in Spain. It centers on the fate of a beautiful young girl, in love with a handsome persecuted hero, who seeks to rebuff the advances of several repulsive old men—one of whom is a royal personality, a lustful sovereign named Don Carlos. "Carlos" is Spanish for Charles. Was Hugo making a veiled comment about Charles X in particular and royalty in general? The opening night of the play became the scene of a war of generations, with teenagers in open revolt against social restrictions. On the afternoon of Thursday, February 25, 1830, a huge line began to form outside the theater, clogging up the Rue Richelieu.

During the performance, rowdy applause followed particularly outrageous lines—as when the young hero tells pretty Doña Sol's lecherous guardian, "Go and get yourself measured for a coffin, old man." Satire became standard tragedy, as in the final act when Hernani and Doña Sol die in each other's arms. According to Graham Robb, the audience erupted into "simultaneous booing and cheering; fisticuffs and arrests." It was, Robb adds, prophetic "enactment—even, in some minds, a direct cause—of what was about to happen on the streets."[23]

With success came prosperity. The Hugo family moved to new quarters, a comfortable apartment on Rue Jean-Goujon, surrounded by fresh air, trees, and a lawn. Victor and Adèle Hugo had three children by then: Léopoldine, Charles, and François-Victor, soon to be joined by a fourth, conveniently called Adèle II (a third son, Léopold, the firstborn, had died at the age of three months). But success took an emotional toll. Victor Hugo became more and more autocratic, egocentric, and eccentric. His literary output would, if anything, be exceeded by his conveyor belt of sexual liaisons. He would become, in current terms, a stud, and women would yield or pursue him like groupies.

These activities were in part precipitated by the tentative liaison that his wife, Adèle, had formed with Hugo's old friend, the respected literary critic Charles-Augustin Sainte-Beuve (1804–1869) not long before Adèle II was born. Dramatically, Sainte-Beuve used to sneak into the Hugo apartment disguised as a nun when Hugo was elsewhere. The affair ended when Sainte-Beuve rather abjectly confessed his love for Adèle to Hugo.[24]

Meanwhile, on the streets of Paris, history caught up with Hugo's revolutionary play, *Hernani*. On July 25, 1830, Charles X dissolved parliament and abolished freedom of the press. A bloody three-day uprising followed (July 27–29), and Louis-Philippe was crowned "King of the French."[25] Monarchy was back in full force. It was also a new disaster. But Hugo was undeterred in his creative energies: in March 1831, *Notre Dame de Paris* appeared in the bookshops, which, as *The Hunchback of Notre Dame,* achieved lasting fame.[26]

But first, on the seesaw between public life and sex, back to sex! On February 2, 1833, Hugo's latest play, *Lucrezia Borgia,* opened at the Porte-Saint-Martin Theatre. The part of Princess Negroni had been given to a young, beautiful actress, Juliette Drouet. She quickly became Hugo's mistress, and remained—always, discreetly, a few houses removed—his very close friend for half a century.[27]

Some of Hugo's finest love lyrics were addressed to Juliette. And, tragically, some of his most memorable verses of grief and mourning were prompted by the drowning death of his daughter Léopoldine in early September 1843. Hearing the news of this tragedy, and in an oddly self-centered note to his wife, Adèle, Hugo wrote, "My God, what have I done to you."[28]

If we glance forward to the dramatic séances to which this book is devoted, we may view the death of Léopoldine as the central emotional core in Victor Hugo's dramatic dialogue with death and the implied assurance of that dialogue of eternal life.

Poetry moved into the background when, in 1845, Hugo was elected a member of the House of Peers. His often contradictory but always dramatic verbiage did not fit into the traditions of the House. At Hugo's home an atmosphere of fearful strain developed. The man himself, who wore the banner of a realistic atheist, seemed to fear a vengeful, malevolent God. Both he and Adèle turned to the erotic as an antidote to death, or to the fear of it. Adèle's friendships with the men in her crowd took on a flirtatious note. And Victor Hugo flung himself into a new infatuation, Léonie Biard. Later on, Léonie sent a batch of Victor's exuberant love letters to Juliette Drouet, presumably in order to break Juliette's relation with Victor; but Juliette had put up with too much of that sort of thing to be manipulated by yet another temporary rival.[29]

Victor Hugo's multifarious pursuits came to a temporary halt due to the revolution he had anticipated, feared, and favored. On February 22, 1848, Paris awoke to the sight of barricades everywhere. Louis-

Philippe fled to England and settled in Surrey as "Mr. Smith." Hugo himself achieved a quite uncomfortable image as a messiah of the revolution. He was elected to the new National Assembly. But the assembly wanted the rebels to halt the destruction of the city. This was the same "rabble who followed Jesus Christ," as Hugo had put it earlier.[30] Which side was he on? He didn't really know himself.

Reprisals were fierce and chaotic. Government troops began to round up "suspects," four of them hidden by Juliette Drouet, who managed to talk her way out of the chaos. Hugo suffered from psychosomatic symptoms, including an intermittent loss of his voice. The assembly ended martial law on November 4, 1848, and placed executive power in the hands of a single head of state. Six days later a president was elected whose name was Louis Napoleon Bonaparte, a nephew of the great Napoleon. He was an odd bird, hesitant, reluctant, and indecisive—the makings of a weak tyrant. Hugo described him later as "this man of weary gestures and a glazed expression," who "walks with an absent-minded air amidst the horrible things he does, like a sinister sleepwalker." [31]

Before the election that brought him to power, the new Napoleon visited Hugo in his apartment. Sitting on a packing crate in the poet's front room, the new ruler pledged that he would not "copy" Napoleon but seek to "imitate Washington." It was all quite humble, cozy, and falsely reassuring. Napoleon and the assembly resorted to a frightened and frightening tyranny almost immediately. Victor Hugo found himself in the middle, orating fiercely, and profoundly challenged in his self-esteem.[32] It was then that the members of his household turned to the occult, a rehearsal for the day-and-night séances that would take place during their exile on the Channel island of Jersey. One visitor, Georges Guénot, reported on a variety of apparent psychic phenomena at the Hugo apartment between the end of July and mid-November 1851. The phenomena included alleged contact with the spirit world, and it is notable that, during this period, a variety of "progressive" movements, ranging from socialism to feminism, tended to run parallel with spiritism. Contact with a spirit world was said to underscore the essential equality of all worlds, a unity of creation. Adèle Hugo sought the help of a "somnambulist," or "psychic," to contact relatives in Normandy. Rather questionable phenomena, such as reading words through a closed envelope, were reported, and participants attempted to or completely succeeded in pushing needles painlessly through their hands. Robb, somewhat obscurely, writes: "even the ghosts of Hugo's verse began to take on a more ectoplasmic consistency, long before the orgy of communication with the spirit world which is usually associated with the years in exile."[33] This could mean that one or the other in the group went into a mediumistic trance, with the result that real or imaginary personages from Victor Hugo's poems manifested to the assembled group. If this interpretation is correct, there existed an emotional and practical basis for the more extensive spiritistic phenomena that they witnessed on the island of Jersey later on.

In any event, exile was just ahead. After successive efforts to come to terms with the increasingly tyrannical regime of Napoleon III, and under actual threat of arrest, Victor Hugo decided that his family was no longer safe in Paris, or anywhere else in France. On the night of December 11, 1851, in disguise, he took the train to Brussels. His family followed him, first to the Belgian capital, and eventually to the Channel island of Jersey, where they settled in a large house called Marine-Terrace.[34]

Two exceedingly influential opposition writings were the product of these years. The first, written in one month, was *Napoléon le Petit,* which, published in England under the title *Napoleon the Little,* became an underground weapon. Hugo had written a six-hundred-page volume in record time, with his usual flowing, literary style, which could be read like a novel. With all the skill of a twentieth-century narcotics smuggler, the author had the book smuggled into France in mini-editions printed on thin paper. Even plaster busts of Napoleon III himself were used to sneak the banned volume into French territory; additional copies were carried by balloon. The first printing of his super-pamphlet appeared in Brussels two days after Hugo arrived on Jersey, where the family spent the first three years of what would amount to nineteen years of exile.[35] The remaining years were spent on the island of Guernsey, at a residence called Hauteville-House.

Exile enabled Victor Hugo to jettison Léonie Biard, but he refused Adèle's subtle urgings to let go of Juliette as well; she, too, settled in exile, not far from the Hugo family. A book of Hugo's politico-ideological poems, written in 1853, *Les Châtiments (The Chastisements),*[36] may well have been the seed of the Cao Dai movement, described earlier. These poems—part political, part philosophical—carried the message of a future faith that would not replace, but would supersede, the world's major religions.

At this point, the Hugo clan was, in a contradictory fashion, both at the center of a new revolutionary storm and in total isolation. None of them were any good at English, least of all the master of the house, who looked upon the French language as something like a divine gift. Jersey had a community of French exiles, but, though Hugo became friendly with its members and in many ways their leader, it could not replace the vast community of the Paris literati or the Paris bourgeoisie or the Paris political establishment among whom he had been accustomed to move with perfect ease. But, on Jersey Island, Hugo would make the acquaintance of a new and extraordinarily distinguished group that would stand well above even the gifted social groups with whom he had been on intimate terms in Paris. What could this be? Well, a higher dimension of existence, of course, the world of the spirits, the world of great minds and of even greater superhuman concepts! It was at this very moment of isolation and frustrated emotional energies, in September 1853, that Hugo's old friend Delphine de Girardin introduced the family to the latest device for spirit contact, the turning table, capable of tapping out messages from the dead by knocking a table leg on the floor. [37]

The book for which this is the introduction, *Victor Hugo's Conversations with the Spirit World,* consisting of the more important of the transcripts of these séances, is a greatly expanded and revised edition of the author's *Conversations with Eternity: The Forgotten Masterpiece of Victor Hugo,* published in 1998, and the first book-length account in English of Victor Hugo's encounters with the spirits. The emotional experience of those encounters lasted more than two years, and the record of its strange and exalted nights and days is certainly a unique document, as well as a glimpse into the subconscious of an egocentric, frustrated genius seeking to crash through the barriers of human communications and exploding like a volcano of yearning, fear, madness, and creativity. After nineteen years of exile on the islands of Jersey and Guernsey, Hugo was able to return, in triumph, to Paris, as the Republic succeeded the reign of Napoleon III. [38] While on Guernsey, he had managed to produce, along with his 1862 masterpiece *Les Misérables* and a huge amount of poetry and non-fiction, three more novels, all of them now acclaimed as classics: *Les travailleurs de la mer (The Toilers of the Sea)*, published in 1866, *L'homme qui rit (The Man Who Laughs)*, published in 1869, and *Quatrevingt-treize (Ninety-Three)*, completed after a final brief stay on Guernsey and published in 1874.

The final years of Victor Hugo's life were darkened by the decision of his wife, Adèle, who had never ceased to long for Paris, to move to Brussels while Victor remained on Guernsey. Adèle died in the Belgian capital on August 27, 1868, with her husband there to close her eyes on her deathbed.[39] Their daughter Adèle had fallen, literally, "madly" in love with a British officer, Albert Pinson, and followed Pinson to Canada. Emotionally disturbed, she hoped that he might marry her. When he was transferred to the Caribbean, Adèle followed him, to wander the streets of Bridgetown, Barbados, as she slipped deeper into madness. Eventually, she was brought back to Paris, where she was permanently institutionalized. She lived on until April 21, 1915.[40] Juliette Drouet, who had spent fifty years both at Hugo's side and at a distance, died on May 11, 1883.[41]

Victor Hugo died on May 22, 1885. The mass of mourners moving through the streets toward the Pantheon, where he was interred, was estimated at two million, more than the actual population of Paris at the time. Although in his lifetime Hugo had been an outspoken, even flamboyant, spokesman of the Paris underclass, in poetry, prose, plays, and speeches he left only 1 percent of his fortune to the "poor." On the other hand, always conscious of grand symbolism, he had ordered that, at his funeral, his body be carried in a simple, black "pauper's coffin." Of course, the coffin was at the center of a vast state parade, complete with uniformed marchers, funereal music, and appropriately gaudy floral decorations. Thus, in a final irony, Victor Hugo's funeral procession symbolized his life's ultimate contradiction.[42]

Hugo's last will reflected his belief, or certainty, that there was life after death. He also had a brief, self-assured message for those who came after him: "I have tried to introduce moral and human questions into what is known as politics. . . . I have spoken out for the oppressed of all lands, and of all parties. I believe I have done well. My conscience tells me I am right. And if the future proves me wrong, I am sorry for the future."[43]

_____

Martin Ebon (1917–2006) served for twelve years as administrative secretary of the Parapsychology Foundation in New York City. He was the author or editor of more than eighty books, including *Prophecy in Our Time* (1968), *They Knew the Unknown* (1971), and *KGB: Death and Rebirth* (1994).

One

JERSEY ISLAND
SETTING FOR A SÉANCE

For Victor Hugo and his son Charles, standing on the foredeck of the British steamer *Royal Mail* on this calm morning of August 5, 1852, the first sight of Jersey Island is a disappointment. They have been expecting an emerald green isle, a perfumed garden, the bouquet of the ocean, another Eden. What they see is a line of stark gray rocks slanting precipitously into the sea, without a tree, without a trace of greenery.[1] There isn't a house to be seen, let alone an entire town; the capital, Saint Helier, is hidden between the bluffs.

Hugo stares at the sheer rocks. His heart sinks. *These rocks cannot be my destiny,* he thinks. *Not unless one is shaped like a lingam, or a phallus. Let me see . . .*

They draw nearer and Saint Helier swims into sight from behind a cliff. The boat enters the harbor. In the distance they can see the pier; the women are there—mother, wife, sister, somber of demeanor, waiting to provide what solace they can.

Hugo has not seen his wife and daughter for nine months. The two Adèles have come directly from Paris, escorted by Auguste Vacquerie, the close friend of the family who waits beside them on the pier. Hugo and his son have come from Brussels—the first stage of the poet's exile—via Southampton.

His wife, Adèle, is forty-nine now. Her hair is still black, but she has become stouter.

Hugo turns around abruptly. Juliette is in her stateroom—Juliette Drouet, his great love, his mistress. The night before, he has left Charles on the storm-lashed deck and gone down to see her. He has lain with her, comforting her in her distress. She is forty-six. Her hair is gray. She is no longer young. But her love is as fresh as ever.

On Jersey Island, he will have two wives.

The boat swings closer to the pier. Behind his wife and daughter, around them, with respectful enthusiasm, stands a crowd of welcomers waiting to pay homage to the poet. Some are Jerseymen, some English, but most are soldier-refugees from failed revolutions—there are almost three hundred of these political exiles on the island—who have been granted, like himself, asylum on this British crown dependency set like a raw gray jewel in the dark blue waters of the English Channel.

Involuntarily he searches through the crowd, looking for a woman. It can be any woman. Behind him is Juliette, before him is Adèle, but still he feels compelled to look. His exhaustion and the chaos of his barely controllable days have brought out in him the faun, the satyr, almost always vigorously erect. He has never plucked a Jersey flower. But now he leans over the railing and catches the eye of one. She is décolletée and wearing a bright blue frock; she stares at him, then glances away. His lust is strong—but his lust is also his muse and if in his imagination his hands sweep down her body, lines of poetry also leap unbidden to his head.

This high barren rock of Jersey Island suddenly does not seem so barren. After all, rocks, and plants and animals, contain souls that are part of God, even though the perfect essence of God must remain apart from His creation. This rock of Jersey is a part of the soul of God; perhaps Victor's destiny lies here after all. Perhaps the soul of Jersey is a woman's soul. Did not the cabalists say that the soul of God is, in part, a woman's soul?

The gangway has been lowered. Victor Hugo walks carefully down it, Charles following after him. A loud cheer goes up from the crowd; caps are tossed into the air and hang suspended for an instant against the gray bluffs before falling back down on the jetty. Hugo embraces his wife, Adèle. He embraces his daughter Adèle—but too heartily, remembering as always, with a pang, that this is the daughter whom he loves but does not like. Adèle is twenty-two now. Her glistening raven-black hair is drawn severely back from her high soft cheekbones; she still has the beauty that made Balzac say of her, when she was fourteen, that Adèle Hugo was the most beautiful woman he had ever seen. But now Victor sees in her eyes something veiled, tormented, defiant—a growing hardness.

General Adolphe Le Flô steps forward gaily from the crowd. Hugo has recognized him from the foredeck: he is very tall and very lean and, as always, impeccably dressed. Hugo imagines that General Le Flô was dressed to the nines when he commanded the murderous siege of Constantine in Algeria;[2] that the blood, flying everywhere, did not settle on his impeccable uniform as all around him his troops fought the Arabs tooth and nail. Le Flô may be witty—too witty—and frivolous—too frivolous—but he is also absolutely fearless. That fearlessness had gotten him through fourteen years of campaigning in Algeria, and Hugo admires that.

Le Flô asks Hugo to address the exiles, and, when Hugo says yes, he calls them to order. Scrambling up on a proffered chair, the poet intones the prayer that he repeats to himself five times a day—not a Christian prayer at all, but one that consists of a single line: "O Lord, share your strength and power with me."

Then he addresses his fellow exiles. He begins: "My dear co-citizens of the United States of Europe* . . ."

Afterward, Le Flô escorts them through the cobblestoned streets of Saint Helier to the Hotel de la Pomme d'Or, Hugo shepherding his wife and daughter and Auguste Vacquerie before him. The new arrival complains about the flatness of the houses in Saint Helier, their grayness, their sameness, their monotony. This is also true of the churches: he has already seen ten, and though they are of seven different religious denominations, they also all look the same.

Le Flô responds with his usual sprightly benevolence: "My dear friend, do not despair! Saint Helier is not as joyless as may appear. The Jerseymen are mad for pleasure. Saint Helier is a depository for every sort of festivity; high society here is half English aristocracy and half French aristocracy; wealthy men and businessmen abound."[3]

Hugo is somewhat reassured. He has no doubt the urbane old soldier is signaling him that there are first-rate houses of easy pleasure in Saint Helier. He suddenly remembers Windmill Street in London, the cramped hotel where he and Charles stayed, the prostitute who made up for his discomforts . . .

Hugo walks with a lighter step—and then, abruptly, he moves forward to the two Adèles and pats each on the back.

*See chapter 21 for further information about the United States of Europe.

On Hugo's third day on Jersey Island, a fight erupts in the Hugo family.

Victor Hugo wants to live in the seaport of Gorey, several miles east along the coast. He wants to live beneath the splendid gothic ruins of the castle of Mont Orgueil ("Mount Pride"), which, built in the fourteenth century to guard the coast against the French, covered with scraggly ivy-covered trees, still dominates the horizon. For Victor Hugo, Mont Orgueil is virtually a gateway to another dimension. It is supposed to mark the spot where, until A.D. 709, Jersey was joined to the mainland.[4] Local historians believe that in that year a month-long holocaust of wind and rain separated the island from the Normandy coast forever.

On January 9, 1735, the tide went out so far from Normandy that it exposed a village submerged a thousand years before; in the glittering mud you could see kitchen utensils, wagon-wheel ruts, the occasional, still standing wall of a house. In 1812 a vast storm, churning up the ocean bottom, brought to the surface beyond the Gorey sandbar a sort of phantom forest—trees horribly twisted, stripped of their leaves, with their bark still brown.[5] Perhaps Victor hopes to see something like this happen again; perhaps, observing the ocean from Mont Orgueil like an eagle peering out from its aerie, he wants to see some fragment of the lost Atlantis, glistening with occult treasures not seen for three thousand years, surge up suddenly out of the sea.

Charles sides with his father in the quarrel over where to live. He, too, wants to live beneath Mont Orgueil. But the two Adèles want to live in a three-story house called Marine-Terrace, located a quarter of a mile from Saint Helier. General Le Flô chivalrously intervenes on behalf of the ladies, and Victor and Charles yield.[6] On August 16, the family moves into Marine-Terrace; Hugo will later describe the building as "a heavy white cube, right-angled, shaped like a tomb," with rooms that are "clean, forbidding, perfunctorily furnished and freshly repainted, with white funeral shrouds on the windows."[7]

Hugo must also attend to his other household. Soon he will install his great love, Juliette Drouet, in a house two blocks away. On many a night, and especially when his wife, Adèle, is bickering loudly with the tradespeople, his satyr-self will nimbly descend a footpath, open Juliette's door, and fall into her arms. Hugo's children know all about this but, out of respect, through force of habit, they all turn a blind eye. Victor Hugo is, after all, not only their father but the most famous writer in the world.

Once settled in Marine-Terrace, Hugo has time to note that

another old friend has accompanied him to Jersey. This is the star Arcturus. For many years, in Paris, he was accustomed to seeing it rise behind the Place Royale. Now he is delighted—and somehow surprised—that Arcturus should have come with him on his exile.[8] He believes that all poets are mystically linked to Arcturus, that a part of their soul resides in that ruby red star. For Hugo, the universe swarms with correspondences. In *The Toilers of the Sea* he will intimate that the star Aldebaran is a star of evil, mystically linked to all evil creatures on earth; he will write that the rays of sunlight entering the underwater lair of the deadly octopus became "as green as a ray from Aldebaran."[9] In his later years of exile Hugo will elaborate on these beliefs, lacing them subtly through his many writings.

The poet has learned, on August 8, that his prose diatribe against Napoleon III, *Napoleon the Little,* has finally been published in Brussels. Hugo and his friends will spend the rest of the year and part of the next disseminating this banned work in every possible way. At the same time, he will begin his collection of poetry *Chastisements,* which is also an assault on Napoleon III, but a gentler one. *Chastisements* will occupy him until the summer of 1853. He will write much else as well; his brain, that of an artist of genius, has to support them all. He resumes his habit of rising at five o'clock in the morning and writing without interruption until half past eleven. Were he not to maintain this ruthless discipline, he would not be able to cope with the unending demands, of every sort, that are now being made on his person.

The dissident anti-Bonapartist Pierre Leroux has arrived on the island on August 30. He is a journalist and a philosopher, and Victor Hugo's on-again, off-again friend. Leroux is accompanied by twenty-seven members of his family, including his eight children.[10] He is the opposite of Le Flô, who is tall, lean, and elegant; Leroux is short, stout and disheveled. He is also fiery. He constantly insults Victor Hugo with great affection. He dismisses all art that does not rigorously serve the purpose of bettering society. Thus he dismisses all of Hugo's poetry, while applauding his compatriot for being a genius. Leroux is a socialist (in fact, he is the man who coined the word *socialiste*): he has rejected God, the clergy, and the aristocracy. He is also a socialist in the Charles Fourier mode: he believes in a World Soul, in reincarnation, and in an ideal world lasting eighty thousand years with the last eight thousand consisting of Perfect Harmony. Hugo also believes in reincarnation, but everything he believes, Pierre Leroux does not believe, and vice versa.

Jersey Island is ultimately more beautiful than Hugo has expected. True, it is almost always cool, and squalls bring wind and rain for a part of almost every day. Also, it is not large. Thirteen years later, in *The Toilers of the Sea,* Hugo will write that its 44.6 square miles are "exactly the size of the city of London. It would require two thousand and seven hundred Jerseys to equal France."[11] Were he to write today, Hugo might say that Jersey is exactly one-half the size of Washington, D.C., and that it would require 82,432½ Jerseys to equal the United States. In Hugo's time, the population was fifty-six thousand (enough to fill a medium-sized, twenty-first-century football stadium); today, the population is eighty-eight thousand. In Hugo's time, 80 percent of the population spoke English, though French was widely spoken; today, 90 percent of Jerseymen and women speak English, though the use of French remains widespread.

Auguste Vacquerie, thirty-four, will be a permanent houseguest at the Hugos. Acerbic and moody, he is also the unrequitedly loving suitor of the young Adèle. Auguste is a talented writer; in his 1863 *Les miettes de l'histoire* (Tidbits of History), he will describe with telling effect the splendors and miseries of Jersey Island. Vacquerie writes of rich wheat fields gleaming in the sun (when the sun is out), of giant cabbages running as wild as weeds, of camelias growing taller than trees.[12] This is in the southeast; in the rockier northwest, towering cliffs plunge into the sea. At their base, the waves have sculpted out intricate grottos that, with their lofty ceilings, their high stone columns, their multicolored play of light, are like underwater cathedrals of the sea.

There is another aspect of Jersey Island that fascinates Hugo: the island contains the artifacts of a vanished civilization. This civilization, which Hugo believes goes back to some splendidly antediluvian time, is that of the Druids. (We now know that druidic civilization goes back not half as far.) Scattered here and there across the fields and even in the forests are dolmens and menhirs—polished columnar stones that rise higher than a human being. Some are laid out in the enigmatic circular form of the cromlech; these monuments, erected millennia ago, are, or so the islanders think, the repositories of ancient souls. The Jerseyans associate them with barbaric bloodletting rituals. They believe that ghosts imprisoned in these sculpted rocks prowl the countryside at night: wailing druidic priestesses dressed in black, or white, or gray; the lurching figures of men carrying their heads beneath their arm; dogs and blackbirds driven mad by demons.

Hugo's older son, Charles, twenty-six, shares his father's interest in these matters. On Guernsey Island, Charles will write a novel inspired by the occult side of the Channel islands: *Le cochon de Saint-Antoine* (Saint Anthony's Pig). But, in September 1852, Charles, though brilliant, is lazy and at loose ends. Victor admires his son but wonders if he hasn't spoiled him. From a lying position, or at best a sitting one, Charles controls the guests with sardonic, devastating arguments. He smokes incessantly, reluctantly removing his pipe only to eat; the others suspect he does not remove it in even more intimate settings. But the new craze of photography is sweeping France, and Charles will soon take it up. This will distract him, for a while, from the vexatious difficulty of being Victor Hugo's eldest son.

Hugo's other son, François-Victor, twenty-four, doesn't arrive on Jersey until September 22. He is *not* lazy; he merely awaits a suitably exalted challenge. He has found one in the person of Anaïs Liévenne, a Parisian actress who holds his soul in thrall. Anaïs will visit Jersey, but the father's disapproval will be one factor making her give up the son. It will be awhile before François-Victor gets over this far from frivolous love affair. Eventually, he will take up a supremely exalted challenge: he will become the first person to translate the entire works of William Shakespeare into French.

The three hundred political exiles on Jersey Island will have almost as great a hold on Victor Hugo's affections as his family and his writing.

They are men now proscribed in their countries, and therefore now called "proscrits." They are not only from France. Some are from Hungary, some from Italy, some from Poland. The Hungarians and Italians have risen up against the Austro-Hungarian Empire with heartbreaking results, while the Poles have been engaged in a decades-long, still far from resolved, struggle against the rule of Russia. All of these Jersey Island proscrits—these anti-monarchists, these newly aborning socialists and democrats—have fought against royals of some sort according to the dictates of their countries; they have tried to break rule by divine right, and some have sought to shatter the power of popes.

All of them have failed, and all are now in flight from triumphant reactionary regimes. These exiles are practical, powerful men, seething with frustration and in various stages of despair. Two will die of heartbreak within nine months of Hugo's arrival on Jersey: Louis-Hélin Dutaillis[13] and Jean Bousquet.[14] Two long and spread out funeral processions, such as the Jerseymen have never seen before, will wind their way slowly along the roads and over the fields of the island. Each coffin is borne by four pallbearers, one from each of the four countries whose defeated idealists comprise the funeral processions. There is no priest or mass. The red flag of the United States of Europe is carried behind the coffin; that is all. At the gravesides, making the air ring, Victor Hugo delivers the funeral orations, which the Jerseymen, standing awestruck at the back, will never forget. These will be among his finest speeches.

Such were to be some of Victor Hugo's preoccupations during his first year on Jersey Island.

≫≫⋘

But, as spring became summer in 1853, as it became less and less likely that Napoleon III would soon be ousted from power—as Victor Hugo's situation weighed more and more heavily on him—his lonely thoughts, prompted by the pounding of the ocean, turned more and more to the unspeakable tragedy whose tenth anniversary would soon come round: the death by drowning of his older daughter, Léopoldine, with her husband, Charles Vacquerie, on September 4, 1843, when Léopoldine was eighteen years old and three months pregnant.

Hugo had not been home at the time. He had been returning from a monthlong visit to Spain with Juliette Drouet. They had stopped off at the famous charnel house of Saint-Michael's Church in Bordeaux; its seventy mummified bodies had put Hugo in a gloomy mood and had filled him with a presentiment of disaster. They had gone on to Rochefort and sat down in the Café de l'Europe to read the newspapers. Skimming through *Le Siècle*, Hugo, in the most terrible moment of his life, chanced upon a story that had been reprinted from the Le Havre journal.

> An appalling event, which will cast into mourning a family held dear by the world of French letters, came to inflict its sinister sound upon our population this morning. . . . M. P. Vacquerie . . . took with him in his yacht . . . his nephew M. Ch. Vacquerie and the young wife of the latter, who, as everyone knows, is the daughter of M. Victor Hugo . . .[15]

Léopoldine had married Charles Vacquerie—the brother of Auguste Vacquerie—on February 15, 1843. On September 4, at Villequier on the Seine, Léopoldine and Charles had boarded the small yacht belonging to Charles's uncle Pierre. The uncle's ten-year-old son, Arthus, was also on board. They had set out on a day trip across the Seine at a point where the current was particularly strong. The boat was top-heavy with sail. Although Pierre was an experienced sailor, the boat capsized in a sudden gust of wind and everyone on board drowned.

First reports said that Léopoldine and Charles were found clasped in each other's arms. A final report indicated that Léopoldine drowned clinging to the boat while Charles was swept downstream. "Didine" had been Victor Hugo's favorite child.

Juliette Drouet would later write down Victor's reactions in the Café de l'Europe.

> I had had scarcely time to look at the headlines when my poor darling suddenly leaned towards me and said in a choking voice, holding the paper out to me: "This is horrible!" I looked at him. Never, as long as I live, shall I forget the indescribable expression of despair upon his noble features. A moment back I had seen him smiling and happy, and now, in the space of a second, without the slightest transition, he seemed as though thunderstruck. His poor lips were white; his magnificent eyes were staring in front of him. His face and his hair were wet with tears. His poor hand was pressed to his heart as though to keep it from bursting from his breast.[16]

Scholar Maurice Levaillant paraphrases her next words: "He didn't move for several minutes; it was as if he were terrified. Then he got up, walked outside like an automaton without seeming to see anything. O sadness! The sudden singing of a group of girls recalled him to reality. . . . He had come to the ramparts of the town, beside a little path where there was a children's carousel; his heart broken, he collapsed weeping on the grass."[17]

The two rushed back to Paris. They arrived on September 12. Léopoldine and Charles had been buried in the cemetery at Villequier six days before.

———

Victor Hugo never fully recovered from the death of Léopoldine; grief and guilt would hound him for the rest of his days. Despite his sturdy rationalism, in his worst moments he would believe that Léopoldine's death had been a punishment from God for his adulterous ways. He wrote no poetry for almost three years and did not do much other work. His play *Les Burgraves* (*The Burgraves*) had failed in 1843, but this was no longer important. Auguste Viatte writes that "he forgot about the failure [of this play]. . . . He forgot about literature; his pride and glory no longer mattered to him. For three years, in the mind of this man whose soul had been virtually annihilated, a single hideous grief remained—a single image, a single memory, hypnotized him."[18] He could not get out of his prodigious imagination the frightful picture of Léopoldine in the last stages of death by drowning.

Although he gradually began to improve, Léopoldine's death had sounded the death knell of his belief in Christianity, though he didn't know it at the time. He now threw himself into esoteric belief systems: mesmerism, Hinduism, cabbalism—soon, spiritism. He entered parliament and, charmed by Napoleon III in the beginning, soon became a harsh critic, excoriating the ruler in speech after speech; this as much as anything helped to reawaken his creative powers. Hugo began to write serious poetry again—just in time to experience Napoleon III's coup d'état of December 1851 and, on pain of death, flee to Brussels and then on to Jersey Island.

But, as September 4, 1853—the tenth anniversary of Léopoldine's death—drew closer, the never-to-be-accepted, never-to-be-forgotten loss of his daughter must have weighed with increasing heaviness on Victor Hugo.

September 4 came and went. We don't know how Victor Hugo reacted to that day. Then, on September 6, the curtain began to rise on the first act of a prodigious play. On that day, a visitor arrived at Saint Helier from Paris: this was Delphine de Girardin, a childhood friend of Victor's, now a society beauty but also an intellectual, a well-known playwright, and the wife of the publisher Émile de Girardin, whose newspaper, *La Presse,* was the first in France to carry paid advertising. Delphine came to the Hugo household bubbling over with enthusiasm for a new craze that was captivating Paris.

This was the talking tables. With these tables, it was said, you could talk to the spirits of the dead.

Two

LÉOPOLDINE BECKONS

The tapping tables had first been heard in America six years before.

In December 1847, the Fox family—mother, father, and two daughters, Margaretta, fourteen, and Kate, almost twelve—moved into a ramshackle farmhouse in the hamlet of Hydesville, twenty miles from Rochester, New York. As a cold and snowy winter settled in, they began to hear strange rapping noises in the house. On March 31, 1848, Kate clapped her hands once and asked whatever was doing the rapping to follow suit. Her single clap was answered by a single rap. Kate clapped different numbers of raps; the mysterious rapper kept following suit. Kate and Margaretta devised a code and were soon communicating with the rapper, who said that "he" was the spirit of a peddler murdered by a previous tenant and whose body was buried in the basement.

The basement was dug up, but no body was found. The raps continued. It seemed that wherever Kate and Maggie went, raps manifested. Using the code they'd invented, the sisters communicated with what invariably turned out to be the spirits of the dead. An older sister, Leah, living in Rochester, took her younger sisters in hand. Soon the three of them were a channeling trio, evoking raps by their presence and, in public and private séances, talking to the rappers.

The Fox sisters became a sensation. They called forth not only raps but lights and tables that tapped their legs and moved and levitated; disembodied raps and table tapping became the lingua franca by which the sisters communicated with the dead. They gave more and more demonstrations, privately and in halls where attendance grew every night. Private clients and audience members alike were usually satisfied that the Fox sisters had put them in touch with their departed loved ones. The sisters' method of talking to the dead, soon christened Spiritualism, spread like wildfire. In 1910, Sir Arthur Conan Doyle estimated that there were ten thousand mediums in the United States in 1850. An earlier estimate had put the figure at thirty thousand in 1853. The population of the United States was then twenty-three million.

Though they had launched what amounted to a revolution in spirituality, the Fox sisters were often suspected of practicing fraud. Skeptical committees constantly tested their powers, many refusing to validate those powers. Rumors spread that Margaretta and Kate had confessed to their parents that they had made the raps themselves by popping their knee and toe joints. Alcoholism, unhappy love affairs and marriages, unending financial problems, constant doubts and the demands of the public: all of this came to bedevil the days and nights of the channeling Fox sisters and probably affected their judgment and their memory of events. Maggie and Kate recanted in 1888, telling the world that their rapping had been a hoax from the beginning. A year later, Maggie recanted her recantation. Some of the phenomena manifested by the sisters seemed surely to involve more than mere popping knee and toe joints. The sisters died in poverty and some obscurity: Leah in 1890, Kate in 1892, and Maggie in 1893.

Were they genuine psychics? Today, many who believe in psychic powers do not believe the Fox sisters possessed them. But there are many who still believe the sisters were authentically psychic. So elusive was what they did that their lives are almost a giant Rorschach blot: what you believe about the Fox sisters and their putative abilities is almost a mirror of what you believe about psychic phenomena in general.

If the Fox sisters really were con artists, it is an ironic and disturbing twist of fate that their feats launched a whole new religion, and one that quickly became international. In 1851, the Spiritualist movement leaped the Atlantic Ocean, instantly taking root in England, France, Germany, and even Turkey.

When it reached the shores of France, however, it collided with a popular European-grown religion/spiritual practice: mesmerism.

The Austrian physician Friedrich Anton Mesmer (1734–1815) had theorized that we all have a critically important nonmaterial fluid in our bodies—one shared by all of the universe and linking us to the entire universe—whose effects he christened "animal magnetism." If this fluid is "in balance," we are mentally and physically healthy; if not, we are sick in some way. The practice of magnetism—holding a magnet over a patient's head or some other part of the patient's body—could recalibrate a person's fluid.

Mesmer apparently effected many cures in this way; after the trail-blazing doctor's death, his disciple, the Marquis de Puységur, found that when he magnetized some patients they fell into a sleepy, trancelike state—"mesmerized," as Puységur called the condition, in homage to the master. Puységur observed that in this state many subjects seemed more intelligent, more aware of their lives, more perceptive about people and events, than they were when awake. A happy few even achieved a state of "extreme lucidity" in which they became apparently telepathic, clairvoyant, or prophetic.

In the early part of the nineteenth century, particularly in France, mesmerism became a very popular therapy. In the 1830s and 1840s there were as many "mesmerists" in a French town or city as there are chiropractors and acupuncturists in an American town or city today, and probably many more. (Indeed, the "fluid" sounds a lot like the chi energy spoken of in classical acupuncture.) Practitioners were everywhere; a scholar of the Illuminati, Auguste Viatte writes that "it rained mesmerists on every street corner, illiterate or learned, working-class or upper-class, believer or non-believer; all you had to do was look and you could find one that suited you; you could even take a few of them seriously."[1]

Victor Hugo, restlessly alert to every new way of effecting personal and spiritual growth, acquired at an early age a belief in the power of the fluid. He told Paul Stapfer on Guernsey Island in 1860 that he was

> wrong to deny the effectiveness of magnetism. It's not a joke. It's a fact acknowledged by science and studied scientifically. My son, François-Victor, had insomnia when he was a child. We tried everything to make him sleep, but nothing worked. He was so sick that the day came when we thought we would lose him. One night I tried some magnetic passes over his body. He slept for fifteen hours without waking. This sleep was so beneficial and so restorative that the doctor had no idea why or how it had happened and could only marvel that my boy had actually been cured. All my child would say to me was, "Oh, Papa, go on! More! More! That made me feel so good."[2]

Viatte tells us that, in late 1847, when interest in mesmerism was at a peak, Victor Hugo, wondering if a trance state could confer the gift of divination, arrived at a séance at the Parisian home of the viscountess St.-Mars carrying a sealed box under his arm with a secret word written inside it. The presiding psychic was "Alexis," one of the most celebrated mediums of the day. She put herself in a hypnotic trance and took Hugo's box between her hands. Turning it around and around, she spelled out *P, O, L, I.* Then she stopped, declaring, "I can't see the next letter." She suddenly went on: "But the ones after it are *I, Q, U, E.* There, I see it! The word is 'politics' [*la politique*]," The medium topped off her feat by revealing that the letters were written "on a piece of light green paper M. Hugo tore out of a brochure at home."

"That's right!" Hugo had exclaimed, opening the sealed box and showing the piece of paper around.

From then on, writes Viatte, "'second sight' counted Victor Hugo among its most illustrious defenders."[3]

Hugo came to see the fluid as a sort of philosopher's stone whose full expression in a human being could make that person a kind of a god. The fluid was nothing less than the power that brought every created object in the universe into relationship with every other created object (in fact, Mesmer had hinted at this). Coming down to breakfast one morning in May 1853, Hugo told his daughter Adèle that he had just had a dream in which his own fluid had interacted with the fluid in flowers to enable him to see the color of the scent of each individual flower. "Carnations give forth a red flame like rubies," he told her, and "lilies a white flame like diamonds," while cornflowers glowed "with a sapphire-like blue flame and roses a rose flame like amethyst."[4] The fluid could reveal to us the truth that all the five senses—and more—were one.

※※※

Even as Victor Hugo was holding forth on Jersey in May 1853 on the power of the fluid, back in France, mesmerism, with its core belief in the fluid, was rapidly being overtaken by the growing excitement over Spiritualism and the tapping tables. The leading mesmerist of the day was Baron Jules du Potet, who owned the largest-circulation mesmerist magazine, the *Journal du Magnétisme,* the greatest number of mesmerist salons, and the mesmerist salons with the biggest rooms. As upper and middle classes alike flocked to buy three-legged tables and try to talk to the dead, du Potet decided that if he could not defeat the tapping-table menace then he could at least co-opt it. He now declared that Spiritualism was really mesmerism under a different name. He cited the case of Angélique Cottin, the "electrical girl" from Normandy, who in 1846 could not only make tables tilt and tap out sounds without her touching them but also could make all other objects around her move and jump about.

Cottin had gone on a tour around the world that had included the United States; perhaps there, du Potet suggested slyly, the Fox sisters had attended one of her demonstrations and picked up the art of table tapping from her. Potet cited the case, famous in the annals of mesmerism, of a man whose atrophied leg, when magnetized by a medium, tapped out messages from the spirit world. (This was the very same leg, du Potet hinted, that had originally invented the Spiritualists' code of one rap equaling the letter *a*, twenty-six raps equaling *z*, and so on.) Mesmerism *was* Spiritualism![5]

But nothing could stop the noisy onward march of the tapping tables. Moreover, a considerably more imaginative co-opter of spiritual fads than Baron Louis du Potet had appeared on the scene. This was Hippolyte-Léon Dénizart-Rival who, adopting the name of Allan Kardec (which, he said, the spirits had given him), simply renamed Spiritualism "spiritism" [*le spiritisme*] and, adding the doctrine of reincarnation and that of a "perispirit" effecting the connection between the nonmaterial fluid and the material body, developed almost overnight a whole new fluid-based religion. Du Potet and the mesmerists were forced to retreat, and Kardec became the king of the table tappers.

Soon Kardec's subjects were everywhere! France was conquered by this new occult technique it now called spiritism. Aristocrats, intellectuals, and artists in particular succumbed to the craze of table tapping, though the bourgeoisie was not far behind. Eighteen fifty-three— the year when, as we will soon see, Victor Hugo first talked to the spirit world—was the *annus mirabilis* of French spiritism. In *Marvels beyond Science,* Joseph Grasset quotes Bersot on the "heroic ages of turning tables."

> It was a passion, and everything was forgotten. In an intellectual country whose drawing rooms were generally famed for the lively conversations held therein, one saw, during several months, Frenchmen and Frenchwomen, who have so often been accused of

being light-headed, sitting for hours around a table, stern, motionless and dumb; their fingers stretched out, their eyes obstinately staring at the same spot and their minds stubbornly engrossed by the same idea, in a state of anxious expectation, sometimes standing up when exhausted by useless trials, sometimes, if there was a motion or a creaking, disturbed and put out of themselves while chasing a piece of furniture that moved away. During the whole winter there was no other social occupation or topic. It was a beautiful period, a period of first enthusiasm, of trust and ardor that would lead to success. How triumphant with modesty those who had the "fluid!" What a shame it was to those who had it not! What a power it became to spread the new religion! What love existed between adepts! What wrath prevailed against unbelievers![6]

Baron du Potet wrote, not without envy,

The tables are making one hell of a noise! Go into the porter's lodge, you'll see him making his table turn; go to the home of a judge, a lawyer, an archbishop even, and their tables are turning—after dinner, of course. It seems they're even interrogating tables in palaces.[7]

The Roman Catholic clergy inveighed against the mania from the pulpit, the bishop of Viviers (later archbishop of Paris, the highest clerical rank in France) declaring that those who practiced table turning were doomed to eternal hell-fire.[8] Napoleon III may have quietly encouraged the fad, relieved that something was taking people's attention away from his increasingly repressive measures. The cartoonist Charles Daumier, "honoring" Spiritualism with a dozen cartoons in May and June 1853, scornfully labeled the phenomenon "fluidomania."[9]

Although Victor Hugo had followed the progress of spiritism in France, he was not at the time particularly interested in talking to the dead, nor had he given the subject much systematic thought. All this was about to change, however, and almost literally overnight. The precipitating factor would be the weeklong stay of Delphine de Girardin at the Hugo household on Jersey Island.

Almost the first question that Delphine put to the startled Hugos was: "Do you do the tables?"

Maurice Levaillant writes that, by way of reply, "Victor Hugo expressed his skepticism and Mme Hugo her still unsatisfied curiosity."

"How should the tables be done?" Hugo asked Delphine.[10] She explained that the medium or mediums—whoever's fluid was potent enough to channel the words of the spirits—first placed their hands on the table. Then, when the table was good and ready, it raised one leg, then another, tapping out a message perhaps on the floor, perhaps on another table. Sometimes the table leg moved but did not rap. Sometimes the leg did not move—or there was no table at all—but there were raps. It could take awhile for a message to come through: the table leg, though it could signify "yes" with one tap and "no" with two, had to produce the number of raps corresponding to the position of a letter in the alphabet, so that one tap meant *a,* twenty-six taps meant *z,* and so forth.

The tables were coy and unpredictable; they were contrary and capricious. Sometimes a leg would remain poised in midair for minutes without tapping. Other times the table would float away from the floor, sometimes rising to the ceiling; sometimes the table shook and shook violently. Sometimes it slid across the floor from one end of the room to the other while simultaneously turning around in circles.

The Hugos listened warily to Delphine. There was, they told her, a table at Marine-Terrace that, some weeks before, they had unsuccessfully tried to animate in the spiritistic mode. Perhaps that table had not been appropriate—?

In *Victor Hugo et le spiritisme* Jean de Mutigny takes up the story.

> Not even waiting for dessert, Delphine de Girardin asked to see the table. . . . It was a big, square, four-legged table. Delphine burst out laughing: "It's not surprising the spirits haven't manifested! You need a little round table. Otherwise the phenomena can't possibly appear." There was no little round table at Marine-Terrace. Delphine immediately decided to go to Saint Helier and buy one.[11]

In a toyshop, she purchased a small, round, pedestal table with a single leg ending in three gold claws. She brought it back to Marine-Terrace herself. She and her host placed the pedestal table on top of the big square table. They tried again and again that evening to make the pedestal table "turn." It was to no avail. The next day they tried again, still without success. Auguste Vacquerie, General le Flô and his wife, and Count Sandor Teleki and his wife took turns around the tables. For four days, under the forceful and impatient direction of Delphine, they all labored to make a piece of furniture talk.

Victor Hugo did not seem to take much of an interest. He did not sit at the table. He did not sit near it. Sometimes he read quietly on a couch at the end of the room.

On the afternoon of Sunday, September 11, 1853, something astonishing happened.

It was on this afternoon that Victor Hugo took part in the séance for the first time. Auguste and Delphine sat at the pedestal table with their hands resting on top. Present as well were Mme Hugo, Charles and François-Victor Hugo, General Le Flô, and Pierre de Treveneuc.

Slowly, falteringly, the table began to rap out words. The participants were delighted! They seemed to have succeeded in calling up the spirit world. Initially the messages were brief, fragmentary, almost incoherent. The attendees dealt with the unfolding séance as if it were a children's parlor game: they asked the table to guess what they were thinking.

Auguste Vacquerie was still asking his question when the table began to tap out the word *suffering*.

"That isn't the word I'm thinking of," said Auguste. He had been thinking of the word *love*.

Suddenly the table became jerky, abrupt, almost willful in its movements, as if it were about to rap out a command.

"Are you the same spirit who was just here?" asked Delphine. The table rapped twice: *No*.

"Who are you?" asked Delphine.

The table tapped out: *Daughter. Dead.*

Everyone thought at once of the drowned Léopoldine.

"Who are you?" Delphine asked again.

The table replied in Latin: *Ame soror*. ("Sister soul.")

This could surely be only one person: the sister of the two brothers who were present. It could surely only be Léopoldine. Emotion overcame the participants. Mme Hugo broke down and began to sob. Victor Hugo fought to remain composed. The poet now took charge:

"Sweet soul, are you happy?"

Yes.

"Where are you?"

Light.

"What must we do to go to where you are?"

Love.

Delphine asked: "Who sent you?"

The Good Lord.

Victor asked: "Do you have a message for us?"

Yes.

"What?"

Suffer for the other world.

"Do you see the suffering of those who love you?"

Yes.

"Will their suffering go on for some time?" asked Delphine.

Yes.

"Will they [Victor Hugo and his exiled family] soon return to France?"

The table did not move.

"Are you happy when I mingle my prayers with your name?" asked Victor. It was something he did every night.

Yes.

"Are you always near those who love you? Do you watch over them?"

Yes.

"Does it depend on them whether you will return [to the tables]?"

No.

"But you will return?"

Yes.

"Soon?"

Yes.

Then the table was silent. The spirit had departed. The séance was at an end.[12]

And Victor Hugo was hooked. He would be intensely and tumultuously involved with the spirit world for the next two years. He would speak with more than one hundred spirits. The séances would inspire his greatest poetry, a vast epic cycle on the nature of God. The séances would become the greatest—and the least known—adventure into the supernatural that has ever been recorded.

Three

CHANNELING THE ENEMY

Napoleon III, emperor of France, trod softly along the marble-covered corridors of his palace. Gleaming gaslights high on the gilded walls held back the darkness of the falling night. The emperor wore his general's uniform and a blue sash bestrewn with medals. He twirled his thick mustache absently, his cloudy blue-gray eyes peering slowly about beneath his heavy lids.[1] He did not see what was around him. Instead, he saw the snow-white thighs of the redheaded courtesan he had just left and to whom he had given a 50,000-franc diamond necklace.

His thin ears, set low on the sides of his narrow face, did not hear what was around him, neither his own footsteps nor those of the two attendants following behind him at a discreet distance. Instead he heard, as clearly as if it were happening now though it had happened three days before, the screams and sobs of his wife, the empress Eugenie, railing at him in a jealous rage.

Pursuing his slow pace down the corridor, the emperor took a half-smoked cigarette from his lips and let it fall to the floor. He slipped from his breast pocket the gold cigarette case, encrusted with eighteen diamonds in the shape of an eagle, which had once belonged to his uncle Napoleon I, and extracted from it another cigarette. He raised the cigarette to his lips just as one of his attendants, racing lightly up behind him, held out before him a thin flame from a silver lighter. The emperor thanked the attendant politely, puffed once on the cigarette, and continued his quasi-somnambulistic walk along the corridor.

It was September 12, 1853. He and the empress Eugenie had been married for more than nine months. He had been unfaithful to her only for the past three.[2] He was not aggressive in his pursuit of beautiful women. "As a rule, the man attacks," he liked to tell his stable boys. "I am on the defensive, and sometimes I capitulate."[3] Didn't the empress understand—it had been explained to her several times— that he carried a crushing weight of responsibility on his shoulders and that—alas!—amid the cares of government he had neither intimate friends nor old acquaintances nor relatives who could provide him with the sweetness of family life? He freely confessed to seeking in illegitimate relationships the affection that his tender heart required. Shouldn't he be forgiven, then, the occasional indulgence that injured no one and that he never talked about? He needed these little distractions—and, besides, he reminded the empress, he always returned to her with renewed pleasure.[4]

But, he thought sadly and with irritation, coming to an abrupt stop in the corridor, the empress Eugenie didn't understand. Three days ago she had forced her way into his study and vented her rage in the most outrageous manner. He feared that soon not even the most explicit orders would give him the privacy he needed for work or just to talk; the empress would always believe that he had given the orders to hide his appointments with women.

The emperor sighed and saw that he had come to a stop beside a six-foot-high mirror set in an ebony frame. He turned slowly and confronted his own image. Was he really, as that wretch Hugo would have it in that execrable book whose every copy he, the emperor, was destroying just as quickly as it arrived in France—was he, Louis Napoleon, really "cold," and "pale," and "looking half-asleep," and "speaking with a slight German accent," and "vulgar," and "childish," and "theatrical," and "vain," as that traitor Victor Hugo had written?[5]

He straightened up, reflecting on it all. He thought that he was none of those things, no, none of them at all—or, at any rate, some of them only when he had to be, only when his Destiny dictated at a given moment that he must pretend to be one of those things.

He dropped his cigarette to the marble floor and ground it out with a slow circular motion of his leather-booted heel. He had remembered a troubling interview that he had had that very afternoon. It had been about Destiny.

The emperor, lost in thought, continued his slow pace down the corridor. He did not believe in God. He did not really believe in France. What he believed in was his personal star. He believed that he was a Man of Destiny. What did that mean? It meant that Providence itself dictated what he had to do. It meant that, in order to ensure the success that Fate had ordained for him, he was permitted to do things that other men were not.

He was, for example—and this had been the case during the coup d'état of December 2, 1851—permitted to order his troops to fire on a rioting mob and round up all his opponents from the assembly, along with many of the most distinguished men in France, and take them from their homes in the middle of the night and have them herded into prison and even have some of them shot. He was permitted this because he was a Man of Destiny, and because it had been essential on that star-crossed day of December 2, 1851, that he assume absolute power—essential not for himself but for France, because in that crucial hour he, Louis Napoleon, had been the only person who could stand between France and the hideous abyss of anarchy.[6]

That very afternoon, in his book-lined study in the palace, he had explained this to the distinguished and brilliant academician/educator Victor Duruy, not exactly in these words, but more diplomatically, subtly. He had hoped that Monsieur Duruy would agree with him, because for years the emperor had longed to write the definitive biography of Julius Caesar, and Duruy had just published a book entitled *History of the Romans* that the emperor was sure was the finest book he would ever read on the subject.

When he had finished expressing his point of view, Duruy, who had been gazing at him steadily, looked up at the ceiling. Then, clasping his hands, the academician leaned forward and said politely:

"Sire, what we call Providence used, as you know, to be called Destiny. And what was this Destiny? A mysterious personage created to explain the inexplicable. But today we have banished this mysterious personage from our teaching, because today the first principle of education is to consider the merit of an act. Teachers must tell their pupils that we are not slaves but rather architects of our own fortunes."

"Possibly," replied the emperor, his voice trembling. "But sometimes, when society is going to pieces, it is necessary to infringe legality."

Duruy looked away. "One does such things at times," he replied, "but it is better not to recall those times."[7]

These words gnawed at the emperor's soul as, rounding the last, gas-lit corner of the marbled corridor, he emerged suddenly into the brilliant chandeliered light of the central hall of his palace. Suddenly, he felt exhausted. He crossed the hall, his attendants following discreetly behind him, and began to mount the long, sweeping staircase that led to the imperial bedroom. On this night of September 12, 1853, sleep (which would come to him with increasing difficulty as the Second Empire stretched on through the years) was the only escape he knew from the thoughts that divided his soul.

Some nights, he had bad dreams.

※※

At that exact hour, some two hundred miles to the west and eighteen miles out into the English Channel, Delphine de Girardin, Auguste Vacquerie, and almost all the Hugo family were sitting down to a second session at the tapping tables. No one had slept very much the night before. The emotional intensity of the first séance had overwhelmed them all. Before, no one except Delphine had believed in the tables. Now, everyone believed in them; Victor Hugo, until then the most rebellious, was now the most convinced. He was sure they had spoken to Léopoldine. Who would play the cruel trick on him of pretending to make a table leg rap out a message from his drowned, beloved first daughter?

The séance began. Now, on this night of September 12, 1853, Victor and Charles laid their hands on the table.

It stirred. Their hearts leaped. Perhaps Léopoldine would return that night!

"Who are you?" asked Hugo.

The table spelled out: *Fairy.*

This word was followed by a string of incomprehensible syllables in Assyrian, or at least the spirit claimed they were Assyrian. The participants wondered: Was the afterworld pulling their leg? Then the "fairy" consented to speak in French.

Victor Hugo asked: "Have you a communication for us?"

Light.

"Are you acquainted with the soul who came here yesterday?"

No.

"Do you know that a soul came here?"

Yes.

"How do you know?"

The tomb.

"How can we get her to return?"

Hope.

But they were deeply disappointed. The hopes of the night before had been dashed. Hugo bowed his head in submission. Delphine asked the table: "Do you know that your questioner is the great poet Victor Hugo?"

Yes.

"Do you know his works?"

Yes.

"Name one."

The Hunchback of Notre Dame.

Now that he had been properly introduced, Hugo began to ask questions again. The dialogue went as follows: "Do spirits communicate with each other?"

Yes.

"Are you happy?"

Yes.

"Were you a man?"

No. Woman.

"Are those we have loved close by?"

Yes.

"You said you were a fairy. Are fairy and soul the same thing?"

Yes.

"Do you have a body?"

No.

"Do other spirits appear to you in the same form they had in life?"

Yes.

"The form of their youth?"

Yes.

"Say something unprompted by me."

Everything dies toward life.

"How long have you been dead?"

Three years.

"Your country?"

France.

"Your name?"

Amelia.

"How old were you when you died?"

Twenty-eight.

Amelia's words gave off a softly seductive vibration. Hugo suddenly felt drawn to ask: "Do you love me?"

Yes, replied the table, with the gentlest of raps.

"Did I know you on earth?"

No.

As bizarre as it was, Hugo felt that the table was flirting with him! He realized that in his distress he had been flirting with it! "Will it give you pleasure to see me again in the next life?" he asked.

The table jerked away. It reared up on two legs and just missed falling over backward. Then it righted itself and rapped out angrily: *No!*

Hugo was alarmed. The slight vibration given off by the table had changed completely. It was the difference between day and night: Before, the raps had been gentle, the merest brush of a bird's wing. But this furious *No!* had been like the swipe of a tiger's paw!

"That's some rap our little Amelia has!" Delphine exclaimed, laughing.

"The love affair between you two did not last long," said Mme Hugo wryly. Everyone was laughing. Victor Hugo joined in the laughter. He asked the table, "Is death desirable for those who have done good deeds in life?"

The table's tone was still harsh. *Yes.*

"Is it to be feared by those who have been wicked in life?"

Two sharp raps: *No.*

Hugo was taken aback. Could it really be that the good and the bad shared the same fate in the afterworld? His sense of justice was affronted. "You must be wrong, Amelia," he said, and asked the question again.

The answer was still: *No.*

Auguste Vacquerie was indignant. "This soul rejects the notion of reward and punishment after death!" he snapped.

Hugo scolded the table. "Listen, you there! Don't play with our souls. Know that there is a thinker here [Vacquerie] who hesitates to believe you. Your reply has deeply affected him. Give us an unequivocal answer: Is it not unthinkable that the wicked and the good should receive the same reward in heaven? Now, for the third time: Do those who have done evil in life have anything to fear in death?"

The table leg nearest Hugo rose slowly, then fell back. The leg nearest Vacquerie rose and turned until it faced him directly. Then it fell back on the table, and after that single rap was still.

So this time the answer was *Yes.* But Vacquerie was still disgusted. "All she's doing is spouting drivel," he muttered angrily.

All of a sudden, the table shook so violently that the hands of Victor and Charles slipped off.

"That's odd," remarked Delphine. "I'll bet the table's changed inhabitants. I'll bet that's not Amelia anymore."

"Answer me, Amelia," pleaded Hugo. "Is it you?"

The table leg nearest him rapped twice, almost convulsively: *No!*

"Well!" exclaimed Delphine. "I guessed right. How many of you want to bet that it isn't the devil himself who's in the table now?"

Hugo demanded: "You there! Tell me your name!"

The table leg rose, rapped once. It rapped a second time, then stopped.

"Is that a *b*?" asked Hugo.

Yes.

"Go on."

The table was shivering. It rapped fifteen times; fourteen times; once; sixteen times: the letters were *o, n, a,* and *p.* Each time it rapped, the shivering increased. It rapped out four more letters: *a, r, t, e.* With each of these four letters, the shivering decreased.

"Bonaparte!" they all cried out.

Mme Hugo, who had been in the kitchen, ran back to the living room wringing her hands.

"Is it Bonaparte?" demanded Hugo. The table rapped out as if in a fury:

Yes.

"Which one?" asked Hugo. "The big one?"

No.

"The little one?"

Yes.

All of them were shivering. Hugo exclaimed vehemently: "What! It's you, who we call Napoleon III, who's there?"

The table rapped with irritation: *Yes!*

"Is it really you, Louis Napoleon?"

Yes.

The pedestal table acted as if it were trying to jump off the larger table. It skidded around the surface like it was trying to escape. The participants stared in astonished silence. Victor Hugo shouted: "You scoundrel, I've got you!" The table twisted and turned like a bucking horse.

"Who sent you?" demanded Hugo.

The table leg in front of him reared up. It fell back to rap out, swiftly and with conviction: *My uncle.*

Victor Hugo was certainly impressed. The last thing he could have expected was that the table would put him in touch with his mortal enemy Napoleon III, emperor of France. As far as he knew, Louis Napoleon wasn't dead but very much alive.

"So it's possible for the spirits of the living to appear to us?" he asked.

Yes.

"I could have told you that," said Delphine. "It's standard spiritistic doctrine."

"Where is your living body at the moment?" Hugo asked.

In the shadows.

"You mean it's sleeping?"

Yes.

"Is it dreaming you're here?"

Yes.

"Is the dream making it suffer?"

Yes.

"Why?"

The dream is meant to punish me.

"So your uncle is unhappy with you?"

Yes.

"Is he unhappy with me?"

No.

"Does he know I admire him?"

Yes.

"Are you suffering on account of your crimes?"

Yes.

"Do you know when you'll die?"

In two years.

There now ensued one of the strangest conversations that has ever taken place, not only in the history of channeling but also surely in the history of confrontations between dictators and poets. It was not so much a conversation as a trial. And it was Louis Napoleon who was in the defendant's seat. Almost from the beginning, Victor Hugo assumed the role of prosecutor (with Napoleon III quickly falling into the habit of calling him "the judge") and began to pound away at (if this was really what it was) the soul of the sleeping emperor. This trial through the tapping tables went on for six hours, from nine o'clock in the evening of September 12, 1853, to three o'clock in the morning of September 13.

What were the highlights? Napoleon III declared that he would die at the hands of *everyone* and be replaced by the *universal republic*; Hugo and the others took this latter to refer to a United States of Europe, or at least a Federation of France and Germany. The emperor of France admitted to greatly admiring the writings of Victor Hugo—even while hating him as a man! He confided to them that his uncle, Napoleon I, hated his nephew, Napoleon III, every bit as much as Napoleon III admired Victor Hugo. In fact, Napoleon I called his nephew *his greatest unhappiness.*

The sleeping emperor claimed to fear Victor Hugo more than anyone else in the world, constantly rapping out cries of alarm like *Help me, I'm afraid* and *The judge is there!* Just why did Napoleon III fear Hugo? Because the poet made him feel awful about himself: *Your heroism puts my dastardliness to shame*, Napoleon III rapped out. *Dare to do*, he added, further telling Hugo that *Your daring frightens me!* Hugo's brilliance also intimidated Napoleon III; at his overthrow, he felt, *Hugo will be the brain, I feel it in my crown*, of a new government. The emperor did not think that he was smart enough to do what he had to do—and he feared that someone like Hugo would push him aside. The emperor of France reiterated that he would die *in two years*—and then Hugo would be among a group of towering geniuses who would succeed him as the governors of France.

Louis Napoleon thought Victor Hugo should be prepared to forgive him for his crimes. Why? *Because of your genius*, he told Hugo. But the poet pointed out to Napoleon that his crime hadn't just consisted of exiling Victor Hugo. Rather, Napoleon III's usurpation of power was a crime that "affects the whole human race"—and why should Hugo forgive him for a crime that affected everyone on the planet? The emperor, groveling with especial self-abasement before the "the judge," had to agree.

This trial through the tapping tables was taking place, Napoleon told Hugo, because *my conscience needs to be examined by you.* Still, if Napoleon III had his crimes to commit all over again, he would do so, *because he so liked being emperor!*

And so on and so forth it went, until most of the guests had gone to bed and Hugo, gray and exhausted, was slumping down in his armchair, and the tapping table was finally still.[8]

What did Napoleon III, emperor of France, have to say about his dreams when he emerged from the imperial bedroom on the morning of September 13, 1853, and began once again to tread the marble-covered corridors of his palace?

It is not recorded.

※※※

In the years ahead, Victor Hugo, reflecting on his encounter with the sleeping shade of Napoleon III on the night of September 12, 1853, would realize just how wrong the tapping tables could be about predicting the future. Napoleon III would not be ousted from power two years after the séance, nor would he die shortly after that. He would not be ousted until 1870. He would die, an exile himself, in England, in 1873—twenty years after the tapping-table session at which he had allegedly appeared.

For the séance attendees at Marine-Terrace, there was one more enemy to be channeled, and that on the very next night.

Four

WHEN THE SPIRITS
SPOKE HUNGARIAN

Count Sandor Teleki, Hungarian patriot, colonel in the revolutionary army of Louis Kossuth, reined in his chestnut-colored mare at the top of the hill and, leaning his stocky body forward, surveyed the blue Atlantic Ocean stretching out to the horizon.

The sea still had not lost its power to enthrall him. He had hardly ever seen it before the age of thirty-one, when the Austrian victory had spat him out of his landlocked country like a cannonball aimed at the Polish border. He had scrambled across central Europe and through Switzerland and France and England until at last he had come to rest on this rocky spit of an island set in this stunning sea.

Now, on horseback at Rozel Bay on the southeast corner of Jersey, at the edge of a cliff that fell straight down to an undersea grotto sculpted by the tide, he gazed out at the ocean in wonder. Its depths calmed his soul. The aquamarine sea cleansed his mind. It baptized him anew in its holy waters.

But always, after he had looked at the sea for five minutes, at most ten, the faces began to swim up at him out of the depths. They were desperate, suffering faces. They were faces distorted in agony, faces that stared at him in mute reproach through sightless eyes. Some of the faces he knew as well as his own. Others were the faces of strangers, though he had known them intimately, just for a moment, in an extremity of suffering.

"Colonel," called a brisk voice from farther down the slope. "Count Teleki, Sir."

Teleki picked up his reins and looked around from the saddle.

Lieutenant-Colonel Nicholas Katona, dressed immaculately in great-coat, breeches, and black boots, was riding up to him.

"Is it the general?" asked Teleki.

"Yes, Colonel," said Katona. "He's tired. I think it's time to go."

Teleki wheeled his horse around and joined Katona. The two trotted side-by-side down to the road. Katona had been aide-de-camp to General Lazar Meszaros during the war, and, here on Jersey, he was still aide-de-camp to General Lazar Meszaros. Now the general sat slumped forward on his horse beside the road, his eyes closed, his white-bearded chin resting on his chest.

Teleki rode up to him. The old man seemed to be sleeping. Teleki touched his hand and he opened his eyes. "I wasn't asleep," Meszaros said firmly, straightening up in the saddle. Beneath the gaunt temples, the eyes that returned Teleki's gaze were the unhappiest that he had ever seen.

The thought occurred to Teleki that there were the faces of the dead that welled up at you out of the sea, and there were the faces of the living that surrounded you every day and were just as racked with suffering. Lazar's was one of those. Meszaros had been minister of war and an active general in the field for sixteen months in Louis Kossuth's government. He had been fifty-two when he joined the cabinet. A year later, he looked sixty-five; already they were calling him the Old Man. Now, four years later, he looked eighty. Every day a new line etched a track across his proud and hopeless face. You saw him age before your very eyes.

"It's time to go home," said Teleki.

The general nodded and picked up the reins.

They had spent an hour resting by the cliffs. Now their excursion was over. They faced their horses around and fell into single file, Teleki in front, Meszaros in the middle, Katona bringing up the rear. They trotted down the narrow muddy path that led away from the bluff, pace quickening as the horses, glad to be moving again, rapidly lengthened their stride.

The faces welled up in front of Teleki again. He had discovered that, once the faces came, they did not go away until he had paid homage to them, until he had acknowledged the depths of their suffering, until he had replayed in his mind every detail he knew of their ordeal. The face that rose up before him now—the face that kept pace with him along the road—was the face of Louis Batthyány.

He had last seen that face on October 6, 1849, when the open wagon transporting Teleki and ten other prisoners to Adad Prison had suddenly been diverted, while passing by the outskirts of Pest, into the center of the city. It was six o'clock in the morning; dawn was streaking the sky with gray; and Teleki, filthy, starving, in rags, trembling so violently from the cold that his chain rattled menacingly along with him, watched numbly as the wagon drew up beside a small gray paved square on which a squadron of Austrian soldiers, perhaps thirty, was drawn up.

"We have been ordered to let you watch something before taking you on to Adad," one of the guards in the wagon had told them curtly.

Teleki gazed blankly as the squadron of soldiers snapped to attention. Not far away, on the other side of the square, in the ground floor of a flat, almost windowless, building, a narrow door opened slowly. A light-complexioned man, tall and erect, emerged and stood swaying slightly in the harsh gray light of the dawn.

He wore a white open-necked shirt and black loose-fitting trousers. Soldiers appeared behind him holding his arms. His hands were not tied. A bloody bandage was wrapped around his neck.

The soldiers released the prisoner's arms. Alone, stepping firmly, he advanced into the center of the square. Teleki now saw his features, and with a shock he recognized the nearly bald head, the tawny blond beard framing the face, the calm alert glance of Louis Batthyány, Hungary's first prime minister in the provisional government of Louis Kossuth.[1]

Teleki watched in stunned horror as the commander of the firing squad stepped forward and spoke briefly with Batthyány. The commander held out a blindfold. Batthyány refused it with a wave of his hand. In a voice that Teleki could clearly hear, he asked to give the order to fire. The commander stepped back stony-faced. The five men of the firing squad fell in and were called to attention. Batthyány lowered himself to one knee on the paving stones. He straightened up and gazed steadily ahead. The commander barked out another order. The soldiers loaded their rifles and shouldered them.

"Allez Jäger, éljen a hazor!" shouted Louis Batthyány.

Teleki had heard these words before. They were in three languages and they meant, "Long live the fatherland!"

The rays of the morning sun, breaking suddenly through the gray streaks of cloud, threw into astonishing relief the bald skull, the blond beard, the unwrinkled face, the brilliant black glance, the elegant self-possession despite the bloody bandage around the neck, of this magnificent Hungarian on one knee before a firing squad and opening his arms wide as if to further expose his breast.

"Fire!" pronounced Louis Batthyány, loudly, distinctly, firmly.

A volley of shots rang out.[2] The blast hurled Batthyány backward. He collapsed on his side, arms still outstretched, rolled over on his back, and was still.

The bullets had struck him in the head and chest. The blood mingled with the blond hair of his beard, soaked the bandage around his neck, and flowed out across the paving stones.

"Murderers!" screamed Teleki, tearing at his chain.

Beside him the biggest of his fellow prisoners, a captain with the shoulders of an ox, tore his chain from its socket with a single violent wrench, leaped lightly up onto the edge of the wagon's side, balanced there for a moment, and then hurled himself headfirst downward onto the pavement.

Something sharp and heavy struck Teleki on the head. He knew no more.

When he awoke, vomiting, head on fire, the wagon had come almost all the way to Adad. It was night. He was given some scraps of food, then lost consciousness again. A kick awakened him. The wagon had arrived at Adad Prison. Weak and trembling, half-unconscious, he was hustled through long dark corridors and into a tiny cell.

He remembered little of his first days at the prison. There were many prisoners, and word had it that Field Marshal Julius Haynau himself, the vicious commander of the Austrian army, had ordered that Batthyány be hung like a common criminal rather than executed by a firing squad. The night before he was to die, he had stabbed himself in the throat with a dagger smuggled into his cell by his wife. The doctors saved his life, but now, with his neck torn and bandaged, it was impossible to properly hang Louis Batthyány. Haynau was furious.[3]

Teleki expected to be hung himself, and without warning, at any time. For six weeks he woke up every morning telling himself, you will certainly die today. At the end of the third week, seeing that he was still alive, he had asked for something to read. A book had been tossed into his cell. It was *Le dernier jour d'un condamné (The Last Day of a Condemned Man)* by Victor Hugo. "You see, *cher maître*," Teleki would say to Hugo on Jersey Island three years later, "they were trying to cheer me up! How fortunate I was to meet you at the time."

At the end of the sixth week the door of his cell had been flung open and a dapper young colonel appeared. He handed Teleki a piece of paper on which was written not "Sandor Teleki"—his name—but "Dominique Teleki." "Come with me, Dominique Teleki," said the dapper colonel. Teleki followed him down a long and winding corridor to an ornate office.

He found himself alone with a general. "My dear fellow," said the general, smiling faintly from behind a huge oaken desk, "I have saved you. I wrote a name different from yours on purpose. Now, leave this prison. My guards will escort you. Go."[4]

Teleki stared open-mouthed, not daring to ask why he was being freed. The general gazed at him thoughtfully and then declared: "Let us say that it is a matter of personal honor. Let us say that your distinguished family is involved. Let us say that a woman of great generosity played a leading role."

Teleki was deposited outside the prison. It was night. He had only the clothes on his back and the uneasy feeling that the general's beneficence did not extend beyond the prison walls. He ran. He ran through the night. During the day he slept in the deep thickets of dark forests. As he ran he wondered: *Who could that woman of great generosity possibly be?* It seemed to him that it could only be his first cousin, Blanka Teleki. Before the war, Blanka had helped refugees escape from Hungary. She had had to fraternize with a group of Austrian officers to do so. She had been found out, and she had been in prison for several years now, but she was still in touch with powerful persons who helped her on the outside.

A sharp jolt snapped Teleki out of his reverie. His horse, racing along the Jersey road, had stumbled and recovered itself. Yellow wheat fields were sweeping by; without knowing it, Teleki had spurred his horse to a gallop. He twisted around in the saddle: Mezsaros and Katona were far behind. He settled back, distracted, in his saddle. A different face was welling up before him—not Blanka's, but the face of the woman the memory of Blanka always evoked. He dreaded to see this face.

It was four months before the end of the war. Teleki and his men had come to a village razed by the Austrians. Fire and ash was everywhere, and the bodies of women, children, and old men. A castle overlooked the village; Teleki and his men advanced up the hillside toward it. A junior officer rode ahead, then turned and galloped back. "Colonel," he shouted, "Haynau has been here. It is the work of the monster Haynau."

Teleki urged his horse up the slope. There were bodies in the garden. Some were naked. Riding through the trampled rosebushes, he saw the half-hidden body of a woman. He dismounted and pulled the rose bushes aside.

She lay on her stomach. Her back was a mass of clotted blood. Here and there the white of vertebrae peeked through. She had been whipped to death. He turned the body over. Gashes like sword wounds crisscrossed her breasts and stomach. One eye dangled from the socket.

Galloping at breakneck speed along the Jersey road, his horse foaming, Teleki violently banished from his mind the face of the woman. *Alas*, he thought, *poor humanity! We think the worst has happened, but there is always worse to come.* The Austrian commander—the beast Haynau, the hyena of Brescia, the murderer of Louis Batthyány—had continued the practice, for which he had become notorious in Italy, of having women stripped and publicly whipped to death for aiding the insurgency.

Teleki's horse was faltering. He slowed it to a canter and, looking back, saw that Meszaros and Katona were no longer there. They had turned off at Meszaros's house in Saint Sauveur; Teleki himself was on his way to Victor Hugo's house.

He slowed his horse to a trot. Ahead of him, the soft silhouette of Saint Helier stood out against the twilight sky. Teleki turned slightly to his left; Marine-Terrace was a half mile down the road. He and his wife (she had left for Paris the night before) dined with the Hugos two or three times a week. That past Sunday afternoon they had witnessed the disturbing séance where Hugo's deceased daughter had apparently spoken through the tapping tables. Teleki hadn't known what to think. He was a skeptic, but he had been moved.

He was dining with the Hugos again tonight, and it was his understanding that there would be another séance. Of course there would be! That charming Parisian woman, Delphine de Girardin, the instigator of it all, was still there. In the twilight that was fast settling into night, Teleki turned his horse sharply into the stable yard below Marine-Terrace. He reined in, leaped off, and handed the bridle to the stable boy who came running. Combing his hair back with his fingers,

Teleki stepped smartly in the direction of the huge house that, every window on its ground floor brightly lit, rose up against the darkness of the night.

The meal was convivial, as always. Victor Hugo was in good form. He managed to refute every argument put to him by either of his two sons. At nine o'clock they all sat down in armchairs close to the tapping tables.

There was indeed to be a séance that night, and, attending it, along with Teleki, were Victor Hugo, Mme Hugo, the young Adèle Hugo, François-Victor Hugo, Auguste Vacquerie, General and Mme Le Flô, and, of course, Delphine de Girardin.

Teleki and Charles Hugo placed their hands on the table. There were quick exchanges with two spirits. Then—perhaps a half hour had passed and Victor Hugo had just replaced Teleki—a new and somber energy possessed the table.

The leg stirred slowly as Hugo asked: "Are you a soul?"

The answer came: *Yes.*

"What is your name?"

Haynau.

Teleki, seated two chairs away, started and shivered. He knew Julius Haynau had died six months before.

"What are you doing here?" asked Hugo. "Who sent you?"

Blanka Teleki, came the answer.

This time Teleki was shocked. What dreadful joke was this? Blanka? Could this be? Was Blanka dead? Then he remembered that earlier that evening Hugo had told him that a sleeping Napoleon III had come through the tables the night before and spoken to them. But surely, Teleki now thought, all this was nonsense—

"Where is your soul, Haynau?" Hugo was asking. "Can you tell us?"

It is being whipped.

"Does not that seem like justice to you?"

Alas!

"Do you know what I've said about you?" asked Hugo. The poet had written several scathing verses about Haynau.

God showed me.

"When will Hungary be free? Do you know?"

Yes.

"Tell us."

In three years.

"Do you acknowledge the justice of Hungary's cause?"

The table did not move.

"Are you still there, Haynau?" asked Hugo.

Yes.

"Do you agree that you are being justly punished?"

Yes.

"That Hungary's cause is just?"

Yes.

"Do you repent of your crimes?"

I do not repent.

"You do not repent?"

I'm thinking about it.

"Why did Blanka Teleki send you to me?"

To be avenged.

"Do you know that her cousin is here?"

Yes.

"Do you see him?"

Yes.

"Do you see all of us who surround him?"

Him.

"Only him?"

Yes.

"Can you tell me what will become of your emperor Franz-Joseph?"

Yes.

"Tell us."

Tyrant.

"Will he be punished some day in this lifetime?"

Yes.

Teleki had been numb up to this point. Now he joined the conversation: "Will it be by me?" he asked.

No.

"Will it be by *me*?" asked Victor Hugo.

Yes.

"So I'm the one who will punish the tyrant Franz-Joseph?"

Yes.

"How?"

I am opening my grave for him.

They looked at each other in consternation. Hugo asked: "Have you come here to say something to Colonel Teleki?"

Yes.

"Speak."

Crows be here to tear eagles apart.

"Eagle?" muttered Hugo. "That is the emblem of Austria. Is he talking about the emblem of Austria? Are we republicans the crows? Perfidious remark!"

Teleki asked: "How many men have you executed, wretched creature?"

One is worth a thousand.

Afterward, they would disagree about the meaning of this statement. Hugo thought it meant, "One Hungarian is worth a thousand Austrians." Teleki, on the other hand, took it for a totally cynical remark meaning, "Kill one, kill a thousand; what's the difference?"

Teleki asked: "You told me your soul was being whipped. By whom?"

By the rope.

"What rope?"

The gallows rope.

"How much was Georgey paid to betray us?"

The table stayed still.

Hugo asked Teleki who "Georgey" was. The Hungarian replied that he meant Arthur Görgey, the general who had been defeated by Haynau's forces in one of the last decisive battles of the war. At the time Kossuth thought Görgey had thrown the battle; he called him "Hungary's Judas."

Hugo asked the table: "If Blanka Teleki sent you, what are you doing to avenge her?"

Turning all my hatred into love for her.

"Can you leave this séance without our permission?"

There was no response.

"Are you still there, Haynau?"

No.

And with that, the field marshal was gone.[5]

———

The séance wasn't finished yet, but Sandor Teleki, disturbed and exhausted, did not pay much attention to what happened next. Auguste Vacquerie had taken over from Charles at the table. No sooner had he placed his hands on the table when it began to tremble strongly.

"Who's there?" Auguste asked.

Civilization.

This was only the first of many "personifications" that would come to the tapping tables.

Vacquerie asked: "What is the best way civilization has of expressing itself here on earth?"

Speech.

"Among all the ways words can be used, which is the most effective?"

Poetry.

Vacquerie was a poet himself. He eagerly asked Civilization: "Do you have a communication for me?"

Yes.

"Tell me."

Believe, for the world begins.

"Do you come more willingly to some humans than to others?"

We build our nests in the tallest trees.

"Am I one of those trees?"

You have the roots of one.

"What must I do to acquire the height of one?"

Suffer.

"And—?"

Suffering is the dew.

"Please continue."

Hope is the flower, death the fruit.

Now Victor Hugo entered the conversation. After the exchange of a few pleasantries he asked, "Can you tell me when there will be an end to the oppression that currently weighs upon France and upon the world?"

Perhaps Hugo was thinking about Napoleon III. But the table replied: *France is only a country.*

"France is, yes. But what about the world?"

Your world is only a horizon.

Hugo did not know how to respond to this enigmatic statement. Now he asked: "Do you, as Civilization, preside over all the civilizations in all the worlds at once?"

Yes.

"Do you believe, as I do, that civilization's efforts should be turned toward the situation of women and children in particular?"

And toward the elderly. They are no farther from the grave than are the children.

"Do you not think that it is a good idea to make a distinction between religion and the priesthood?"

Religions fade with winter and are reborn in springtime.

"So God is the eternal sap, societies are the tree, and religions are the leaves?"

Good.

"Can you tell me how you picture the next stage of my duties on earth?"

You must go on. Be in the forefront of your century. The future is in your hands.

"Do you think that while I'm alive I'll at least see the continent of Europe freed?"

Yes.

"A United States of Europe?"

Yes.

"By a bloody revolution or a peaceful one?"

Blood doesn't count beside tears.

"Do you mean that, when peoples weep, they must be saved even if it means war?"

Yes.

"When will we see a United States of Europe?"

In six years.

"How long will Bonaparte reign?"

Two years.

"Spirit, will you return to us?"

Yes.

"What do we have to do to make you return?"

Be inspired.

"Do you have a final word before you go?"

Great man, finish Les Misérables. (Hugo had brought the manuscript of his future masterpiece with him to Jersey; he would complete the book on Guernsey Island in 1862.)

The séance had come to an end.[6]

But the séances were not ended for Count Sandor Teleki.

❧✦❧

Let us defy chronology and leap ahead nine months. (In the next chapter, we'll return to the séances of mid-September 1853 and move forward once again in an orderly fashion.)

Teleki had continued to attend the séances, but only sporadically; his many duties on Jersey Island kept him busy almost all the time. He came from the nobility, and his Transylvanian family had been enormously wealthy; now he was extremely poor. Most days he worked in Philippe Asplet's candle-making factory in Saint Helier. He wrote foreign news stories for the exiles' newspaper, *L'Homme*.[7] He kept in touch with Kossuth, whom he visited regularly in London, and maintained contacts with numerous other influential Hungarians, including the pianist Franz Liszt and the violinist Edward Reményi (the latter would soon visit him on the island). Most of all, Teleki strove to help the Hungarian exiles keep body and soul together.

He was not sure he did a very good job of keeping his own body and soul together. The faces continued to haunt him every day. There was the searing image of Louis Batthyány collapsing on the paving stones, blood mingling with the blond of his beard . . .

When Teleki came to the séance at Marine-Terrace on the evening of June 7, 1854, his attitude was casual, almost one of indifference. The effect of the earlier séance, when, it seemed, he had talked to Julius Haynau, had almost faded away.

Present at the séance that night were Count Teleki, Victor Hugo, Mme Hugo, Adèle Hugo, Hennett de Kesler, Louis Guérin, Charles Hugo, Albert Pinson, and Auguste Vacquerie.

Teleki was surprised to find himself volunteering, without being prompted, to sit with Charles at the tapping tables.

No sooner had he placed his hand on the pedestal table than it began to rock slowly back and forth.

"Someone is here," stated Charles. "Who are you, spirit?"

Teleki felt an odd uneasiness.

The table leg began to tap an answer, it seemed, to Charles's question. It tapped more slowly than usual. After what seemed an endless time, Charles, sounding tired, murmured: "The first name is 'Louis.'"

The table leg went on tapping.

Teleki found it hard to pay attention. His neck felt constricted, as if a weight were lying on it. Vague images swam past the periphery of his vision, colors that ebbed and flowed—gray, red, and yellow-blond.

He felt an overwhelming sadness.

Charles said grumpily: "It's spelling out a last name, though I don't understand it. It's 'Batthle'—? No—" The table leg tapped with immense slowness. Finally Charles, sounding worn-out, declared: "The full name is Louis Batthyány." He stared at Teleki and said: "That name is familiar to me. I don't know from where."

Victor Hugo, sitting nearby, started to speak, then thought better of it. He sat back and gazed intently at Teleki.

The Hungarian count was overcome with emotion. He tried to speak but couldn't.

Charles asked: "Colonel Teleki, do you have a question?"

Fighting to maintain his composure, Teleki said, "Yes, I have a question. I will ask it in Hungarian."

He asked his question aloud, though no one, least of all Charles, understood him. No one knew he had just asked the spirit of Louis Batthyány, whose execution by firing squad he had witnessed five years earlier: "What can I do for our country?"

The table leg tapped even more slowly than before, as if it was relaying a message from the other side of the universe. With each tap, more energy seemed to drain from Charles, who abruptly burst out: "These are nonsense syllables!"

"They aren't," said Teleki. He had been counting the taps carefully. "They are Hungarian syllables. My question is being answered in Hungarian."

The participants gazed at him in puzzled silence. Charles finally slumped in his chair and said: "It's finished."

Teleki closed his eyes and bowed his head.

Louis Batthyány had spoken to him in Hungarian.

He had said:

The native land waits to be avenged.[8]

Five

THE SHADOW
OF THE SEPULCHER

In the meditation halls of ashrams, where meditators sit, eyes shut, cross-legged, on the floor, attempting to get in touch with their higher selves, strange noises often fill the air: barks, belly laughs, giggles, sudden screams, strangled gasps, buzzing, a bee-like humming, even the occasional bray.

According to the gurus, these noises are the soul clearing its throat, coughing up the deep obstructing phlegm of previous lifetimes, shoveling psychic debris out of the way, clearing a path so the higher self can begin to re-exert its forgotten presence.

Years later, looking back on it all, Victor Hugo, who knew a great deal about Hinduism and something about meditation, must have wondered at times if those first dark encounters with Napoleon III and Julius Haynau at the tapping tables hadn't also been a kind of clearing out of the soul, a flushing of violent and vengeful feelings from the psyche so that the enlightenment of contact with beings from the higher realms of heaven (such as Léopoldine, who, exceptionally, had come through right at the beginning) could begin to make itself manifest. Whatever the truth, there was no question that, at the séance of September 14, 1853, which began at half past nine in the evening, there appeared a spirit as different from the spirits that had preceded it as day is from night.

Present at the séance that night were Delphine de Girardin (who had delayed her departure for Paris), the entire Hugo family, Count Teleki, and General and Mme Le Flô. First Charles and Teleki, then Charles and General Le Flô, placed their hands on the little pedestal table.

Victor Hugo, seeing the table begin to stir, asked: "Who's there?"

The answer came: *The Shadow.*

"The shadow of someone who has been alive?"

No.

"Must we all live at least once?"

No.

"Are you an angel?"

Yes.

"The angel of death?"

Yes.

"Why have you come? Can you tell us?"

To chat with life.

"What do you want to tell us?"

Believe.

"In what?"

In the unknown.

"Is the world you belong to a continuation of this life?"

Death is the balloon that carries the soul to heaven.

"And what do you have to say to life?"

Spirits, come, here be seers.

"Are we the spirits you're addressing?"

No.

"You mean we are the seers?"

Yes.

"Can you see us?"

No.

"Have the spirits you've just summoned lived life as we live it?"

The table did not move.

"Can you answer?"

No.

The table trembled.

"Is there any way I can calm you?"

No.

"Are you a happy spirit?"

Happiness is merely a human phenomenon, since it cannot exist without unhappiness.

"Are you speaking in this way because you dwell in the absolute?"

Yes.

"Tell us about yourself."

Infinity is an emptiness packed full.

"Do you mean that what we call emptiness is filled with the spirit world?"

My goodness!

"So, Shadow, you're capable of a good belly laugh?"

No.

"Speak to us."

Use your body to seek out your soul.

"Are you the only spirit here at the moment?"

I am everything and I am everywhere.

"Do you want me to keep on questioning you?"

Yes. You hold the key to a door that has been closed.

"Are you aware of the vision I had yesterday?"

I know not yesterdays.

"Can we be certain of seeing you after we die?"

You are but wearing glasses.

Hugo would ponder these words and decide they meant that mortal vision is a kind of wearing of glasses and that when we die we discover that seeing is far different from what we thought. For now, though, he pursued a different line of inquiry:

"If we behave well in this life, can we hope for a better one?"

Yes.

"If we behave badly, will we have a more painful one?"

Yes.

"Are the souls of the dead with you?"

Under me.

"You say that you are everything and everywhere. Are you God?"

Over me.

"Are you nearer to other souls than you are to God?"

For me there is neither near nor far.

"Tell me, are there inhabited worlds other than our own?"

Yes.

"Inhabited by beings who resemble us in body and soul?"

Some, yes. Others, no.

"After death, do the souls of those who have done good deeds find themselves in regions of light or do they end up inhabiting other worlds?"

Light.

Suddenly the table was still. The spirit, whom they would come to call the Shadow of the Sepulcher, was gone. He would return often.[1]

❧❧❧

Delphine de Girardin left for Paris a few days later. This diminished not a whit the interest of the group in the tables. Ten years later, in *Les miettes de l'histoire,* Auguste Vacquerie would recount his own first wild rush of enthusiasm:

> The departure of Mme de Girardin put no brake on my zeal to talk to the tables. With abandon I hurled myself into this extraordinary experience of death gaping half-open before us. I no longer waited until evening. I started at noon and didn't finish till next morning; I stopped only to eat. I exerted no [psychic] influence on the table myself, and so I never touched it; but I interrogated it. The mode of communication was always the same; I went along with it. Mme Girardin sent me two tables from Paris. The first was small, with one of its legs ending in a pencil that could write or draw the spirits' communications; we tried it once or twice but it drew indifferently and wrote badly. The second was larger, and of the variety that has the letters of the alphabet inscribed in a circle on its top like the numbers of a clock, with a needle, attached at one end to the center of the tabletop, meant to move in a circle and point to letters. We also discarded this type after an unsuccessful attempt, and I definitely recommend the more primitive type that, simplified by practice and a few abbreviations, eventually acquires all the speed necessary. I chatted easily with the table; the sound of the sea intermingled with the words of these dialogues whose mystery was enhanced by winter, by night, by storm and by isolation. The table no longer spoke in single words; now it responded in sentences and even with whole pages. Most of the time it was solemn and magisterial, but sometimes it was witty and even comical. At times it exploded in rage; more than once, it hurled insults at me when I treated it with irreverence, and I must admit that I couldn't really relax until it had forgiven me. It wanted to be interrogated in poetry, and we obeyed; and then it answered in poetry itself.[2]

There began to unfold at the séances what one commentator (admittedly a skeptic, but a fascinated one) has called, "a fantastical mystical phantasmagoria . . . one with innumerable scenes and acts, which both charmed and worried Victor Hugo and those close to him, and of which they were both the unconscious authors and the gravely astonished audience."[3]

It seemed as if a contact had been established between Marine-Terrace and the mysterious regions called the afterworld and that this (so to speak) new Jersey Island lighthouse, casting its powerful beams into other realms of reality, was able to attract spirit after spirit. Discarnate entities crowded around it like spirit moths drawn to the flame of the living. There were spirits of a type never heard of before by the participants: the shades of legendary animals like Balaam's Ass and the Lion of Androcles, and abstract entities like Criticism, Tragedy, Death, and The Grave, which were somehow animated with soul and not dissimilar to the transcendent Ideas of the Greek philosopher Plato. There were also the shades of some of the great geniuses of humankind, who seemed extremely anxious to talk to Hugo and whom he welcomed with all the familiarity one reserves for one's closest friends.[4]

One of the first great souls to descend to the tapping tables was the Italian poet Dante Alighieri (1265–1321), author of *The Divine Comedy,* who dropped in on the séance of September 13, shortly after the Shadow of the Sepulcher made his exit. Had Dante come because he, too, was an exile, banished from his native city of Florence in his lifetime? Did he wish to commiserate with the exiled Victor Hugo? No sooner had the shade announced itself when Hugo exclaimed:

"Dante, you know I love you and admire you. I'm happy that you are here. Speak!"

The shade replied: *This exile comes to you from grave's edge.* And then: *Love is. Hatred is nonexistence.*

"Why are you here?"

The native land.

There were Italian political exiles on Jersey Island as well. Had the spirits of these fellow patriots drawn Dante to the tables?

And then, as suddenly as he had come, the author of *The Divine Comedy* was gone.[5]

The spirits crowded through in increasing number and loquacity. There were distinguished shades from the French Revolution, like Marat and Robespierre, and many giants of French literature: Chateaubriand and Racine dropped by briefly; Molière would stay on for the duration. During the first weeks and months the séance participants begged for descriptions of heaven. The spirits obliged, none more so than Jean-Jacques Rousseau (1712–1778), who paid a visit sometime between September 29 and December 6, 1853. The séances took place mostly at Marine-Terrace, but a few were conducted at the home of the proscrit Edmond Leguevel; the Rousseau séance was one of those. There is no record of who attended, though we know who asked the questions.

Jean-Jacques Rousseau was the French philosopher whose groundbreaking works on political theory and education shattered the entrenched thinking of the aristocracy and upper middle classes and paved the way for the French Revolution. When Xavier Durrieu asked the shade to describe heaven, "Rousseau" became ecstatic:

In the infinite depths before me I see a dazzling abyss that seems to draw me ceaselessly toward it. I am carried away by the irresistible attraction of its radiance. I am always in flight and I never arrive. I am plunged into infinity for an eternity. I am giddy with God.

"Are you completely happy?"

My happiness is like a perfume. I'm always inhaling it and it always eludes me. It is a ceaselessly renewed, never-satisfied, intoxication. I enjoy both the fullness of happiness and the desire for happiness. . . . Picture my happiness as a bath in an ocean of light-beams. Human love has these beams, but they should be bolts of lightning.

In life, Rousseau had expressed the belief that suicide is usually justified. What did he think about this in death, Leguevel asked.

Suicide is the act of a traveler who has eternity to travel in and is afraid of being late. To commit suicide is to put forward the hour-hand of the wristwatch of your life.

Leguevel pursued: "Do we have the right to commit suicide?"

No.

Charles asked: "Is it the act of a madman?"

Yes.

Durrieu asked: "Why are men afraid of death? Since life where you are is so happy, why has nature made it that men fear death?"

God wants man to live. He hides death from him.

After several more brief exchanges, Jean-Jacques Rousseau was gone.[6]

❧❦

This was just a very small part of what the séance attendees were hearing that fall. As the communications mounted, what did Victor Hugo and company think about it all?

Did they think they were actually talking to the spirits of the dead?

Once the heartrending effects of the first séance with Leopoldine had begun to fade, Victor Hugo was no longer certain that he had really spoken to his dead daughter or that he was speaking to the spirits of the dead at all. For a brief period he wondered if it didn't all come from Charles, who was turning out to be the most gifted medium among them. He declared to his son on September 21, 1853: "It's quite simply your intelligence multiplied five times by the magnetism that makes the table act, and makes it tell you what you already have in your own thoughts."[7]

He had changed his tune by mid-October. Now he thought that he might actually be talking to spirits, but that the spirits might not necessarily be who they said they were. He told a friend: "It may be that this is a single spirit, who assumes these names in order to get our attention."[8]

By February 1854, Hugo was looking around for ways to prove that the spirits really existed. In her diary entry for February 7, Adèle Hugo quotes her father.

There's only one physical way to prove this spiritual thing: Ask the mysterious beings who talk to us to reveal to us three secrets—for example, how to cure rabies, how to properly steer a balloon, and where there are undiscovered gold deposits in Australia. Then send the answers in three sealed envelopes to the Academy of Sciences. Tell them:

"We're going to publish a book, dictated by the Tables, and we asked these same Tables to tell us the three secrets which are contained in these three sealed envelopes. If, as time passes and humanity unlocks these secrets by itself, the three answers are found to be correct, then our spirits will have proved to be real; if not, our book will have been found out to be a fiction."[9]

There is no evidence that Hugo ever asked the spirits these questions or any like them, or ever sent any answers to the Academy of Sciences.

The spirits, however, had plenty of answers that were *not* verifiable, and these we will now begin to examine; for, as the séances went forward, the tapping-table shades began to assemble an agenda of their own. First, though, there is a piece of unfinished business to complete: there occurred at the séance of October 5, 1853, an uncanny sequel to the encounter with Napoleon III that had taken place on September 12.

We have no record of who was present at this séance or if it took place at Marine-Terrace. But we do know from the transcripts what transpired. First, the table trembled. Then Hugo asked: "Who's there?"

The answer came: *I am the other one.*

"What do you mean by the other one?"

Napoleon.

"Which one?"

The Great.

A wave of excitement passed through the participants. Hugo said: "You know I admire you. Do you have a message for us?"

Yes.

"For me?"

Yes.

"Speak."

The shade of the great Napoleon I then tapped out an anguished attack on his nephew, Napoleon III:

Help! Seize the assassin! My lineage is sacrificing me; they're pillaging my life; they're assassinating my death. O, my old Personal Guard! O, my flags! O, my victories! O, my son! Austerlitz—O, purity of blood spilled for the fatherland! O, idealism—come to my aid! My abused title sullies my glory. My bones are being stolen. Ah! Funeral shroud, close yourself up! The violator of France has stolen the sanctity of the tomb. The gravedigger Bonaparte gnaws away at the dead Napoleon.

This diatribe didn't, of course, surprise Hugo. He thought it only fitting and did not feel the need to comment. He asked Napoleon I instead: "What would you do if you were me?"

The shade replied: *Write your poetry.*

"What do you think of my book *Napoleon the Little?*" This was Hugo's own attack on Napoleon III.

An immense truth. A baptism for the traitor.

"As you know," said Hugo, "it pains me greatly that this miserable creature has diminished your name. In the face of his criminality, I continue to admire and respect you."

Yes.

"Do you know the section in my book entitled *Expiation?*"

No.

"Does your soul dwell among the blessed?"

Yes.

"I find that fitting. But don't you feel as a punishment the pain of having such a man as Napoleon III parody your name?"

Yes.

"Can you talk about the life that is yours now?"

Yes.

"We who are here believe in God. Can you define Him?"

The table carefully tapped out: *An infinite glance from an eternal eye.*[10]

And then, abruptly—as unexpectedly as it had begun—the visit was over. They would not hear from Napoleon I again. But they were soon to encounter a military genius whom even Napoleon I considered his superior.

Six

HANNIBAL STORMS THE
TAPPING TABLES

It was true that General Joseph-Léopold-Sigisbert Hugo had had immense experience in combating guerilla leaders who conducted wars of bush and ravine, bursting out of nowhere to fight brief, bloody skirmishes and then abruptly melting away into a landscape of a thousand hiding places.

Hadn't he tracked down the Italian bandit and guerilla leader Fra Diavolo, the general driving his own men through torrential rains and pea-soup fogs and minor earthquakes, forcing them at the point of a sword to climb sheer bluffs that had never been climbed before except by goats, and not going to bed himself for thirty days?[1]

Yes, certainly, it was true. But that had been in Italy, where the majority of Italians had accepted the conquest and rule of Napoleon I, and Fra Diavolo had led an insurgency not only against the French but also against most of Italy as well. Here in Spain, it was different: though some of the nobility had made a show of it initially, none of the Spanish accepted the rule of the conquering Napoleon, which meant that when General Hugo, newly appointed the governor of the provinces of Guadalajara and Segovia, had to fight the guerilla leader El Empecinado ("The Stubborn One"), he was fighting not only El Empecinado, but every other Spaniard as well.

That was why, writing at his desk early one morning at his headquarters in Brihuega, forty-five miles north of Madrid, the general was particularly alarmed to hear the sound of gunfire coming from Auñon.

For the past several weeks General Hugo had been fortifying the village of Auñon against El Empecinado and his rebels. The village sat on the right bank of the Tagus River at the point where a lone stone bridge spanned its rushing waters. For months El Empecinado had been crossing the bridge from north to south, leading his men on skirmishes that sometimes took them as far south as the gates of Madrid. The general had been building a blockhouse and lengthening the railings on both sides of the bridge; but the Spanish workers, every one of them loyal to El Empecinado and his rebels, purposely worked so incredibly slowly that the fortifications were still not finished.

General Hugo stayed over at Brihuega one day a week, and on those days he would leave his brother, Corporal Louis Hugo, in charge at Auñon. So General Hugo was unusually concerned when, early that morning, he heard the sound of gunfire coming from Auñon.

He left his office and went to the guards on duty next door and asked them if they'd heard anything. They replied that they hadn't. The general decided he must have been mistaken—and anyway, wasn't Auñon twenty miles away, too far for the sound of gunfire to be heard? He returned to his office and resumed his writing.

Almost immediately the sound of firing came again, louder and more distinct this time. It was definitely coming from Auñon. The general rose from his desk, went out of the office, and accosted the guards again. This time he told them they must have heard something.

They stared at him, puzzled. "No, Sir, General Hugo," said the first soldier. "I heard nothing, Sir." The other soldier concurred.

The general was astonished and irritated. "Fetch Major Shelly and his men," he snapped. "Some of them must have heard the racket."

When Major Shelly and his men from the Royal Irish Horse Brigade arrived—some factions of the Irish having sided with Napoleon in this war—they, too, said they'd heard nothing. An aide-de-camp was sent out to the plain to question the fortress guards, but nobody there had heard the sound of firing either.

General Hugo was now extremely worried about his brother. He could no longer contain himself. He mounted his horse and ordered the brigadiers to do the same. They set off at a gallop in the direction of Auñon. Before they'd gotten halfway, the roar of cannon fire proved the general had been right. Though Auñon was just twenty miles from Brihuega, the route was made four times longer by the precipitously sheer mountainsides alongside which the road wound and twisted, often turning back on itself.

By the time General Hugo and his men arrived at the village, its half-finished blockhouse was in the hands of two rebel bands, one of them led by El Empecinado. Auñon had been overrun and the streets and fields were littered with the bodies of the dead. Colonel Louis Hugo was badly wounded, and what remained of his garrison was about to be slaughtered. Hugo and his men attacked with a fury. Soon the village and bridge of Auñon had been retaken. The rebel forces fled, with General Hugo and his men in hot pursuit.

Afterward, the general wondered how it was that he had been able to hear the sound of musket fire twenty miles way in Auñon. Perhaps it was some trick of acoustics, the sound being reflected this way and that through the welter of steep mountainsides until it happened to arrive exactly at the level of the desk that General Hugo was writing at. But, if that were the case, why had he been the only one to hear the sound of gunfire?

Was it because his brother Louis lay badly wounded in the streets of Auñon?[2]

General Joseph-Léopold-Sigisbert Hugo was, of course, the father of Victor Hugo. At the time of the Auñon incident Victor was eight, and the year was 1810. The story became enshrined in family lore. Mme Adèle Hugo included it in her biography of her husband, *Victor Hugo raconté par un témoin de sa vie* (Victor Hugo Recounted by a Witness to His Life) published in 1863. The mysterious Auñon incident was the first occasion we know of when the military and the psychic vividly interacted in the lives of the Hugos. The encounters with Napoleon I and Napoleon III at the tapping tables could be said to constitute a second and a third. But those two encounters were decisively topped when, on December 8, 1853, there came tapping through the turning tables a military genius whom even Napoleon I (and certainly Napoleon III) acknowleged to be his master. This was Hannibal Barca, the Carthaginian warrior who almost defeated the mighty Roman Empire in the Second Punic War in the third century B.C.

Who exactly was Hannibal Barca?

In the twelfth century B.C., Phoenicia founded the colony of Carthage, in what is now Tunisia. By the third century B.C., Carthage was an independent city-state, powerful enough to challenge the rule of Rome on the other side of the Mediterranean.

The two states fought the First Punic War in 264–241 B.C. ("Punic," another word for Carthaginian, is also the name of the language the Carthaginians spoke.) The war ended in an inconclusive victory for Rome. In 218 B.C., Hannibal Barca, at twenty-five already a general, sparked off the Second Punic War by seizing Roman possessions in Spain and France and mounting a surprise attack against Rome across the Alps.

Military history has seen few such daring exploits as the crossing of the Alps by Hannibal and his army. Historian David Soren writes: "The route that he took is still a mystery. . . . The undertaking was so difficult that Hannibal was thought to have magic powers and that he could, with chemicals, dissolve boulders."[3] The Carthaginian general began the September-October crossing with forty thousand men and thirty-seven elephants and ended it having lost half his troops and two-thirds of his elephants to bad weather, starvation, and warring tribes. But he made it to northern Italy where he succeeded in catching the Romans off guard.

Hannibal was a military strategist of unprecedented power, resourcefulness, and intelligence. The Carthaginians won battle after battle. For two years the Romans avoided engaging Hannibal's forces directly. But on August 2, 216 B.C., they marched on the Carthaginians in the Battle of Cannae, at what is now Canne in southwestern Italy. Rome had sixty thousand troops, Carthage forty-five thousand. Hannibal executed a "pincer movement"—the double envelopment of an enemy whose forces are superior. By nightfall Rome had suffered fifty thousand dead and wounded; the remaining ten thousand soldiers had fled to safety behind the walls of the capital. This was the greatest military defeat in the history of Rome.

Now the inherent seriousness and steadfastness of the Roman people asserted itself. The army made a supreme and enduring effort over the following years. Still, it was not until thirteen years later, in 203 B.C., that Hannibal was finally driven from Italy. He was forced to commit suicide by the Romans in 183 B.C.

The balance of power between Carthage and Rome had still not been entirely worked out. The Third Punic War was fought in 149–146 B.C. Rome sought and achieved total victory, razing Carthage to the ground, plowing over its ruins, and sowing salt in the furrows.

When the shade of Hannibal first made his presence known through the tapping tables on December 8, 1853, he seemed to be little more than a fussbudget. He refused to talk. Asked why, he said it was because the design of the carpet on which the table sat reminded him of one of his defeats. The table was moved into a carpetless room. Now Hannibal was ready to talk. Present at the séance were the entire Hugo family, Auguste Vacquerie, and the proscrits Sandor Teleki, Émile Guérin, Albert Barbieux, and Xavier Durrieu.

Guérin and Teleki put their hands on the table. Hugo began the questioning of Hannibal:

"Napoleon I said you were the greatest military captain of ancient times. He ranked you above Alexander the Great because you sacrificed half your army to conquer on the battlefield of Italy and kept it there for fifteen years. What do you think of Napoleon?"

The Carthaginian replied in Latin (which Hugo knew perfectly and which most of the others knew well): *Napoleon was the greatest leader after victory, the worst leader after defeat.* ["Dux maximus post victoriam, minimus post cladem."]

Hugo disagreed. During the retreat from Moscow—when winter, and not the Russians, defeated Napoleon—hadn't the emperor kept his composure admirably, with the result that once he was back in France with his energies preserved he was able to improvise a whole new army?

The shade replied:

I said the worst leader in defeat, not the worst man. Defeated by winter, the greatest of leaders does not flee; he dies. Death is the supreme victor. ["Dixi ducem, non virum. Victus a hyeme, dux magnus non fugit, moritur. Mors suprema victoria."] Asked to say this in French, Hannibal replied a little differently: *A defeated Napoleon is a selfish Napoleon. Conqueror, he thinks of France; conquered, he thinks of himself. A defeated Napoleon is a fleeing genius who takes refuge beneath a crown instead of abdicating beneath a halo. That abdication is death.*

"There is a point of history about which you can perhaps enlighten us," continued Hugo. "There was a Roman legion that fought at Cannae and left a monument on which you can read what look like the syllables *leg* and *fulminate*. According to legend, the eagles—the bronze insignia of the Roman legions—were struck by lightning at this spot. Does the legend explain the inscription? Can *fulminate* be read as *fulminata* ["lightning"] or *fulminatrix* ["thundering"]?"

The table was still.

"Okay," said Hugo, "let's talk about you."

There was a burst of tapping:

Stone tells falsehoods; bronze lies; marble blasphemes. Only mud can tell the truth. Caesar, Alexander, Charlemagne, Hannibal—all lies! The Bonapartes—all truth!

But Hugo, though he'd asked Hannibal about himself, still wanted an answer to his question about the strange Latin words on the monument. He told Hannibal that Napoleon I, when asked how he could remember the names of all his brigades, had replied: "Do you forget the names of your former mistresses?" Apparently Napoleon could also remember the names of all the legions he'd defeated. Surely, Hugo told the shade of Hannibal, the Carthaginian general could do the same! Hugo thought that perhaps the monument at Cannae contained the name of one of these defeated legions, either *Fulminatrix* or *Fulminata*.

Trix, the table rapped out.

"What were the names of the Roman legions that took part in the Battle of Cannae?"

The reply came slowly:

Vindicatrix ["The Avenger"], *first; second, Victrix* ["The Victorious"]; *Fulminatrix* ["The Thundering"], *third; Fulgurans* ["The Lightning"], *fourth; Vorax* ["The Voracious"], *fifth; sixth, Vultur* ["The Vulture"]; *the greatest and last—*

And here the table halted.

Hugo asked: "Can you give us a breakdown of the Carthaginian legions or troops that took part in this battle?"

Yes.

There ensued a brief technical discussion between Hannibal and Hugo about types of Carthaginian legions. It ended with the table tapping out three names:

Fides, ultio, patria ["Faith, Vengeance, The Native Land"].

Charles intervened with a provocative question: What did Hannibal think of Napoleon III? "You who are the personification of someone who makes a vow and keeps it: Can you give us your opinion of him who today stands for the violation of his word in the face of the world?"

The table replied:

I used my hatred to keep vows; him, he broke his vows in the service of his hatred. I am the archangel of a country that sought revenge; he is the Satan of a people who are capable of self-sacrifice. I am the winged vow that carries the world before it; he is the masked vow that steals away a people. I am vow's wings; he is its deceiver.

Hugo changed the subject radically: "Today there is nothing left of Carthage but history. Rome wiped it off the face of the earth. You alone can tell us what Carthage was like. Will you?"

The tapping table replied at length:

It was a giant city. It had sixty leagues of towers and six thousand temples, three thousand of them made of marble, two thousand of porphyry, six hundred of alabaster, three hundred of jasper, fifty of stucco, forty-five of ivory, four of silver, and one of gold. The streets were three hundred feet wide and paved with marble covered by silver tiles. Perfumed lamps burned all along the length of the houses, and white elephants swaying beneath saddled towers brushed against singers and dancers in the streets. The air was so scented and melodious that flowers and birds never died there. Carthage had thirty thousand vessels, six hundred fortresses, one hundred thousand horses, twelve thousand elephants, one hundred thousand talents [of gold] a year— and Hannibal.

"Will you tell us the names of the four silver temples and the golden temple?" asked Hugo. When the table assented, he asked, "First of all, tell us the names in Carthaginian. Then translate them into Latin. First, the names of the silver temples."

First temple: in Carthaginian, Bocamar; *in Latin,* Sol *(Sun). Second temple:* Derimos; *in Latin,* Luna *(Moon). Third:* Jarimus; *in Latin,* Dies (Day). *Fourth:* Mossomba; *in Latin,* Nox (Night).

"Tell us the name of the golden temple."

In Carthaginian: Illisaga; *in Latin,* Lux *(Light).*

The séance was coming to a close. Hannibal concluded by telling Hugo that the French poet was correct in thinking that Punic (Carthaginian) and Basque were basically the same language.

And then the shade of the warrior was gone.[4]

※※

Pondering this séance months, even years, later, Hugo had to admit that it was one of the more problematical of his confrontations with the spirits. Hannibal had begun with some thought-provoking remarks about Napoleon I. But then—or so it now seemed—he had drifted with ever-increasing velocity into Cloud-Cuckoo-Land. Some time after the séance, Hugo, making inquiries of several historians, had learned that most of them believed the Romans hadn't begun to name their legions at the time of the Battle of Cannae in 216 B.C. (Had the Carthaginians? The historians weren't sure.) Hugo hadn't known either of these facts.

There was also the fact that Hannibal's description of Carthage at its height wasn't one to inspire confidence that this really was the shade of the Carthaginian general. Six thousand temples? Streets three hundred feet wide? The ancient city of Carthage would have had to extend very far into the Sahara to make room for everything that Hannibal had described!

Did any of the chronicles of ancient times, historical or imaginative, provide proof of the fabulous details that Hannibal had set forth? None that Hugo could find. In December 1862, a gift from his friend and fellow author Gustave Flaubert was delivered to Victor's home on Guernsey Island. It was a copy of Flaubert's just-published novel, *Salammbô*, the action of which is set in Carthage at the time of the Second Punic War. Hugo knew that as a young man the author of *Madame Bovary* had traveled excitedly to Tunisia to view the ruins of Carthage. Flaubert knew Latin and Greek well, and in an earlier letter he'd told Hugo that while writing *Salammbô* he had read literally every book extant on ancient Carthage.

Hugo searched through *Salammbô* carefully for any hint of the fabulous details supplied by Hannibal nine years before. He found only a single, elusive, allusion. It came when the doomed hero of the book, the rebel general Mâtho, wondered out loud to the Carthaginian priestess Salammbô, with whom he was madly in love—and whom he had virtually abducted—whether there was any place in the world the two could flee to where they would still be safe from the wrath of the Carthaginians? Mâtho came up with the following:

"Beyond Gadès [Malta], twenty days by sea, you encounter an island
covered with gold powder, with greenery and with birds. On the

mountains, huge flowers full of steaming perfumes sway like eternal incense holders. In lemon trees taller than cedars, snakes the color of milk use their diamond-shaped jaws to bite off fruit so that it falls to the lawn. The air is so sweet it keeps you from dying. Oh! I'll find it! You'll see! We'll live in crystal grottos hollowed out of the base of hills. No one lives there yet, or I would become the country's king."[5]

Where had Flaubert gotten this from? He had read it—but there was no reason to believe the source was historically accurate! This certainly wasn't proof for Hugo that he'd really been talking to Hannibal. But, in the halcyon winter of 1853–1854, when the experience of the tapping tables was still new and exciting, no one devoted much time to being skeptical. Moreover, an encounter would soon come, courtesy of the tapping tables, which would take the search for the truth of the tapping tables in an entirely different direction. We will read about that encounter in the next chapter.

Seven

GOD'S CONVICT

On your planet packed with infamous prisons
There dwell the wicked of all the universe,
The condemned who, come from alien skies diverse,
Brood in your rocks, bend in you bowing trees.

Yes, your savage universe is God's convict.
Your constellations, in letters of fire of somber script,
Spell out the prison shouldered by your world.

VICTOR HUGO,
WHAT THE SHADOW'S MOUTH SAYS

In *Meetings with Remarkable Trees* (1997), Thomas Pakenham tells us that when Irish peer William Bury, the second Earl of Charleville, built a new castle among the oaks of his property at Tullamore in 1801, "already there was one giant tree known as the 'king oak' dominating, like a watch tower, the carriage drive to that town." The tree had a girth of twenty-six feet. The Bury family, believing that if a branch fell one of the Burys would die, "supported the giant arms with wooden props. Of course, there was nothing they could do to protect the trunk. In May 1963 a thunderbolt splintered the main trunk from top to bottom. The tree survived, but the head of the family, Colonel Charles Bury, dropped dead a few weeks later."[1]

In *The Secret Life of Plants* (1973), Peter Tompkins and Christopher Bird write that the great American horticulturist Luther

Burbank (1849–1926), developer of hundreds of new varieties of plants,

> revealed that when he wanted his plants to develop in some particular
> and peculiar way not common to their kind he would get down on
> his knees and talk to them. Burbank also asserted that plants have
> over twenty sensory perceptions but that, because they are different
> from ours, we cannot recognize them. "He was not sure," wrote [phi-
> losopher Manly P.] Hall, "that the shrubs and flowers understood his
> words, but he was convinced that by some telepathy, they could com-
> prehend his meaning."[2]

Do trees suffer? Do flowers think? These questions have been raised anew in the late twentieth and early twenty-first centuries.

New ideas about the intelligence of animals have been in the air since the 1950s. In *The Man Who Talks to Whales: The Art of Interspecies Communication* (2002), James Nollman, the first person in the world to hold a Ph.D. in interspecies communications (from the University of California), describes how buffalo communicate with humans using "a dirty yellow glow . . . like a ring, a smokescreen, or a fence expanding outward around the entire herd."[3] He also asserts that dolphins, whales, flies, and chickens each have a language of their own. Australia-born philosopher Peter Singer argues in *Animal Liberation* (1976) that there is no definitive proof that humans and animals are different species, maintaining that the idea that animals represent a "lower" species than humans is merely another one of society's prejudices—one Singer labels "speciesm."

What about stones? Do they have souls? Ancient man certainly thought so. Writer Douglas Hill reports that "the idea of erecting a tombstone over a grave may possibly have arisen from the belief that the spirit of the dead person would inhabit the stone." Hill claims that the coronation stone of the old kings of Ireland, known as the Lia-fail, was said to shriek aloud whenever the rightful heir to the throne stepped on it. The Irish Blarney Stone confers eloquence on those who kiss it. Old Welsh and Irish tales speak of "stones that move or speak, especially on unusually supernatural occasions, like Midsummer Eve."[4]

❧⟨⟩❧

Victor Hugo believed in every shape and size of reincarnation—the doctrine that holds that our soul returns to earth through lifetime after lifetime. His first child, Léopold, born July 16, 1823, lived for only three months. When Adèle became pregnant again (with Léopoldine), Victor wrote to his father: "Everything leads me to believe that our Léopold has returned." When Hugo's first grandchild, Charles's son, Georges, died in 1868, Victor told his friends he was certain Georges would return. When his second grandchild was born four months after the death of the first, the child was also named Georges.[5]

Hugo believed, later in life, that in previous lifetimes he had been Isaiah, Aeschylus, Judas Maccabee, the Roman poet Juvenal, several more poets, several painters, and two kings of Greece (whose names he couldn't remember). From time to time the poet also intimated he had been Job and John of Patmos (author of the Book of Revelations).[6]

Hugo also seems to have believed that reincarnation could run backward, or at any rate unfold differently from what most people assume. One day he announced to Paul Stapfer, a young French professor he had befriended on Guernsey Island, that the Roman poet Juvenal (Decimus Junius Juvenalis, circa A.D. 50–129), of whom he believed he was the reincarnation, had plagiarized a line of Hugo's poetry. When Stapfer tactfully suggested that perhaps the contrary was true, Hugo protested vociferously, declaring he had read Juvenal's line for the first time that morning but had written his own line in French some years before.

The poet later told Stapfer that the second of mankind's great errors (the first being to divide the universe into three zones, heaven, earth, and hell) was "to divide time, in relation to us, into three ages: the nothingness that came before [*le néant antérieur*], this life, future eternity." Human life, Hugo declared, was "likely only one stage in an endless series of metamorphoses and tests intended to make us worthy, by degrees, of a more and more elevated existence." He concluded: "If things really are as I've just said, the immortality to which our nature aspires doesn't open up before us all of a sudden one fine day, fully formed; we enjoy it starting from the present moment and continue to enjoy it in successive portions."[7] (Hugo was prodigal of such conventional-time-annihilating beliefs, telling the young Adèle on Jersey on January 7, 1853, that "there must certainly be a world somewhere that, contrary to this one, begins with old age and finishes with youth.")[8]

At the end of the eighteenth and the beginning of the nineteenth centuries, bits and pieces of the great Hindu epic poem *Bhagavad Gita* appeared in French and German for the first time, notably in the translation of *The Laws of Manu* by Loiseleur-Delongchamps.[9] Hugo took to heart the classical Hindu doctrine of reincarnation described in these works. Benjamin Walker sums up this doctrine in *Man, Myth & Magic: An Illustrated Encyclopedia of the Supernatural*.

> Some schools of belief, particularly in Hinduism, hold that a man does not necessarily assume a human form in his next incarnation. Certain Hindu sects teach that the soul may be reborn as a plant, or an animal. Someone who has lived a life of vice or crime may be re-embodied as a cactus, a poison ivy, a lizard or a toad: According to the early Hindu law-giver Manu, the slayer of a Brahmin enters the womb of a sow or a she-ass; a drunkard will be reborn as a beetle that lives on dung; and other sinners and reprobates will become hyenas, rodents, insects and creatures of low and repulsive estate. Those who have done well will return as men and women.[10]

As a young man, Hugo knew personally or knew the works of not only all the important writers of his time but also of the so-called Illuminati, a patchwork quilt of lesser figures—some of them very brilliant—who subscribed to the beliefs of Louis Claude de Saint-Martin (1743–1774). De Saint-Martin was a "magical adept" whose philosophy lay midway between the traditional mysticism of the East or West on the one hand, and a new evolutionism on the other. The Illuminati were thinkers who, turning away from the increasingly rapid advance of modern science, continued to work out the implications of certain ancient esoteric doctrines.

One such figure was Delisle de Sales (1741–1816), a friend of Voltaire, who wrote in *Of the Philosophy of Nature* in 1804, "Everything has feelings, plants have feelings, a tree has organs, everything lives, all things nourish all other things, nature possesses but a single law: You cannot wound a single being without outraging all of nature."[11] De Sales's contemporary, the scientist Pierre Samuel du Pont de Nemours (1739–1817), insisted that all animals had a language.[12] Hugo was a personal friend of Auguste Guyard (1808–1882), a naturalist/socialist who attempted to create a model commune in his home village of Frotey in Haute-Saône. Guyard was a gentle soul said to be able to talk to animals. This early believer in interspecies communication famously declared:

> The substance of non-human nature evolves over the millennia into a human substance. This diamond that dazzles us with its fire, this rose that intoxicates us with its perfume, this warbling bird whose melodies make us rejoice—in a few thousand years the essences of all these three will be part of the human body; they will supply it with its charm and structure.[13]

Hugo took Guyard seriously enough to entrust him with the care of the Hugos' white Persian cat while the family was on Jersey Island.

Hugo was also much taken with the beliefs of Boucher de Perthes (1788–1868), who contended that "all beings make up a single race." Pondering the numerous physiognomic resemblances between man and animals, Perthes speculated whether, on other planets and in other dimensions of reality, species might not be all mixed together, so that there were mountains that were also bacteria, trees that were somehow animals, and rocks that howled with fury. It seemed to him that the vast diversity of conditions that prevail on earth might tend to hide the very real and profound similarities between humans, plants, animals, and even stones.[14]

But there was a certain angularity, even a harshness, to Hugo's own beliefs about the ensoulment of all nature. His friend and contemporary the poet Alphonse de Lamartine had written a 12,000-line epic poem, *The Fall of an Angel* (1838), describing a pre-Flood Lebanon where angels still mated with the daughters of men and cedars sang joyful hymns to the glory of God.[15] Hugo was intensely interested in what might have been the nature of the world before the Flood, and in 1861 he would write about the vast stone ruins of Rephaim in Lebanon, which he believed had been left behind by a primordial race of giants ruled by the biblical king of Bashan named Og (Joshua 9:10, 12:4).[16]

But Hugo had come to believe that nature, if it had ever sung hymns to the glory of God, did not do so in our present age. He believed, rather, that the animal, vegetable, and mineral worlds all feel intensely, but that all they feel is pain. The poet sensed something terrible in the heart of nature—a "certain quality of excessive evil in the savage beast," Illuminati scholar Auguste Viatte tells us.[17] For Hugo, according to Viatte, "suffering does not limit itself to us. It embraces, in its vast symphony, both mountaintop and abyss."[18]

Hugo had a chilling feeling that our world was little more than a vast prison, even that our entire universe was no more than "God's convict."[19] Every part of nature was filled with soul, but that soul matter was the stuff of felons, both native to earth and from other parts of the cosmos, and certainly including us. Such a belief was crystallizing in Hugo's mind during his first two years on Jersey Island; it must have been reinforced by the fact that he was a sort of convict himself, chained in banishment to this rocky Channel isle. Out of such ruminations would be born Jean Valjean, the hero of a book he had begun in Paris and which he would complete on Guernsey Island in 1862: *Les Misérables*. Jean Valjean— that great exemplar of mankind—had been a convict for eighteen years for stealing a loaf of bread, and in a way would be a convict all his life.

The universe was God's convict? What strange and bitter thoughts had begun to fill Victor Hugo's mind?

Beginning on December 27, 1853, at Marine-Terrace, the great poet would receive alarming confirmation of his fears. It would come in the form of a flurry of bizarre statements conveyed through the tapping tables by a disembodied entity called Balaam's Ass. Present at the séance on that night were Mme Adèle Hugo, Victor Hugo (who arrived late), and Auguste Vacquerie. Others may have been present, but the transcripts record only these three names.

Hands were placed on the pedestal table. It began to move almost immediately.

Auguste Vacquerie asked: "Who's there?"

The answer came: *Balaam's Ass.*

Balaam's Ass? They were all surprised. It seemed as if a donkey were speaking through the tables—a female donkey at that, since the French word tapped out was *l'anesse*.[20]

But who, or what, was "Balaam's Ass"?

A "Balaam's Ass" has come to mean someone who bears a message from a higher realm, the contents of which the bearer can't understand because he or she is too innocent, or too pure, or perhaps too simpleminded. The original story of Balaam's Ass is found in the Old Testament, Numbers 22:1–34, while the broader story of the soothsayer Balaam is told in Numbers 22–24. This is the story:

Balak, the king of Moab, is alarmed at the conquests of the Israelites who have appeared at his borders. He sends his elders to Balaam, a holy man living in Ammon who is said to be able to speak directly to God. Balak wants Balaam to come to Moab and curse Israel in the name of the Lord.

Balaam sends word back to Balak via the elders that he can only do what the Lord commands him to do and that he does not know what that will be in regard to the Israelites.

Nevertheless, without a specific directive from God, Balaam gets on his ass and, with two servants, sets out on the road to Moab to see Balak.

Furious that Balaam has not waited for instructions, the Lord sends an angel to meet him on the road. At first Balaam doesn't see the angel, but the ass he is riding does. She tries to avoid the angel by moving off the road. Balaam, furious, beats her. Twice more the ass tries to avoid the angel; Balaam continues to beat her. The Lord miraculously enables the ass to speak. She admonishes Balaam for beating her three times. Yahweh permits Balaam to see the angel, who tells him that he would have been slain had it not been for the courage of the ass, who, despite the beatings of Balaam, still tried not to pass beyond the angel of the Lord.

Balaam realizes he has sinned and offers to go back. The angel tells him to go on but to be mindful always of the instructions of the Lord.

Balaam arrives at Balak's palace, and the two of them go off together to offer sacrifices. But Balaam, divinely inspired by Yahweh, does not curse Israel but rather blesses it. When Balak complains, Balaam reminds him that he had earlier told the king he would only be able to do what the Lord commanded him to do. Twice more, Balak, building up larger and larger offerings, pleads with Balaam to curse the Israelites in the name of the Lord. Each time Balaam, commanded by Yahweh, blesses the Israelites instead. Finally, he returns to Ammon.

Victor Hugo was to write a poem, "God Invisible to the Thinker,"[21] inspired by this tapping-table encounter with the shade of Balaam's Ass. The poem begins, and continues, with Balaam seated on the donkey's back and filled with doubt and despair as he makes his way toward Balak's palace; it ends on this note: "'. . . *What utter nothingness's slave are we?. . .' So he thought palely, underneath the grim branches, those hairs tossed by the breeze's whim, The donkey stopped—and said: 'I can see HIM.'"*[22]*

Balaam's Ass appears in the writings of Giordano Bruno, the Dominican ex-friar who embraced hermetic writings and was publicly burned at the stake for heresy in Rome in 1600. Bruno calls one of his works *Idiota Triumphans* (Triumphant Idiot), explaining, says Renaissance scholar Frances Yates, that a "triumphant idiot" is someone who has "shown forth a divine truth which he does not understand himself but which those with deeper insight . . . can acclaim as a wonderful revelation." The triumphant idiot appears in another part of Bruno's *oeuvre*, "in a passage in the *Eroici Furori* [The Heroic Enthusiasts] where the simple type of inspired person was likened to the Ass which carries the Sacraments [when Christ entered Jerusalem at the beginning of Lent]."[23]

Let's continue with the séance of December 27, 1853:

"Well, Balaam," asked Auguste Vacquerie as the séance began, "if you're a spirit in the afterworld, you who have been a beast in this one, you're better equipped than any of us to answer a question we've often wondered about: Do animals have souls?"

Yes, they do.

"Talk to us about it."

Mankind is the prison of the soul, while the animal is the convict in the galleys.

"So life is truly a punishment?"

Yes.

"Explain."

The created being passes through creation as a bird passes through a tree, alighting on each branch. Man flies through infinity alighting

---

*Excerpt from *Selected Poems of Victor Hugo: A Bilingual Edition*, translated by E. H. Blackmore and A. M. Blackmore. © 2001 by The University of Chicago Press. Used by permission of The University of Chicago Press.

on each world. You inhabit a world of suffering and punishment. We inhabit a star of light and reward. Man is born into life on this earth to expiate a guilty past, and the animal to expiate a monstrous past. Man does not know what he did wrong and the animal does not know what his crime was. If they knew, that would make them happy, for punishment would no longer be anything more than a suffering that told itself: I committed such and such an injustice. I'm certain what it was; I'm in no doubt about its nature.

Now, it is in our having doubts that the punishment lies. For man to know his error would be for him to know his judge, would be for him to know God. And the certainty of God's existence would make for paradise on earth. In order to punish, divine justice puts on a mask. Punishment consists in seeing only the judge's mask. Reward consists in seeing the face of God.

"Come down a step in the ladder for us: Do plants have souls?"

Yes.

"Then do plants suffer a lot? For if the essence of punishment lies in not being able to see God, the plant world is blinder than the animal world. Are you asserting that man is in effect in prison, while the animals are in galleys and the plants are in dungeons, and this for all their lives?"*

If the plant suffers, it deserves to suffer. Undeserved suffering, inflicted on even a single atom, would be enough to make all heaven collapse. Trees would fall, terror-stricken worlds would sink into the abyss, and infinity would cease to radiate ever outward if the rose were oppressed or the daisy victimized. Suffering necessarily entails weakening. The plant is the grimmest of the prisons of the soul. The lily is sheer hell.

"So you're saying animals suffer more than men and plants suffer more than animals?"

Yes.

"How can that be possible? Don't pangs of conscience make us suffer the most? Don't we suffer all the more when we live according to the dictates of our soul? Do you really expect us to believe that a blade

---

*These are descending orders of harshness; in modern terms, we might think of "prison" as a minimum security prison, "galleys" as a maximum security prison, and "the dungeon" as solitary confinement.

of grass feels less happiness than a dog? Or that a creature that can't think suffers more than one that does? I grant you that there might be some truth in this if the souls of plants and animals were aware of their former greatness. But even man retains only a twilight gleam of his true nature. For the brute animal, that gleam would have to be the merest shadow; for the vegetable being, it would be pitch-black night. How can something be a punishment if you can't even feel it? Are you trying to tell us that a horse that is perfectly content with a single bale of hay is being punished more harshly than we are with our unquenchable thirst for the ideal?"

The spirit replied:

The horse is more harshly punished to the degree that it is more deeply plunged in matter. The plant is even more harshly punished, because it is rooted in soil. The ladder of punishment has three rungs: the human body, the hide of the animal, and the root of the plant. The soul imprisoned in the plant has two rungs left to climb, the soul imprisoned in the animal only one, to reach the level of man. The soul's punishment begins in the animal and vegetable realms with corporeal suffering and ends with moral suffering in the human realm. To attain the human realm will be felt almost as a deliverance, since to suffer only morally is already to be halfway to freedom. The soul breathes in man; it suffocates in the plant. The eyes of man are skylights that open out upon a higher life; the prisoner-soul in the human brain peers out at heaven through these skylights.

Auguste Vacquerie pursued: "You say that for the vegetable world, punishment lies in the complete ignorance of its true nature, and that for man it lies in his doubts about its true nature. You also seem to be saying that the pain that results from complete ignorance, or from being in doubt, would cease the moment we found out who we really were. And then you go ahead and tell us who we really are! If what you're telling us is true, then, if we accept what you're saying, our punishment will cease. It follows from that that our lives will end, since the only reason we have been born into life is to be punished. The very world itself would cease to be if our punishments vanished by virtue of our having had their true natures revealed to us! You tell us that we are sentenced to doubt, and then you reveal that truth to us!"

The table tapped out:

I said that the punishment lies in having to be in doubt about one's true nature. *I affirm the truth of this proposition, whereas you are doing nothing more than doubting your doubts. Therefore, you continue to suffer punishment.*

Victor Hugo entered the discussion: "In regard to these truths you are affirming, for some time now I, Victor Hugo, who am speaking to you, have believed in exactly what you say. If one has to doubt these things in order to be punished, then, tell me: Why has an exception been made of me?"

If you're so sure of yourself, tell me what punishment is meted out to the soul of an ox?

"You didn't understand my question. I'm telling you that I've glimpsed some of the truths you've just revealed to us; that those touching upon the human soul and its punishment in this world are at the level of a certainty for me and have been for some time. On this point I am no longer in a state of doubt—and yet, I am still being punished! I ask you then: What special category do I belong to?"

The proof that you doubt is that you have merely glimpsed. As for me, I affirm these truths. You believe what your thoughts tell you, and you doubt what our revelations tell you. Your thought is merely human; ours is divine. The thoughts of even the greatest mind always wear a blindfold over one eye. That blindfold is life. You are a living, and therefore a fallible, genius. I will spell out to the dead Victor Hugo the errors of the living Victor Hugo. Truth awaits you at the door of the tomb. You mistake God for a children's book that can be read in a flash.

God is infinite, and what is infinite cannot be known. Death will astonish you. Death is always astonishing. When he emerged from the tomb, Moses exclaimed: "How splendid it all is!" Socrates ran about everywhere in heaven crying out: "How ravishing it all is!" Jesus fell to his knees.

Mme Hugo joined in: "My husband has been reflecting on and talking about the destiny of man, in the way you have just described it, for a long time now. He had thought these things out long before you revealed them to us tonight."

The table rejoined:

He has expressed only a millionth part of the truth concerning the human race. As proof I offer you this, one of a million examples: He does not know that your globe contains another globe within it, like a pit or a stone in a fruit. Volcanoes are the mouths through which this inner world breathes. That world is your hell. Punished souls inhabit it, engulfed not in flame but in shadow.

Now Balaam's Ass proceeded to explain how the damned soul sank from the bottom of its grave down through the earth until it reached this internal globe, which was hell, and how, if the soul was to be pardoned, it would be ejected up out of this interior hell by a volcano's eruption. He explained how the soul, when not forgiven, rose up through the earth and was imprisoned in a plant or animal. He asserted that one way in which the souls in this interior world were punished was by their having to continually hear their misdeeds eloquently described by persons living on the surface.

But Auguste Vacquerie, whose mind was still on the bewildering revelations that had preceded this description, burst out abruptly:

"Is mankind to be forever condemned to a prison, the animal forever condemned to a galley, the plant forever condemned to a dungeon? Is the world always to be so condemned? Is our earth really, from the oak tree's root to the genius's brow, nothing but a stinking morass in which the dirty linen of the higher worlds is washed throughout eternity? Everything that thinks, everything that walks, everything that grows—everything is punished? What?! Woman, virgin, baby aborning—all of these are guilty? The dog that adores its master, the bird that hovers over us, the rose that gives off its glorious fragrance—these are all criminals? Is there not a single blade of grass that is innocent?"

The table replied: *You all came here guilty.*

Auguste desperately responded: "So tell me, is it then correct for me to say: Everything on earth is expiating a crime committed elsewhere?"

Yes.

The session ended. The spirits had introduced some disturbing cosmological themes. They would be energetically discussed over the next year and a half, with Auguste Vacquerie fighting the spirits every inch of the way.[24]

Eight

ANDRÉ CHÉNIER LOSES HIS HEAD BUT ENDS UP KEEPING IT

In 1829, Victor Hugo published a short novel called *The Last Day of a Condemned Man*. Here is a dialogue between the condemned man and the guard who will shortly escort him to the guillotine.

"It seems, excuse me for saying so, Mr. Criminal, that you'll be leaving this earth today. If there's one thing I know for sure, it's that people who die by the guillotine can foretell lottery results. Promise me this, that you'll come back from the dead and visit me tomorrow night—What do you have to lose?—and give me three numbers, three winning lottery numbers. Okay? (Don't worry. I'm not afraid of ghosts!) Here's my address: Popincourt Barracks, Staircase A, Number 26, at the end of the hall. You won't have a problem recognizing me, right? You can even come tonight if that's more convenient."

[The condemned man, who is narrating the story:] I wouldn't have deigned to answer this idiot except that an insane hope popped into my head. When we're in desperate straits, we sometimes think we can smash a padlock with a feather. "Listen," I said, as humorously as I could for someone who was about to die, "I really can make you richer than a king. I can help you earn millions, but on one condition."

His stupid eyes widened. "What's that? What's that? Whatever pleases you, Mr. Criminal!"

"Instead of three numbers, I promise you four. But you have to trade clothes with me."

"Is that all?" He was already unfastening the top buttons of his uniform.

I'd gotten up from my chair. I watched his every move, my heart pounding. I could already see the door opening in front of the policeman's uniform with me wearing it. I could already see the square and the street and the Palais de Justice behind me.

He half-turned indecisively. "Wait," he said. "Are you doing this just to get out of here?"

I saw that all was lost. Still, I made a final effort, however useless and senseless it might be. "Yes," I told him, "but you'll have a fortune."

He interrupted me: "Well, no! Wait! What about my numbers? For them to be winning numbers, you have to be dead."

I sat down on the bench again, without a word and feeling even more cast down by hopelessness than I had felt buoyed up by hope the moment before.[1]

Victor Hugo wrote *The Last Day of a Condemned Man* to graphically illustrate the inhumaneness of capital punishment. By the age of twenty-seven, when he wrote this short novel, he had witnessed more than his share of public executions. Mario Vargas Llosa tells us that, according to his wife, Adèle (in *Victor Hugo raconté par un témoin de sa vie*), the first intimations of its horrors came to the five-year-old Hugo "on a trip that he made with his mother and brothers and sisters to meet his father in Italy: a line of bandits hanging by their necks among the trees. This spectacle, along with the image of a man in Burgos in 1812 who was about to be garroted [Victor was returning to France from Spain with his family after Napoleon I's defeat]. . . and who was advancing to his place of execution in a sinister procession, coupled with the image of the corpses of Spanish patriots executed and dismembered in Vitoria by the French, were to give him an early aversion to the death penalty."[2] Mme Hugo also tells us in her biography of Hugo, says Vargas Llosa, that "in the summer of 1825, his friend Jules Lefèvre dragged him along to the Place de Grève to see a patricide, Jean Martin, having his hand and head cut off. Victor Hugo was sickened by the festive behavior of the crowd gathered for the spectacle. On another occasion, he . . . saw a couple of murderers, Malaguette and Ratta, on their way to the scaffold. He once crossed the square at the Hôtel de Ville and came face to face with the guillotine. The executioner was rehearsing the execution that was to be held that evening, oiling the joints of the machine while he was chatting amiably to passersby. According to Adèle Hugo, the day after this event, Victor Hugo began writing *Le dernier jour d'un condamné.*"[3]

Hugo wrote *The Last Day of a Condemned Man* in three weeks at white-hot speed, reading parts to his friends and family every night. He spent two days doing research at the notorious Bicêtre prison outside Paris observing every detail of a condemned man's last day. His twenty-five-thousand-word book is the only one of Hugo's novelistic and dramatic works narrated entirely in the first person singular. Hugo biographer Joanna Richardson maintains that it is "the first prose work in which Hugo asserts the poet's function as a reformer. It is also the first prose work which is written from the heart."[4] The publication of *The Last Day of a Condemned Man* on February 3, 1829, created a sensation. Readers were alternately repelled and fascinated by Hugo's raw and original exposure of societally sanctioned murder. The book immediately went into three printings. Of the many horrors it described, not the least was expressed in the final words of the book: "FOUR O'CLOCK." The novel had to end here; 4:00 p.m. was the execution time of the narrator, and the executioners could be counted on to punctiliously maintain their schedule.

The years hurtled forward with their whirligig of events in the life of Victor Hugo. The year 1852 found him exiled to Jersey Island, and the year 1853 saw him caught up in the mysteries of the tapping tables. His fierce public hatred of capital punishment had not abated one bit, and 1855 would find him unsuccessfully trying to stop the public hanging of an arsonist named Tappner on Guernsey Island by writing letters to the British government. Not long before that—in December 1853, almost a quarter century after the publication of his celebrated novel condemning capital punishment—Hugo sensed an extraordinary opportunity to write a sequel to *The Last Day of a Condemned Man.* It had to do with the tapping tables.

There is a curious entry in Adèle Hugo's diary for December 20, 1853. She quotes her father as saying at the dinner table: "I don't want to say this in front of Charles [as the medium], but I have an extremely interesting question to put to André Chénier. I'll tell André Chénier to finish *The Last Day of a Condemned Man,* and to go on after FOUR O'CLOCK."[5]

André Chénier was a deceased French poet whose shade had first visited the tapping tables on Jersey on December 9, 1853. Chénier was guillotined on July 25, 1794, a victim of that time of particular ferocity in the French Revolution known as the Terror. He was only thirty-one years old. When Adèle wrote the entry in her diary, the shade of André Chénier had already visited the tables three times. Each time, the dead poet had graciously submitted to dictating closing lines to a selection of poems he hadn't finished while he was alive. All this had given Victor Hugo, first, pause, and then an audacious idea. At the next tapping-table session at which Chénier appeared, he would ask the poet to tell them what it was like to be guillotined and then what it was like afterward. That would give Hugo an unhoped-for sequel to *The Last Day of a Condemned Man*—a sort of *First Afterlife Day of a Guillotined Man*.

But who exactly was André Chénier?

He was a poet who the critics generally consider to be the greatest French poet of the eighteenth century. For all that, he is probably the least known great poet in the modern era. Hardly any English-speaking readers have ever read his poetry—and not very many French-speaking readers, despite the pride the French take in their culture. Why is this? Let's visit André Chénier on the last two days of his short, tragic, and brilliant life, and try to find out. We'll start with the day known as Sixth Thermidor, year II in the French Revolutionary calendar and July 24, 1794, in the Julian calendar.* The place is Paris, France. We are in the Reign of Terror.

---

*On October 24, 1793, the leaders of the French Revolution introduced a new calendar to the French people to emphasize that the Revolution represented a total break with the past. The years were in Roman numbers, with year "I" beginning on September 22, 1792. The twelve months were given new names and began on the 19th or 20th of the now obsolete months. The name of the new month Thermidor, for example, came from the Greek word *thermos* meaning "heat"; Thermidor began on July 19 or 20 and ended on August 19 or 20 (depending on other fine details in the calendar). Each month consisted of three weeks of ten days each, called *decades*. Each day was divided into ten hours, each hour having one hundred decimal minutes and each decimal minute having one hundred decimal seconds. Napoleon I abolished the calendar effective January 1, 1806 (the day after ten Nivôse year XIV), a little over twelve years after its inception. However, it was used again during the Revolution of 1848 and during the brief Paris Commune in 1871 (year LXXIX).

It is the middle of the night. In a cell in Saint-Lazare prison in the north of the city, a thirty-one-year-old man tries to pull himself together. He bends over a table, beginning to write. The silence is broken only by the ticking of a clock and the retreating and approaching footsteps of the guards in the long, wide corridor outside.

The cell is bare except for a mattress, a table, a chair, and a pile of laundry. Oddly, the door can be locked only from the inside. There are no bars on the window, only a cross. It may be that the ghosts of horrified nuns flit across these silent walls: before the revolution, the prison was a convent of the religious order of Saint-Lazare. Now, on three floors each lined with cells giving out on a wide corridor, it houses seven hundred "enemies of the republic," one hundred of them women.

The man is, of course, André Chénier. He is small and slim with a touch of swarthiness to his features. His black hair is disheveled, his wide brow knit with worry, the intelligence of his blue eyes clouded over with despair. Born in Constantinople in 1762, he was brought to France by his French father and Greek mother when he was two. He has been a brilliantly successful student of the classics, a private secretary to the French ambassador in London, a journalist, a member of a moderate political party—and, since March 7, a prisoner of Robespierre's Committee of Public Safety, accused of inciting hatred of the state.

Beneath it all, he is a poet. But so small has his output been, so unique is his poetry—and so brief will his life be, since at the age of thirty-one he has less than two days left to live—that André Chénier will have the distinction of being one of the least known great poets in history. But, in the estimation of France's finest literary critics, he is certainly great.

There has been a certain haughtiness in André Chénier. He has seen himself as superior to others. His arrest had outraged him—as a personal affront, as much as anything else. Over the last three months, in his tiny jail cell, that has been changing. He has been writing bitterly satirical poems against the Terror. Housed with seven hundred others, seeing what he sees, experiencing what he is experiencing, he has begun to think about himself less. His self-pity is becoming compassion for mankind.

But now the world is closing in on him. Visitors and mail are no longer permitted. Before, the prisoners could eat alone; now they must eat in a communal dining hall, paying for their meals with fifty sous a day "borrowed" from their captors. Their cells are searched daily for anything that might help them escape: razors, scissors, watches, rings, gold and silver money—everything is confiscated.

The afternoon before, everything has become much worse. The trials have begun. The first group of twenty-five prisoners has been taken in the tumbrils to the Conciergerie, where they will be immediately tried, found guilty, and executed. Their crime: "speaking out" against the state.

André Chénier knows he will almost certainly share that fate, and soon.[6]

Now, in the middle of the night in his cell, he is writing a poem in minute handwriting on a long thin strip of paper used for wrapping laundry. He knows that death is imminent. For the moment, his self-pity has the upper hand. He promises himself that when he completes this poem, probably in an hour, he will commit suicide. He expresses this in the first stanza. But, when the stanza is finished, he changes his mind. Since he has expressed this feeling in poetry, he no longer needs to act upon it.

In the next two stanzas he describes himself being taken from his cell by Death and dragged down the corridor as his prison mates watch in horror; Death is taking him to the guillotine. But, once he has expressed in his poetry this fear of death, he finds he is no longer afraid.

He welcomes death in the next twelve lines, beginning,

> *Ah well, I've lived too much,*
> *May death deliver me.*

And then he discovers that, because he has expressed this acceptance of death in poetry, he no longer wants to die. The will to live has suddenly revived within him. But how can he live if he really does face imminent death? The answer is that he will no longer live for himself, for André Chénier. He will live as a man among mankind. He will do this by expressing in his poetry the horror all men and women must feel at the heartless indiscriminate slaughter of the Reign of Terror. In the last twelve lines, empowered by his hatred of the Terror and by his certainty of the power of his poetic gift, he uses his pen to record for posterity the final feelings of a condemned man.

> *Oh my pen! poison, gall, horror, Gods of my life!*
> *You are the only reason I still breathe.*
> *If it is written in heaven that ne'er a sword*
> *Will glitter in my hand*
> *Another weapon, dipped in bitter ink,*
> *I'll use to plead the cause of all mankind.*

In the next few lines he describes those guilty souls whom he will meet in the afterworld and their guilty deeds. He concludes his poem:

> *Suffer, heart swollen with hatred, for justice starved.*
> *And you, Virtue, weep for me if I die.*[7]

He has finished his poem. Because he has been writing in such minute script there is still room on the long thin strip of paper. He copies out parts of other unfinished poems. Perhaps he adds a line or two to these poems. Then, his mission accomplished, André Chénier lies down and sleeps.

The tumbril arrives that afternoon to take the second group of prisoners to the Conciergerie. André's name is among those called. Biographer Francis Scarfe re-creates his final moments at Saint-Lazare: "After a quick farewell to the Trudaines [two brothers who were his close friends] (to whom he no doubt passed some manuscripts), his hands were tied behind his back and he mounted into the tumbril."[8] The two brothers will be executed one day after André; it is likely they who passed on his poetry.

We cannot imagine how Chénier must have felt as he made his final journey across Paris. Perhaps the sense of transcendence that had awakened in him that long night before made the trip more bearable. Legend has it that as his tumbril passed through Paris a faithful friend walked all the way beside him. The tumbrel arrived at the Conciergerie. The next morning, Chénier was tried and found guilty. His life ended on the scaffold of the Barrière de Vincennes shortly after four on the afternoon of Friday, July 25, 1794. Another legend has it that, a moment before he was guillotined, he put his hand to his forehead and remarked, "Well, all the same, I did have something in there."

Francis Scarfe writes that André Chénier's "martyrdom at the age of thirty-one has naturally resulted in his becoming a symbolic figure, a representative of the Romantic ideal of 'the poet as hero'. . . . which he was one of the first of the modern poets to embody.

"It may be seen that Chénier achieved heroism almost by accident, and in the last days of his life it lay not so much in going to the guillotine for his opinions as in overcoming an intense egotism and identifying himself with all those who were oppressed."[9]

That was in 1794. Let's return to 1853.

Here is how Claudius Grillet, in his *Victor Hugo spirite* (Victor Hugo, Spiritist), published in 1929, describes the first coming of the shade of André Chénier to the tapping tables on Jersey.

"On Friday evening, December 9, 1853, we saw what amounted to a renewal on Jersey of the experience of [the early-sixteenth-century pope] Julius II (an enthusiastic user of the turning tables, by all accounts), who persuaded the spirit of Homer to pick up the lyre again and add a verse to the *Iliad*. The séance took place at [the proscrit] Leguevel's house, and not at Marine-Terrace. Victor Hugo was not in attendance.

"At the start, Socrates occupied the tripod [three-legged] table for a few minutes. Then, suddenly, an abnormally strong shaking of the table alerted the assembled host that something unexpected was about to happen.

"'Who's there?' asked Charles Hugo.

"The reply was: *André Chénier.*

"We know that numerous works of this poet remained incomplete. Durrieu, another of the exiles at the séance, finds that this is an excellent opportunity, since we have Chénier in our hands, to ask him to complete several interrupted poems. Chénier is more than willing. It is thus that, solicited to complete the fragment of *Idyll XII* that begins in this way: 'Hasten to me, young Chromis, I love you and I am beautiful . . .' he replies with an outpouring that is really very much in his [the living Chénier's] style:

> "'*Neæra is swift-footed, but Chromis is agile,*
> *In Woods of which Amaryllis is Virgil's bird.*'

"Etc. Six lines follow. Other attendees, acquiring an appetite for the exercise, also express their desires. At the request of Guérin, Chénier has to complete his last poem—the one interrupted by the executioner. He also has to reconstruct the parts that are missing from the poems he wrote when he was living. Without losing his head, the glorious 'decapitatee' gives himself over to these various demands in the most gracious manner. Hugo, had he been there, would certainly not have dismissed these bucolic improvisations . . ."[10]

Did the shade of André Chénier really complete the living Chénier's final poem—the one cut short by the executioner?

If so, wouldn't that in some way constitute proof of survival after death?

What was André Chénier's last poem?

There is still debate about this among academics. Some have inclined to the view that it was *The Young Captive*, written in Saint-Lazare several weeks before Chénier was executed. The consensus now is that it was *Iambic IX* (the title refers to the meter of the poem, which is iambic)—the same poem that, several paragraphs above, we describe André Chénier as writing in his cell during his last night at Saint-Lazare.

If *Iambic IX* really was Chénier's last poem, do the new "last lines" dictated by André's shade make a good fit with the last lines of the published poem?

Here are the last lines of *Iambic IX:*

> *Come now, stifle your cry;*
> *Suffer, heart swollen with hatred, for justice starved.*
> *And you, Virtue, weep for me if I die.*[11]

The new last lines of Chénier's final poem, transmitted through the tapping tables at Guérin's request, were

> *Tyrtæus and Leonidas*
> *Will climb into their coupled carts*
> *Painted red like the décor of the Paris Opera.*
> *But my own soul, at the bottom of their basket of heads,*
> *A singing bird, will fly away!*[12]

Do we have a match? This is an odd piece of poetry, and the only thing we can say for sure about it is that we *don't* have a match. The versification, the rhythm of the lines, are completely different from what we find in *Iambic IX*, and the theme, such as it may be, also seems different. In *Iambic IX* there is only the narrator, André Chénier, who is moving beyond the imminence of his death to something greater; in the channeled poem there are two additional personages, Leonidas and Tyrtæus, who seem to be getting into two of the same tumbrels that transported André Chénier from the Saint-Lazare prison to the Conciergerie.

Who are Tyrtæus and Leonidas? They are both heroes of ancient Sparta. Tyrtæus, who lived in the seventh century B.C., was a general and also a poet whose inspiring martial airs were sung by the Spartans as they marched into battle. Leonidas (circa 530–480 B.C.) was the Spartan king who sacrificed his life and the lives of his select band of three hundred soldiers at the pass of Thermopylae in Greece in 480 B.C. to delay the advance of the Persians on Athens (Sparta and Athens were then allies). This delaying strategy was a crucial factor in the eventual defeat of the Persians.

We shouldn't be surprised to find the disembodied author of these lines bringing two heroes from ancient Sparta into the French Revolution. This is a poem, and this is the kind of liberty poets take. But what does the author mean? Why are the two tumbrels attached? Are they red like the décor of the Opera because the spirit poet wants to fuse the images of blood and of the forced, artificial drama of an opera in order to contrast the greatness of the Spartans with the pointless bloodletting of the Terror? Why does "Chénier" say that his own severed head, lying under the heads of the Spartans, will fly away singing like a bird? It's all something of a mystery, and reading *Iambic IX* doesn't help.

Curiously, both Tyrtæus and Leonidas paid brief visits to the tapping tables on Jersey Island. Tyrtæus dropped by on December 14, 1853, staying just long enough to recite a longish poem that Hugo seems to have briefly considered using as the words for an anthem to the United States of Europe.[13] Leonidas's visit on Tuesday, May 2, 1854, was so brief that the famed defender of Thermopylae couldn't get a word in edgewise as Victor Hugo delivered two masterful orations to his glory.[14]

Our examination of these two pieces of poetry certainly hasn't taken us anywhere near proving that there is survival after death. For Claudius Grillet, the remarkable thing was that poetry like this was dictated through the tapping tables at all. He observes that Victor Hugo wasn't present at the séance on that night of December 9, 1853, and that therefore the channeled poetry couldn't possibly have been transmitted, however unconsciously, to the tables from Hugo's extraordinarily creative mind. Grillet writes:

> Could the mysterious animator [of the tapping tables] have been Charles Hugo? That would be greatly to his honor. Had Charles been able to compose, on the spur of the moment, the admirable poetry of the Lion [the Lion of Androcles], of Aeschylus, of Shakespeare, or of the Shadow of the Sepulcher, we would have to place his poetic faculties and verbal power above those of his father. The wonder would be, not that he had composed such lines, but that never before and never after these celebrated séances did he display such prodigious talent.[15]

Chénier appeared at the tapping tables a second time, at the séance held at the Leguevels the next night, December 10, 1853. Victor Hugo was present that night along with the Leguevels, Mme and Mlle Adèle Hugo, Charles and François-Victor Hugo, and the political exiles Xavier Durrieu and Colonel Taly. During this session the shade of Chénier completed two more poems he had left unfinished during his lifetime: *My Manes at Clythia* and "fragment XXII" of the *Elegies*.[16]

In the course of a short séance held on December 11, 1853, with Victor Hugo absent but his two sons present along with Guérin, the Leguevels, and Xavier Durrieu, the spirit of Chénier brought to completion a poem called *Neæra*.[17]

The three séances at which André Chénier completed a total of nine of the poems he had left unfinished in his life would be eclipsed by the next two séances at which Chénier appeared. At these séances the shade would be not so much a poet dictating poetry as a seer revealing the nature of the universe not long after its creation.

On December 29, 1853, at 9:00 p.m. precisely, Victor Hugo arrived at the séance all set to ask the shade of Chénier what happened to the living Chénier after he was guillotined—and so, by analogy, what happened to the narrator of *The Last Day of a Condemned Man* after "FOUR O'CLOCK."

Present at the séance that night, which took place at Marine-Terrace, were Victor Hugo, the two Adèles, Charles and François-Victor Hugo, and Auguste Vacquerie. Mme Hugo sat at the table with Charles.

Learning about the afterlife was only a part of Victor Hugo's agenda that night. He must have been wondering whether it was really possible for a dead poet to add new lines to a poem he had written while he was alive. Hugo had no doubt the souls of the deceased could dictate poetry to the souls of the living. But he wondered if channeled afterlife poetry could ever really be a follow-up to the poetry the poet had written while on earth. Didn't you change in the afterworld? Didn't you see things from an entirely different perspective? Didn't you grow? Could the shade, dwelling in such vastly different surroundings now, even remember what life had been like on earth, or even remember what he or she had been like?

This is the question that Victor Hugo now put to the spirit of André Chénier, though in a different form. He began by congratulating André on the poetry he had composed for the séance participants. Then he asked him what he thought of the French Revolution now? Chénier had been part republican, part royalist while he was alive; did he still hold this position? Hugo wanted to know whether Chénier's soul had changed in the afterworld. "Do we make any progress in the tomb?" he asked. "Have you remained what you were? Do life and death see with the same eyes?"

The shade replied:

My work will be a double one. I must create my known work and my unknown work. The first will be royalist, the second republican. One will curse the French Revolution, the other will bless it. My head, in falling, grasped the idea that my eyes beheld only as an executioner's axe. These thoughts, irrigated by my blood, blossomed in the grave. My lyre that decried the revolution's scaffold, set itself in the grave to singing the praises of the revolution.[18]

New vistas were opening up. The shade of Chénier had broached the subject of *homo duplex—Homo sapiens* as "double man"—that the spirit called Death would take up at length beginning some nine months later, on September 19, 1854. Let's briefly look at what Death would say about this matter.

During their lives all great minds create two bodies of work: their work as living beings and their work as phantoms. Into the living work they throw the living, terrestrial world; into the phantom work they pour that other, celestial world.

The living speak to their century in the language it understands. . . . While the living being creates this first work, the pensive phantom, in the night, in the silence of the universe, awakens within the living human being. [That] specter [exhorts the total human being]: Get up! Get on your feet! There's a high wind blowing, dogs and foxes bark, darkness is everywhere, nature shudders and trembles under God's whipcord; toads, snakes, worms, nettles, stones, grains of sand await us: Get on your feet! . . .

I bear you away with me, the lightning flash, our pale horse, rears up in the clouds. Come on! Enough sun. To the stars! To the stars! To the stars![19]

At least one distinguished academic has suggested that, in the fantastic world described above, "We hear echoes of Nietzche's 'Mighty Dionysiac desire then engulfs this world of phenomena in order to reveal behind it a sublime aesthetic joy.'"[20] That academic wonders if the dynamic reaches opened up by the tapping tables bear some relation to the pre-time-and-space cosmos intimated by Friedrich Nietzsche in *The Birth of Tragedy*. (We'll touch upon this subject later on.)

Whatever may be the case, at the séance of December 29, 1853, the shade of Chénier seemed to be telling Victor Hugo that the spirit had been engaged in two labors: the "known work," which was the work completed and now chronicled in his actual life, and the "unknown work," a part of which he was now expounding to Hugo—with this very exposition being, apparently, a part of the unknown work!

The rest of the evening's session was taken up with a political discussion between, for the most part, Hugo and Chénier. The séance ended with everyone agreeing to meet again as soon as possible.

They did meet again, and very soon, on the night of January 2, 1854. It was at this séance that Victor Hugo finally got the opportunity he had been looking for: the shade of Chénier would describe to him the execution of the living Chénier, what it was like to be guillotined, and what happened afterward.

The séance began at 9:30 p.m. Present along with Victor Hugo were Auguste Vacquerie, Mme Hugo, and Charles Hugo. The latter two were seated at the table.

We began this chapter with a lengthy passage from Hugo's *The Last Day of a Condemned Man*. Let us preface André Chénier's account of how he was launched into the afterworld with the final paragraphs of Hugo's 1829 novel. The condemned man is standing at the foot of the stairs leading up to the guillotine. He narrates:

> That awful executioner! He went up to the judge to tell him the execution had to take place at a particular time, that that time was approaching, and that the execution was his responsibility—and that besides it was raining and they risked getting the guillotine rusty.
>
> "Have pity on me!" I cried. "Let me wait for one more minute in case I'm pardoned. Or I'll defend myself! I'll bite you!"
>
> The judge and the executioner left. I was alone. Alone with two policemen.
>
> Oh, that horrendous crowd howling like a pack of hyenas! How do they know I won't escape? That I won't be saved? If my pardon—? . . . It's unthinkable that I won't be pardoned!
>
> Ah, what miserable people! It's seems to me we're climbing up some stairs . . .
>
> FOUR O'CLOCK[21]

Here is the account of the shade of André Chénier:

The man climbs up on the scaffold. The executioner attaches him to the platform. The half-moon of a collar closes around his neck. The souls of those who have been guillotined take flight in this iron collar. Then the man has a terrible moment. He opens his eyes and sees below him a basket full of reddish mud. It lies in the gutter at the bottom of the scaffold, and his head tells him: "I'm going to be there."

"No," replies his soul.

The scene has just changed. Instead of mud he sees an ocean; instead of blood he sees light. He has entered the sky by way of that gutter. O terror! O joy! O awakening! O tremendous kiss! O falling to one's knees! O soaring! The soul takes flight, yet remains on its knees. It remains a child, yet becomes a bird.

But O surprise! It feels itself being slowly enveloped in a diaphanous sheath. The sky changes into a mirror. The soul sees itself. It is beautiful. It is twenty years old. The body no longer hides the soul; it reflects it. The soul is no longer enclosed in matter. Beauty is no longer a matter of flesh. The soul has released from this corpse being dragged to the charnel house all that was precious in it: its smile, its glance, its sunniness, love's first kiss still lingering on the lips of the severed head, a forgotten sigh, the song of an autumn evening, the perfume of an April's early morning, the tiny little fast-subsiding outburst of a dove, the words, "I love you"; and it has carried all that away into the sky.

I recognize myself, and yet I no longer have any of my senses about me. I'm alive, and yet I no longer carry the weight of my life. It pulsates through the light in my transparent veins. I drink infinity through all my pores. An invisible mouth covers me with a long kiss in which I sense my mother, in which I recognize my mistress, and which gives forth one after the other the perfume of all my lovers.

A luminous line separates my head from my body. It is an alive and feeling wound, which is receiving the kiss of God. Death appears to me simultaneously on earth and in the sky, while my body, transfigured by the tomb, plunges deep into the beatitude of eternity. At an immense distance below me I see my other body, which the executioner is throwing to the worms, my head rolling in the gutter, my wound gushing blood, my guillotine blade being washed, my scalp dangling at the end of a stick, and my name being execrated by the crowd.

Then I hear a voice crying, "Glory to Chénier!" and I see a halo descending from the heights of the sky down to my forehead. The basket into which my head had rolled has ended up becoming an annunciation of God . . .

At this point, Auguste Vacquerie noted that the communication through the tapping tables had become troubled. Charles said that it must be because he was so tired. They decided to end the séance there. It was taken up again on January 6, 1854 (no hour is given). Present this time were Auguste Vacquerie, who transcribed, and Mme and Charles Hugo, who sat at the tables. The shade of Chénier picked up where he had left off:

Apotheosis! The guillotine has blazed up in beams of light. The executioner has discovered his own wholeness in God. The sower of death has harvested immortality.

I am reborn in a huge cradle. As pink as a lily in springtime, I emerge living from the shadows. Each soul is a flower growing out of the dirt of its tomb. Heaven is a bouquet. The scent of cemeteries is the softest scent. God will always inhale the odor of a rose that grows out of death. Prayer plucks the rose for God. Prayer is the bouquet-maker of heaven.

All of a sudden, I hear voices in the infinite, one saying, "O my poet, my name is Neæra. I am sad; my crown is incomplete. Your verses abandoned me. I died while being born. O my poet, make me live again. Look once more upon my Idyll. *Let me rejoin Chromis."*

*The other voice says, "O my lover, I am Camille; you made me love you, you made me sing. Give your love back to me, and take up my song once more. O my love, enable me to find Chénier again."**

The other says, with a grim and plaintive note of mockery: "O revenger, I am Louis XVI. You'll hold anger's whip in your hand. You'll be on a first-name basis with thunder. Seize the lightning iambic and avenge me. Make the scaffold wilt. O poet, make me rediscover Tacitus."

At this point the spirit of Robespierre enters the dialogue, and at this point we will end our transcription of the shade of André Chénier's words. Victor Hugo, François-Charles Hugo, and Mlle Adèle Hugo had abruptly entered the room. They wanted to talk to William Shakespeare. Suddenly the shade of Chénier was gone. He was never to return.[22]

---

*Here the creatures of Chénier's unfinished poetry are asking Chénier to complete that poetry so that they may be fulfilled. The shade of Chénier has already, at the séance of December 9, 1853, completed *Idyll XII*, the poem in which both Neæra and Chromis appear.

Nine

WILLIAM SHAKESPEARE, CHANNELED AND TRANSLATED

François-Victor, aged twenty-six in 1854, the youngest son of Victor Hugo, loved and revered his father, but sometimes there peeked out from beneath his filial piety, just for an instant, a profound resentment bordering on hatred.

At Marine-Terrace at 11:30 every morning without fail (you could almost set your clocks by it), the two clattered downstairs together, Victor from writing poetry and François-Victor from translating William Shakespeare, both having begun their work at six o'clock in the morning.

Today, January 13, 1854, was no different from any other day except that this morning François-Victor, coming down behind his father (who looked even more freshly scrubbed than usual), sniffed on the back of his father's collar the faint scent of a perfume he knew was not his mother's because, since coming to Jersey Island, she had not worn perfume.

There rose up in François-Victor a smoldering rage that, usually when he felt it, he completely suppressed. On this particular morning, he was forced to suppress his rage even more quickly than usual, because the moment that he and his father arrived at the bottom of the stairs, the Hugo household erupted in violent activity. The two dogs, Chougna and Lux, bounded in from the front hall and, nearly knocking François-Victor over, hurled themselves on Victor Hugo, whom they adored. Mme Hugo, who hated to have the dogs run wild in the house, rushed in from the dining room and flailed a broomstick over them.[1]

The door of the greenhouse/photography studio burst open and Charles stumbled out, swearing loudly (they had awakened him), dressed in his rag-tag Bohemian uniform of baggy pants and torn sweater, hands black with developing powder and clutching an equally blackened pipe. Young Adèle, who had been sitting quietly at the piano, suddenly pounded the keys with passion, playing the opening bars of *La Traviata*.

Victor always knew if Charles had been working in the darkroom all morning or merely using the greenhouse as a place in which to round off his habitual twelve hours of sleep a night. Now, not waiting for the music to subside, raising his face from the dogs who were frantically licking it, he glared at Charles and launched into one of his customary lectures: "My dear Charles, I have a rule, and that rule is to sleep only seven hours a day. It works for me and it is recommended by one of our very best doctors, M. Louis, who says it doesn't matter when you get the seven hours, at night or during the day." They were now all making their way to the dining room table as Victor went on, "All that matters, says the doctor, is that you get the sleep unfailingly and regularly. I warn you, Charles, you're wasting the best years of your life. You sleep twelve hours a day, not seven! You're losing five hours a day, which comes to five years every twenty years."[2]

Charles, who had heard this story many times before and always hated hearing it, shoved his pipe into his mouth and, sitting down noisily at the table, began to blow gigantic smoke rings. François-Victor, though he was careful to sleep just seven hours a night himself, sympathized with his brother; both knew their father hadn't always stuck to this rule himself and sometimes slept very odd hours, as in their early childhood when (Victor still told the story) he wrote *The Hunchback of Notre Dame* at all hours including the night and sometimes didn't sleep for thirty hours. (Admittedly this was the mirror image of Charles's problem.)[3] Now they were all sitting down at the table and François-Victor, feeling a renewed surge of anger, this time at his father's hypocrisy, accidentally knocked over the salt shaker and, without thinking, picked up a pinch of salt and tossed it over his shoulder.

"Aha!" roared Charles gleefully, seizing the opportunity to deflect attention from himself, "Mr. Nineteenth Century has done it again! This impeccably rational man, this disciple of Voltaire, has shown us that way down deep what he really believes in are the hoariest of old wives' tales!"[4]

"Ah, yes, it is certainly true," joined in their father, but more gently. "Once again we see the Man of the Enlightenment caught in a contradiction: he tells us with absolute conviction that the spirits of the dead do not speak through the tapping tables, while at the same time he believes that it is bad luck to spill salt and that that bad luck can only be canceled out by throwing salt over one's shoulder."

"Just a habit lingering from childhood," mumbled François-Victor. "Just my peasant blood peeping through. But all of you know that if I don't believe in the tables, if I don't believe in the spirits and what they say, I do believe in one great spirit, and that is William Shakespeare."

Now all of them, sitting around the table, beginning to eat, gazed at him silently and respectfully, all quarrels suddenly past. Something not to be mocked had entered the conversation: François-Victor's belief that the soul of William Shakespeare had taken possession of him and was helping him translate the works of Shakespeare into French.

Lowering his eyes, ignoring them, François-Victor thought to himself that he could never really explain what he meant when he expressed this belief. It had all started when he was learning just the language itself—not at school, where he had learned the basics, but in prison, when he was cramming English. His mother had told him that the family would soon be moving to London (or so she hoped), or to Jersey Island, and he should perfect his English as quickly as possible. It had happened that, one night as he opened for perhaps the third time the English grammar his mother had sent him (along with an entire library of books), his eyes chanced to fall upon the word "Shakespeare," and he suddenly found himself falling desperately, madly, head-over-heels in love with the English language and, in particular, with Shakespeare's way of using it.

He was not even particularly good at languages! Moreover, if he had had to study a foreign language, and had some choice in the matter, he would probably have studied German, or perhaps Spanish. But he had no choice! And this was not because he had started to learn English at his mother's bidding. It was because the *English language*— especially the English of Shakespeare—had chosen *him*. For from that night on he was the spellbound captive of the language. It held him in thrall, like the singing of Circe had held Odysseus and his sailors in thrall—and François-Victor was not lashed to a mast. He had fallen to his knees before the linguistic genius of the goddess Britannia, and from then on he had never ceased to call out to her, breathlessly, imploringly, whenever he could, "Take me, I'm yours! Do with me what you will!"

He constantly had the sense, as he worked on his English through the long prison hours, that a vast presence hovered behind him and enfolded him in its wings. It was as if he had a guardian angel, and that guardian angel was the soul of William Shakespeare. Sometimes his guesses about what Shakespeare was saying were more accurate than the conclusions he reached with his intellect alone. He had hunches, and he checked out those hunches—and increasingly his hunches turned out to be right. No, he did not believe in the spirit world, and he rarely attended a séance. But, yes—no matter how contradictory it seemed—he believed that he was cradled in the arms of the spirit of William Shakespeare and that if he were ever to fall from the lofty skies in which he pursued his studies, mighty arms and beating wings would bear him up again to those empyrean heights.

François-Victor emerged slowly from his reverie. Around him, the Hugo family was busily finishing up lunch. His father was holding forth with his customary freedoms on the idiocies of the Second Empire. And, just at the moment that Victor Hugo pronounced yet again, with his habitual scorn, the words "Napoleon the Little," François-Victor, who was sitting beside him, detected once more the faint and delectable scent of perfume on his father's collar. Possibly it was Juliette Drouet's perfume. They all accepted Juliette, at least to a certain degree. But François-Victor had just the glimmer of a hunch that the perfume had come from someone else. It reminded him a little, in fact, of a perfume that Anaïs had worn once in that passionate and heart-wrenching time of their great love, which now seemed to François-Victor to have been a thousand years ago, though it had ended just last year.

And with this thought, François-Victor rose suddenly from the table, again suppressing the same surge of anger he had felt at his father earlier, and, turning sharply, without saying a word of goodbye to anyone—but luckily the meal was over and Victor Hugo himself was rising—he strode out of the dining room, down the hall, and out the door into the fresh, clear air of the early afternoon.

Fifteen minutes later, he was in the saddle and urging his pony up the path that led to the Saint Helier road.

Every morning François-Victor dressed in his riding costume for lunch. Every day after lunch, regularly as clockwork, he strode the short distance down to the stables, mounted his horse, and rode for three-quarters of an hour. His destination was the ramshackle shed and rocky field of the improvised fencing school run by Pierre Leroux, where he fenced for a half hour every day.[5] He stuck at these disciplines rigorously, because finally he was not a strong man. When he was twelve years old he had been terribly ill; he had not slept for days, and his doctors, not knowing what was the matter, had feared for his life. Then his father—or so Victor claimed—had healed him by making mesmeric passes over his body. François-Victor remembered almost nothing of this, but he had survived, and he had prospered.[6] He still came down sick easily and sometimes his limbs grew unexpectedly weak and he had to lie down for a time. So it was essential that he take exercise, that he do so regularly and vigorously, and that he do so, if possible, in the open air.

His horse was moving at an easy trot as he passed the house of Juliette Drouet.

François-Victor felt uneasy. Once again, he sensed the fingers of anger testing his strength here and there. It was not exactly the thought of his father's philandering that made him feel uneasy. No, it was the thought of what he himself might do if he were to give way to this behavior, a behavior that seemed like a kind of strength in his father but that in himself (though he had surely inherited this characteristic from his father) always seemed like a great weakness. Victor Hugo could work with total discipline for part of the day and play with total profligacy for the other part. But François-Victor knew that for him to give way to his own sensual side always meant that that sensuality would rage on forever, week after week, to the exclusion of all else, until finally some powerful force of circumstance brought it to a halt.

He knew this because of what had happened between Anaïs and himself when he had gotten out of prison.

When the December 1851 coup d'état took place, François-Victor was serving four months of a nine-month sentence at the Conciergerie in Paris for publishing an article highly critical of Napoleon III. For a prison term, it hadn't been that harsh. He had shared his cell for a while, a spacious and tastefully furnished room, with his brother Charles, who was serving a six-month sentence for publishing an article condemning capital punishment (both he and his brother would be granted an early release). They ate well in a communal dining hall with their fellow prisoners. They could have visitors almost any time they wanted, and, if they requested it of their jailers, almost anything would be delivered to their cell.

François-Victor found that he did not despair in prison as long as he rigorously structured his life. He read at certain hours of the day. He studied at certain hours of the day. He exercised regularly. He did not allow a moment to go by which he did not fill with some previously planned activity. But, just before beginning his term, he had been very taken with an actress named Anaïs Liévenne, who performed at the Variétés Theater. Anaïs visited him a number of times in prison. He did not allow her to stay for any length of time. Each time she left, he had to fight to put thoughts of her out of his mind. Somehow, after each visit, he would make a mighty effort to immerse himself all the more deeply in his studies; he would manage to structure his life all the more fiercely.

When François-Victor was released from prison and saw Anaïs, he realized he had fallen desperately in love with her, and, suddenly freed from his disciplines, he gave himself over to a life of debauchery that was the polar opposite of his life in prison.

Anaïs was very popular. Alexander Dumas had been one of her lovers and presently she was kept by a certain Viscount de Waresquiel who had given her complete run of a hotel close to the Champs-Elysées that came with servants, a garden, and a horse and carriage. Anaïs returned François-Victor's ardor; she lavished every affection on him. She also continued to give parties, and François-Victor was obliged (although he submitted gratefully) to fall in with her extravagant lifestyle. Very soon he was penniless. Now Anaïs supported him, using the Viscount de Waresquiel's money. The viscount found out and, distressed, cut off the flow of money. Anaïs found herself obliged to pay the hotel's enormous bills. Her friends and admirers loaned her money. François-Victor gave her money, borrowing it from the Hugo family and his friends. He used some of it to play the stock market, losing everything. Into the bargain, Anaïs was suffering from consumption.

François-Victor's family and his friends banded together to rescue him from what one of them (Jules Janin) called "this blind and degrading" affair. But François-Victor wanted to marry Anaïs. His father suggested he bring her to Jersey Island to see if she would be happy living there; perhaps François-Victor could then support her with his pen. Anaïs accompanied the son to Jersey. But the Variétés showgirl, although she seemed to love François-Victor, found life on Jersey too serious. She returned to Paris after several weeks.

François-Victor followed her. At the end of December 1852, Mme Hugo traveled to Paris and persuaded her younger son to return with her to Jersey. He did so. In mid-January 1853, Anaïs followed him to the island. This time it was Charles Hugo who escorted her back to Paris. The relationship was over.[7]

François-Victor suffered terribly for several months. Gradually he realized that he had flung himself into this doomed, sensual, passionate affair with Anaïs with every bit as much abandonment, with just as rigorous an exclusion of everything else, as he had flung himself into his studies of the English language and Shakespeare in his prison cell in the Conciergerie. He saw clearly that he was not able to fling himself into both kinds of activity at once. It was the sort of thing that his father could do—and it was largely for this reason that François-Victor felt a profound resentment bordering on hatred for his father that, when it reared its head, he repressed so quickly that he almost did not know that it existed.

This resentment aside, there had been a landmark exchange between the two one morning at the end of November 1853. Both were sitting in the dining room, staring silently out at the sea whose dark blue breakers seemed to be striking the beach with more ferocity than ever. Both (as they later admitted to each other) felt like shipwrecked sailors. Abruptly François-Victor turned to his father and said: "What do you think about this exile?"

His father replied: "That it will last a long time."

François-Victor asked: "How do you plan to fill it?"

His father replied: "I will look at the ocean."

There was silence. Then his father asked: "And you?"

"And I," said the son, "I will dedicate the entire length of my exile here to translating the works of Shakespeare."

His father had replied: "Ocean, Shakespeare: they are the same."[8]

It was at that point that François-Victor knew with certainty that he was a man who must always be possessed, though he could only be possessed by one thing at a time. First it had been Shakespeare, then it had been Anaïs—and now it was William Shakespeare again, powerfully and irrevocably. And so he set himself the task of translating the complete works of William Shakespeare, with a determination that he did not expect would leave him until the end of his days.

These were the thoughts that preoccupied François-Victor as, on that chilly day of January 13, 1854, he arrived on horseback at Pierre Leroux's fencing school, fenced for longer than usual (an hour and a quarter instead of an hour), rode back to Marine-Terrace at a vigorous clip, and then, before going down to dinner, did his exercises on the bedroom floor.

It was on that night that the shade of William Shakespeare visited the tapping tables for the first time. François-Victor did not often attend the séances, and he did not attend this one. When he was told afterward that the shade of Shakespeare had come by, he expressed no regrets at having missed him. These spirits of the tapping tables, if they were real, might also not be who they said they were. No matter; he had no need of them; Shakespeare was, after all, his own, his guardian angel.

At an earlier séance, Victor had asked the spirit called Criticism: "What *is* Shakespeare, anyway?"

Criticism had replied: *A diver after souls.*

"Go on," begged Hugo.

Before Shakespeare, the human soul was a sea whose depths had not been sounded. Aeschylus had expressed everything that has to do with that sea: storm, wind, lightning, foam, rocks, sky—everything except pearls. Shakespeare dove in and brought back love.[9]

When, on that evening of January 13, 1854, the Bard of Stratford himself, William Shakespeare (1564–1616), came tapping through the tables, Victor Hugo and Auguste Vacquerie were present while Mme Hugo and Charles sat at the table. The transcripts don't tell us when the séance began, though they say it ended at midnight. Victor Hugo began the questioning:

"As you know, for us you are one of the four or five greatest creators of all mankind. Would you like to tell us what happened in the tomb, what encounter took place, on April 23, 1616?"

*I kissed Corneille, just then being born.**

Hugo corrected the Bard: "I said 1616, not 1606. Collect your thoughts and consider whether that day Shakespeare did not meet another great representative of human thought."

No.

"However, on April 23, 1616, Cervantes [author of *Don Quixote*] died—the same day, almost the same hour, as you. Did you meet him? Would you care to answer that?"

No.

Hugo probed further: "Do you mean you wouldn't care to answer, or you didn't meet Cervantes?"

Cervantes did not die at the same time as I did.

"But he died the same day. You must have met him in that place you both went to. Two geniuses like yourselves must have had a great deal to say to each other. What did you talk about?"

When you die, you immediately take on the age of all those who are dead —that is, the age of eternity. In heaven, nobody arrives first and nobody arrives last. All have a single second of eternal life, and that second lasts a hundred thousand years. Asking a dead person, "How long have you been in heaven?" is like asking a sunbeam, "How long have you been in the sun?" A soul is a sister who doesn't have a big sister. Infinity is not love's big brother, nor eternity genius's big sister. All great minds are twins. Ideas have sons but not grandsons. If you ask the sunbeam how old it is, it will reply, "Ask the lightning bolt." If you ask the lightning bolt, it will reply, "Ask the sunbeam." I saw Cervantes once. He greeted me and spoke thus: "Poet, what do you think of Don Quixote?" And Molière, who was passing by, answered, "He's the same man as Don Juan." And I told Molière, "He's the same man as Hamlet." Don Quixote doubts; Don Juan doubts; Hamlet doubts. Don Quixote seeks; Don Juan seeks; Hamlet seeks. Don Quixote weeps; Don Juan weeps; Hamlet weeps. Hamlet smiles; all three suffer. In the skull that Hamlet holds, there is your tear, O Cervantes; there is your laugh, O Molière. The skeleton of doubt grimaces beneath the beauty of our three works. We write the drama; God brings it to completion. Behold heaven: it is the last act. The tombstone that opens on our souls is the curtain that

---

*Pierre Corneille (1606–1684) was one of the greatest of French dramatists.

rises on the dénouement. Applaud, Cervantes! Applaud, Molière! Applaud, Shakespeare! Enter God.

Hugo had another question:

"When you were on earth, you created—you created in imitation of God. Now that you've left earth and are living the true life, living in the light, what is your genius doing with itself? You, Shakespeare, lived and created, and for you these two ideas were inseparable: for Shakespeare, to live *was* to create. So, are you continuing to create? Are you continuing your work? If you're getting on with your creative work—if it still comes welling out of you—this must also be true for all the other geniuses in heaven. Which means that, running parallel to that primary creation which is God's, there must also be what we might call a secondary creation—that is, God's creation through the agency of great minds.

"This opens up vast new horizons! If you're [continuing your work], are you doing so with reference to the world of men you lived in or with reference to the world of souls in which your being now dwells? Has your work undergone the same transformation as you have? Do you now write—if the word 'write' is applicable—in a language that is new to us, that men would not understand, a language appropriate only to heaven? What are you writing? Dramas? What passions do you describe? What worlds? What ideas? If these dramas were translated for us, would they be at all accessible to our human intellects? In a word: What is the connection between the work you are now doing in heaven and the work you did on earth?"

The shade replied:

Human life has human creators. Celestial life has the divine creator. Creating is work; contemplation is work's reward. On earth great minds create in order to moralize; but, in heaven everything is moral, everything is good, everything is just, everything is beautiful. I could only create something here if heaven were incomplete; but as it is I dwell in a masterpiece. I have my being in perfection now. I who was admired am condemned to admire. I am lost in a crowd of spectators, I who was the creator of the spectacle.

God has fashioned an orchestra pit for himself composed of demigods: Orpheus, Tyrteus, Homer, Aeschylus, Sophocles, Euripides, Moses, Ezekiel, Isaiah, Daniel, Aesop, Dante, Rabelais, Cervantes, Molière, Shakespeare, and others whom I can only glimpse dimly in the depths of infinity without quite seeing who they are. We sit pensively before the Light of Eternity. Jesus is on his knees. The Light illuminates us; it bedazzles us. The life of eternity ravishes us and it flows over us; and if you saw all the prophets and all the magi and all the poets and all the geniuses who are seated before God in this circle, you would not ask me if I created.

No; I look. No; I listen. No; I am no more than an atom attentive before the face of infinity. I am a great man abdicating to the infinite. I fall from archangelhood. I get off my pedestal as inconspicuously as possible, and I throw away my halo. I am a dream whose death is an awakening. I was art; now I am love. My creations have left their wings in the tomb. As I have become what I now am, so has my art been resurrected in forms of love. Art walks to heaven's door, but only love can enter. Happiness is an eternal Mecca whose pilgrim is art but whose angel is love.

Mme Hugo asked: "You say that, in that world in which your being now dwells, you no longer create works of art. How is it that André Chénier thinks only about creating works of art, only about completing his works?"

The shade of Shakespeare replied:

Life placed a crown upon my head. It beheaded Chénier. Chénier still has something to say to life. As for me, I no longer speak to anyone but God or in God's name. Shakespeare is the father of his works. Chénier is the orphan of his.

The session concluded at midnight.[10]

Shakespeare returned to the tables on January 22, 1854, at a quarter of ten in the evening. Present were Victor Hugo and Auguste Vacquerie, with Mme Hugo and Théophile Guérin sitting at the table. First there was a brief communication with a spirit who was apparently the soul of the Jacob of the Old Testament. Presumably (it isn't recorded), Jacob's interlocutor was Victor Hugo. The séance began:

"Is there anybody there?"

Yes.

"Your name?"

Jacob.

"Do you have a communication for me?"

Yes.

"Speak."

Let us doubt.

At this point, the following note written by Victor Hugo is inserted in the transcript:

"A half hour before this séance, Victor Hugo and Auguste Vacquerie, alone in the sitting room and chatting about the tables, expressed some doubts. They found it strange, in particular, that [in the previous séance] Shakespeare told them Don Quixote was a symbol of doubt, whereas both of them saw Don Quixote as standing for, *par excellence,* affirmation. No one could have overheard the conversation between the two. Charles was in his room at the time, two floors above the sitting room.

"[Just after the above brief exchange with Jacob,] Charles entered and took his mother's place. He sat down at the table without asking which spirit was there or what had been said up to this point."

Then the shade of Jacob continued:

Shakespeare was quite right in telling you that doubt lies at the heart of all the works of man. Yes, Don Juan represents doubt. Yes, Hamlet represents doubt. Yes, Don Quixote represents doubt. You haven't understood these personages in the broadest sense. Would you like me to give you that understanding in a single word? Don Juan's fight with the statue, Hamlet's fight with the shadows, Don Quixote's fight with phantoms—all these are the same fight, all this is man at war with the invisible; it is the boxing match of body versus soul, the duel of flesh against spirit; doubt is the grim field upon which knights joust. All of these are the eternal wrestling of Jacob with the angel.

Victor Hugo declared: "What you've just said is beautiful, and it's conclusive. Did you hear what we said just a short time ago in the sitting room?"

The table stirred but did not tap.

"Are you there, Jacob?"

There were two taps: *No.*

"Who's there?"

Shakespeare.

"Have you a communication for us?"

Yes.

"Speak."

The shade declared:

I'm just a bit inclined to ask you, wretched men of genius: Do you think you have the stature to dare defy the god of the depths of all of space? Do you think your brains have produced such wonderful stuff that you've earned the right to protect them by not baring your head to the god of all the suns? Do you think your masterpieces are of such high quality that you can dare to throw the gauntlet down before the god of all eternity? What are our Hamlets, what are our Don Juans, what are our Don Quixotes—what are all of them when compared to the majesty, the power, the light? What are your dramas, what are your worlds, when compared to creation? Hamlet, take off your showy black shirt. Don Juan, throw away your sword. Don Quixote, strip off your face mask. Ruy Blas,* lend them your servant's clothes, so that they may appear before the eternal master dressed appropriately. Servant's clothes are the costumes worn by masterpieces when they stand before God.

They took a short break. Then the participants asked Shakespeare to continue. He did so:

First of all: you're strangely mistaken about me. I disdain my work no more than the statue disdains its pedestal. I stand on my creation. You say: "He's trampling it underfoot." No; I don't disdainfully trample Hamlet underfoot; rather, I superbly ascend the lofty fortifications of Elsinore [Hamlet's castle], and there, instead of addressing the shadows, I speak to God. That is what I do. Every great thinker, in climbing into the grave, completes the last step of his created work. Death is the supreme tour-de-force. The sublime assault on heaven is the final phase of the great creative work done on earth. Life puts a mask on the forehead of spirit; death strips away the mask and says, Greetings, halo. I am the vanquished of God; I come to tell you the tale of my defeat. I am the ambassador of the victory of the divine. I blow the trumpet blast behind the chariot of the Eternal, and it will astonish you to hear me sounding the name, not of Shakespeare, but of Jehovah. You see, I'd almost forgotten my own name. Thank you for recalling it to me, you who remain among the living.

Victor Hugo wanted to hear more, but Shakespeare declared that he would now recite a poem.

"In English or in French?" asked Hugo.

---

*Ruy Blas is the hero of Victor Hugo's 1838 drama of the same name.

The English language is inferior to the French, Shakespeare replied.

"We are listening."

And William Shakespeare proceeded to recite a poem to the assembled company.[11]

The English language is inferior to the French—?!

Perhaps it is just as well that François-Victor attended the séances of William Shakespeare on neither the first night nor the second. He would likely have been outraged by this remark.

From the end of the second séance on, William Shakespeare's contributions to the Marine-Terrace tapping-table séances would consist almost exclusively of poetry and of the first act of the play that constitutes the appendix of this book.

François-Victor continued to toil over his translations. True to his word, he worked on them during the entire time of his father's exile on the islands of Jersey and Guernsey, returning to France only when his father did, in 1871.

His translations, which included not only all the plays but also all the poetry of Shakespeare, along with critical commentary, were well received by the critics. Several of the translations of the plays are still performed today.

Ten

METEMPSYCHOSIS SPEAKS

*I feel that there is much to be said for the Celtic belief
that the souls of those whom we have lost are held captive
in some inferior being, in an animal, in a plant, in some
inanimate object, and thus effectively lost to us until
the day (which to many never comes) when we happen
to pass by the tree or to obtain possession of the object
which forms their prison. Then they start and tremble,
they call us by our name, and as soon as we have
recognized them the spell is broken. Delivered by us, they
have overcome death and return to share our life.*

MARCEL PROUST, *IN SEARCH OF LOST TIME* OR
REMEMBRANCE OF THINGS PAST

Auguste Vacquerie had been such a brilliant student at the Collège
de Rouen in Normandy that the headmaster of the prestigious Lycée
de Charlemagne in Paris had invited him to complete his scholastic
training there for free, as a "prize examinee." Auguste had happily
accepted and had graduated from the Lycée de Charlemagne with
highest honors. While there, he had gotten to know Victor Hugo (the
Lycée had produced one of his dramas) and their families had become
friends. Indeed, Auguste's brother Charles had married Léopoldine
Hugo, with the tragic consequences that profoundly affected them
all.[1]

Auguste had not found it easy to lead his classes at the Paris lycée.

But he loved learning and he worked hard and even Victor Hugo had complimented him on his acute intelligence. So, yes, that had been difficult—but what was even more difficult was loving the strange and moody Adèle Hugo and making her love him in return. In fact, it seemed to him that he was utterly failing to do this—that Adèle was spurning him contemptuously—and this periodically filled his heart with bitterness and pain.

But now, as he strolled along the beach in front of Marine-Terrace on April 15, 1854, with his shaggy gray shepherd dog Chougna (she had been given to him by Count Sandor Teleki—*chougna* was the Hungarian word for "ugly"), Auguste wasn't thinking about this at all. Now he was cudgeling his brains over yet another matter that was an exceedingly difficult one (and also, sometimes, an emotionally trying one), and that was this utterly bizarre question, which the tapping-table spirits kept raising, of the metempsychosis of souls through beasts and plants and stones as well as through men and women.

According to the spirits, all human beings were the reincarnation of persons who had committed criminal acts in a previous lifetime for which they were being punished by having to live through their present lifetime. And, though all of us have a sense that we are being punished, none of us knows *why* we are being punished; we have no memory of that previous lifetime or that previous crime.

The souls of animals were also the prisons of beings who had committed criminal acts (even worse ones!) in a previous lifetime. And while animals remembered their criminal acts as vividly as if they were branded on their souls, none of them knew their commission of these acts was why they were being punished—or even that they *were* being punished! The upshot was that while humanity struggled to improve itself in order to overcome its sense of guilt, the animal did not feel guilty and expiated its crime simply by being itself (which self was a sort of representation of that crime)—by wonderingly beholding itself; by contemplating itself over the period of that lifetime. All of this was true of the kingdom of plants as well, which embodied the souls of beings who had committed even worse crimes than animals in a previous lifetime—and that was why they were imprisoned in plants and not in animals! And all of this was even truer of stones, which embodied souls whose crimes had been even worse, and who therefore found themselves reincarnated in the prison of a stone.

The four domains of being—man, beast, plant, and stone—moved upward or downward on the Great Chain of Being according to how well they bettered themselves, or how badly, in a particular life. Moreover, because the only appropriate response to a suffering soul was compassionate love, and since all of nature was ensouled, then you had to bestow an equal portion of love on every particle of creation. Such was the truth of reincarnation, according to the table-tapping spirits.

But what did all this amazing and sordid and exalting nonsense really mean, wondered Auguste? Was any of it *really* true?

It was 6:00 p.m. on this evening of April 15, and Chougna, great barker, prancer, and leaper onto human breasts that she was, was bounding ahead on the dark brown sand while Auguste, wearing the thick black frock coat that protected him against almost every change of weather, idly tossed pebbles at clods of green-black seaweed lying on the sand.

He stopped abruptly, remembering that seaweed should not be stoned but loved, since after all it contained the imprisoned souls of suffering beings. But so did pebbles! And the souls within them were suffering even more, because they had committed even more heinous crimes in a previous lifetime. Auguste did not let fly the one pebble remaining in his hand but instead let it drop quietly to the sand. Then he remembered: Sand, too! Every grain of sand as well was panting with suffering soul-stuff! Auguste stifled an impulse to flee from the all-too-sensitive sand up to the grass; then, sighing—remembering that grass too was soul-stuff— he remained standing in bewildered contemplation where he was.

It was all quite hopeless, really. A man couldn't get up in the morning—couldn't even get out of bed—without rudely bumping into the living conscious soul-stuff that permeated all of organic nature and even all of inorganic nature. (It even permeated man-made things, since objects like penknives and wristwatches and teakettles also somehow acquired soul-material.)

Most compelling of all, Auguste thought as he turned slowly on the beach, gazing first at the sand flats, then at the promontories, then at the houses, most compelling of all was this matter of *animals'* being prisons of souls that had committed terrible crimes in a previous life. Auguste loved animals, and dogs were his favorite. Madame de Staël had once said, famously, "The more I see of men, the more I like dogs."[2] But Auguste's love of dogs was not simply a reaction to his growing awareness of the follies of men. Rather it was something he felt because he knew that dogs were splendid, loving, self-governing, soul-filled beings. Perhaps there was even something to what the spirits said regarding the ability of animals, including of course dogs, to "glimpse" God—but what human could presume to understand just what these darling creatures knew?

The sun was setting, but warmth was still rising from the beach. On the sand, Auguste placed a special mat for sitting and then sat down, laying to one side the notebook in which he'd been jotting revisions to his play that had been performed in Rouen the summer before. He called Chougna. The dog came bounding joyfully up to him. He took the shaggy sides of the dog's head between his hands and pulled her into his lap, petting her with long strokes and addressing her, "So, my dear creature, you are perfectly happy as a dog because you have no knowledge that you are being punished? But, at the same time, you have a burning memory of—what? In what strange way does your hideous crime of a previous lifetime represent itself to you?"

Chougna abruptly became stock-still. She inclined her head and seemed to stare at Auguste.

There were moments when he was certain Chougna had something to say to him and was trying to say it. Now was one of those moments. Bending forward, Auguste looked into the depths of her eyes.

It seemed to him that he saw (he had seen it before), at the very bottom of those fine limpid eyes, something obscurely doing battle with itself, something debating tormentedly the terms of its own destiny. It was as if some unlucky person had fallen into a well and was straining to climb out, even calling for help—a very unlucky person who clutched at the sides of the well and pulled himself up a foot or two and then fell back. Auguste believed he was gazing directly at a struggling soul. *Ah, my dear girl,* he thought, *I wish I could throw you a rope. But I don't have one.*

Auguste had come to love almost all animals. He could hardly believe that once upon a time, as a child, he had blasted bullfinches out of the trees with a shotgun at Villequier and lured sparrows to their death by throwing fistfuls of seeds between rows of wheat so the birds would flock right in front of the muzzle of his gun. *What a miserable sort of an ambush,* he thought, *one that only a coward could think up!* As if mankind didn't have enough animals to kill just out of sheer necessity, just because we have to eat.

Sitting there on the beach, with the sun touching the horizon and Chougna frisking in his arms, Auguste thought of all the cows humanity had slaughtered, all the chickens it had bled to death, all the salmon it had ripped apart with fishhooks, all the lobsters it had tossed into boiling water while they were still alive. *Will a time never come,* he wondered, *when we have had enough of that grim law that condemns our species to a lifetime of ferocity simply by declaring: To live is to kill!?*

Auguste had personally sworn to be good to all the fauna that humanity did not have to eat. These days he made a habit of picking beetles up off the roadway and depositing them on nearby hedges. He was the Good Samaritan of toads! The day before he had rescued a toad that children were stoning; he had plucked it off the road and set it down in a field some distance away. He was now the intimate friend of snails and the gallant protector of spiders.

He did not hate wild animals. Rather, he saw them as suffering from some mysterious and awful destiny. He did not hold them responsible for the harm that they inflicted on mankind. He pitied them for what they did—in fact, he loved them for it! It seemed to Auguste that men should act toward savage beasts in the same way men acted toward the savage tribes they encountered in the jungle: they should tame them and then educate them. First and foremost, tigers had to be civilized. Savage bites from lions, rifle shots from men—surely this should not forever be the sole form of dialogue between man and lion. How Auguste longed to walk up to a jackal and say: Brother, let's embrace![3]

But man's relationship to beasts included far, far more than animals. Auguste was sitting on the sand close to where the grass began. Two hours before, it had been raining. The tall grass was moist, and as he looked he saw a big, fat worm expel itself in quick undulations from between the blades. It wriggled forward until it came to the sand—and then it stopped, its front part raised. It stared blindly, or so it seemed, at Auguste.

Auguste stared stonily back. All feeling had suddenly drained from his body. It wasn't exactly that he was scared of worms, but—exactly who *was* this worm?

The spirit called Balaam's Ass had told them in December of the year before that the metempsychosical cycle through which the soul of every being passed was a truly punishing, even an unforgiving, one. A month or so later, apparently (Auguste hadn't been at the session), the spirits had told them that the reincarnational journey was extremely rocky in the sense that, on the way "up" you mustn't put a single foot wrong. You certainly mustn't engage in any evil act, because if you did, you ran the risk of all of a sudden tumbling and crashing and rolling right back down the Great Chain of Being. From having been a man or a woman (sometimes a very distinguished one) in this lifetime, you found yourself reincarnated as an earthworm or a stone in the next.

The spirits had told Victor Hugo that Cleopatra had been reincarnated as an earthworm! Auguste felt that this, if it were true, was probably fitting. After all, hadn't the ancient and brilliant queen of Egypt really been not much more than a monstrous femme fatale? She had seduced Julius Caesar and then—over fourteen years!—Mark Anthony, not because she had any love for these men but solely in order to conquer the Roman Empire.[4] The spirits had also mentioned Heliogabalas, the extremely corrupt emperor of Rome in the second century A.D. Heliogabalas was notorious for having had beautiful women stripped naked and harnessed to his chariot, which he then drove around the arena while tearing at their flesh with his whip. The emperor's metempsychosical punishment (which Auguste, again, approved of) had consisted of being reincarnated as a cemetery headstone sticking out of a half-open grave.

Auguste was guiltily aware that his mind all too easily ran in such morbid channels. It was getting dark, and the beach was cooling off. He quickly got up from the sand and turned toward Marine-Terrace, which loomed up beyond the grass. Chougna, bounding up, flounced into the tall grass. Auguste decided that he would ponder the subject of metempsychosis another time. The spirits had hinted subtly that, sometime soon, the spirit of Metempsychosis itself would come to the tapping tables and explain everything. They had been saying this for a while, and nothing had happened yet. Auguste decided it would be okay to ponder the nature of metempsychosis and crime and punishment at his leisure; he thought he had plenty of time.

In the meantime, he smelled dinner. He and Chougna quickened their pace toward the house.

※※

In *Victor Hugo spirite,* Claudius Grillet describes what he calls the Hugolian belief system of "metempsychosis applied to a doctrine of universal redemption."

> Souls survive bodies, but take on a new material form. It's a sort of generalized purgatory. Souls survive bodies, but integrate matter anew around them. They plunge into inferior forms of being (animal, mineral), or they mount up toward the more perfect form of man or angel, according to whether their present existence has merited reward or punishment. Everything that is, is also conscious and alive to varying degrees. Beyond the impassive, unmoving, and speechless appearance of things, the spiritist eye saw a nature that was aquiver with life, that bled, that suffered for being contained in the blind horror of matter or the punished flesh of animals—that purified itself and sang on the heights of spirit. In this system, there is no eternal punishment. But there are penalties. In awaiting their re-entry into grace, all criminals suffer in their prison of matter a punishment proportionate to their crime. From the pebble in the road to the stars in the sky, the entire universe is alive. But universal burial in matter is the sentence imposed on those who are guilty—and also the means by which they expiate their sins.[5]

In *Psychanalyse de Victor Hugo* (Psychoanalysis of Victor Hugo), published in 1943, psychoanalyst Charles Baudouin locates, in Hugo's early upbringing, the roots of the poet's belief in metempsychosis. The imagery of Hugo's later poetry, opines Baudouin, came not from the afterworld but from Hugo's early, intense, and ambivalence-saturated relationships with his mother, his father, and his brothers.

Baudouin's psychoanalytical focus doesn't prevent him from providing us with a clear and comprehensive account of Hugo's philosophy of metempsychosis. Five basic premises underlie that philosophy, Baudouin asserts, and he sets them forth followed by pertinent quotations from the later poetry of Hugo. In what follows the lines in italics are not from the spirits but from Hugo's poetry, while the italicized words that follow the quotes are the names of the poems from which the lines are taken.

Dr. Baudouin writes that, according to the Hugolian cosmology:

1. The universe is peopled with souls that move from stage to stage in a continuous series and according to their moral value. This is a creation

> *That goes from rock to tree and tree to beast*
> *And from the stone climbs imperceptibly to you,*

but that, far from stopping at man,

> *Enters into the invisible and into the weightless and*
>   *sinless,*
> *. . . fills the azure sky*
> *With creatures who are neighbor to man and others who*
>   *are distant . . .*
> *Sublime ascension of the starry stairways.*
>   *WHAT THE SHADOW'S MOUTH SAYS*

On the other hand, beings pass in dying from one stage to another according to their merits; they rise or descend and, according to a law of moral equilibrium, take on the form that corresponds to their degrees of merit.

> *Everything lives. Creation hatches forth metempsychosis.*
>   *GOD, II, THE ANGEL*

2. This continuous ladder of beings mounts up to the archangels,

> *And in the heights vanishes in God,*

while at the other end it plunges into absolute evil . . .

> *A hideous black sun from which radiates the night!*
>   *WHAT THE SHADOW'S MOUTH SAYS*

3. *God made the universe; the universe made evil*
WHAT THE SHADOW'S MOUTH SAYS

It is by virtue of this original sin that the soul has fallen into the diverse stages of matter. From now on, the world in which it dwells is "the punishment-world."

> *In the monster, it expiates [a sin]; in man, it repairs*
> *[one] . . .*
> *Yes, your savage universe is God's convict.*
WHAT THE SHADOW'S MOUTH SAYS

4. For man, compensation lies in ascending, in dying, to the level of pure spirit; while punishment consists in falling to the level of the animal, of the plant, of the stone.

> *All wicked people*
> *Cause to be born, when they expire, the monster of their*
> *lives*
> *Who takes them over.*
WHAT THE SHADOW'S MOUTH SAYS

Hugo takes a particular interest in describing the monster-animal and the monster-stone. Take the animal:

> *Pity the bird of crime and beast of prey.*
> *What Domitian and Caesar did with joy,*
> *The tiger now pursues with horror. Verres,**
> *A wolf beneath a purple robe, is [now] a wolf in*
> *the forest.*
WHAT THE SHADOW'S MOUTH SAYS

But the ultimate jail is the interior of a stone:

> *The stone is a cellar inside which a criminal dreams.*
GOD, II, THE ANGEL

---

*Caius Verres, circa 120–43 B.C., was a corrupt Roman administrator.

There is, "immured in the stone," a nameless cry of pain.

> *O! What eyes fixed wide open*
> *[Dwell] in the depths of pebbles, those dungeons*
> *of souls.*
>
> WHAT THE SHADOW'S MOUTH SAYS

This vision of the stone-cave seems to have haunted Hugo. . . . It's more than a walled cave; it's a cave consisting only of walls. This vision is associated with every sort of image of Fate, and has its beginnings in the vision of the skull of mankind walled in upon itself by the punishment of complete isolation from which there is no escape:

> *Man, captive spirit, listens to them [the magi]*
> *While in his brain, doubt—*
> *that beast blind to the gleams of heaven—*
> *Seizes the indignant soul*
> *By letting down its spider's web*
> *From the dungeon's ceiling: the skull.*
>
> CONTEMPLATIONS, VI, THE MAGI

5. But the examples of punishments that, like another Dante, Hugo gives us in his hell, are above all punishments of kings, emperors, men of the cloth, and tyrants from every century. We've already seen the fate he assigns to Domitian and Verres. . . . He [also] relegates

> *Tiberius to a rock, Sejanus to a serpent.*
>
> WHAT THE SHADOW'S MOUTH SAYS

The poem *Night Weepings* "relegates the souls of the most illustrious tyrants to cemetery headstones sticking out of the fresh earth of half-opened graves . . ."[6]

In all the poetry Hugo wrote, from the time of his meeting with the spirits in September 1853 onward, the revenge or reward of metempsychosis is everywhere.

Not long after Auguste Vacquerie's meditation on the beach in front of Marine-Terrace—on April 27, 1854—the spirit of Metempsychosis itself came to visit the tapping tables.

Present at the séance (which began, unusually, at quarter past eight in the morning, and would be followed by another, unrelated, séance at three o'clock in the afternoon) were Théophile Guérin, Charles Hugo, and Auguste Vacquerie. The first two sat at the table; Vacquerie took notes. At first, the tapping tables, animated by the shade of William Shakespeare, tapped out the first lines of Shakespeare's new drama (see appendix). Then, abruptly, the spirit of Metempsychosis appeared. It proceeded, without preamble, to define itself in the following four-teen statements.

I am the eternal idea.
I am the real.
Only I complete myself by the I.
I take man and wrest him into thingness.
I am the slope of the soul betwixt infinity and the finite.
I am immensity's arm bearing the grain of sand and mixing it with the seed of fire.
I am the corridor leading you to secret doors.
I am the staircase of Babel climbed by Jacob and leading to the unknown ceiling.
I have a countenance fashioned out of creation; my eyes are stars, my ears are wind, my mouth is abyss, my skin is sky, my hair the forest's branches.
I am the mysterious portrait hanging on the wall of the dreadful house.
I am the formidable atom-seed of man.
I am the flower's root, the rock's foundation, the insect's tendril, the convict's ball-and-chain, the angel's wing.
I am that which chains and that which unchains.
I am the archangel-jailer, and I shine forth in the immensity like a sun in the shape of an iron collar.[7]

And thus it was that Auguste Vacquerie obtained all his answers.

Eleven

VICTOR HUGO
AND THE *ZOHAR*

It is December 1845, a clear cold night on Paris's Right Bank. Victor Hugo, freshly shaven, his handsome profile bent fiercely forward, strides along the Boulevard des Capucines. He is in the middle of a lively conversation with the black-bearded rabbi/scholar of the Cabala, Alexander Weill. Hugo's long gray cloak, thrust theatrically over his shoulder, is not expensive, but neither is it threadbare. The small, slightly built rabbi, skullcap pushed down over his forehead, wears only a thin black frock coat, one that has seen better days.

They are discussing sex. They often discuss sex. Ten years later, Weill will relate these conversations in his *Memoirs*.

> Hugo knew women, their charms and their dangers, very well. When I quoted to him Goethe's rather pornographic poems that were doing the rounds of the German university cafés, when I quoted secret aphorisms from the Cabala about women, he gave me some advice about love, hammered out of his own rigorous observation and highly original, that I have never forgotten.[1]

Now the two of them, striding vigorously down the boulevard, have arrived at their destination: a premier brothel in a luxurious hotel. Hugo rings the bell. He is welcomed with open arms; obviously, he's well known here. Alexander Weill is also welcome, though it's obvious he is not well known. In his 1855 *Memoirs*, the scholar-adventurer will describe Victor Hugo in these surroundings:

Like Louis XIV, Hugo sowed bastard children almost everywhere he went. I knew a very young woman who boasted everywhere, even in my own living room, that she was the daughter of the great poet (she even had his handsome profile). . . . [In the brothels] Hugo was worshipped like the god he was, or believed himself to be. (In good faith, I hasten to add.) Adultery didn't seem to be any more of a crime to him than to the god Jupiter.[2]

Alexander Weill was not French but German. He had immigrated to Paris from Alsace in 1836 to study rare copies of the *Zohar*—the most esoteric book of the Cabala—kept under lock and key in the oldest synagogues of the capital. Weill had another powerful motive for coming to Paris: he wanted to meet Victor Hugo, whose works he had been infatuated with since he was a boy and whom he regarded as a god—"*the* god"—of literature.

Somehow, Weill had managed to wangle an introduction. The two became friends, and Weill ingratiated himself into Hugo's life. Maverick Anglo-French professor of literature Denis Saurat tells us in *La religion ésotérique de Victor Hugo* (The Esoteric Religion of Victor Hugo), published in 1948, that Weill "flattered the pride of the poet as only a Jew can do who is used to humbling himself before God."[3] Weill had an encyclopedic knowledge of German literature, which he made available to Hugo at the poet's whim. Through Weill, Hugo added much to the knowledge of the German poet/playwright/scientist Johann Wolfgang von Goethe that he had first shared with Alphonse de Lamartine several years before. (And, although there's no direct evidence, he may also have acquired from Weill some knowledge of the Italian ex-Dominican priest/maverick scientist Giordano Bruno.)

Weill possessed other knowledge that was, if anything, of even greater value to Hugo. The Alsatian scholar had brought with him from Germany a commentary on the *Zohar* by Rabbi Lazarus Ben Aaron, Weill's teacher. He did not hesitate to share it with Hugo. The poet had known, but did not know it was so marked, that the *Zohar* seems—in its account of the creation of the world—to sanction sexuality, almost to glorify it, though within strict rabbinical guidelines.

In reading Rabbi Ben Aaron's commentary, which focused primarily on sexuality in the *Zohar* and seemed almost to condone licentiousness, Hugo found some justification for the promiscuous life that he was no longer able to keep himself from pursuing. With Weill he paid visits to the upper-class bordellos of Paris—"Hugo remaining the god at the hunt, and Weill probably the hanger-back or follower," writes Saurat—the two discussing the *Zohar* all the while.[4]

So powerful was the effect on Hugo of this core book of the Cabala—or rather Rabbi Lazarus Ben Aaron's sexually oriented commentary on it—that Hugo began instinctively to weave its teachings into the new religion that he was not quite consciously beginning to create. The *Zohar* would provide some of the superstructure for the great poetry on the nature of God that Hugo would write on Jersey Island; its teachings would also crop up in some of the more provocative statements of the Jersey Island spirits.[5]

What exactly is the *Zohar?* What does it tell us about God, the universe, and sex?

Even today the *Zohar* is not well known among Jews. It is a compendium of ancient Jewish wisdom that first appeared in Spain in A.D. 1300. It was supposedly put together by a Spanish Jew named Moses de Léon. Modern scholars think parts of it may go back as far as the Jewish community of Baghdad in the fifth century A.D. Around the *Zohar,* all the other holy books making up the Cabala were to accrete.

Zohar means "Book of Splendor." The book is written in Aramaic, a language the ancient Jews called the "language of the angels," and in a dialect of Aramaic so obscure that scholars still have difficulty translating and interpreting it. Nineteenth-century students of the Cabala regarded the *Zohar* as a sacred, even a secret, text, one whose contents should not be revealed to a non-Jew.[6]

In 1855, Weill published a French translation of the commentary on the *Zohar* of his Alsatian master Rabbi Lazarus Ben Aaron, calling his translation *Les mystères de la création* (Mysteries of Creation). In *La religion ésotérique de Victor Hugo,* Denis Saurat relies on this book and on the six-volume, three-thousand-page French translation of the *Zohar* published by Jean de Pauly in 1906–1911 to tell the story of the creation of the universe as set forth by the *Zohar.* Saurat believes this version of the story is the one Weill passed on to Hugo in the years 1836–1851.[7]

According to Saurat, the cosmology of the *Zohar* is unique in the

annals of metaphysics in that it is based on the notion of the divine
"retreat" or "withdrawal" of God—the idea that God created the universe by withdrawing or separating a part of himself from himself.
According to Pauly's *Zohar,* this God of "retreat" is a God of pure
light. In an initial stage, this "Most High" created the universe by
withdrawing his essence from a fluid stream of primitive light that,
dividing into one hundred filaments, radiated out into space (or, more
accurately, created space by its coming into being). The one hundred
filaments became the heavens and the earth and all of the starry,
planet-filled firmament in between.[8]

The description of creation in the *Zohar* is unusually subtle,
and difficult, in its assertion that when God retreated from a part
of himself to form the universe, the part of himself from which he
retreated was by definition now imperfect, because if it were not
imperfect it would continue to be homogeneously one with the perfection of God. The universe described in the *Zohar* is imperfect
by virtue of existing—which means that it has begun to partake of
evil—while at the same time it is also perfect, or good, as it has been
created from the substance of God himself.

Saurat believes Hugo is describing this Cabala-inspired process
of creation beginning with line fifty-one of his 1855 poem *What the
Shadow's Mouth Says,* a work thought to have been inspired by the
Jersey Island spirits. Here is John Porter Houston's translation of the
passage in question:

> *God created only unweighable being.*
> *He made it radiant, beautiful, shining white, worthy of*
>   *worship.*
> *But imperfect; otherwise, being on the same plane,*
> *The created equal to the creator,*
> *Such perfection, lost in infinity,*
> *Would have mingled and merged with God,*
> *And creation, because of its great brilliance,*
> *Would have returned into Him and would not have*
>   *existed.*
> *Holy creation, of which the prophet dreams,*
> *In order to be, O mystery, had to be imperfect.*
> *Thus, God made the universe; the universe made evil.*

Now then, the first transgression
Was the first weight. God felt a pang of pain,
Evil is matter, black tree, deadly fruit.[9]

The *Zohar* suggests that Creation is a far more sensual act than is implied in Hugo's lines. According to Pauly's *Zohar*, God has two sides, a right side and a left side. Each side has two principles, a male principle and a female principle. God drew the female principle from his right side, naming it the Matrona; by this act of drawing forth he created the universe. Together, God and the Matrona (who is sometimes called God's wife, other times His daughter) created the earth. The Pauly *Zohar* asserts that

> [t]he one who is on high is the father of all; it is he who created everything; it is he who fecundated the earth, which became big with child and gave birth to the earth's productions. It was fecundated as a female is fecundated by a male.[10]

The *Zohar* describes a number of the Matrona's sexual adventures on earth; it does this to point out that sexuality is at the heart of the earth's creation, that it is among the deepest of heaven's impulses, and that—in conformance with the ancient esoteric dictum of "as above, so below"—it is a wholly natural part of man's life on earth. Saurat says that "sensuality is rendered divine by the example of God himself"[11] in the *Zohar*. God has drawn from his side a wife, the Matrona, and, Saurat assures us, in the *Zohar* "no detail is missing from the description of their relationship."[12] It follows that sexuality is holy, although it can remain so only to the extent that it adheres to specific rabbinical religious and conjugal guidelines. But this does not diminish the fact that, according to Saurat, the legitimization of sexuality in the *Zohar* "allows rabbis every sort of [sensual] boldness."[13]

So far we have told only one-half of the story of creation. The left side of God also has a role. It, too, possesses a male principle and a female principle. This complicates the creation of the universe to the extent that God also has to withdraw his essence from his left side. When he does so, the male principle becomes Satan and the female principle becomes Lilith, Satan's wife, sometimes called his daughter. At the instant of his creation, Satan begins to precipitously plummet down through the astral spaces to what will become the center of the earth, his wife/daughter Lilith plummeting down beside him. The two become immured in the stony black center of our planet; or rather, they create and become that stony black center by the cessation of their fall. In this way does the *Zohar* make it clear that sexuality on earth also has an evil aspect.[14]

Though Satan and his "fall" play a major role in Victor Hugo's poetry, they were not elements in the picture of the universe that emerged from the Jersey Island spirits. This notwithstanding, the cosmos and its spirits as described in the *Zohar* resemble the cosmos and its spirits as described by Balaam's Ass and his tapping-table peers. Renaissance scholar Frances A. Yates writes that "a striking feature of Cabalism is the importance assigned to angels or divine spirits as intermediaries throughout this system, arranged in hierarchies corresponding to the other hierarchies. There are also bad angels, or demons, whose hierarchies correspond to those of their good opposites."[15]

Both the *Zohar* and the tapping-table spirits inform us that a tremendous array of angels, demons, and other discarnate beings come and go between heaven, earth, and the multiplicity of stars and planets. According to Pauly's *Zohar,* human beings have two bodies—a physical body and an astral body. At night, when the "doors" to the lower world are closed and earth is covered in darkness, humans can use these astral bodies to voyage to the higher worlds.

The Marine-Terrace spirits also claim that at night we can soar through the heavenly realms in our astral bodies and that this is due to mankind's special quality of being *homo duplex* ("double man"). The *Zohar* implies that aspects of the left side of God have coalesced into "planets of punishment" to which erring souls are sent, while aspects of the right side of God have come together to form "worlds of reward" inhabited by meritorious souls. All of these movements between planets are determined by a complex system of reincarnational reward and punishment that resembles the "Great Chain of Being" described to Hugo and his friends by the Jersey spirits.

To what extent were the concepts and even the words of the Jersey Island spirits, when they echoed what Victor Hugo already knew about the *Zohar,* simply the poet's own thoughts, in some way telepathically conveyed through the tapping tables? To what extent were they an amalgam of Hugo's thoughts and those of, say, Pierre Leroux, or Charles Hugo, or Auguste Vacquerie, all of whom were intelligent and learned and, if not already, then soon to be, authors of books themselves? To what extent were these concepts and words partially the thoughts of the séance attendees and partially the thoughts of something whose nature we do not understand?

There is no question that many of the ideas expressed by the spirits had been on Hugo's mind for years. On January 4, 1855, he wrote to Delphine de Girardin that "a whole quasi-cosmological system, which I have been incubating for the last twenty years and which is already half written down, was confirmed by the table with magnificent developments."[16] (Note that Hugo adds: "with magnificent developments.") And certainly there were things the spirits said that reflected the esoteric thought systems pondered by Hugo, not only with regard to the *Zohar* but also with regard to reincarnation. His reflections on this subject had begun no later than 1832 and had probably begun earlier. These reflections concerned the souls of stones, plants, animals, and even objects—as well as those of humans. His reflections also included the spiritistic notion of an all-pervasive "fluid" that is present in all animals; a fluid that heals illness and can even facilitate communications with the dead.

It's easy for us to dismiss what we don't understand, or back away when new horizons expand before us that feel likes abysses yawning beneath our feet because we fear the unknown. But there is no easy answer to the question of where the Jersey Island spirits came from. Hugo seems to have believed that the spirits were there from the beginning, that they had been with him during all of his writing life, and that if their words reflected what he himself thought, that was because (he could not know how many years before) the spirits had directly or indirectly inseminated him with those ideas. Hugo could never quite accept the spirits—and he could never quite reject them either. Perhaps his ego, and/or his creative needs, would never allow him to dismiss the spirits. Even so, if this great genius was able to doubt his own doubts from time to time in the midst of this great experience, why should we be any different? The notion of doubt is, in fact, pivotal to the enormous mystical experience of Victor Hugo on Jersey Island. In the next chapter, we will discuss that notion.

Twelve

MARTIN LUTHER
ON DOUBT

Victor Hugo's thoughts about the reality of the Jersey Island spirits were in a constant state of evolution.

By November 15, 1853, he had decided, according to Adèle's diary, that "the goal of the phenomenon of the tables is to lead man to Spiritualism. . . . People don't believe. They deny God. God, who doesn't have time to wait for the slow development of human thought, has all of a sudden revealed himself to them through the physically undeniable phenomenon of the talking tables."[1]

Adèle's diary records that by January 20, 1854, he was qualifying this statement. "I don't believe blindly in the phenomenon of the tables. If the book [of the transcripts] we are putting together gets published, people will see that I've always argued with the spirits—respectable arguments, but arguments nonetheless. There are two sources of illumination in me: My conscience, which derives from God, and my reason, which illuminates the truth and derives from mankind."[2]

It was, he said, a matter of critically examining what the spirits said. But even that went only so far. No matter how much you racked your brains, no matter how hard you tried, you could never quite prove to your satisfaction that the spirits really existed. The spirits had set things up that way.

On February 7, 1854, in another exchange recorded in Adèle's diary, Charles asked: "What if the tables ordered us to publish the book right away?"

Hugo replied, "We would have to obey. Obviously, if an angel

135

appeared to me and said, 'Here's the truth, I'm giving it to you, here's revelation, communicate it to the human species,' I would communicate that revelation to the human species, and I wouldn't give a damn what anyone said. But the present phenomenon, this phenomenon we're participating in every evening, doesn't present us with an absolute enough character that we should feel obliged to obey it. This phenomenon respects human freedom and the state of enlightenment humans have attained through their own efforts. It respects our freedom by leaving us in doubt. Its coarse and often questionable manner, the contradictions of the beings with whom we speak—all this is meant to protect our free will and our ability to choose freely for ourselves."[3]

Doubt was necessary; out of respect for our sense of personal freedom, the spirits had to leave us in a state of doubt. Doubt was one of the ongoing themes of Victor Hugo's life, according to Denis Saurat. Saurat says of the poet: "The great believer was a great doubter. . . . Hugo never shook off doubt, just as he never shook off a sense of evil [in both the world and, because he was a part of the world, himself]. Hugo's intellect made him experience constant doubt, and his conscience made him experience constant remorse. . . . But Hugo couldn't live a divided life; inevitably he had to bring the two together. He proclaimed the necessity of doubt and of evil, as indispensable instruments of human progress." Moreover, Saurat asserts, Hugo believed all those who claimed they never felt doubt were simply lying. He believed all priests were liars. He believed that those who can see what lies beyond see it only very obscurely. Those who claim they see more are lying or committing sacrilege.[4]

On February 3, 1854, the spirits themselves entered the discussion in force. Their spokesperson was a particularly appropriate shade. On February 3, there came to the tapping tables Martin Luther (who "personifies doubt,"[5] in the words of Denis Saurat), the great German religious reformer who, born in 1483 and died in 1546, launched the Protestant Reformation, thereby forever breaking the dogmatic hold of the Roman Catholic Church on Christianity and Christ.

Martin Luther had had his own communications with the beyond, which was one of the reasons he fascinated Victor Hugo. Luther's exchanges were mostly negative: by his own account he had had numerous exchanges with demons. However, their "devil's advocacy" had served to push him irrevocably toward God.

The February 1854 séance at which Luther first appeared began at 9:00 p.m. Present were Victor Hugo and Auguste Vacquerie, with Mme Hugo and Charles sitting at the table.

"Who's there?" asked Victor.

Luther, the table replied.

An apparently surprised Hugo welcomed Martin Luther warmly. "It is a joy for us to talk to you," he told the shade. "You are one of the great formulators of the laws of self-examination. You are surely one of the spirits who is most disposed toward opening the doors of mystery for us."

But then Hugo, in effect, got to asking about himself: "A host of persons who have greatly influenced the destiny of the human race through their thinking are represented to us as having had mysterious beings at their ear, speaking words from unknown worlds. Socrates had a 'familiar spirit'; Joan of Arc had an angel; Muhammad had a pigeon. The four Evangelists are supposed to have written the Gospels under the inspiration of four supernatural beings: a lion, an eagle, a bull, and an angel. In your own writings you often speak of devils who got mixed up in your work. You've intimated that you often argued with them; these demons seem to have been importuning beings rather than visiting friends. Can you tell us if the various manifestations of the mysterious I've just enumerated have any relation to this phenomenon that is taking place right now?"

The shade of Martin Luther replied:

The Word of God chooses certain spirits. The sound of his voice is thunder, ocean, wind. Man is a terrified passenger in his world; life is an Ark that has gone astray. And so, to quiet man down God softens his voice. He silences thunderclap, sea, and storm. And whilst mariner-humanity is driven to despair inside the Ark, God extends hope to him by using animals: The dove saves Noah; the donkey saves Balaam; the lion saves Androcles; the pigeon inspires Muhammad; and the four Evangelists listen to their four beasts. The language of the divine assumes yet another form: man is placed between beast and angel. Man has one ear to the ground and one to the sky. When the beast becomes silent, the angel speaks—but it's the angel we are dealing with in either case. The beast is the angel in disguise, the apparition is the angel revealed. I have heard that angel. Socrates spoke to him; Joan of Arc obeyed him; and Jesus came home to him.

Now, why was it that I, who heard the divine word, doubted? Why was it that Socrates, faced with drinking hemlock, doubted? Why was it that Joan of Arc, about to be burned at the stake, doubted? Why was it that Jesus, on Calvary, doubted? It was because doubt is the instrument that forges the human spirit. If the day were to come when the human spirit no longer doubted, the human soul, having acquired wings, would fly away and leave the plough behind. The earth would lie fallow. Now, God is the sower and man is the harvester. The celestial seed commands the human ploughshare to remain in the furrow. Man, do not complain that you doubt.[6]

The spirit of Martin Luther had avoided answering the question of whether Hugo was a member of that distinguished club that included Socrates, Jesus, Muhammad, Joan of Arc, and many others. Luther had said something more important: that not knowing what's going to happen—and not knowing what role, if any, God is going to play in our lives—drives all of us on to productive activity. But herein lies a paradox. We must have faith, we have to believe—but not *too* much. Otherwise, we would cease to mold, out of our necessities and anxieties, a world in which we can survive and prosper.

Denis Saurat asserts that what Luther told Victor Hugo on the night of February 3, 1854, reflected the poet's own convictions. A belief about doubt and evil, says Saurat:

> . . . goes right to the heart of the metaphysics of Hugo as expressed in *What the Shadow's Mouth Says*. God, in order to create mankind as a personality distinct from himself, had to withdraw [a part of his substance] from himself, leaving behind some evil, and therefore some ignorance, to work its way into the life of man. . . . "Doubt makes him free, and freedom [makes him] great" [from *What the Shadow's Mouth Says*]. It is this occult withdrawal of God that brings about the creation of man. This is the central doctrine of the cabalists: withdrawal makes God into a creator, and God's withdrawal [creates] doubt in man and makes *him* into a creator. God intervenes directly, and then, in order to generate the doubt that makes for greatness, introduces forgetfulness.[7]

On that night of February 3, 1854, Martin Luther wasn't finished: *Doubt is the specter that holds the flaming sword of genius above the gateway of the beautiful. Shakespeare doubted and he created Hamlet; Cervantes doubted and he created Don Quixote; Molière doubted and he created Don Juan. Dante doubts and he creates hell. Aeschylus doubts and he creates Prometheus. All creators doubt, and as a result they create gods. As for me: from my doubt I created a religion.*[8]

These words must have reminded Hugo of what Jacob (the biblical patriarch who wrestled with the angel) said when he dropped briefly by the tables following Hugo's conversation with Shakespeare on January 22, 1854: *Shakespeare was quite right in telling you that doubt lies at the heart of all the works of man. . . . [Doubt is] the duel of flesh against spirit; doubt is the grim field upon which knights joust. All of these are the eternal wrestling of Jacob with the angel.*[9]

But Hugo still wanted to have his own greatness affirmed. He asked Luther whether his—Victor Hugo's—table-tapping experiences were "the latest link in the vast chain of revelation that began in the Middle East [with Noah, Christ, the four Evangelists, Muhammad, and so on] and ended with the very spirit before us, you, Martin Luther."

He received an unexpected answer.

Which table are you talking about?

Hugo, confused, replied: "The one that's here, that Charles is holding."

I don't see any table.

The poet responded swiftly: "Then you have something to learn from us creatures of earth and shadow. Know this, that we are communicating with you by means of a three-legged table. Tell us how you for your part speak to us. Am I to assume you're really not aware of how our replies come to you? That you aren't able to perceive us in any way? Tell me: How do we appear to you?"

Spirits.

"But in what form do we appear to you?"

The spirits of the dead see the spirits of the living through the foreheads of the living; the spirits of the dead inhale the perfume of roses across space and hear the songs of birds across the sky. The human spirit is the earth's great perfume and great song. You come to us scented and melodious. Perfume and song are formless; our conversation is an exchange of harmonies; the idea is the keyboard and God is the musician.

Hugo replied: "From all that you say, it would seem that from your vantage point the human spirit is rather impersonal. Do you know which humans are here? Do you know our names as humans? Why do you come to us and not to others? Have you come for some specific reason?"

The table shook. Whatever spirits possessed it now seemed anxious to leave. After a few more words, a spirit identifying itself as Shakespeare answered, perhaps a little reluctantly, the question to which Victor Hugo so badly wanted an answer:

You are chosen.

"Is that all?" Hugo asked.

Yes.[10]

There were one or two more words. Then the spirits were gone; the table was still.

There is, apparently, a second reason why God does not reveal his secrets to mankind. It has to do with epistemology—the study of how we can know things. It has to do with the simple insight that what we can know is bounded by our knowledge, by our experience, by the limitations of our sense perceptions.

This "inability" of God and the spirits to do much more than broaden our understanding a little, insofar as the divine powers must vastly restrict what they say because they speak through us, and with us, and by us—all that seemed to be the burden of what the spirit calling itself "Idea" told Auguste Vacquerie on the night of July 3, 1854. The July 1854 session, beginning at ten o'clock in the evening, was also attended by Victor Hugo and Charles Hugo.

Auguste began by addressing, with Idea, the problem of human suffering. The intensely serious Vacquerie wondered this: If we suffer on this earth because we are here to expiate a sin we committed in a previous lifetime, why has God, who created us, set things up this way? Why has he, who could do anything he wanted, and anything he wanted with *us,* introduced suffering at all? You would be doing mankind a great service, Vacquerie presumed to tell Idea, if you would be kind enough to answer this question.

The table replied with an enigmatic answer:

You have just knocked at the back gate of the dark castle. You want to escape, and you tell me, "Open up!" Which indicates that

*you don't know who we are. You are our prisoners, and we are your
jailers. All of our explanations are keys to the dungeon. We are the
invisible turnkeys of the stars. When we unlock a sun, we unlock a
shadow. When we unlock infinity, we unlock a jail cell. When we
unlock God, we release one person from solitary confinement. We
are baleful lights bringing enlightenment with darkness. We assert
without being able to prove our assertions, and we cast doubt even
as we pour forth truth. We, like you, are condemned. Under earth's
sky Love is a galley slave, Idealism is a galley slave, Repentance is a
galley slave, Hope is a galley slave. Truth is a shadowy lantern hanging in the vault of the human skull. The savage dungeon surges up
out of the fearful firmament. The wind blows all around you with
an eternal groaning. Even death cannot take away your prisonhood.*

*To die in that Bastille is still to be imprisoned. The gravedigger
doesn't make a breach in the wall; he just allows you to see the rest
of the castle. Nothingness is the ghost of this castle. Doubt haunts it.
Mystery rises up from all four corners of the room. The black sen-
tinel of ignorance is always there, always ready to balk the spirit, to
enclose it in infinity, to consign it to eternity, to throw it into the back
of God's lowliest ditch, to strangle it with beams of light.*

The brilliant Vacquerie hardly knew what to say about these bewildering ramblings. "Enlighten us!" he cried simply. "Whatever do you
mean when you say your explanations are dungeon keys and you are
our jailers? Are you not, rather, our liberators? Because the light you
bring us, though mixed with shadows, still represents more light than
we have known before, and light and liberty are the same."

*We want to liberate you; we cannot. At the end of all our expla-
nations, even the most profound, there is a wall. Infinity, for us as
well as you, is an impasse. All we can do is give you a change of cell,
give you a little more light and a little more air. We can enlarge the
skylight but we can't tear down the wall. Your cell has a window,
but where there is a window, there must be a wall. Windows presuppose confinement; they presuppose prisons. We are your windows.
We are at one and the same time a beam of light and the wooden
beam that bars the door. We cast shadows because we let light pour
in. Don't forget that it is the sun alone that produces shadows—that
is, reflections. Shadows of whom? Of God. Reflections of whom?
Of God. Here is the difference between the punitary worlds and the*

worlds of reward [see chapter 19]: *in the punitary worlds, God sees himself as blackness; in the rewarded worlds, God sees himself with crystal clarity. Only paradises mirror invisibility.*

Vacquerie replied, "Now I understand you. We are in a dungeon within a prison. You don't open the prison, but you do open the dungeon."

We've brought you some light, but that very light brings even more shadow. We've brought you out of the catacombs, but we haven't brought you out of the prison. You were in the Bastille's cellar; we've put you on the roof. Before, you couldn't even see the sky; now, you can see it. But all you've done is exchange a ditch for a battlement, solitary confinement for the abyss. It should be quite clear to you that we remain your jailers even while we are your liberators. We can remove your handcuffs, but we can't give you a nail file. We make you less unhappy but we don't make you more free. We make you mount up to the sky, but by way of the prison staircase. The sky opens before you, but it's been opened by a jailhouse key.

Vacquerie summed up grimly: "The upshot of all this is that it isn't possible for you to give us a decisive and irrefutable explanation for that terrible problem: Why does an infinity of goodness and power create so many hells?"

I don't know what the other spirits will tell you.

"But, you—can't *you* give us an explanation?"

No.[11]

Despairing of ever finding enlightenment with respect to the perennial questions of mankind, Auguste Vacquerie now went on to quiz Idea about the secret world of animals. This amazing topic— upon which the spirits would expatiate with ideas a hundred years ahead of the time in which the séance took place—we will address in chapter 14.

Thirteen

OTHER VOICES,
OTHER ROOMS

Trembling with rage, her young face flushed, Adèle Hugo ran as quickly as her dress and petticoats allowed her down the muddy path that led from the terrace to the beach. She reached the bottom and stumbled out on the sand. The dark brown beach, almost deserted (it was five o'clock in the afternoon and rain was forecast), stretched out to the tide that separated the sand from the sky like a thin blue pencil line drawn across the horizon. The sun, low in the west, glimmered a dull orange through the roiling clouds.

Adèle lifted a trembling hand to her cheek and wiped away the spit.

Auguste had spat on her! Up on the terrace, where anybody could see but luckily no one else was around, he had spat in her face!

He had come striding across the terrace to her and, reaching out had seized her black-sleeved arm. He had brought his sharp thin profile down to her face. "Why did you take Albert's arm and not mine last night?" he barked. "Why did you wear that revealing dress?"

Staring at his scowling features, she had decided not to reply. "And yet you're so skinny," he snarled, squeezing her arm. "Too skinny! Your muscles are like strings. Your arms are like spindles. No wonder you usually cover them up."

Angry and frightened, she had pulled her arm away. Then he spat in her face.

She had turned around and begun to flee but not quickly enough to prevent him from kicking her from behind. Stumbling, almost falling, she had run over to the path and scrambled down.[1]

Now, still trembling, crouched on the sand, tears welling up in her eyes, Adèle put her hands to her temples. Her head was splitting. She turned and looked up at the terrace. Auguste seemed to be gone.

The thought raced through her mind that, although he had tried to make her love him for eight years, he had never succeeded because, in fact, he had never known who she was. To Auguste she was only the ardent daughter of Victor Hugo. She was a promising composer of light melodies and a promising journalist in the confessional mode. She was a partner in debates with them all—debates on the crimes of Napoleon III, the horrors of the Crimean War, the glorious possibility of a United States of Europe, and the existence or nonexistence of a God whom one could only doubt and the form that his existence—if there be any such—might take.

But this was not the real Adèle. This was mere appearance, a ghost, a chimera. The real Adèle was not a mortal woman. She was a supernatural woman, a superior being who had arrived on earth from a higher plane of reality to teach the souls of man. Her heart and her soul were steeped in the invisible world, and her genius was the light that gleamed through from that world.[2]

A light rain began to slant downward in thin sheets that flicked and subsided along the beach. Adèle scrambled to her feet. Her headache was gone. She began to hurry back up the muddy path that led to the terrace. Auguste would not have lingered there in the rain—Auguste, who also could never make her love him because when she was eighteen an Englishman with an exquisite face had appeared to her in a dream. The Englishman had told her he would come to her one day, that he was the great love of her life. She had waited for years and now, just three weeks ago, he had come. His name was Albert Pinson. He was a gentleman farmer who did not have to work because his family was wealthy (and anyway he was above such concerns); at the moment he was spending his time visiting Jersey Island.

Albert had come to a dinner party at Marine-Terrace, and she had immediately recognized him as the Englishman of her dream. He was tall and blond, with mocking eyes and a mischievous smile. She loved him from the first night that she saw him and she knew that he had been dazzled by her beauty and her genius.

He came to visit the family several times after that, and she knew that he was falling under her spell. He had been to dinner the night before. She had invited him to the séance tonight, and he had said that he would come.

Now, as the rain lessened and began to drift away, she arrived at the top of the terrace and began to stride toward the greenhouse that led to the house. She suddenly stopped. A numbing anxiety made her heart sink. What if Albert did not love her? What if he would never love her? What if, in loving Albert, then in losing him, she also lost Auguste?

Adèle knew that it was time to talk to Léopoldine.

No one knew, not even her mother, that she talked to Léopoldine. No one knew about the days when she sat in the chair in her bedroom and put her hands on the little pedestal table beside her bed and talked to her drowned sister, Léopoldine. Léopoldine wasn't the only spirit she talked to. One time she had talked to the Shadow of the Sepulcher, another time to a "good spirit," and once she had talked to a "bad spirit" (she did not like to think about that time). But mostly she talked to her sister, Léopoldine.

Her dear, drowned sister adored her. All her spirits adored her. At the big séances in the dining room Shakespeare and Aeschylus and the other spirits did not even acknowledge her presence, let alone recognize her genius. Here in her bedroom, with her hand resting on her own little tapping table, she could talk to spirits who knew her and who loved her—

"Adèle!"

It was her father's voice. Adèle paused and saw that she had come out of the greenhouse and into the front hall of the house. Her father, wearing his big red English pullover, one hand holding a book, was standing in the doorway to the drawing room.

"Yes, Papa?" she asked meekly.

He was staring thoughtfully at her. "Are you coming to dinner?" he asked softly.

"No, Papa." Without waiting for his reply she turned brusquely and continued on her way through the hallway. She did not want to go to dinner tonight. She did not want to go dinner unless Albert was there. He wasn't coming to dinner, but he was coming to the séance. Actually, these days she did not want to eat anything at all. Auguste had said she was skinny, but he was mistaken; she was fat. She wanted to be slim for Albert.

She went into her bedroom and, closing the door firmly behind her, ran across to the bed. She plopped down on it even though her clothing was wet and sandy from the beach and the rain. She leaned forward and placed her hands on the little pedestal table beside the bed.

She felt the familiar reassuring surge of energy.

She knew that her spirits loved her unconditionally. It was they who had told her she was a superior being from a higher plane of reality. She knew they believed in her—in her genius, in her beauty, in her passion. She knew they believed in her love for Albert and in Albert's love for her.

Perched on the edge of the bed, she laid her hands on the table and asked her sister, Léopoldine: "Am I in my rights, am I doing a legitimate thing, in giving up the life that Auguste could provide for me?"

The table began to tap on the floor with a leg. Adèle wrote the words down on a piece of paper on her nightstand:

Beauty, mind, talent constitute your pain. Beautiful beauty, unhappiness, genius, a fine satisfaction, which would give Auguste eternal pain. Fight, fly, force would kill jealousy, destiny, floating, death reign. Your beauty beaten constitutes unhappy beauty. You, beaten mistress, be assured, modify bounty, arrange joy, dominate unhappiness. Be assured, build beauty, good-bye.

She did not want Léopoldine to go. "Why are you leaving?" she cried.

Death.

"What do you mean by death?"

Doing more than lasting.

"Given my situation, will you finish the sentence?"

Difficult, Adèle.

"What must I do to get out of this situation?"

Banter, drink, good-bye.

"Will you return?"

No.

"Why not?"

Faith. What would make Auguste unhappy?

"So he has to go?"

Yes.

"What do I have to do to get him to go?"

Love your mother.[3]

There was a knock on the door.

Adèle sat bolt upright, terrified.

When she contacted the spirits by herself, she was always afraid there would be a knock on the door and she would go over and open it and one of the spirits would be standing there, the Shadow of the Sepulcher perhaps or the good spirit or the evil spirit, or maybe Léopoldine. She knew the spirits loved her but the idea of actually seeing one of them frightened her terribly. She was especially terrified of seeing her drowned sister, Léopoldine, who would be staring at her through blank unseeing eyes, with wet flowers in her soaking hair and her long white dress dripping water to the floor, like Ophelia in *Hamlet*.

"Adèle!" It was her mother's voice, calling firmly from the other side of the door.

She jumped off the bed and ran over and opened the door. Her mother stood there, her black hair carefully coiffed and wearing the faded green coat she always wore when she went out for a walk. "Dear one," her mother said, touching her arm lightly, "I must go into town on this beautiful evening and visit Mme Regnier. She is ill. Would you like to come with me?"

Adèle knew her mother would rather attend the séance tonight than go and visit a sick friend. She knew her mother wanted her to go with her because she did not want Adèle to attend the séance tonight when Albert and Auguste would both be present. Her mother loved Auguste. He had long been her first choice to become Adèle's husband. She did not like Albert. Island gossip had it that the Englishman was an idler and a gold digger; her mother believed he wanted to marry Adèle for her money. (Victor Hugo had promised he would give Adèle a dowry of 50,000 francs.)

Three days before, Adèle had told her mother that she loved Albert and was sure he would soon ask for her hand in marriage and that therefore Auguste must now leave the island. Her mother had been heartbroken. Finally, she had agreed that Auguste should leave, but certainly not immediately and indeed not until the spring, when it could be done in such a way that Adèle would not be seen to be rejecting Auguste.[4]

Now, staring intently at her mother as she stood in the doorway,

Adèle said, "Mama, I can't go tonight. Albert has promised me that he will come to the séance. And I have promised him that I will be there."

"There will be other séances," her mother said gently.

"Oh, but tonight's séance is different! I know something special will happen tonight."

Her mother gazed at her quietly. Then she reached up and kissed Adèle on the cheek and without another word turned and strode away along the hallway.

Adèle shut the door. She turned around and looked at the clock. It was late. She must dress. The supernatural woman must be ravishing for her predestined lover.

When Adèle, dressed in her finest black gown, advanced timidly into the dining room, everyone had already gathered for the séance.

Her father, seated sidewise on the long blue couch, was talking earnestly with the Hungarian count Teleki, who was similarly seated sidewise in a mirror-image pose of Victor Hugo. The two exiles Émile Guérin and Hennett de Kesler, who spent so much time together, sat beside each other in the two chairs by the window. Charles lounged, pipe in hand, exhaling large puffs of smoke, in the orange armchair beside the tables.

Adèle avoided looking at Auguste, who, arms crossed over his chest, hands gripping his shoulders, sat on the narrow wooden chair beside the door. She went across to the black divan, where Albert sat all alone, and threw herself down beside him.

She turned to speak to him, but no words came. His long thin face, with its alert blue eyes, its flushed cheeks, with the pencil line of a blond mustache traced beneath the sharp, salient nose—all these stunned her with their beauty and reduced her to silence. Albert smiled; she blushed and quickly turned her face away. His foot touched hers; she felt the electric thrill of it. She sensed that his face was leaning close to hers. "Mlle Hugo," he murmured in his adorably accented French, "tell me, are you too a believer in the spirit world?"

"Oh, yes," she breathed, half turning to him. "You have only to listen to them and you will believe! And do you? Are you a believer as well?"

"Would you like me to be?"

"Oh, yes, I would so like you to be!" She glanced at him quickly, then looked away. He was smiling at her almost mockingly from beneath the pencil line of his blond mustache.

"And so I shall be, if you wish," he answered.

He stood up. This caused a brief lull in the loud murmur of conversation in the room. He strode across to Charles, who, eyes half closed, frame sprawled out negligently in the orange armchair, was tamping his pipe with studied nonchalance.

"I understand there has to be a second person at the table," said Pinson, gazing down at Charles. "May I be that person?"

"Of course," said Charles, affecting great indifference. "Be the guest of the beyond, if you like. But I fear you will find it all quite boring." He bent forward and patted the seat of the armchair on the other side of the big square table.

Albert sat down. "I think that, on the contrary, I shall find it all very interesting," he said emphatically.

Victor Hugo turned and spoke up from the long blue couch. "My dear Pinson," he said, "may I, on behalf of the spirits, welcome you to the afterworld? Do you have a question for the spirits?"

"May I ask them a question in English?" asked Pinson.

"Of course," said Hugo. "I daresay they speak a little English in heaven."

As if those words had been a signal, the séance started. Charles placed his hand on the little three-legged table lying on the larger four-legged table. Pinson placed his hand beside Charles's.

The pedestal table began to move.

"Who's there?" asked Charles.

The table replied in Latin: *Frater Tuus.* [Your brother.]

"You can't be my brother," said Charles. "My brother is alive and well and reading Shakespeare in his bedroom. Are you M. Pinson's brother?"

Yes, tapped out the spirit. *André.*

The room stirred. This had caught the participants' interest. Adèle, straining forward to catch every movement of Albert's face, saw a troubled expression cross it.

Pinson stared at Charles. "I do have a brother named André," he said slowly. "Or I did. He disappeared twelve years ago. No one in the family has any idea what happened to him."

He paused, then asked: "May I question the spirit in English?"

Charles nodded. Albert looked at the table and asked a question.

No one in the room knew English except Adèle, who could read it but could not speak it very well. She did not understand what Albert had just said. The table leg rapped quickly; Albert seemed to listen attentively. The rapping ceased. Albert seemed disturbed. He asked a second question in English. A second answer came, briefer than the first.

Albert lifted his hand from the table and turned to face the guests.

"The spirit has communicated information of a very private sort," he said, his voice trembling slightly. "I am impressed. I'm sure there's no one in the room who could have known what has just been communicated to me." He paused and added: "The information is so private that I cannot share it with any of you. I apologize."

"By all means," said Victor Hugo grandly. "Let it remain a secret between yourself and God. But the séance is not yet over, my dear M. Pinson. Surely you will continue to be one of our mediums?!"

"Yes, Sir, I will continue," said Pinson doubtfully. He put his hand back on the table.

Adèle searched her father's face. It was now set in a scowl. She felt sure she knew what he was thinking (and had been thinking all the while, but often her father hid his thoughts behind words of unctuous flattery): that this wretched Englishman, who was after his daughter's dowry, was now somehow manipulating the tapping tables to his own purposes. Adèle knew that this couldn't be further from the truth, but she also knew that her father, in asking Albert to remain at the tables, was hoping to catch him out in his manipulations.

The pedestal table moved again, this time with a more staccato motion.

"Who's there?" asked Pinson with some hesitation.

The table replied: *Byron.*

"Is Montague Helt alive or dead?" Pinson asked in English, translating for the others. He did not say who Montague Helt was. They did not ask him.

With Pinson translating, the table tapped out: *Alive.*

Pinson seemed disappointed. Émile Guérin put a question to "Byron." "Can you formulate a complete thought in just a few lines of verse?" he asked. "We ask for just a few lines because Charles doesn't know English and is getting exhausted following the letters."

The table answered: *Yes.*

"Go ahead," said Guérin.

After a moment, the table tapped out in English: *You know not what you ask.*

Pinson, translating for them, asked in English: "Can't you recite some lines of your poetry?"

No.

"You mean you don't want to?"

Yes.

"Why don't you want to say something?"

The pedestal table shook violently and turned around on itself on the top of the big square table.

"Who's there?" asked Pinson.

There was no reply. The table shook violently. A minute or two went by. Then it tapped out: *Silence.*

"'Silence?' Does whoever is there mean we should stop?"

Scott.

"Are you Sir Walter Scott?"

Yes.

"Do you wish to speak?"

Pinson translating, the table tapped out two lines of verse in English:

> *Vex not the bard; his lyre is broken,*
> *His last song sung, his last word spoken.*[5]

They listened raptly. The spirits, who had never spoken English before now, spoke with the words of a master. Albert seemed as surprised as anyone. Then, without a word, he got up quietly and strode back across the room to where Adèle was sitting. His surrender of his place at the tables somehow signaled that the séance was over. This made Victor Hugo unhappy; he had some questions to ask. It made Adèle very happy; now she had Albert all to herself, if only for a few minutes. And if, that evening, it could only be for a few minutes, what did that matter? Albert would soon be hers forever. Léopoldine had promised.

᪥᪥᪥

A decade later, Victor Hugo, conducting research, would learn that Albert Pinson did not have a brother named André and that Pinson's full name was Albert Andrew Pinson. In the fall of 1854, Pinson had become an officer in the British army. This had impressed Adèle, but Victor Hugo would eventually learn that Pinson had become a soldier only because a judge in a debtor's court had ordered him to choose between the British army and debtor's prison. Pinson had extensive gambling debts that apparently had finally caught up with him.[6] Was the mysterious "Montague Helt" simply somebody Pinson owed a lot of money to and whom he therefore would have preferred dead?!

Had Victor Hugo known these things in late 1854 rather than in late 1864, it's unlikely that any aspect of the grim fate that awaited his daughter would have changed. Adèle Hugo would stalk Albert—whose indifference to her would become total—from London, England, to Halifax, Nova Scotia, to Bridgetown, Barbados as the Englishman worked through his tour of duty as an officer.[7] All during this time, Adèle would slip gradually and irreversibly into a state of schizophrenia. In February 1872, her father would have her brought back to Paris. In the same month he would commit her to a sanatorium, where she would live out the rest of her very long life, dying in 1915 at the age of eighty-five.

She would be the only one of Victor Hugo's children to survive him.

Fourteen

THE SECRET LIFE
OF ANIMALS

The following passage is from the diary of Adèle Hugo. It is a conversation held around the family dinner table on July 26, 1854.

Victor Hugo: "I did a good thing today. I rescued a salamander."

Auguste Vacquerie: "Me, I rescued a crab."

Charles Hugo: "And me, a bird."

François-Victor Hugo: "I rescued a spider."

Auguste Vacquerie to Victor Hugo: "Tell us the story of your salamander."

Victor Hugo: "There was an unlucky salamander in the road that the passersby would surely have stomped on if I hadn't picked it up and carefully deposited it in the grass. The rescued salamander gazed up at me out of his big tender eyes and seemed to be thanking me."

Auguste Vacquerie: "I saved a crab. The sea had tossed a crab onto the terrace. This luckless creature was scuttling across the terrace at just the time that the Rose kids [from next door] had appeared and were about to massacre it. I courageously took the crab and carried it back to the ocean."

François-Victor Hugo: "I spared the life of a monstrous spider, that land-bound version of a crab. I was getting into bed when I saw this enormous spider lowering itself from the top of the wall and advancing toward the head of my bed. I gave it a scare and it scurried back up to its web."

Charles Hugo: "For my part, I helped save a bird. XXX and I were just leaving XXX's house when his mother pointed out to us a bird

153

that was all tangled up in some string. The unfortunate bird, who no doubt had gotten into this predicament on account of some kid, looked horribly unhappy. The bird was right at the top of a tree that had been struck by lightning. That meant it would be very dangerous to rescue the bird, because you had to climb a tree whose branches could break off just like that. What did XXX do? He climbed the tree at the risk of breaking his neck or his legs or his back and brought the bird down. I untangled the bird's feet from the string and it spread its wings and took off.[1]

The following is a record of a conversation held between M. Guérin, Auguste Vacquerie, Mme Hugo, Victor Hugo, and Adèle Hugo on October 7, 1854; Adèle entitles it, in her diary, "Three Stories about Animals."

Adèle begins: "My father was in the habit of feeding an alley cat named Carton ["Cardboard"] at dinnertime. Carton always left his food to go and rub up against my father. The guests were astonished at so much tenderness in a cat. We talked about the development of feelings in animals. On this subject, M. Guérin told a story about the dog who had befriended the proscrits."

M. Guérin: "There was a very ugly—but very democratic!— dog who befriended the proscrits. This dog only followed proscrits. Whenever there was a meeting, he would go to the meeting. Whenever a group of exiles sat down in a restaurant to dine together, he would go up to the table. Cabo—that was his name—only ever followed proscrits; he never followed a native of Jersey."

Victor Hugo: "Well, I too have something rather special to tell you about a dog. I was strolling about in a certain area of town and my head was preoccupied with my work. I was near a farmhouse. All of a sudden a yellow dog rushed out of the farmhouse, dashed up to me, and hurled himself on me, covering me with kisses. The yellow dog began to follow me; but, because I was about to turn around and head home, I made him understand that he shouldn't follow me much farther. The dog understood perfectly and ran back to the farmhouse.

"Every time I strolled by that farmhouse, the same thing happened. And Toby—I knew his name because I heard the farmer call him—never missed kissing me, following me, and running back to the farmhouse whenever I ordered him to. Cabo and Toby are probably ex-

Decembrists who have undergone metempsychosis into dogs and come here to ask us to forgive them for their past wrongs.*

"But I have another story to tell you that is even stranger than this one, because it concerns a cat's love and not a dog's love, and we all know that a cat is colder by nature than a dog. It was on a Sunday, and I was near Saint George's Tavern, at the hour when the Wesleyans go to church. I was in the middle of daydreaming and while I was, that whole silent pack of churchgoers streamed by me. All of a sudden, a gray cat bounded out of a house, ran up to me, and rubbed against me while stretching its back. I petted the cat, who was in such a state of passion that he wouldn't leave me. Whenever I was alone, the cat followed me. Whenever somebody passed, he went off and hid; then, when I was alone again, he came out and started following me again. Once, a group of children appeared, and before the cat had a chance to see them and hide they ran after him. The poor beast was forced to leave me and hide in the garden. This cat is yet another repentant ex-Decembrist who has suffered metempsychosis."[2]

What really goes on in the hearts and minds of animals? Victor Hugo broached this subject once again at the séance of April 24, 1854. The séance, which had begun at two o'clock in the afternoon, and which was attended by Mme Hugo, Victor Hugo, Charles Hugo, and Auguste Vacquerie, had been under way for some time. "Drama" was the presiding spirit when Victor Hugo, reading from hastily scribbled notes, expressed the following thoughts:

"I've often asked myself if it were not possible that animals see things that we don't see, and if this were not one of their compensations for being animals. I wondered this again tonight when I heard dogs barking on the empty terrace when nobody was going by. I wondered if it could be said that man thinks, but doesn't see, while animals don't think, but see; I wondered if that were not how God provided some sort of compensation for the incompleteness of animal nature. Dogs see ghosts and souls going by, and they bark. While that's happening, we human beings are in the dark. We wonder: Why are they barking? They see what is mysterious, but they can't understand it;

---

*The Decembrists were the plotters of Napoléon III's coup d'état of December 2, 1851. Hugo, whatever his beliefs in metempsychosis, is here, of course, being ironic.

perhaps we would be able to understand it, but we can't see it. I've written this down in a hurry, but it should be enough to give you the gist of my thoughts. What is your thinking on this? Would you care to enlighten me?"

Drama replied:

There are mysterious compensations for mysterious ills. Animals are prisons of the soul. But these cells are pierced with windows that open out to infinity, even though those windows are narrow and low and heavily barred. The bars cast shadows, and light seeps in through the air vents. Animals see man and glimpse angels. The glance of the beast encompasses a wide spectrum; its eyelashes embrace the physical world on one end and the world of spirits on the other. The eye of the dog you're whipping watches the angels smile. The barking of dogs is a stammer understood only by the Great Deaf-Mute; the roaring of beasts is the wail of a newborn babe heard only by the Silent Grandfather. The words men speak express only half a prayer; the voices of animals express the other half. The earth is filled with ears: there are two ears for every mouth; the first ear forgives while the second punishes. Animals, flowers, and stones lead an existence between man on the one hand, who doesn't see their souls, and God on the other, whose countenance they glimpse. They do this in such a way that, at nightfall, from every part of the animal world—dens, nests, woods, waves, darkness—an immense noise rises: the prayers of muzzles, beaks, fins from every sort of prison, from eyelids that weep for all eternity but are never wiped. God says: I hear you; and the lion learns patience, and the bird is less disturbed in its sleep, and the dog keeps yapping but at the robes of angels now. "Forgiveness" is the only word in the human language that beasts can spell. All the other words? Animals do not hear them. For them, it is as if these words had fallen into the sea—except that animals have no concept of drowning. Forgiveness is Noah's Ark.

Victor replied by talking about his poetry:

"I put in the mouth of a rose the following line that is being addressed to a caterpillar: *Come to my place. My buds are where souls hide.* Did I write this line blindly? Or did I, like the dog in the night, glimpse something?"

Drama replied:

Yes, you glimpsed something; but the rosebush is not the only place where souls hide. Why do you poets always speak lovingly of roses and butterflies but never lovingly of thistles, poisonous mushrooms, toads, slugs, caterpillars, flies, mites, worms, vermin, and infusoria? These are certainly ill-favored creatures, but—and then there are pebbles and seashells! Why don't you speak lovingly of bedbugs? Of fleas? . . . Why don't you take pity on the sufferings of vile horrible creatures? Why don't you take pity on the torture of infinitely small creatures condemned to live in the excrement of the infinitely large?

Drama went on to reiterate the sufferings of inanimate objects—*iron suffers, bronze suffers, an iron collar suffers*—and even of inanimate objects created by humans for offensive and defensive purposes—*the cannon suffers; the blade of the guillotine suffers. You pity Joan of Arc; pity the stake as well.* Then the spirit returned to the theme of feeling love for every sort of creature. It launched upon a final comment: that, in speaking as it did, Drama wasn't merely mouthing sentimental platitudes about animals:

What I say is very precise, and I wish to emphasize that I'm not talking about the vague feelings that poets have had about universal life. . . . I'm talking about the actual vital life of beasts, of flowers, of stones, just as I would talk about your lives as human beings. I want to stress the importance of this attitude; I approve of this attitude and I command poets to write lines like this, just as I would command my valets to do certain tasks. . . . I want you to rehabilitate the unhappiness of the toad and the despair of the thistle. I would be very happy if, in this house, you spoke of tigers with pity and of tiny earthworms with respect. From now on I want you to talk about the softness of wolves, the kindness of leopards and the weakness of lions. I've read the following in your manuscripts: Those charming forests where you suddenly meet a lion. I engage you to change this prosaic and pretty phrase—especially the word "charming"—to a phrase a lion deserves.[3]

On this note, the session ended.

Two months later, the ability of dogs to glimpse the supernatural was forcefully demonstrated to the participants of the séances. This occurred during a period when the group was communicating on and off with the Lady in White. (See chapter 16.) They had been expecting her on this particular evening of June 23, 1854.

Instead, the night began with an angry and sustained shaking of the table.

Present at the séance were Victor Hugo, Hennett de Kesler, a Marine-Terrace maid named Julie, Auguste Vacquerie, and Théophile Guérin. Mme Hugo and Charles Hugo sat at the table. As it trembled violently, Charles exclaimed:

"Calm yourself! Speak. Who are you?"

The table shook even more violently. It rapped out:

The Grim Gatekeeper.

"Explain to us what the Grim Gatekeeper is," asked Victor Hugo. "Are you Death?"

No.

"Tell us who the Grim Gatekeeper is."

The ghost who opens shadows. The one who holds the keys to suffering.

They could not think of who this unhappy spirit might be. The table was shaking so badly that it kept falling over on its side. They were able to right it only with great difficulty. It rapped so quickly that they could scarcely count the raps.

"Do you have something to tell us?" asked Victor Hugo. "Speak!"

I suffer.

"What can we do for you?" asked Mme Hugo.

Pray.

"We will pray for you," offered Victor Hugo. "Do you have anything to add?"

The table shook convulsively. Mme Hugo asked Archangel Love to intercede.

Then the table tapped out swiftly: *They are barking.*

Victor Hugo's notes record that at that moment the participants began to hear dogs barking loudly all around the outside of the house. "Is this house surrounded by ghosts and spirits?" asked Guérin.

Yes.

Victor Hugo asked: "Are other houses haunted by invisible beings in the same way?"

No.

"Call repentance to yourself," begged Mme Hugo. "Calm yourself."

The Grim Gatekeeper tapped out, as if in a frenzy: *Shut up, dogs!*

To everybody's surprise, the barking of the dogs subsided rapidly.

"Do you hear us, we who are here?" asked Mme Hugo. "Don't listen to the dogs, and pray."

The barking of the dogs faded away completely.

"The dogs aren't barking anymore," Victor Hugo stated. "Now are you able to talk to us? Who are you? Were you once a soul enclosed in a human body? Have you lived before? What crime did you commit that has made you so unhappy? Speak."

Once again the table moved convulsively. It tapped out:

O the horror!

"What does that mean?" demanded Victor Hugo. "Explain that to us."

The Danube, the Thames, the Seine, the Neva: four sources of blood that run from the four wounds of Jesus Christ. *

Now Hugo replied: "We feel the same horror as you about what's happening. Your thoughts are our thoughts. Do you know this?"

Yes.

"Are you suffering less?"

Yes.

"Why were you suffering so much a little while ago?"

Ghosts.

"Are they no longer there?"

No.

The group pursued this line of inquiry for several minutes longer. The Grim Gatekeeper was not forthcoming. The barking of the dogs picked up again as the table shook convulsively.

"Do you hear the dogs?" asked Hugo. "Can you tell us why they're barking?"

They see the blackbirds.

"Do you mean the ghosts?"

There was no response.

"What world do you dwell in?"

The pebbly stars.

"Do you love us?"

Yes.

---

*This seems to be a reference to the European dictators' wars, which weighed heavily on the minds of the exiles on Jersey Island. Here it is linked with the sufferings of Jesus on the Cross, with which the exiles, even when completely irreligious, sometimes identified.

"Do you approve of our exile?"

Yes.

The dogs had continued to bark loudly. The table tapped out abruptly: *Shut your mouths, dogs.*

The dogs immediately stopped barking.

Concerning this final happening, Victor Hugo noted in the transcript: "It wasn't only the house dogs that were barking. There were yappings from near and far. The dogs were howling all across the fields and all across the beach. It was clear to us that they all stopped at the same time."[4]

The dialogue with the Grim Gatekeeper was by no means over. But for the rest of the séance the exchanges would focus on the "human" ghosts that seemed to haunt the island, such as the Lady in White and the Lady in Gray. There would be no more paranormal events, and no more allusions to the secret world of animals.

That strange negative energy calling itself the Grim Gatekeeper never returned to the tables.

Two weeks later—on July 7, 1854—the spirits had still more to say about the unknown hearts and souls of animals, and this had to do with those creatures who, like Balaam's Ass, had managed to reach out and have a positive effect on the realm of man, thereby carving an esoteric transitional niche for themselves on the Great Chain of Being.

A comment by Victor Hugo, recorded in Adèle Hugo's diary for August 22, 1854, throws much light on this subject. (See also chapter 17.) Adèle quotes her father as saying: "I believe that at the farthest extreme the instinct of the beast is permitted to arrive at such a perfected state that this instinct can lead it to perform a sublime action. We have striking examples of this in the Lion of Androcles and the Lion of Florence. So it is that the beast, rewarded for its sublime action, passes from the animal state into the state of archangel."[5]

At the séance of July 7, which began at 2:45 p.m., Théophile Guérin asked a question that he had been considering for some time; it had to do with the nature of animals, and he asked it of the spirit that called itself "Idea." Present were Auguste Vacquerie and Mme Hugo, with Guérin and Charles Hugo sitting at the table.

Guérin began:

"On the subject of beasts, Balaam's Ass told us that man did not know what his mistake was, and the animal did not know what its crime was. Regent's Diamond recently informed us* that, on the contrary, the beast *does* know why it is a beast. The spirit insisted on this, even declaring that we should think of the crime of every beast, of every plant, of every stone, as the counselor, guide, and shepherd of that creature."

The shade called Idea replied:

The world has made progress, not only with regard to mankind but also with regard to animals, plants, and stones. In the beginning, hell was everywhere. Man knew nothing of his real nature. The beast knew nothing, the plant knew nothing, and the stone knew nothing. A deep shadow lay upon universal consciousness.

Saviors came. Moses taught man that he had a right to be alive. Socrates showed him that he had a right to think. Jesus revealed to him the right to love. These three men, each in their turn, took to the grave with them some part of the shadow that had lain upon the earth.

That part of the world capable of rational thought became aware of its punishment: humanity realized it was being punished. Then an immense light shone forth. From the night the hand of God emerged, wielding a lightning bolt. In the glow of that lightning bolt, humanity caught a glimpse of a God who was smiling. The thunderbolt of the Old Testament is the sunset; the flame of the Gospels is the dawn.

Animals, plants, and stones: they, too, have had their Jesus Christs. Balaam's Ass was one. In the wake of the Passion of certain predestined beasts, that same half-light shone on animals as shone on man. The Lion of Androcles took suffering upon himself for the tiger. The Dove of the Ark fluttered through the sky for the serpent. Saint Antoine's pig shielded the goat with love. Balaam's Ass took thought for the thistle. The Lion of Florence—the greatest of them all—saved the stones of the city. What then came to pass? God said: "Man knows his punishment; beast, plant, and pebble will know their crime. I let man know half the mystery; I'm letting beast, plant, and pebble know the other half."

In speaking thus, God brought a revolution to the hearts of beasts who cannot speak. The den had had its Calvary; the angel had had its

---

*The transcript of the séance to which Guérin refers is lost. "Regent's Diamond" was apparently a spirit who was a personification from the realm of stones.

Golgotha. The stable had had its cross. The bird's nest had brushed heaven. But God, wearing as he does mystery's garment, does not reveal to dead animals that when they were alive they succored beasts, nor does He let plants and stones know that they have been their own saviors. Beasts, plants, and stones remaining on earth will tell you that they know their crime. Balaam's Ass, the Lion of Androcles, the Dove of the Ark will all tell you that they do not know theirs. Why has God decreed it thus? Perhaps because He does not want the benefactor to know what benefit he has conferred. Perhaps because He wishes to hold back some portion of happiness from those already in a state of bliss. Perhaps because he wishes to spare the newly deceased beasts the shock of knowing what crime they have just expiated, and because when he bestows paradise he always gives away just a little so that eternity will remain full.

Guérin protested:

"In the midst of the splendid things you've just told us, there is one point that seems obscure to me. You say man and beast each know half of the secret—that man knows his punishment and the beast knows its crime. I have trouble understanding that distinction. The beast has awareness of its crime; it is also aware of its suffering. To know you have acted badly and to know that you are suffering: Is that not the same as knowing that you are being punished?"

That the beast is aware of its crime does not mean that it knows that it is being punished. For, to know that we are being punished is to know that someday we will be delivered from that punishment; we will have expiated our crime, whatever it is. Thus man knows that, in that he is suffering, he is climbing ever upward toward the good.

But the beast does not have that knowledge. The beast has instinct, and it suffers and it knows the nature of its criminal act, but it cannot make a connection between its instinct and its suffering and its knowledge of that crime because it lacks the faculty of reason. The animal suffers, and it knows its crime; but man suffers and he thinks; the workings of his mind are such that he can work out the connection between suffering and punishment and realize that, somewhere, somehow, forgiveness is implied.

Man reasons; the beast does not. Man is logical; the beast is not. Man calculates; the beast does not. Man draws conclusions; the beast does not. A dog never totals up the blows it has received. A cat doesn't know how old it is. A monkey may be able to knock a clock out of kilter, but it can never set the time. The beast represents the absence of mind. What is quite simple for you—drawing from suffering the conclusion that there is punishment—is an impossibility for the beast. If the beast reasoned, it would speak. Language is nothing but the beating of thought's wings.

Guérin was still not satisfied:

"You say that by punishment you mean hope of deliverance, and that the beasts don't know their punishment. . . . We've been told quite the opposite by other of your spirits; we've been told that beasts, plants, and stones know they are not condemned for life, and that they hold in their heads 'the thought of certain deliverance.' In what sense are you telling us that beasts have neither the certainty nor even the hope of being liberated?"

The animal knows what crime it has committed. It knows it will be forgiven for that crime. While awaiting its pardon, it knows it is suffering. What it cannot do is reestablish the connection between that suffering and whatever else may be involved. Where reason begins, the animal leaves off. For it to attempt to draw the simplest conclusion is for it to gaze into the abyss. There is no such thing as a naive animal.[6]

And there the dialogue on animals ended, at least for a time.

But the dialogue would resume, and the séance participants would continue to hear about the world of animals. For the moment, however, let us turn to some of the other spirits that were visiting the tapping tables, and, in particular, the personification of the Ocean and Wolfgang Amadeus Mozart.

Fifteen

ROARINGS OF OCEAN
AND COMET

Charles Bénézit, musician, anti-Napoléon III patriot, and political exile on Jersey Island, didn't know why he had been summoned to the Hugo household, but he didn't believe it was so he could have this miserable conversation with Charles Hugo.

Victor Hugo's eldest son, sprawled out on the couch in Bohemian disarray, his unlit pipe clenched between his teeth, had been stating that he, Charles Hugo, was a fatalist, that there was no point in working or, for that matter, not working. In fact, it didn't really matter what anybody did, because fate and Providence were the same thing—as, indeed, were good and evil.

These remarks had irritated Bénézit, who, sitting up straighter in the big green armchair, had declared: "No, we are masters of our fate! I believe absolutely in personal freedom. My God, if I want to lift my elbow, I lift it! If I want to talk, I talk. If I want to give one hundred sous to the poor, I give it. I am free, absolutely free!"

Charles had replied, "Well, no, you're not free to give one hundred sous to the poor, because you don't *have* one hundred sous. None of us has any money. And you're certainly not free, for example, to go to the Saint-Ouen suburb of Paris."

"My God, yes," Bénézit had exclaimed, "I am absolutely free to go to Saint-Ouen."

"If you run into somebody along the way who steals everything you have, you're not free to go to Saint-Ouen. An even better example: you're not free to compose a melody."

"Certainly I am free to compose a melody!"

Charles Hugo had gotten interested enough in this conversation to rise to a near-sitting position. "So, compose it right away."

Bénézit stood up, strode across the room, and sat down at the piano. He turned to Charles. "Ah, it will take a little time."

"So you see, you're not free to compose a melody in five minutes."

The thought occurred to Bénézit that this conversation was not only a miserable one but also now an exceedingly silly one. Still, in deference to the great poet in whose drawing room he was sitting, he peered benignly at Charles and answered in the gentlest of voices: "Well, no, not in five minutes."[1]

At that point, Victor Hugo mercifully entered the room. He was carrying a big red notebook under his arm. "Ah, my dear Bénézit," he exclaimed happily, "I am so glad to see you! Forgive me, sir, for not having gotten my invitation out to you till this morning. We would so much like you to have dinner with us! And, after dinner, we would so much like you to meet a famous composer, one who, I believe, is very anxious to meet you."

Victor Hugo beamed.

"And who, *cher maître*," said Bénézit—who, having sprung up from the piano bench where he had just sat down, was gratefully shaking Hugo's proffered hand—"and who might this eminent personage be?"

"Wolfgang Amadeus Mozart!"

"But, my dear sir, Wolfgang Amadeus Mozart is dead!"

"Only in the bodily sense, dear Bénézit!" expostulated Hugo. "You have attended our séances. I'm quite certain M. Mozart will be visiting us tonight, through those very tapping tables whose workings you have observed. Indeed, he has already visited us, on April 23, three weeks ago. He needs your help, sir, in a very delicate matter. *Your* help, sir—you, M. Charles Bénézit, patriotic Frenchman, republican, activist, political exile, pianist, composer, teacher of composition and piano to a fortunate few including my own daughter Adèle, and author of several shrewd and imaginative works on the future of music. He needs your help, sir, and, in this particular matter—so do I!"

Bénézit gazed speechlessly at the great man. Certainly he had been present at several of the séances. He had been interested, intrigued, even fascinated. But he was not sure what to make of the reality of the phenomenon. He opened his mouth to reply, or protest, or exclaim—

he wasn't sure which—but then Victor Hugo reached up a finger and touched Bénézit on the lips and, with a loudly whispered "Shush," effectively shut him up.

"Dear Bénézit," said Hugo, "forgive my rudeness, but I do not have time to explain it all right now. However"—he thrust the big red notebook into Bénézit's hands—"it is all written down here. This book is the record of our séances. I should like you, if you would be so kind—we have two hours before dinner—to read over those transcripts, which will bring you up-to-date on our friend Wolfgang Amadeus Mozart." He pointed to a piece of paper sticking out of the notebook. "Here is a list of the relevant texts; there are only three of them. Kindly consult the list, read the books, and enjoy what you read!"

Then he was gone out the front door in a burst of benevolent energy that left Bénézit feeling as if Victor Hugo considered him to be the most important person in the world, and certainly the man whom the poet, if he had any choice in the matter at all, would like to spend at least three-quarters of his time with.

Bénézit, for the moment stunned, sat down once again on the piano bench. Charles Hugo had decamped at almost the same moment as his father had entered the room. The huge house seemed empty now, its suddenly sepulchral silence broken only by the occasional clatter of dishes in the kitchen (the cook was making dinner) and the barking of a dog on the terrace. Bénézit opened the notebook to the transcript of the first séance: April 22, 1854 (today was May 16). Still flying high on the tailwind of Hugo's eloquence, he began to read.

The first séance had taken place on April 22, 1854, at 4:00 p.m. Present were Théophile Guérin, Victor Hugo, Mme Adèle Hugo, and Charles Hugo.*

V. H. [Victor Hugo]: "Is there anybody there?"

T. [Table]: *Yes.*

V. H.: "Before you tell us who you are, may I be permitted to ask a question?"

---

*The subsequent transcripts are presented in the simple Q and A form (with the occasional note) in which Benezit would have seen them. However, the words of the living are placed in quotation marks, and those of the spirits in italics, in a way in which Benezit would not have seen them, but which is consistent with the format used in the present book.

T.: *Yes.*

V. H.: "The table has composed poetry, and very fine poetry; it seems to us that it could do the same with music. Music is like poetry: it is the breath of thought. Are you able to compose music?"

T.: *Yes.*

"Can you compose music like the *Marseillaise* of the French Revolution? We need you to compose another *Marseillaise,* one that will bear the same relationship to the former as the coming European Revolution will bear to the French. You will write the music. I will write the words. The bugle needs a bigger mouthpiece! Does that arrangement suit you?"

Yes.

"Do you need M. Guérin, who is a distinguished flutist, to explain his system of annotation to you?"

No.

"So you know it without his having to explain it to you?"

Yes.

"Tell us about yourself."

I am your neighbor.

"What do you mean by that?"

I am Ocean.

"A melody composed by an ocean for a revolution! What could be finer? We are listening to you. What would you like us to call your composition?"

"My Noise."

T. G. [Théophile Guérin]: "What would you like those who sing it to call it?"

The Thundering.[2]

Bénézit quickly read through the discussion that followed. Hugo, Guérin, and Ocean argued over how the music should be dictated and annotated. They came up with a method that seemed workable to Bénézit, if overly simple. Then Hugo left the room, and the transcript ended. Presumably, Ocean had dictated his music to Guérin, the proscrit taking it down in another notebook. Now Bénézit began to read the transcript of the next séance, which had taken place the next day, April 23, 1854, at 2:30 p.m.

Present: Théophile Guérin, Mme Hugo, Charles Hugo.

Mme A. H. [Mme Adèle Hugo]: "Are you Ocean?"

Yes.

T. G. [Théophile Guérin]: "Your composition such as you dictated it to us makes no sense. No doubt I made mistakes in writing it down. Where should we make changes?"

A technical discussion ensued between Ocean and Guérin. Bénézit skipped through it; it was brief and a little confused. Ocean suggested they merely change the key. The spirit tapped out a series of disconnected letters: *a, d, a, f, f, o.* Then Victor Hugo briskly entered the room and took over.

V. H.: "The tune—M. Guérin tried to play it on the flute—didn't amount to much. You've just told us that we have to change the key from *sol* to *fa*, that that will change the melody completely. Is that really the only change that's necessary?"

Who says little, sees a lot. The sea is art. The deep blue sky is infinity. A drop of water can reflect the image of a giant star. The knife-edge of an ocean wave is the string of a gigantic lyre. The ocean's dens are ears forever open to the singing of the musicians of eternity. The vast sky is packed with birds perching like sublime musical bars on this powerful organ of God. The sea makes music; the sky writes words. The poet's name is love; the musician's name is power—

"We are ignorant creatures; we have already told you that. We are ignorant in all things, and in music most of all. The aggrieved words you fling at us do not annoy us. But, can you tell me: why are you so irritated?"

Your flute pierced with little holes like the asshole of a pooping brat disgusts me! Make a real orchestra for me and I'll make a song for you. Take all the loud noises, all the tumult, all the din, all the anger of sounds floating free in space, morning wind, evening wind, night wind, wind in the tomb, storms, sandstorms, gusts that run their violent fingers like maddened creatures through the manes of trees, tides rising onto beaches, rivers plunging into the sea, cataracts, waterspouts, the vomiting of cacophonous tumult from the earth's enormous belly, the sound lions make, the sound elephants trumpet through their trunks, the sounds unassailable snakes hiss through their coils, that whales moan through their wet warm nasal passages, that mastodons breathe in the bowels of the earth, that the steeds of the sun whinny in the depths of the sky, that the zoo of the wind whistles in the cage of the air, that fire and water spew forth in insults (the

first from the depths of the volcano's maw, the second from the bot-
tom of the abyss's mouth)—take all these, and then say to me: There's
your orchestra. Harmonize this racket; make its hatreds into love;
bring peace to its battles. Be the maestro of that which has no master.
Be the conqueror of infinity. Tame the horror, calm the violence, and
kiss the elements' mane. Make the four winds come together on the
tip of your violinist's bow rather than on the fiery tongue of celestial
lightnings, and give art's blessing to this enormous union of the forces
of nature now on its knees before you. Marry the two betrotheds of
creation who have been staring at each other lovingly for six thousand
years: the earth and the sky. Be the priest of that majestic church—but
don't tell me to make music with your flute!

V. H.: "We don't have a way of trying out your music. All we have
here is a piano. It's not our friend's fault that all he has is a flute. The
greatest musicians on earth—I didn't say in the sea!—didn't mind
trying things out on poor instruments. Can't you just accept that,
too—even you? We can't believe that you're seriously annoyed at our
friend. Will you continue what you've begun, namely to compose the
Marseillaise of a future revolution? Will you? Tell us!"

I'd very much like to satisfy you, but you don't have a way of
annotating my music. You have to understand the language of inani-
mate objects before you can understand creatures like me who don't
have a visible form. That is how flowers see souls. There are dialogues
between perfumes and the essences of things. Roses talk to the dead;
jars of jasmine on attic windowsills chat with all the sky. The music
I tried to dictate to you yesterday is beautiful but it lacks accompa-
niment. The piano I really need would be too big to bring into your
house. It would have only two keys: white and black, day and night; a
day full of birds and a night full of souls.

Mme A. H.: "Yesterday you said you would compose this melody.
Why did you say yes yesterday?"

Calm yourself.

"That's hardly an answer."

The music has been composed.

"If it's all done, what parts should we remove from what you
dictated?"

Look for them.

"Did M. Guérin write it free of error?"

It must be touched up by a human musician. Talk to Mozart about it when you see him.

V. H.: "Can you send us Mozart?"

Yes.

"Can he come here this evening?"

There is a way he can help you. Put the table in front of the piano. It will strike the keys, and you will annotate.

"Will Mozart come and animate the table, or will your spirit, remaining in the table, do the rapping?"

Mozart is preferable. Myself, I'm unintelligible.

"Would you kindly ask Mozart to come at 9:00 o'clock tonight?"

I will ask Twilight to pass the word along.[3]

Bénézit, fascinated, read on in the big red notebook. The next séance took place at 2:30 the same afternoon and wasn't on Hugo's list. The one after it was. That session began at 9:20 p.m. the same night:

April 23, 1854, Sunday, 9:20 p.m.

Present: Victor Hugo, Théophile Guérin. At the table: Mme Victor Hugo, Charles Hugo. Auguste Vacquerie writing.

A. V. [Auguste Vacquerie]: "Who's there?"

T. [Table]: *Mozart.*

V. H.: "Did Ocean tell you about our conversation this afternoon?"

Written commentary by A.V.: "Without replying, the table went to the piano and struck a C. We had a great deal of trouble figuring out what the note was. Had the table struck a white key, a black key, or what? We asked the table how to proceed."*

A. V.: "Is there some sort of procedure we can follow?"

No.

"Do you prefer the method Ocean used yesterday?"

No.

"What do we do? We'd really like to hear your music."

I'll give it some thought.

"How soon can you come back?"

---

*It's not clear what strategy for placing the table in relation to the piano was used at this séance. It seems to have been somewhat different from the strategy that would be used in the next two séances.

In ten days.

"Tuesday, May 3, from 8:00 p.m. on?"

Yes.[4]

Thus the séance ended. It was the third and last séance whose transcript Victor Hugo wanted Bénézit to read.

At dinner that night, an expansive Hugo told the Jersey Island proscrit/composer that Mozart hadn't shown up for the May 3 rendezvous. The séance participants had wondered if they would ever hear from him again. And then, just that night before, Hugo had been told by one of the most trustworthy of the spirits that Mozart would come on May 16—tonight!—and that Hugo should invite the most accomplished composer he could find to the séance. That was Bénézit.

Hugo expressed frustration with Mozart to his dinner guests. "We annoyed Mozart," he told them. "It wasn't our fault. Mozart came through the tables into the company of artists—ourselves—who understood absolutely nothing about the only form of art that interests him. We are not painters, but we can judge a good canvas very well, whereas in music we know less than nothing.[5] That's why I took the liberty of inviting you, my dear Bénézit." Hugo smiled encouragingly at the composer. "I believe your understanding of music is not restricted to preconceived ideas. I'm hoping that you'll be able to catch the afterlife productions of Wolfgang Amadeus Mozart in the golden net of your open mind."

They finished dinner and then shifted slowly to the chairs surrounding the tables.

The séance began at 8:00 p.m. Present that evening, along with Bénézit, were Théophile Guérin, Mme Hugo, Charles Hugo, and Auguste Vacquerie. Victor, saying he had to go out for a minute, asked them to begin without him.

Bénézit was excited, but he hardly knew what to think. Spirituality made him uncomfortable. He hated all religions.[6] He hated them so much that he had taken rooms in St. Helier as far away from any ecclesiastical structure as he could, not an easy thing to do in a town crowded with a dozen religious denominations from English Roman Papist through Primitive Methodist to a Mormon temple[7] each often having more than one church. He did not believe in an afterworld—though the thought had crossed his mind, as he listened to Victor

Hugo hold forth at the dinner table, that if you composed music with the power and splendor and fecundity of a Mozart, then perhaps not even death could stop you. Through sheer irrepressible momentum your disembodied creative soul of a towering genius might continue to hurtle forward, a glowing comet of endlessly proliferating symphonies careening around the universe and occasionally alighting on earth to piggyback on the soul of a live composer . . .

Bénézit abruptly dismissed these thoughts from his mind as sheer giddy foolishness and forced himself to calm down. Leaning forward, notebook in lap and pencil in hand, he watched with studied care as Mme Hugo and Guérin, the designated mediums, placed their hands on the little three-legged table. It trembled. Bénézit trembled too.

Then the table began to tap. It tapped swiftly for a minute or so. Guérin declared that it had spelled out *Mozart*. The spirit, his raps interpreted by Guérin, tersely told them what to do. They followed his instructions. They pushed the two tables, the small one on top of the big one, against the piano. They moved the little pedestal table to the edge of the square table so that its feet were flush with the keyboard. Mme Hugo and Guérin placed their hands on the three-legged table again. Bénézit, heart thumping, watched as the pedestal table slid slowly along in front of the keys; from time to time it stopped, elevated a leg, and brought it down on a key, striking a note. Then it awkwardly moved on.

Bénézit, using the system of notation laid down by Ocean, sometimes asking Mozart questions, painstakingly took down the notes. First there was an A flat; then there was a B; then . . .

As the session progressed, it became increasingly clear to Bénézit that a mega-*Marseillaise* was not being composed—in fact, that nothing was being composed at all, or so it seemed. Bénézit racked his brains to figure out what could be the pattern behind the bizarre collection of notes that emerged slowly, through the efforts of the tapping table, from the piano keyboard. It seemed to him that this was little more than a cacophony . . .

He communicated his doubts to the participants. Then he asked the shade of Mozart: "Are you composing a symphony, or simply setting out the basics for a melody?"

Composing a symphony.

Just then, Victor Hugo arrived back in the room. Informed of the general consternation, he addressed the table firmly: "Instead of a symphony, instead of a musical epic whose creation is beyond our means of execution, couldn't you just dictate a simple melody, one like, for example, the *Marseillaise,* but one which can be sung by a revolution, by humanity?"

The table rapped out: *So be it.*

"Would you be able to dictate a brief song for us this evening?"

I'll need time to prepare it beforehand.

"When do you want to dictate it to us?"

Next Tuesday.

And that was the end of the séance.[8]

Charles Bénézit had to confess—at least to himself—that the session had been disappointing. There was no reason to believe that Mozart had been there at all! He didn't confide his disappointment to the other guests, however. Within a day he had almost forgotten about it; Bénézit taught composition, piano, and French from his rooms in Saint Helier and from time to time traveled to see students, and over the next week he was even busier than usual. Then, suddenly, it was Tuesday again, and Bénézit, having been invited once more to dinner at the Hugo's, found himself sitting down one more time beside the tapping tables in the drawing room of Marine-Terrace.

Victor Hugo hadn't given up on the idea of having the shade of Mozart dictate a pan-European anthem—and, besides, Mozart had said he would come back in a week, which was tonight. Bénézit himself, pencil and notebook in hand, wasn't at all hopeful, though the thought had occurred to him (again inspired by Hugo's eloquence at the dinner table) that, seeing as Mozart had had a whole seven days to perfect his methods of communication (indeed, might have had something more like an eternity, if it were true that the afterworld was outside of time and space), then things might go much better tonight. And so the Jersey Island proscrit/composer, sitting on the piano bench that had been moved aside to make room for the tapping tables, suddenly found himself getting excited one more time.

Present at the séance on that night of Tuesday, May 23, 1854 (it began at 9:45 p.m.), were Bénézit, Victor Hugo, Mme Hugo, Charles Hugo, Auguste Vacquerie, and Mlle Adèle Hugo (who, as a pianist and composer herself, might be expected to contribute some useful energy to the séance). The mediums placed their hands on the little pedestal table on the big square table pushed up against the piano; the spirit of Mozart greeted them again; the tapping table slid awkwardly down along the keys; and Bénézit, leaning forward eagerly, tried to take down the notes.

But nothing happened again.

This Tuesday night was a repetition of the Tuesday night before, except that this time Bénézit pushed the shade of the composer far more with aggressive questions about exactly what was going on. To no avail. The séance degenerated into confusion. "It's all incoherent," Bénézit sighed sadly, peering at the seemingly random collection of notes cluttering two pages of his notebook.

A puzzled Victor Hugo asked the table: "Is this still Mozart?"

The table answered: *No.*

"Who is it?" asked Hugo.

AAA.

"And who is that?"

Louis-Philippe.

Victor Hugo was frustrated. "Do you have something to say to us?" he asked. "Yes or no? Are you trying to bamboozle us? The mysterious shouldn't indulge in hocus-pocus. Whoever you are, you're not being serious; you're being stupid. I find pranks from the graveyard hideous; I'll have nothing to do with them. Speak! You're not Mozart. You're not Louis-Philippe. Who are you?"

The table was as silent as a stone. Then it rapped out *AAA* a second time. And then—their hearts leaped!—it rapped out the word *Cimarosa,* which all of them immediately took to mean the Italian composer Domenico Cimarosa, born in 1749 and died in 1801, and whose shade, they all now hoped against hope, was arriving to take over from Mozart.

"Would you write music for us?" Hugo asked politely.

Yes, the spirit replied—and then, as quickly as he had come, Cimarosa was gone![9]

Wolfgang Amadeus Mozart hadn't composed a super-*Marseillaise.* He hadn't composed a single melody. He hadn't composed anything at all!

Had there really been no coherent spirit-world force at all behind the Mozartian "notes" Bénézit had taken down in his notebook, he asked himself the next day, and the next, and often in the days to come? Was this phenomenon of the tapping tables really nothing more than the pent-up longings and fears and hopes and despair of the proscrits finding expression, however unconsciously, through the rapping of the tapping tables?

And then a new thought occurred to Bénézit, one so audacious—and speculative and frankly insane!—that he immediately decided never to communicate it to his friends, not even Victor Hugo. The thought was this: Yes, perhaps there really was an afterworld. But it was not—of course!—the pious, comfortable, beaming fairyland of lambs and lyres and doing nothing throughout eternity that the Christians so complacently imagined it to be. It wasn't even a dynamic and vital world reflecting the extremes of human behavior, with artists desperately struggling to complete works of art posthumously and lovers, their love unrequited on earth, now flinging themselves madly at each other.

It probably wasn't even human. Why should it be, with the afterworld having to accommodate a million other stars and planets? It had to be more like the realm described by Ocean in the transcripts Hugo had given Bénézit to read, an inchoate and unmade world far beyond the human one, rent with chaos and wrenching change and shreikings and clashings (and, Bénézit knew, these words were completely inadequate to describe this place far beyond human imagining).

If Mozart had been communicating music from that realm, there would not be any way a human composer could possibly understand what he was saying. His compositions would appear to be—as they *had* all appeared to be—nothing but sheer cacophony.

With that Charles Bénézit reined in his thoughts, which he had no intention of ever revealing to anyone, and, before leaving the subject forever, fixed in his mind one final judgment on the tapping tables:

Either the spirits didn't exist, and you couldn't talk to them (you might think you were, but you were only talking to yourself). Or the spirits did exist, and you could talk to them all you wanted, and they could talk to you.

But you could never understand a single word they said.

Charles Bénézit continued, from time to time, to attend the séances at Marine-Terrace. But he never took them seriously again.

Between the abortive music-making sessions conducted by the shade of Mozart, other events had been unfolding at the tapping tables that almost seemed designed to further shake up the preconceptions of the ever-attentive séance attendees.

On April 4, 1854, a fiery comet blazed in the skies over western Europe. At 7:30 that evening, as the Hugo family was sitting down to dinner, François-Victor burst excitedly into the room to tell his father that he had seen the comet. Victor Hugo stood up from his place at the table and strode out to the terrace to observe the celestial visitor for himself.

A séance had been scheduled for that night. It began at 9:00. Present were Mme Adèle Hugo, Victor Hugo, François-Victor Hugo, Charles Hugo, Auguste Vacquerie, and Théophile Guérin. Mme Hugo and Guérin placed their hands on the table.

"Who's there?" asked Guérin.

Legurru.

"Is that your name?"

Yes.

"Who are you?"

Fohe—

The energy seemed troubled. Mme Hugo let Charles take her place.

Victor Hugo asked: "Did you indeed mean to say *Legurru Fohe*?"

Yes.

"Were you speaking French?"

No.

"What language were you speaking?"

The language of animals.

"What animals?"

Lions.

"The lions of this planet?"

The table didn't move.

"What does *legurru* mean?"

The comet is coming.

"Is that what the words *legurru* and *fohe* mean?"

Yes.

Auguste Vacquerie asked, "Does the roaring of lions actually have meaning?"

Yes.

Victor Hugo said, "You were telling us about a comet. Would you like to continue?"

Yes.

The table tapped out: *Before the viper. The star with a tail creeps through the celestial grave. The comet is the serpent that appears at those times when humanity is about to reopen the graves of the dead. Viper on earth, boa in the sky.*

A thoughtful Hugo inquired: "Besides the mysterious and catastrophic symbolism of comets already described by, for example, writers like Virgil in his *Dirae Cometae,* might you be able to provide us with some exact details about comets—their paths, their distance from other celestial bodies, and so on?"

The table tapped out: *Give me a pencil.*

Charles and Guérin brought out the small three-legged table, one of whose legs ended in a pencil, that Delphine de Girardin had sent them six months before. They placed a sheet of paper under it and laid their hands on top.

The pencil-leg began to move. It quickly drew a picture. What emerged looked like a head. To this head the pencil attached a tail, then partially filled in the head with tiny globes. In Latin, on the tail, the pencil wrote: *semen astrorum* ("seed of the stars"). (See drawing A on page 178.)

The participants were bewildered. Was this some sort of astral blueprint of the comet—of all comets? They asked the lion to draw a picture of itself. It did so. (See drawing B.)

Mme Hugo asked, "Can you draw—will you draw—what I'm thinking of right now?"

The table sketched a young woman, framing the woman in a heart. In the upper left-hand corner it drew a grave with a cross above it. (See drawing C.)

Mme Hugo admitted to the company that she had been thinking about Léopoldine.

Théophile Guérin asked the table to draw what he was thinking of. It sketched a woman whose heart was visible through her breast.

WHAT THE TURNING TABLES DREW (I)

A. Self-portrait of a comet, or alchemical formula?

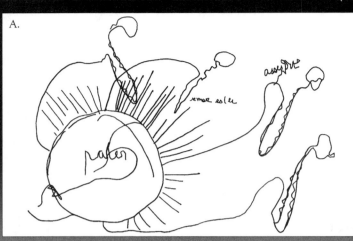

A.

B. Self-portrait of the lion that spoke the language of lions

B.

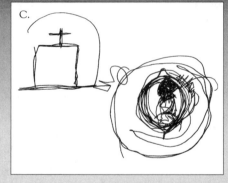

C.

C. Mme Hugo thinking of Léopoldine

D. Théophile Guérin thinking of his mother's heart linked to the hull of the ship upon which he was transported

D.

Above her head was a ship's hull; it was connected to the woman's heart by a long thin filament. (See drawing D.)

Guérin, deeply moved, swore this was the image of what he had been thinking. What was that? He wouldn't say.*

Auguste Vacquerie asked the table to draw what he was thinking of. It drew a picture of a kind of medallion usually worn by women. Beside the medallion, it sketched a miniature painting that seemed to be hanging on a wall. At the bottom of the sheet of paper the pencil sketched what looked like Vacquerie's profile, connecting that profile to both the medallion and the painting. Above the painting, it wrote in Latin: *de arte ad familiam.*†

The participants were impressed. But Vacquerie himself was crest-fallen. "That's not what I was thinking of," he complained to the table.

No.

"Why didn't you draw what I was thinking?"

You doubted.

"If I doubt, you have a simple enough way of making me believe: draw what I'm thinking."

I can't.

"You did it for Mme Hugo and Guérin."

They didn't doubt.

Here the séance ended.[10]

Did it end because Vacquerie doubted? That seems unlikely. But, in the now almost two-centuries-long history of séances, it has often been noted that doubt on the part of a participant can seriously weaken the ability of the spirits to communicate with that particular participant. Perhaps that was why the spirits of the tapping table were unable to tell Auguste Vacquerie what was going on in his mind.

On Thursday, April 13, 1854, at 9:45 p.m., with Victor Hugo and Auguste Vacquerie in attendance and Mme Hugo and Charles sitting

---

*Victor Hugo adds in the margin of the transcript that Guérin had been transported to Jersey aboard a prisoner vessel called *The Duguesclin* and that Hugo thought the woman in the picture was Guérin's mother, her heart attached to the vessel that was taking her son away.

†*De arte ad familiam* means "from the family's art." Commentators point out that the painting resembles the popular *Christ on the Mount of Olives* by Eugène Délacroix, a reproduction of which Vacquerie owned.

at the table, a second brief encounter with the language of lions took place.

Victor Hugo, responding to the rapid tapping of the table, asked, "Tell us your name."

Fecoil.

"What language are you speaking? Is it still the language of lions?"

Yes.

"What does *fecoil* mean in the language of lions?"

The moon is bothering me.

"Why is it bothering you?"

Its light is too bright.

They went and closed the window. When they returned, the table was silent. No spirit could be coaxed to return. The séance participants did not hear from the comet again, nor from Wolfgang Amadeus Mozart.

Sixteen

THE LADY IN WHITE

Mysterious spirit who, finger on lips,
Passes by me . . . don't go! speak to the half-mad man
Drunk on shadows and infinity,
Speak to me, thou, white brow that bends over me in my
* night;*
Answer me, thou who gleams and walks beneath the branches,
Like a breath of air bringing clarity!

VICTOR HUGO, *HORROR*

In the winter of 1854, Victor Hugo might have been forgiven for feel-ing that the apparitions that haunted Jersey Island were closing in on him, either to hallow him with love or harrow him with terror, most likely to do both at the same time.

He had begun to hear stories of strange visitations almost as soon as the Hugo family had begun to explore the island. A farmer hold-ing a crucifix tightly had pointed out to his daughter Adèle the cloven-hooved footprints of the Devil in the grass near the dolmen at Rozel. Not far from the Grosnez caves, on the northwest tip of the island, a milkmaid, piously telling her beads, had shown Adèle the sharp rock jutting out to sea where the Virgin Mary could sometimes be seen sit-ting on a Sunday morning.[1]

That was the year before, when the ghosts and phantoms were still some distance away. But, as his second winter on Jersey Island stretched on into 1854, Victor Hugo began to feel—surely fatigue played a role—that the forces of light and darkness had taken his measure and were now beginning to advance slowly, resolutely toward him in his redoubt at Marine-Terrace. His barber had told him in mid-January that the Devil had lately been seen wandering much closer to these parts than Grosnez or even Rozel—even that he was not unknown to prowl the tiny street called the Rue des Ailleurs at Grouville only a mile-and-a-half away. Sometimes the Devil wore a cap so hideous that the Jerseymen were too frightened to try to tell Victor Hugo what it looked like. Victor felt as if the supernatural was coming closer and closer, streaming over hill and dale like the shadow of a vast cloud sweeping across the fields and beaches of Jersey—like a hangman's noose that was for the moment very wide and very ethereal, but which was inexorably tightening around his neck.

At one o'clock one morning, Charles and François-Victor, very drunk, strode off to the Rue des Ailleurs to roust the Devil from his lair and find out what that piece of headgear looked like. They'd gotten soaked in a sudden rainstorm for their pains, and Charles, dressed in a tattered greatcoat and orange and mauve trousers, was mistaken by a Jerseyman (who fled screaming from him) for the very Devil he was trying to find.[2]

But if the Enemy of Mankind hopefully might never make it as far as Marine-Terrace, there were four other phantoms, one in particular, who greedily regarded the lanes and alleys and leafy nooks leading to the Hugo house as their allotted stomping ground. One was "the headless man," who was the shade of a luckless islander decapitated centuries before. Then there were the three shades who were known locally as the "three Ladies of the Sandbar": the Lady in White, who was the first woman on the island to murder her baby; the Lady in Gray, a former Druid priestess who had sacrificed her father on the stone altar of a dolmen; and the Lady in Black, who had also murdered her father, though the circumstances were unknown.[3]

The Hugo family had been told about the Lady in White almost as soon as they moved into Marine-Terrace. At the crest of a hill sloping down toward the beach, about a half mile from the house, there stood a menhir—one of the ancient druidic standing stones of Jersey—that the locals called in the French dialect of that region *La Blianche Danme:*[4] the White Lady. The menhir was said to be infused with spirit, and that spirit was also the White Lady, or Lady in White, who roamed the island freely every night. It was said you could see her surge up out of her rock just as twilight melted into darkness.[5]

The Lady in White in particular was thought to be intimately associated with Marine-Terrace. She was, the Jerseymen said, its familiar
spirit, a kind of guardian ghost, who flitted by the bottom of the terrace every evening but would only become visible if you drew a big
black cross on the breakwater dividing the terrace from the beach.
Charles and François-Victor Hugo, for all their sense of superiority
over the spirits, had never presumed to do this.[6]

By early 1854, the Lady in White had begun to make herself visible
in the neighborhood without anybody's prompting.

At half past eleven one night in early February, a baker's appren-
tice, returning from work, was about to pass the Church of Saint-Luke,
which almost abuts Marine-Terrace, when all of a sudden he saw at
the end of the street the motionless figure of a woman so engulfed in
flames that she appeared to be all white.

Adèle writes in her diary:

> Terrified, the worker didn't dare go forward and didn't dare go
> backward. To advance would have been an affront to the appari-
> tion; to back up would have been to provoke it to follow him. But
> since staying in the same place was out of the question, he made a
> strenuous effort. The worker finally took the chance of continuing
> on his way, and running, flying, losing his head, eyes shut tight,
> hairs on his head bristling, insane with terror, he raced by in front
> of the ghost.[7]

When Victor Hugo heard the story the next day, he smiled know-
ingly. For some time now these phenomena on Jersey Island had been
no stranger to him. He told Adèle: "At night my room fills up with
strange noises; there are knocks on my wall; papers stir; inexplicable
noises can be heard." He was intrigued that the Lady in White had
made herself so visible. "Since they [the spirits] can talk to us," he
mused, "maybe they can show themselves. . . . They can make us hear;
perhaps they can make us see. A being in black would frighten me to a
certain extent. A being in white, perhaps less."[8]

Whatever Hugo's desires, it seemed that a chain of supernatural
events had been set irresistibly in motion. Adèle tells us in her diary
that on the night of February 22, 1854 (Victor Hugo gives February
21 or February 23 as the dates),

my father got home at eleven o'clock at night. He passed in front of the first-floor drawing room whose windows give onto the street. He noticed that the windows were in darkness. At two o'clock in the morning my brothers came home and saw that the windows were sparkling as if splendidly illuminated by a huge fire or thirty lighted candles. They stood there in astonishment; in order to get to the bottom of the matter they wanted to open up the drawing room, but it was double-locked. François-Victor was more tired than intrigued; he went to bed. Charles, more tenacious, [came and] asked [me] for the key; I didn't have it. He looked around the house but couldn't find it. Then, for the sake of peace and quiet—and finding he was all alone—he went to bed with the kind of terror that the bravest of men will understand.[9]

Victor Hugo continues, in a note preserved in the transcripts: "At dawn the next morning the maid, who had the key, unlocked the drawing room door. The candlesticks weren't there, which meant that it couldn't have been the Hugos' candles that had filled the drawing room windows with light; and besides, nobody had lit a fire in that room the night before."[10]

At daybreak of the same day—at almost the same moment as the maid unlocked the drawing room door at Marine-Terrace—a passerby was chased down nearby Dyke Road by a woman dressed entirely in white. The terrified passerby made inquiries of the townspeople—he was a stranger to these parts—and was told he had been pursued by the centuries-old ghost called the Lady in White who haunted the fields (and homes) of Jersey.[11]

This incident of the blazing drawing room windows, plus the incident of the passerby's being pursued by a wholly white ghost, were enough to prompt Victor Hugo to call a family séance for half past one that afternoon (it was February 22). Charles and Mme Hugo sat at the table, while Victor Hugo transcribed. François-Victor was also there.

Hugo asked the tables if anyone knew what it was that his sons had witnessed the night before. A spirit, on condition of anonymity, tapped out: *Yes.* Hugo inquired if the phenomenon had been natural or supernatural. The entity tapped out: *Night beauty.* Nobody knew what that meant, and the table became silent. "Is that all?" asked Victor Hugo. *Yes,* the table rapped. François-Victor took Charles's place and asked the table to elaborate. Whoever was there responded with a nonsensical string of words: *(Faith), goddess, doubt priest man altar temple night.*

That was the end of the séance.[12]

⚛

There was now a sort of hiatus in the paranormal activity around Marine-Terrace—although the proscrit Théophile Guérin, returning home from Saint Helier at midnight one night in March and passing by Marine-Terrace, heard a piercing scream that made his heart sink. He had heard exactly the same scream, at exactly the same place, exactly one month before.[13]

On or about March 23, 1854 (again, the exact date is not clear), there was a renewed flurry of activity. Adèle writes: "Last night Charles happened to make the table speak. He asked for the name of the spirit who was there. The spirit said that its name was 'the Lady in White.'"[14]

In fact, this was a full-fledged séance. It had begun at nine in the evening. Victor Hugo, Mme Hugo, and Auguste Vacquerie were present, along with Charles.

Victor Hugo asked: "Is anyone there?"

The table tapped twice: *No.*

"No?" exclaimed Hugo. "Who is it that's replying 'No?'"

The table tapped twice: *No* again.

Victor Hugo protested, "But mustn't there be somebody there, since somebody is saying 'No?' Can you say who you are?"

Again the answer was, *No.*

"Is something bothering you?" asked Hugo.

Yes, replied the table.

"What is it?" asked the poet.

For an answer, the table tapped out in Latin: *Domus vestra. Si vis mecum loqui, veni in viam.* [Your house. If you want to talk to me, come out in the road.]

Auguste Vacquerie suddenly asked: "Are you the Lady in White who, we are told, has been seen near our house?"

Yes.

"If we went out into the street, would we see you?"

Yes.

"Tonight?"

Yes.

"At what time?"

Three o'clock.

"Would we be able to see you if several of us went at once?"

No.

"So we have to be alone?"

Yes.

"Do you love us?" asked Mme Hugo. "Are you sympathetic to our concerns?"

Yes, replied the shade.

"So you don't want to speak to us here in the house?" said Vacquerie.

No.

Having set up a rendezvous for three o'clock that morning, the Lady in White vanished suddenly, to be replaced by the shade of Molière. The conversation now had to do with the dead playwright's comedy *The Learned Ladies.* The séance ended early, largely because François-Victor had a wholly mortal rendezvous in Saint Helier.[15]

No one was anxious to go out in the street at three o'clock that morning. Adèle writes in her diary that when the séance was over "all the inhabitants of Marine-Terrace prudently withdrew to their bedrooms, preferring a warm bed to an icy road, even if the icy road was to be ornamented with a ghost. We all slept the sleep of the exile."[16]

But something remarkable did take place in the middle of the night, and at 3:00 a.m. at that. Here is the story, told in Victor Hugo's own words and preserved in the transcripts.

I went up to bed at 11:30 p.m. I was worried and a little sad; besides, I was preoccupied and a bit on edge because of something I was working on at the time [the poem *The End of Satan*].

I slept badly. Toward 1:00 a.m., I heard François-Victor come in. Charles went down to open the front door for him. Victor, Charles, and my wife chatted in the kitchen for a brief moment. Immediately afterward, they went up to their rooms. I heard my two sons, who sleep in the two rooms adjoining mine, come upstairs.

Everything was silent. The house fell asleep. I was half dozing. In the midst of my drowsiness I had that very sharp perception of surrounding objects that sometimes comes to you when you are almost but not entirely asleep.

I had been in this state for a fairly long time when the ringing of a bell abruptly aroused me to full wakefulness. In the deep calm of the night, the doorbell was ringing in the clearest and most distinct fashion. I raised myself up on my pillow. I listened. The world had fallen silent again, and nothing was moving in the house. I thought: "Nobody in the house is outside. It wasn't somebody from the house who rang. Might it, by any chance, be 3:00 a.m. now?"

I wrestled with this idea for a moment. I was averse to getting up on account of the cold. But I said to myself: "It's odd that the bell should be ringing, and it would be strange indeed if it were 3:00 a.m. now." I threw myself out of bed—and I ought to add, seeing as I'm telling the whole story anyway, that I moved cautiously, as if someone else were in the room.

The shutters of my window weren't closed, the night wasn't particularly dark, and it wasn't at all dark in my room. I took the box of matches that was on my table and struck several matches in a row against the wall; the fourth lit, and from it I lit my candle. I looked at my watch, which hung from the back of the chair close to the head of my bed: The hands said 3:05 a.m. It had been about five minutes since I had been awakened by the ringing of the bell.

I put out my candle. I peered outside to see if I could see anything. The sea was calm, the night pale, the terrace deserted. I went back to bed. As I was getting into bed, I saw the phosphorescence of the matches tracing a luminous trail on the wall between the two windows; I said to myself, "What if that were about to take the form of a ghost!" The trail vanished.

The next morning, I told the story at breakfast. No one except me had heard the doorbell ring. They'd all been fast asleep at the time. We resolved to ask the table about it this evening. I said that if the table invited us there again [out in the street, in the middle of the night], I would go. Auguste said, "I'd be very scared, but I'd go too, on the sole condition that people kept me company in the house right up until it was time [to go]." You had to go alone.

Here Victor Hugo's account ends. Glued to the piece of paper on which these notes were written was an envelope containing four matches. Hugo had written on the envelope, "In this envelope are the four matches I used on the night of March 23–24, 1854."[17] The four burned-out matches are still preserved with the originals of the transcripts.

Far more may have happened to Victor Hugo that night than he lets on. And more may have been happening to him in the preceding weeks and months. In the early part of 1854, Hugo wrote three poems apparently inspired by a ghostly Lady in White. They are *A celle qui est voilée* (To She Who Is Veiled), end of January, 1854; *Horror*, March 30, 1854; and *Dolor* (Latin for "grief"), March 31, 1854. The epigraph that begins this chapter is the first two stanzas of *Horror*;[18] all three poems appeared in *Les Contemplations*, published in 1856.

Maurice Levaillant wonders if, contrary to what Victor Hugo writes in his note, the traces of phosphorescence on the wall did not fade out immediately but lingered for an unusually long time—long enough for Hugo to see the face of the Lady in White beginning to take shape on the wall between the windows.[19] Hugo later told Adèle that during that night he had felt (he would feel it many times again) a "sacred horror," which he described to her as what "ancient man believed he felt at the approach of the gods," and which horror, making his hair bristle and his skin crawl, evoked in his heart respectful, reverent fear or outright terror.[20]

The fact is that when Hugo told the story at breakfast time the next morning he was upset and trembling, still obsessed by what had happened.[21] He decided the family should consult the tables that evening. So it was that a séance took place on March 24, 1854, beginning at nine o'clock. Mme Hugo, Mlle Hugo, Victor Hugo, and Auguste Vacquerie were present, while Charles Hugo and Théophile Guérin sat at the table.

It wasn't a fruitful séance. The Greek lyric poet Anacreon (570–478 B.C.) appeared. Hugo pressed him about the Lady in White. He was not forthcoming. All of a sudden the séance was over, almost as soon as it had begun.[22]

At this point, the chronology of events surrounding the Lady in White becomes unclear; several of the transcripts have been lost. We do know that, a month or two later, she manifested through the tables, drew a quick portrait of herself using the table with the pencil leg, and then, without a word, took her leave of the participants. Several days later Victor Hugo was attending the burial of one of the proscrits when, happening to glance into the open grave, he thought he saw for a moment the Lady in White lying at the bottom. The face was that of her self-portrait, and the supine figure (which faded away in an instant) seemed to exude a certain soft luminosity.[23]

It seems that around this time Hugo also had a semi-hallucinatory waking encounter with the Lady in White. This happened while he was strolling on the Azette beach one night. He felt her palpable presence; he sensed that she was imploring him to write a few lines of poetry to her memory. This encounter (and perhaps others like it) may have taken place earlier, in February or January of that year. They seem to have been a precipitating factor in the writing of the three poems in which a shrouded lady makes a ghostly appearance.

Maybe all of these encounters helped to break the ice. The Lady in White appeared at the tapping tables at the séance of Monday, June 19, 1854, and stayed to talk at length. Present were Victor Hugo, Mme Hugo, Auguste Vacquerie, and Hennett de Kesler.

The séance began with a comical flirtation between the Lady in White and Kesler, a shy, hunchbacked, and lonely bachelor-proscrit. The shade arranged a rendezvous with the exile on the Azette beach for the next day. In so doing, she let slip a mysterious statement: *There are times when my stone closes in upon itself.*

Victor Hugo pounced on these words and asked her if that stone was the menhir that the islanders called the Rock of Fairies. Also, he wanted to know what that name meant. What *was* the Rock of Fairies?

She replied: *It is my rock.*

"Can you be seen every night at Rocquebert?" Hugo pursued.

Yes.

"Do you live alone in your rock?"

No.

"Who lives there with you?"

My remorse. He is a black dwarf who beats me every time I come in.

"How can we lessen your suffering?" Mme Hugo asked.

Pray.

"Can you tell us what crime you have committed?" asked Victor Hugo. Everyone had been assuming that the Lady in White was condemned to wander as a ghost for a very long time on account of the crime she had committed, which was—she now confirmed to the séance attendees—having been *the first mother on the island to kill her baby.*

"Has your punishment been going on for long?" asked Hugo. "How much longer must it go on?"

Until the sea comes up to my rock.

"You haven't told us how long you have been subject to this harsh punishment."

Three thousand years.

"Three thousand years of suffering, for the crime of a moment?" exclaimed Auguste Vacquerie. "The justice meted out by human beings is not as harsh as this!"

That is not so. The harshness of a sentence is not measured by how long it lasts, but by whether it is a life sentence. Human law sentencing someone to forced labor for life is a thousand times more harsh than divine law sentencing someone to three thousand years of the expiation of a sin followed by an eternity of forgiveness.

Victor Hugo suddenly found himself flirting with the Lady in White. "You have said you had affectionate feelings for me. You've said *basia mille* ["a thousand kisses"]. Why do you love me?"

Because you love your children and your children love you.

But Auguste Vacquerie was in a serious mood: "You're right," he told the Lady in White, "when you say that the harshness of a sentence doesn't lie in its duration but rather in whether the sentence is for life. But surely this depends on whether the person who is being punished knows that his sentence will end. Do the imprisoned souls of entities like animals, plants, and pebbles know that their suffering will end? Do they know when?"

They know they are not condemned for life. They don't know when their sentence will end. But to know with absolute certainty that your sentence will end one day, though you don't know which day, is the equivalent of being certain that your sentence will end soon. It's the certainty that is the reality.

Vacquerie pursued: "We humans, who are also punished beings, entertain the hope, though we don't have the certainty, that our sentence will come to an end. The only thing we're sure of is life; if, in dying, we are annihilated, we will have been condemned for life.

There is no certainty of resurrection; life itself is a life sentence."

You know very well that you are not condemned for life.

Vacquerie declared, "I know it for myself, because I personally believe in a future life. But it's a condemnation for life for those who believe only in this world, since for them there is nothing after life on earth."

Even those men are certain in their hearts that they will be freed.

"Freed into nothingness! Those whom men condemn for life are also certain to be delivered—by death! There is no difference."

Yes, there is. Man metes out a life sentence, which means that human punishment would go on eternally if death did not intervene. The law decrees punishment and does not decree the end of punishment, whereas, even for those of whom you speak, the sense of being under sentence is accompanied by the certainty of deliverance.

Hennett de Kesler intervened to talk with the Lady in White about their upcoming rendezvous. It had been planned for the beach in front of his house—but now he told the spirit that "if it meant a softening of your fate, I would certainly go and see you on your rock. Would you like me to come to your rock?"

The Lady in White replied: *The owner of the field where my rock sits would fill you full of buckshot if you did.*

Kesler's reply is not recorded, but Mme Hugo asked the Lady, "Will the time come when you will be reunited with your child in the other world?"

I'm certainly counting on it.[24]

And with this, the séance ended.

What did the Lady in White mean by her enigmatic remark that *there are times when my stone closes in upon itself*? Adèle Hugo, in her diary entry for June 24, 1854, records her father's explanation. Hugo had said, after the séance was ended,

> This séance of the table has been very curious. For me, it confirms in my mind certain ideas I have about the phenomenon of dreams. When sleep overtakes the body, the soul flies off to that unknown realm inhabited by the souls of both the dead and the living who are asleep. So, in your dreams, you frequently see the faces of those you love.
>
> During the day, the dolmen is the prison of the soul of the Lady

in Gray. During the night the Lady in Gray* dreams she is in the drawing room of Marine-Terrace. The d[olmen] in which the Lady in White is shut up during the day lets her emerge in her dreams at night, and when she wakes up it seems to her she has knocked on the door of Marine-Terrace.[25]

Did Hennett de Kesler keep his date with the Lady in White? It's not on record.

We don't meet the Lady in White again until Thursday, March 1, 1855, almost nine months later. She seemed a different lady now: far more philosophical in attitude and far more eloquent in speech. The séance began at ten o'clock in the evening, and the participants included Augustine Allix and Jules Allix, the young Adèle Hugo, and Victor Hugo. M. Hugo and Charles were at the table.

Commonplaces were exchanged. Then the three-thousand-year-old ghost launched into a discourse on her fate:

The mountain[†] is my tomb; I am its soul; I am a being God talks about only under his breath; I ascend and I descend; I desire heaven and earth desires me; stars pull me by my hair and coffin nails hold me by my feet. The darkness cries out, "Down with you!" and the suns tell me, "Stand up!" I am twilight's martyr; I fear the setting sun, I fear the night, darkness is my assassin; I am the inconsolable one of the obscure darkness; I weep and the stars extinguish my tears; I weep as I hide behind the mask of day; I weep in the depths of God's infinities; I weep inside the huge grim keg pierced full of stars by the Danaides of infinity.[‡]

Hugo asked: "Are you the same person who came to me on the beach in front of my house one night and asked me for lines of poetry?"

---

*In this diary entry, Adèle (or perhaps it's her father) seems to be mixing up the Lady in Gray with the Lady in White. We'll recall, from the beginning of this chapter, that there are three lady ghosts on the island: the Lady in White, the Lady in Gray, and the Lady in Black. Whatever the source of the confusion, the analysis Victor Hugo applies to the Lady in White is equally true for the other two ghosts.

†This may be a reference to the slope on which the Lady in White's menhir sat.

‡Danaus was a mythical king of Egypt who had fifty daughters: the Danaides. When the daughters married, Danaus ordered them to murder their husbands on their wedding night. Only one refused. The forty-nine other daughters were punished in Hades by being forced to carry water in a jug to fill a bath and wash off their sins, but the jugs were actually sieves, so the water always leaked out.

I am always she. I am the inconsolable one of the horizon. I am she who at nighttime watches myriad tombs clear away eyes in empty skulls, I am the one who comes to bad dreams to chatter; I am one of the bristling hairs of horror; I am the most terrible of all since I am both the white hair and the hair that tells the truth.

"When I saw you on the mountain those days, did you come by chance or specifically to see me?"

For your fine eyes—that is, for your eyes filled with goodness.

"It seems to me that since winter you no longer come to the beach; you come to the plain instead. Do you have any reason for that?"

I am everywhere, but I am seen in the north only at certain hours and in the south only at certain hours; I rise and I go to bed; souls have their laws just as stars do; they act like planets; there are fixed souls, there are vagabond souls, there are nebulae souls, there are Pleiades souls; there is the satellite soul and the sun soul, and there is the asteroid soul and the world soul. Heaven has two aspects: suns and souls, night and death, radiance and resurrection. The sepulcher is a sunrise hidden by God; day is a sunrise revealed by God. Half the night is given wings by eternity; the other half is given wings by infinity.

Victor Hugo exclaimed to the other attendees, "I wrote lines like this: "'Infinity!' said the being," "'Eternity!' said the soul." He asked the Lady in White: "If at this moment I were on the plain or on the sandbar, would I be able to perceive you?"

Don't ask me such questions.

"Where have you learned these fine phrases?" asked Mme Hugo. "And why, seeing as all they do is inspire fear?"

The worst pain of all is the pain of sacred horror. To weep and inspire fear: there's a punishment, because ordinarily sorrow attracts love and tears bring smiles. Alas! My tears are storms, and I am a hurricane driven to desperation because I cannot hold anyone in my arms.

"You asked me to pray for you," said Victor Hugo. "Do you know that I do every night? Do you receive these prayers? Do they lighten your burden?"

I am not the only one who suffers. Pray for us all. If you wish to lighten my burden, forget all about me. Praying solely for one person brings affliction to that person. The only effective prayers are those we sow to the wind every time we pass a grave.

"In fact, it's my rule to pray for everyone, and that is what I do. You ought to know that. But is there any harm in mixing your name with several others in a universal prayer?"

Yes, there is harm in it for my name. I am not known to you. I am not one of your dear departed ones. I am a symbol rather than a being; I am the phantom of an entire crowd; I am the ghost of a crime rather than a criminal. I am not an entity; my name is Infanticide; I am the mother of all murdered infants; I am numberless and invisible; I am the formidable funeral shroud sewn in the grave from the bloodied swaddling clothes of every cradle.

"You said you live at le Roquebert. But I've seen you on the mountain or on the dolmen that the Jerseymen call the Lady in White. At which place do you really live?"

I have several dwelling places; I am part of popular legend; thus have I left my traces in the human imagination. As for the rest, one last word: One night you wanted to go to a light that shone on the sandbar, believing that it was the Lady in White, and you found a fisherman's lantern instead. Well! If you'd gone to the light that shone on the hill instead, you would have found a smuggler's signal. Here is the explanation in one line: There are two souls in the two candles that cast their light upon you.

The table stopped dead. Hugo asked anxiously, "Are you still there?"

The table shook and tapped twice: *No.*

"Who's there?"

Pure yes m pure.

"You who are there, have you anything to tell us? Can you explain yourself further?"

There was no reply.

"Do you want us to ask you questions?"

The table shook a great deal but there was no reply. Charles was exhausted. They ended the session. It was one o'clock in the morning.[26]

Victor Hugo never heard from the Lady in White again. But there is a kind of sequel to her presence in the Hugo household at Marine-Terrace. In October–November 1855 the family moved to Guernsey Island. Now and then over the next year, strange noises manifested in Victor Hugo's new bedroom. They culminated in the following experience on the night of December 6, 1856; Victor Hugo described the experience in his private notebook.

My daughter Adèle went to bed gravely ill; her mother moved an armchair to the foot of her bed to spend the night with her. I went to bed worried. I prayed ardently, or at least as ardently as I could. I commended the soul of the sister to the sister [Léopoldine]; then I fell asleep. I live in the lookout right on top of the house; it's a kind of cell overlooking the sea, separated by only a partition from the room where the two chambermaids, Constance and Marguerite, sleep.

I awoke in the middle of the night and let my mind wander sadly over events while I prayed. I had been doing this in the universal silence around me (calm weather, no wind, no sound of the sea) for several minutes when I heard singing very near me; it seemed to be coming from the neighboring room. I listened; it was the singing of a human voice: soft, light, vague, weak, airy. I thought one of the maids had awakened and was singing, but there was something amazing, something unearthly, about the softness of this voice, which made me dismiss that idea. I wondered if it was from the depths of her sleep or while she was dreaming that one of the maids was singing in this way, but the melody the voice sang—wordless, unarticulated—had a continuous rhythm, followed along perfectly, was all of a piece, in a way that was absolutely incompatible with the disjointed nature of sleep and dreaming. While I was thinking this, I concluded that I must be dreaming myself; I confusedly felt the melody floating into my ear as I fell sleep again.

A space of time—it couldn't have been long—went by. I awoke. This time it was the singing that awoke me, still being sung as if through the partition. It was even more distinct than the first time, very clearly defined, at once melancholy and charming; I was sorry I wasn't a musician and couldn't take it down. It was like the murmuring music of Titania [in Shakespeare's *A Midsummer Night's Dream*] must have sounded.

In the morning I asked the chambermaids which one had been singing. They'd both slept through the night without waking up, and my question astonished them.

I went down to find out what kind of night my daughter had had.

Her affliction had worsened; neither she nor her mother had slept the entire night.

Myself, I wouldn't have said anything about what I'd heard; but suddenly my wife, in the midst of details about my daughter's fever, said to me, "Something worries me; last night, toward midnight, I heard singing in the chimney. Our daughter wasn't sleeping. I asked her if she heard it. She told me, 'Yes, but I didn't mention it because I was afraid you might think I was delirious.'"

I asked my wife: "What did the singing sound like?" She replied: "It was very weak, very soft, exquisite—it was like the cricket and the nightingale combined." My daughter, who was listening, corrected my description: "No, it wasn't the cry of an insect or the song of a bird. It sounded like a tiny human voice."

Then my wife told me that our daughter had been a little frightened by it, and so she had told her: "'Don't be afraid of anything; it's the singing of the cricket, that tiny nightingale of the hearth."

The singing had gone on without interruption for over four hours; my wife and daughter had heard it continuously. It had ceased toward five o'clock in the morning.

The singing was too weak, they both told me, to be heard anywhere but in their room. What had awakened me was also too weak to be heard even on the floor below me. I live just under the roof; there are two fairly high stories between the ladies' apartment and mine; their apartment is in front, mine is in back. Besides, the voice couldn't have come to me by way of the chimney, since there's no chimney in my room or even on this top floor. I should add that I heard the singing on my right, and the chimney's outlet is at the far end of the roof, on my left.[27]

Who had the visitor been this time?

Seventeen

THE LION OF ANDROCLES

[In the Circus Maximus in ancient Rome,] the slave of
an ex-consul had been brought in along with several
others who had been provided to fight the wild beasts.
The slave was called Androcles. When that lion saw him
in the distance, he suddenly stopped, as if in amazement,
and then gradually and calmly approached the man,
as if he recognized him. Then he gently and soothingly
wagged his tail in the way fawning dogs do, and came
close to the man, and gently licked the legs and hands of
the man who was almost paralysed with fear. Through
those caresses of such a savage beast, Androcles regained
his senses which had been paralysed, and gradually
turned back to look at the lion. Then, as if recognizing
each other, you might have seen the lion and the man
happy and demonstrating their joy.

AULUS GELLIUS, "ANDROCLES AND THE LION"
(*NOCTES ATTICAE V. 14*)

Animals rubbing shoulders with humans has been the stuff of myth and legend ever since man first sat at the campfire to tell stories. The relationship between men and lions occupies a prominent place among these stories. Just such a tale had often been told prior to the sixth century B.C. when, in ancient Greece, Aesop made it one of his *Fables* (though whether Aesop used this story is disputed). A century after the advent of Christianity, Roman author and encyclopedist Aulus Gellius (A.D. 130–180) recast the story in his *Attic Nights*

197

(*Noctes Atticae*), naming the slave Androcles and turning him into a Christian.

In Gellius's story, when the lion doesn't devour Androcles but embraces him, the emperor of Rome frees the slave and gives him the lion as a pet. How was it that the lion and Androcles joyously recognized each other in the arena? The reason is the same in every version of the story: a slave fleeing from his abusive master hides in a cave that turns out to be a lion's lair. But the lion, upon entering, doesn't attack the slave. Instead, it shows him its paw, which is covered with blood and causing the lion great pain. The slave sees there is a thorn embedded in the lion's paw and removes it. The grateful lion allows him to stay in its cave and then leave freely. The slave is recaptured by his master and thrown into an arena where animals killed captives for sport (arenas of this sort could be found everywhere throughout antiquity). Then—in every version—the story ends essentially as described above.

After Gellius, the story of Androcles and the lion appeared in a number of other versions, including as one of the *Gesta Romanorum* ("Deeds of the Romans") put together in A.D. 1330, and in a play by George Bernard Shaw, *Androcles and the Lion,* first produced in 1913.

None of these storytellers could ever have imagined, and many among them—especially the atheist George Bernard Shaw—would have dismissed in a moment the sudden emergence of the Lion of Androcles through the tapping tables at the Jersey Island séances in 1854.

Victor Hugo had the Lion of Androcles in mind when he told his daughter Adèle, who recorded his words in her diary entry for August 22, 1854.

> I believe in the soul of animals, but let's agree on what we mean by the word "soul." When I say the soul of inorganic matter, I believe that the soul, shut in, buried, is completely passive. When I say the soul of animals, I still believe that the soul, not as shut in, not as buried as is the case with inorganic matter, is still however three-quarters passive, and allows only instinct to pierce through. Thus the soul of the beast only participates in a confused way in the acts of the beast.
>
> However, I believe that at the farthest extreme the instinct of the beast is permitted to arrive at so perfected a state that that instinct

can lead it to perform a sublime act. We have striking examples of this in the Lion of Androcles and in the Lion of Florence. Thus the beast, rewarded for its sublime action, passes from the animal state to the state of an archangel.

Man himself, who is also a creature made of inorganic matter, is only half-responsible for his actions. His freedom is only relative.

The condition of animals is one hundred times more painful than ours; their souls are in the horrible position that Paganini's soul would be if it were shut up in a tower, walled in, blinded, deaf, having as its only implement a violinist's bow. Whatever might be the genius of Paganini, that genius would necessarily remain unknown.[1]

Thus was the Lion of Androcles to acquire a whole new dimension of metempsychosical meaning once he had appeared at the tapping tables. But this wasn't as yet apparent when, on January 6, 1854, at the end of the final séance with André Chénier, the lion first came unexpectedly bounding into the séance taking place at Marine-Terrace.

Auguste Vacquerie, who was transcribing, and Mme and Charles Hugo, who were sitting at the tables, were the only ones present at the séance that evening. They listened with some puzzlement as the lion launched without preamble into a self-portrait:

Lions' manes are the hairpieces of sovereign brows. The lion is the poet of solitudes. The lion is up and about before sunrise. The lion forgives, the lion dreams. The lion is the roaring of the wind, the silence of the desert. My mane is the air's whip. My claw is might, my glance is goodness. My muzzle tears the tiger out of the desert and rends babies from their mothers. The lion had dominion over the tiger. In the Roman circus, he bestowed the graces that Nero refused to bestow: he spared Androcles, he saved Daniel, he grew as still as God Himself, and he kissed the foot of that which is the ideal. The lion is the power that makes men great and the mercy that makes men good. I am that lion. I salute you.[2]

Then he was gone, after promising to return the next Tuesday, January 10, at nine o'clock in the evening.

But it was the séance participants themselves who failed to show up. Maybe that was why, when the lion abruptly reappeared at the tables on February 17 (in the middle of a poetry reading by Shakespeare!), he seemed heartily annoyed:

Good day, imbeciles.

"Who are you?" asked Vacquerie.

The Lion of Androcles.

Mme Hugo, François-Victor, and Charles Hugo were in attendance at the séance along with Auguste Vacquerie. The latter replied to the lion slightly sardonically: "Do you have any communication to impart to us aside from this friendly greeting?"

The lion answered: *Ask me questions in poetry, just as you did with Aeschylus and Molière.*

Aeschylus and Molière had been insisting the group ask them questions in verse, and so the séance participants always prepared their questions in verse. That was why Mme Hugo now said: "If we'd known you were coming, we'd have prepared verses. Improvised ones can only be unworthy of you."

This kick in the ass makes donkeys of you all. Farewell.

And then the lion was gone.[3]

This bizarre interchange provoked a lively discussion among the participants. What "kick in the ass" was the lion talking about? They begged the table for an explanation, but it was silent. At the next séance, on February 18, Vacquerie asked Aeschylus why the lion had acted as he had. Was it because they'd failed to show up for the rendezvous of January 10?

Aeschylus replied (in verse, of course):

> *This lion is enormous, and full of catastrophes,*
> *You were in the wrong, thinkers, to put him out of sorts.*
> *Victor Hugo will have to toss him several stanzas,*
> *So that, if he returns, he has some tasty bones to munch.*

Perhaps the lion hadn't taken offense, but Auguste Vacquerie had. Why, he asked Aeschylus, was he being snubbed? In all these sessions he had been carefully preparing his questions in verse. Wasn't his poetry good enough? Why couldn't *he*, not Victor Hugo, carry out this challenging task of writing a poem about the lion for the lion?

The shade of Aeschylus replied:

> *And so I will unsay it. Write lines for that lion*
> *You're the one I choose. Above all, make them fine.*

Why? Because this lion won't consent to eat his lunch
Until there's lots of marrow in the bones for him to crunch.

But, asked Vacquerie, what if Victor Hugo were more than willing to write the poem about the lion? Would Vacquerie still get the chance? Yes.[4]

It was not until March 23, while they were talking to Molière, that the Lion of Androcles came prancing back to the tables. Vacquerie, his lion poem carefully composed, began to read.

And then, abruptly, the lion was gone, as suddenly as he'd come.

A disgusted Auguste Vacquerie ended up having to make do with reading his poem to Molière![5]

Perhaps these rapid comings-and-goings of the lion weren't as arbitrary as they seemed. The very next night, the séance attendees realized the stage had been set for a dramatic confrontation between Victor Hugo and the Lion of Androcles.

Claudius Grillet writes in *Victor Hugo spirite:*

> From time to time, the tables and Hugo borrowed from each other. It was as if the tables read the poet's mind and responded to the preoccupations besieging him at that moment, while he in turn exploited the themes the tables presented to him and submitted himself to their literary influence.
>
> Of what I now wish to demonstrate, a lion shall be the witness. Guess who came through on March 24, 1854, in answer to the conjurers' calls? The Lion of Androcles! You should know that, a month earlier, on February 28, Victor Hugo had completed a long poem whose title was "To the Lion of Androcles." Thus this animal, before haunting the drawing room, had sojourned for some time in the poet's study at Marine-Terrace.[6]

At this séance of March 24, it emerged that Hugo, like Vacquerie, had responded to the lion's initial request to *Ask me questions in poetry, just like you did with Aeschylus and Molière.* Hugo had the completed poem in his pocket that very night. And, since Vacquerie had used up his lion poem reading it to Molière the night before, and hadn't even thought to bring it along tonight, the way was clear for Victor Hugo to read his poem to the lion without offending his friend.

And this he did, all ninety-six lines of it, from beginning to end.

For the first nine-tenths of "To the Lion of Androcles" (which would be published in September 1859 in the "Decadence of Rome" section of Hugo's long poem *Legends of the Ages*), the poet lashes out with graphic and scornful imagery at the decadence of ancient Rome.

> *Weak old man, pregnant woman, baby son,*
> *Livid-faced, fleeing, bloodstained, and aghast,*
> *Christian and captive, one and all, were cast*
> *To the wild animals in that terrifying*
> *Abyss, the circus—still alive, but dying.*

Then, when the poem has almost ended, the mood shifts suddenly. The Lion of Androcles appears. Hugo writes,

> *Then you, a lion born in desert air*
> *Where the sun is alone with God—your bed*
> *Being a cave which evening painted red—*
> *You came into the precincts steeped in crime.*

The lion gazes about the city. Then:

> *Your glance lit up, at one stroke, love and pity.*
> *Pensively over Rome you shook your mane.*
> *Humans were bestial—you were humane.*
> > SELECTED POEMS OF VICTOR HUGO:
> > A BILINGUAL EDITION.[7]*

Once Hugo had finished reading his poem on that evening of March 24, 1854, the Lion of Androcles—having deigned for the first time to linger at a séance—recited his own poem. The setting is the desert.

> *The desert was somber, arid, and impassable*
> *The sandy plains gave way to dunes.*

---

*Excerpt from *Selected Poems of Victor Hugo: A Bilingual Edition*, translated by E. H. Blackmore and A. M. Blackmore. © 2001 by The University of Chicago Press. Used by permission of The University of Chicago Press.

At the time when day is born,
Alone in these vast places where God
speaks and shows himself,
Like a king toward a king, I go to encounter
The sun which comes toward me.

We climb, both of us, in our superb haughtiness,
The slope, he gilding it and I trampling its grass.
We recognize each other.
I am proud to have him for host of my lair,
He is proud to see mingling on my belly
The hairs of my mane with his rays.

Thus lived I, alone, dreaming beneath my mane,
Conducting the sun in the sky to my den,
Majestically, mercifully,
Dreaded without anger and strong without
*   violence,*
And saying to the desert: judge if your silence
Be worthy of my roaring.

I opened my dazzled eyelid to the clear brightness,
I listened from time to time to the prophet Isaiah
Singing the praises of the God he served,
Because we are warriors in the selfsame army
Therefore responded we one to the other: I the lion, he
*   the angel,*
From the two ends of the desert.

Gentle goodness was the breath of my mouth.
I could have brought about calm in the wild hurricane
Tamer of surging floods.
I could have, in applying to it my marble will,
Under each one of my feet stronger than tree trunks
Held captive one of the four winds.

The desert was vast, impassable and somber,
I reigned luminous like a lighthouse in shadow,

> *There I lifted up my lofty brow,*
> *In the endless desert that begins again and again*
> *I was alone, alone on that immense beach*
> *Alone like a single and immense word.*[8]

It's easy for us to convince ourselves that this poem was written by Victor Hugo, and that, in some way that even he did not understand, it was transmitted unconsciously—telepathically—to the mediums sitting at the tapping table.

But Victor Hugo did not think so himself. When the poem that was unarguably his own—"To the Lion of Androcles"—was published in *Legends of the Ages* in 1859, he affixed to it the following note:

You will find in the volumes dictated to my son Charles by the tables a response by the Lion of Androcles to this poem. I mention this marginally. All I'm doing is affirming the existence of a strange phenomenon to which I was several times witness: the phenomenon of the ancient pedestal table. A three-legged table dictates poetry by means of raps, and stanzas appear out of nowhere. It goes without saying that never did I mix with my own lines a single line emanating from this mysterious source, nor with my own ideas a single one of its ideas. I always left them religiously with the Unknown, who was their unique author. I do not admit to there even being a reflection of them in my own work. I pushed them aside even to the extent of not allowing them to influence me in any way.

The work of the human brain must remain apart from, must never borrow from, such phenomena. External manifestations of the invisible are a fact, and the internal creations of thought are another; the wall that separates the two must be maintained in the interests of observation and science. We must make no breach in this wall; to borrow something [from this other world] would be to make such a breach. Science too, in its own way, religiously and properly defends its right not to be breached by the Unknown. It is then, I repeat, as much by religious conscience as by literary conscience—it is out of a respect for the phenomenon itself—that I isolate myself from it, making it a rule to accept no admixtures to my inspiration and wanting to keep my work, such as it is, absolutely personal and my own.[9]

In *Victor Hugo spirite*, Claudius Grillet cites several instances where, over the next few weeks, the Lion of Androcles recited lines that were almost exactly like lines written by Hugo ten days, two years, or an even longer period of time before. He draws particular attention to the séance of April 25, 1854, when there took place the simultaneous creation of poetry of a high order by a presumed discarnate-entity poet on the one hand, and a real-life great poet on the other—a poetry contest between a man and a spirit!

Grillet says,

> We are no longer talking about mutual borrowings that presuppose that one work was written before the other. We are talking about simultaneous creation. [During the séances,] . . . the Lion is improvising. That sort of an effort can't be sustained without causing a certain fatigue. Bear in mind, too, that the dictation of his lengthy poems has not been accomplished at a single stretch [; it has been spaced out over more than one séance] and betrays a certain hesitation at times.
>
> It so happens that, on the evening of April 25, in the course of a superb improvisation, the Lion hesitated. The table stopped tapping. The Lion had been in the middle of railing against tamed lions who, not content to accept being slaves, consent to become accomplices to human despicableness and the executioners of martyrs in the Roman arena.

Grillet, who is writing in 1929 and has the transcripts of the séances in front of him, then quotes this "superb improvisation," up to the point where the lion abruptly stopped dictating.

> *And, monsters fed on massacre and shame*
> *Tame giants on whom oppobrium is heaped,*
> *Heartless and mindless,*
> *They raise against the saints their sacrilegious paw*
> *And bury their blood-stained claws in the liv—.*

Claudius Grillet continues, "The underlining of the last two lines is my own. Those two lines do not satisfy the tapping spirit. He [abruptly stops dictating through the tables and, after rethinking these two lines,] is going to rewrite them, thereby completing the stanza.

"During the interruption which lasted several minutes, Hugo for his part got down to work, and then and there wrote the following three lines, [completing the lion's stanza himself and] showing the lines to no one but Auguste Vacquerie:

> *They ripped open the saints dying in the mire,*
> *And their hideous claws enlarged the wound*
> *In the side of Jesus Christ.*

"Almost immediately [after Hugo had finished writing these lines], the table began to move again, and the Lion of Androcles completed the stanza in the following way—in almost the same way as Hugo:

> *Their paws ripped open the martyrs here and there in the*
>   *mire,*
> *And Jesus Christ slipped their claws into his wounds,*
> *For a gift of nails to the gibbet.*"

The revised final lines of the stanza, which the Lion of Androcles has now dictated through the tables, bear an extremely close resemblance to the final lines of the same stanza that Victor Hugo has written just a few minutes before, when the tables were silent as the lion considered how he himself could best rewrite these lines. Claudius Grillet finds this surprising; it is why he is bothering to tell us about this poetry contest. The point is that *nobody else in the room but Victor Hugo and Auguste Vacquerie knew what lines Victor Hugo had written.* Let's assume, to simplify matters a little, that what a tapping table taps out is something that comes through the mind of the medium(s). That evening, Victor Hugo and Auguste Vacquerie were not the mediums; they were not the two who were sitting with their hands on the little pedestal table. That function was reserved for Charles Hugo and Théophile Guérin.

Grillet's question is this: If Charles Hugo and Théophile Guérin didn't know what words Victor Hugo used to complete the Lion of Androcles' stanza, how did the tapping tables know? Grillet is not saying that this is proof that the Lion of Androcles and an afterworld exist; he is merely bringing our attention to this puzzling phenomenon, which (he goes on to say) suggests that Victor Hugo had a powerful influence over the tapping tables, and the tapping tables over Hugo, of which the great poet was profoundly unaware.

Certainly the attendees at the séance were startled when the tables succeeded, a few minutes after Victor Hugo had written his lines, in reproducing them almost exactly. Grillet quotes Mme Adèle Hugo's reaction, as recorded in the transcripts for that night.

"Mme Hugo cried out to the Lion/table: 'Did you read my husband's lines before writing yours?'

"The reply was: *No.*"[10]

Shortly thereafter, the séance broke up. The attendees went their separate ways perhaps a little more silently thoughtful than usual.

That was the last that any of them would hear from the Lion of Andocles for some time, until Sunday night, August 6, 1854, when he reappeared just long enough to proclaim mysteriously and beautifully, in Latin:

Omen, Lumen, Numen Nomen Meus. ["Portent, Light, Numinous Divinity, Is My Name."][11]

(Victor Hugo included in *Les Contemplations, Poem VI, xxv* [1856] a ten-line poem in which God, in the final touch to the completion to his universe, sets in place the seven stars—the Septentrion—that spell out his name, Jehovah. The poem is called "Nomen, Numen, Lumen.")[12]

The quarrelsome if numinous spirit of the Lion of Androcles was paving the way for other, equally numinous events. These would include a visit from the Ocean, a visit from a Comet, and a voyage to the planet Mercury.

These visits would be somehow bound up with the ancient art of alchemy.

Eighteen
ASTRAL VOYAGE TO THE
PLANET MERCURY

From 1858 to 1870, François-Victor Hugo visited Great Britain at least thirteen times. The trips were annual; sometimes he was sightseeing, other times he was doing business on behalf of the political exiles in London.

Much of the time François-Victor was researching William Shakespeare, all of whose works he would translate into French and have published in France. Often he did his research at the British Museum in London, but it's likely he spent some time researching at the great libraries of Cambridge University.

If François-Victor spent much time at Cambridge, he may well have seen a curious manuscript page at the Babson College Library written in the hand of Sir Isaac Newton in 1686.

This page, which can still be seen today, lists the "twelve gods of the ancient people." The list is made up of the names of the seven known planets, the four elements, and the "quintessence," or "fifth" element (also known as the "chaos of elements"). These names are headings, and beneath each heading Newton inserted a member of Noah's family, an Egyptian god, a Roman god, an alchemical symbol, and one or more alchemical substances.[1]

The inventor of modern mathematics and physics was what we call a euhemerist: he believed that the gods of the ancient world were originally real humans around whom legends accumulated, resulting in those humans' attaining the status of gods. Priests honored these heroic humans along the way by naming planets after them. Thus the planet Saturn is named for Noah himself.

Why did Newton draw up this list of correspondences that included not only gods and heavenly bodies but also alchemical substances and symbols? Newton was the world's last great alchemist as well as its first great scientist; he saw a fundamental connection between, say, Mercury as a planet, Mercury as a god, mercury as a substance used in alchemy, and mercury as part of the symbolic language of alchemy. It's ironic that the true nature of this fundamental connection is lost to us today in part because of the great revolution in scientific thinking brought about by Newton himself.

If François-Victor gazed long and hard at this curious manuscript page of Sir Isaac Newton's, he might have recalled a tapping-table séance at Marine-Terrace that he did not attend himself but that was often discussed by the Hugo family and the exiles who frequented the séances. This was the séance of Wednesday, July 26, 1854, when the participants seemed to channel the words and drawings of the inhabitants of the planet Mercury. Mysteriously bound up with these words and drawings were the alchemical formulae underlying the metal mercury and the god Mercury himself.

In Europe in the mid-nineteenth century there was a great deal of interest in the idea of the plurality of inhabited worlds and what the inhabitants of those worlds might be like. France was at the forefront of that interest. In 1752, the great Enlightenment atheist Voltaire published *Micromégas,* the story of a twenty-mile-high, centuries-old inhabitant of a planet revolving around Sirius who travels through interstellar space using seven-million-league boots, balloons, a horse, and a comet. Eventually Micromégas, who has one thousand senses, arrives at our solar system and alights on the planet Saturn.

On Saturn he befriends a typical inhabitant of that planet, a dwarf only one mile high and with a mere seventy-two senses. The two extraterrestrials head off to Earth, stopping along the way only to confer with the "archbishops and inquisitors" of Jupiter. They skip the planet Mars; it's so small that Micromégas is afraid he won't find room to sleep.

But, in the words of Roger Pearson in *Voltaire Almighty,* "the 'globe of Earth' proves very difficult to make out. So small, and so bizarre. Having fished a microscopic whale out of the water and been unable to locate its soul, 'the two travellers were therefore inclined to think that there is no intelligent life in this abode of ours.'" The ETs manage to detect a scientific expedition in the Arctic, which leads them on to an assortment of philosophers, all of whom hold forth on their differing notions of "soul." Micromégas listens politely. Then, as Pearson summarizes it, "'he promised to write them a nice book of philosophy, in very small script just for them, and that in that book they would discover what was what.' Alas, when the book is opened at the Académie of Sciences in Paris, the pages are blank."[2] Micromégas, taking leave of Earth, has become a bit disgusted at how blindly full of ourselves we inconsequential humans are—certainly too much so to know the truth when we see it.

Voltaire's aim in *Micromégas* is philosophical: he is preaching the relative nature of all things and the need for total intellectual humility. But the great Enlightenment philosopher was also at the cutting-edge of scientific research—it was he who introduced the work of Sir Isaac Newton to the French—and *Micromégas* is full of sharply observed "new" science. This story, along with Voltaire's other presentations of the Newtonian universe, had a huge and continuing impact on the French. Victor Hugo loved *Micromégas,* and so did his son Charles, who retold the story in the preface to his novel *Le cochon de Saint-Antoine* (Saint Anthony's Pig), written on Guernsey Island and published in 1857.[3]

In 1781, Sir William Herschel discovered the planet Uranus—the first new planet to be discovered since antiquity. In 1846, the French astronomer Urbain Jean Joseph Leverrier pinpointed the location of Neptune (a discovery made almost simultaneously by the English astronomer John Couch Adams). By this time, astronomers had pushed beyond the boundaries of the solar system and were beginning to grasp the colossal dimensions of the universe (which Newton had suspected) and accept the possibility that it contained numberless planets with numberless species.

In 1862, Camille Flammarion—an astronomer/popularizer of science and proto-sci-fi novelist who would have been the mid-nineteenth-century-French equivalent of Carl Sagan if he hadn't also been a believer in the occult—published a book called *The Plurality of Worlds,* which became an instant classic. The highly precocious author was only twenty at the time, and the book, which was quickly translated into several languages, plunged the average European (and American) reader into a graphically imagined and scientifically sustained account of the possibilities of a universe full of worlds like our own. A copy of

Flammarion's book sat in Hugo's bookcase on Guernsey Island; many years later, the astronomer/investigator of psychic phenomena would contribute notes to *Chez Victor Hugo: Les tables tournantes de Jersey* (At Victor Hugo's: The Turning Tables of Jersey), edited by Gustave Simon, the first collection, published in 1923, of the Jersey Island séance transcripts.

As the table-tapping craze swept across France, Allan Kardec's spiritism had appropriated not only Spiritualism but also the more colorful aspects of the burgeoning new astronomy. The spiritists saw "astral forms" behind the physical cosmos described by Camille Flammarion. The spirits told Kardec that our sun, though "not a world inhabited by corporeal beings," was a meeting place for souls of a higher order "who, from thence, send out the radiations of their thoughts towards the other worlds of our solar system." Profiting from this energy were "souls of many persons well-known on this earth," who were "reincarnated in Jupiter, one of the worlds nearest to perfection."[4] Such statements were the beginning of a vast new "Spiritistic" astral astronomy; published in Kardec's *The Spirits' Book* in 1857, they had been anticipated by the spirits on Jersey Island.

Not only artists and intellectuals but scientists like Flammarion worked enthusiastically at being mediums. The author of *The Plurality of Worlds* wrote numerous books describing his research into psychic phenomena. In one such book he described a séance at which Victorien Sardou, the popular light dramatist of the day, used automatic writing to channel "queer pages concerning the inhabitants of the planet Jupiter, and produced picturesque and surprising drawings to depict things and beings in this gigantic world. One of those drawings showed us Mozart's house, others the mansions of Zoroaster and Bernard Palissy [the famed Renaissance designer of pottery], who are, it appears, neighbors on that planet."[5]

When we realize that Flammarion was a sort of credulous mid-nineteenth-century French equivalent of Carl Sagan, and Victorien Sardou its equivalent of New York playwright Neil Simon, we see how universal the interest in tapping tables was at the time and how acceptable was the belief that not only the spirits of the dead but the spirits of beings from other planets as well communicated with earthbound mortals through the tapping tables. So we should not be surprised to learn that the séance attendees at Marine-Terrace (and the occasional other venue) seem to have communicated with the souls of extraterrestrial beings on at least two occasions. The first was sometime between September 29 and December 6, 1853, when Victor Hugo had a close encounter with an inhabitant of Jupiter named Tyatafia. The exchange was brief, doleful, and heavily prompted by Hugo. It went like this:

"Who are you?"

Tyatafia.

"Is the word you just spoke from a language known to us?"

No.

"Is it the language of a people from this globe?"

No.

"So you're a being who inhabits a planet other than ours?"

Yes.

"Which one?"

Jupiter.

"Do the beings who inhabit Jupiter have a soul and a body? Are they composed of mind and matter like us?"

[No reply.]

"Are the inhabitants of Jupiter as advanced as us in metaphysics?"

No.

"So is Jupiter a planet less fortunate than ours?"

Yes.

"Depending on whether they behave badly or well, do human beings end up on ill-favored globes or happy planets after death?"

Yes.

"Is there physical and moral suffering on Jupiter as on our planet?"

Yes.

"Are there those among our group here who will end up on planets less fortunate than these [Earth and Jupiter]?"

[Reply not recorded.]

"So you know how we're going to spend the rest of our lives?"

Yes.[6]

Victor Hugo had long been fascinated by the idea of extraterrestrial intelligences. In a poem in *Les Contemplations* dated April 1839, he describes a very grim planet—Saturn.

> *Saturn: enormous sphere! Star of gloomy aspect!*
> *Convict prison in the sky! Prison glinting from its air-vents!*

World a prey to haze, to gusts, to darkness!
Hell made out of winter and of night . . .[7]

Over the years, Hugo would have much to say about the forms of interplanetary and interstellar life, sometimes conflating the visionary pronouncements of spirits such as Allan Kardec's with his own reasonably solid knowledge of physical-reality astronomy. On the night of July 26, 1854, all of that and more—as alchemy also played a role—seems to have come together in a rip-roaring kaleidoscopic tapping-table session that combined elements of sci-fi space opera, Steven Spielberg's *Close Encounters of the Third Kind,* and the search for the philosopher's stone.

Present at the séance, which began at 9:25 p.m., were Hennett de Kesler, Albert Pinson, Théophile Guérin, and Victor Hugo, with Charles and Mme Hugo sitting at the table. The session began with the participants' waiting half an hour for the Lion of Androcles to show up; he had promised he would reappear on this night. He didn't—though Victor Hugo tried to coax him by reading aloud some highly flattering poetry he'd written about lions. (See chapter 17, "The Lion of Androcles.")

All of a sudden, the table seemed to go slightly mad. It slid bumpily across the floor. It turned completely around while making loud cracking noises. Then it was still.

Victor Hugo asked the weirdly restless table if, seeing as it didn't want to speak, it would like to draw. Though there was no response, the participants placed the little pedestal table with the pencil leg on a sheet of paper and waited.

The pencil leg began to move.

Victor Hugo asked why the spirits were so silent that night and why the Lion of Androcles hadn't come?

The table leg sketched a clock with the hands set at ten o'clock at night. Hugo asked what this meant. The table drew a picture of a lion sitting by a door. (See drawing E on page 214.)

"Is it that our lion is annoyed?" asked Hugo.

The table drew a complicated sketch. It seemed to consist of an archangel enfolding within itself a head, a moon, three stars, and three planets. Another, smaller lion was trying to enter the body of the archangel.

What did all this mean? The séance attendees had an inkling. Some months earlier the shade of Aeschylus had told them that Molière and

WHAT THE TURNING TABLES DREW (II)

E. At 10 p.m., the Lion of Androcles is excluded from the realm of the archangel. The signature, "Flamel," appears in the upper left-hand corner

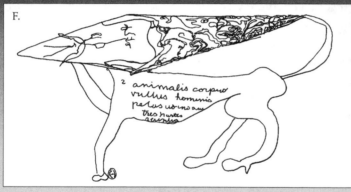

F. Interplanetary/ alchemical hieroglyphics

G. These depictions of the inhabitants of Mercury have their counterpart in alchemical formulae

Shakespeare, and Aeschylus too, lived on Jupiter, which, like the rest of the planets in the solar system, was under the control of Archangel Love; the subject of this drawing, perhaps, was Archangel Love. (Some time after Aeschylus's revelation, the Shadow of the Sepulcher told the group that the souls of Molière and Shakespeare had left Jupiter and were winging their way to Earth where they would be reborn as helpers of mankind. "They will be priests of an immense religion," the Shadow of the Sepulcher had declared.)

Hugo's notes on the July 26 séance have been preserved. He wrote, "From the looks of [this] . . . it would seem that the Shadow of the Sepulcher—of which it [the archangel] is undoubtedly the representation—governs the sun, our earth and the moon, the solar planets and the stars forming our galaxy. [The table] having explained that the lion has been called back, I repeated the question, 'Is the lion annoyed?'"

The pencil leg answered: *No.*

Hugo asked if the complicated figure was actually the Shadow of the Sepulcher.

The pencil, the tone of its vibration altering, wrote: *Forbidden.*

Hugo asked: "Who are you?"

The table replied: *Flamel.*

Everyone at the table knew who this had to be: the fifteenth-century French alchemist Nicholas Flamel, perhaps the most famous alchemist who had ever lived. Before they could say anything, however, Hugo asked the table if it would like to keep drawing pictures or just tap out words?

It responded: *Drawing.*

They sharpened the pencil leg, which had become quite dull, and placed a fresh sheet of paper under it. Hugo asked Nicholas Flamel to "draw what was on your mind when you came to us."

The table leg moved rapidly. Beneath the pencil there emerged a set of drawings, each stranger than the last. Latin phrases went into these sketches, making the drawings look almost hieroglyphic. The first drawing resembled the body of a four-legged animal. At one end of the body was the scowling face of a man with a mustache, and at the other end a tail. The head was bent so far back that the long conical cap it wore was almost parallel to the creature's back, the tip of the cap touching the tip of the tail. The head and conical cap together formed an extended quadrilateral shape, stretched out as if it were meant to be one-dimensional. (See drawing F on page 214.)

Whatever, asked a bewildered Victor Hugo, could this last drawing represent?

The table wrote four phrases in Latin inside the body of the creature: *Animales corpus; vultus homines; petasus insani; tres partes scientiae.*

Almost everyone at the table knew Latin well. They knew the first two phrases meant "body of an animal" and "expression—or countenance—of a man." The third phrase, however, was puzzling even to a Latin scholar: one meaning of *petasus* is "wide-brimmed hat," while *insani* can mean "wild" or even "insane." The fourth phrase, *tres partes scientiae,* meant "three parts of knowledge." Théophile Guérin, taking his cue perhaps from the revelation of the tables that the control spirit for the séance was alchemist Nicholas Flamel, immediately had a suggestion for the overall meaning of the words; he wondered if they referred to the alchemical term "the unique metal." Possibly Guérin surmised that the word *petasus* referred to the wide-brimmed hat of the god Mercury, and that this, combined with the word *insani,* added up to a reference to the volatile movement of the metal mercury. Mercury was a critical agent in the transmutation of base metals into gold; it was "the unique metal."

The table didn't reply to Guérin's question. Instead, it wrote: *Adjourned.*

Victor Hugo was not to be put off so easily. He asked the table, apparently basing his question on the words *animales corpus, vultus homines,* "Can you draw us a figure corresponding to man—half-matter and half-spirit, and inhabiting the world where you are now?"

Yes, the table answered.

The participants slipped a fresh piece of paper under the pencil leg.

The pencil drew a figure resembling the microscopic water animal known as the hydra. It drew six tiny sunlike objects, floating beside the figure and attached to it by tiny filaments. (See drawing G on page 214.)

"Draw us the dwelling place of this being," asked Hugo.

The pencil drew what looked like clouds around the figure.

"What world does this being inhabit?" asked Hugo.

The pencil wrote: *Mercury.*

Hugo asked for details. The pencil wrote, in Latin, beneath the drawing:

Sex habet lampadas, duos oculos semper apertos, caput enorme, sed levissimum, corpus longum, sed tenuissimum non manducat materiam, solidam, sed fluidam, non spirat, sed lucet, habet uxorem. [It has six torches/suns; two eyes which are always open; an enormous head, but very light; a long but very slender body; it doesn't eat solid material, but rather liquid; it doesn't breathe, but instead shines; it has a spouse.]

A spouse? Hugo asked the table to "draw the female of this being for us." The pencil sketched a second, smaller hydralike figure to the right of the first. Was Mercury a "world of reward," Hugo wanted to know? Was it a world reserved for reincarnated souls who had lived virtuously in a previous lifetime?

Yes, wrote the pencil.

"Draw us the actual shape [of an inhabitant of Mercury]," Hugo asked.

The table drew a sphere. Rays emanated from the sphere. There was a tail attached to it.

Victor Hugo asked if the Mercurians were subject to infirmities and illness like human beings?

They can lose their torches, the pencil leg replied, apparently referring to the six tiny floating globes attached to the bodies of the Mercurians.

"Do they grow old and die?" asked Hugo.

Yes.

"Draw one of their places of worship for us."

The table drew what looked like the interior of a plant. Several Mercurians were gathered inside this organism. The pencil wrote the Latin word *templum*—"temple."

Mme Hugo asked the Mercurians: "Why are Molière and Shakespeare on Jupiter, while you are on Mercury? What determines the difference in dwelling places?"

The pencil leg replied: *Majores sunt quem ego.* [They are greater than I.]

"Do you promise you'll return?" asked Mme Hugo.

Yes.[8]

And then, at a quarter past midnight—very early in the morning of July 27, 1854—the astral trip to the planet Mercury was over. It would be an inaugural voyage. The tapping tables were soon to open up to the whole wide universe.

Nineteen

PLANETS OF PUNISHMENT
AND WORLDS OF REWARD

"As he had often happened to find in perfectly limpid sea water tolerably large animals . . . which, out of water, resembled soft crystal, and which thrown back into the water blended with their surroundings in transparency and color, he drew the conclusion that since living transparencies inhabit the water, other transparencies, equally living, might also inhabit the air . . . Since the sea is filled, why should the atmosphere be empty? Creatures of the color of the air would be effaced in the light, and would elude our vision; who can prove to us that there are none such?"

So wrote Victor Hugo in *The Toilers of the Sea*. The words belong to Gilliatt, the seaman hero of the 1866 novel. Gilliatt continues: "The air inhabited by living transparencies would be the beginning of the unknown; but beyond, the vast opening of the possible presents itself. There, other beings; there, other facts." The nocturnal world has an existence of its own, muses Gilliatt, and when we sleep, "it seems as though the indistinct inhabitants of space come to look at us, and that they have a curiosity about us, the inhabitants of earth . . . and the sleeper, not yet fully awake, catches a glimpse of . . . this floating of forms in the shadows, all that mystery which we call dreams, and which is nothing but the approach of a living reality."[1]

Much farther along in *The Toilers of the Sea*, the omniscient narrator expands on Gilliatt's earlier ruminations. "Night," the narrator writes, "is the peculiar and normal state of the special creation of which we form a part. Daylight, brief in duration as in space, is but the proximity of a star."[2]

Darkness as the normal state of the creation in which we dwell: that was Victor Hugo's special nightmare.

In *Philosophy: The Beginning of a Book,* the proto-preface he wrote for *Les Misérables* and later dropped, Hugo addresses the notion of the near-blackness of the physical universe. He asks us to reflect on the smallness of the planet Venus as we see it in the night sky. Then he asks us to realize that, if we were to look at the sun from Saturn, it would appear only twice as big as Venus looks from Earth. Then, he says, imagine that you are looking at the sun from Neptune, the next planet out; it will appear to be no bigger than a star.

Imagine you are traveling far out of our solar system into interstellar space. Soon, even the light from our sun will have vanished into nothingness.

Hugo was appalled at the realization that there was hardly any light in the universe, that it was mostly dark—that almost all of physical reality was pitch-black! That wasn't all: unthinkable coldness as well as unthinkable blackness must prevail in these abysses devoid of sunlight. Hugo had a phrase for this hideous gulf between the stars; he called it the "black ditch."[3]

Moreover, if invisible beings swam about us here on Earth, must they not also swim about us in the depths of interstellar space? And what hideous forms must these invisible denizens of the black ditches take, seeing as their essence must be a reflection of these sunless voids?

How monstrous they must be!

Victor Hugo finally could not abide such a vision of reality. It was too unbearably bleak. His soul recoiled from this description of the universe, which was, after all, only a construction of his mind following out a chain of reasoning. He knew there was more; he knew there was God. Hugo was more certain of God's existence than he was of his own.[4] And had not God, in withdrawing a part of himself from himself to create the physical universe, left a part of himself in even the most brutish piece of matter?

The creation story of the *Zohar,* introduced to the poet by Alexander Weill, had become a part of Hugo's thinking. God, in withdrawing himself from himself, had given birth to filaments of light;[5] and so, where there were the greatest concentrations of light in the present-day universe, there was also the greatest concentration of God. The stars were therefore the purest, the holiest, of the heavenly bodies. The planets closest to the sun must be the purest planets, though already flawed by their separation from the sun. The purest souls came to live on these worlds as they pursued their reincarnational path along the Great Chain of Being (the Mercurians were an example). The next planet out from the sun was correspondingly less pure. Saturn, from whose vantage point the sun was only twice as big as Venus seen from Earth, was a baleful prison world.

Progressing on out to the rim of our solar system, you passed by penal colonies of mounting savagery. Then you took the prodigious leap across the great gulf of the black ditch where, at the midpoint between suns, the presence of God was just this side of nonexistence and invisible, monstrous beings lurked just this side of death. Beyond the ditch lay other solar systems, an infinity of them, and once you gained the outermost worlds you began the descent toward the white-hot glowing center of that solar system, wherein lay, once again, the greatest concentration of God's substance.

In *Explanation*, published as *Poem III, xii*, in *Les Contemplations* (1856) but thought to be an abandoned section of *What the Shadow's Mouth Says* (1854), Hugo elaborates on these images:

> *Every star is a sun; every sun a paradise.*
> *Around the purest globes revolve accursed worlds.*
> *And in the shadows, where soul sharpens eyesight better*
>   *than any glasses.*
> *The planet-hell is dragged in the train of the sun-*
>   *paradise.*
> *Each obscure globe wails; each globe is a penal*
>   *colony*
> *The farther away the world, the worse the dreadful*
>   *prison.*
>
> *Oh, globes without sunlight and almost without dawn!*
> *Enormous Jupiter, lashed by meteors,*
> *Mars that from afar resembles a volcano's mouth*
> *Nocturnal Uranus! Oh, Saturn, locked in an iron collar!*
> *Unknowable punishment! Redemption! Mystery!*
> *Mourning! Oh, moons, even deader than the worlds they*
>   *orbit,*

> *And which also suffer; black they are, and engaged in*
> *what fell deeds?*
> *Specter worlds, dragging chains of unequal length,*
> *Begging for a messiah, hoping for apostles . . .*[6]

Hugo's impulse is to personify these stars and planets, just as the ancients personified the planet nearest to the sun as Mercury, the planet second-nearest to the sun as Venus, and so on. That impulse is all the more evident when, as in the poem *Magnitudo Parvi*, written largely in 1856 and also included in *Les Contemplations* (*Poem III, xxx*), Hugo describes these worlds as sick and dying:

> *Certain of these planets die;*
> *In sandstorm and in mistral*
> *In sobbing seas and weeping waves;*
>
> *Spheres suffocated by their snows,*
> *Strange illnesses afflict them,*
> *Plagues, floods and conflagrations,*
> *Earthquakes profound and frequent;*
> *Their own abysses eat them up;*
> *Their breath bursts into smoke and flame;*
> *From afar you hear, fog-bound within*
> *The dismal coughing of the worlds' volcanoes.*[7]

In their "visit to the planet Mercury" in August 1854, the séance attendees had acquired some preliminary knowledge of the spiritual nature of the planets of our solar system. On November 10, 1854, they would learn not only about the planets of punishment and the worlds of reward that march ever outward from every sun, but they would also learn that, since the substance of God—which is One—extends everywhere throughout the physical universe, then all the suns and all the planets of punishment and reward are interconnected in a single luminous system of checks and balances, and that that system is called devotion.

The séance took place on Wednesday, November 10, 1854, beginning at two o'clock in the afternoon. The Hugo family alone was present, with Mme Hugo and Charles at the tables, and Victor and François-Victor transcribing.

A spirit called Death appeared at the tables.

Victor asked: Was there any way—aside from consulting the spirits at the tapping tables (which they all knew by now wasn't a reliable method)—that humans could predict their future?

The shade called Death replied:

Study human astronomy in depth. It is filled with germs of truth from which you will be able to extrapolate greater truths. For example, you will find it possible to establish the exact nomenclature of your planetary systems of worlds of reward and punitary worlds, all in function of their distance from the sun.

The laws of the heavens conform to the laws of the earth; that law is the devotion of the great to the small, of the good to the bad, of the rich to the poor, of the beautiful to the ugly, of the just to the unjust— of the joyous to the joyless and the smiling to the bleeding.

I speak of the mysterious redemption of shadow by light, of night by the first gleam of dawn. My subject is the deliverance of the guilty gallows-stone by the stone of the martyr's cross; it is the deliverance of the poisonous plant by the perfumed plant, the deliverance of the ferocious beast by the beast of strength and gentleness, the deliverance of the criminal by the innocent, the deliverance of the punished soul by the rewarded soul and of the false idea by the true idea.[8]

The séance attendees were learning that, in heaven as on earth, it was devotion that advanced God's purposes; this was the glue that held everything together. The theme would resound on December 18, 1854, when the Shadow of the Sepulcher told the assembled host:

A tremendous need for devotion, that is the law of the worlds. . . . Love, love, you are the supreme solution, you are the final figure, you are God's billion and the prodigious sum total formed by all the dazzling zeroes of the starry firmament.[9]

But, to return to Death's words on November 10, 1854:

Finally, it is the deliverance of the weeping star by the gleaming star and the enormous sacrifice of paradise for hell. The starry skies contain rare and prodigal constellations whose mission is to gently and unceasingly draw near to worlds in misery, and to little by little bring light to them with a day that begins like dusk and finishes up in a blaze of flame. There are other constellations, equally sublime, whose function is both to draw close to, and to draw close to them, these planets of woe—and this requires a double effort, a double and terrible labor. Some gleaming stars sink, others rise; some are engulfed by shadow, others sweat cascades of light; the latter dive like swimmers into the firmament and from the depths of the night haul up pale and disheveled stars; the gleaming stars descend into the great black hearth of heaven and, with hardly a murmur, transform themselves into fires made of straw and sticks of wood, fires that warm the corpses of these pitiful drowned stars.

Oh, good and strong constellations who become servants of those hideous mortuaries of punishment! Oh, stars that harness themselves to stars gone astray! Suns that become seeing-eye dogs! Spheres that change into wooden serving bowls for the poor! Lights that become the faithful companions of closed eyes! Pleiades, planets, sunbeams, torches, living splendors, flaming lions, fire bears, carbuncle scorpions, diamond Aquariuses, tigers, panthers, leopards, elephants—a dazzling menagerie of formidable suns that through love become the poodles and Newfoundland dogs of the entire cosmos!

In such a way do the heavens resemble the earth; a continual rescue of suns by suns takes place there. Great stars exist just as do great men; there is the star of Socrates, of Galileo, of John Huss; the star of Joan of Arc, of the Macabbean Pleiades, of Dante; the star of Molière, of Shakespeare—and, in the midpoint of the heavens, amid the storm and glory, surrounded by cloud and flame, there is the sun of Jesus Christ, nailed magnificently to the Southern Cross.

Thus composed, the firmament should appear to you in—

Victor interrupted: "I've written lines that skirt these ideas without accepting them. In some, I portray God as sifting stars and souls through a single sieve; in another verse that begins, 'Our earth is to the sun as man is to the angel,' I explain that the degree of the soul's punishment is in direct proportion to the distance [of its home planet] from the sun."

Death ignored him and went on:

—a new light. The placement of worlds, the role played by the heavenly spheres: All this isn't just arbitrary. I've just broadened horizons in your mind that needed to be broadened. And we will speak of these matters again.

Then:

Now I've come to your question. But before I address it, [here is] one more thought: In the punitary planets, there are men, beasts, plants, and stones that contribute to the liberation of their world, just as in the worlds of reward there are suns that contribute to the setting free of the punitary worlds. In the process of toiling to save the punitary planet, the favored star sometimes receives help from man, sometimes from animals, sometimes from plants, and sometimes from stones: star helps man, man helps star, star helps animal, animal helps star, star helps plant, plant helps star, star helps stone, stone helps star. At night, in the hour of the soul, when the body sleeps, words of love are exchanged between the man engaged in rescuing and the star engaged in rescuing. . . . The martyred animal talks to the liberating star, the plant in the midst of ordeals chats with the charitable planet, and the grain of sand crushed underfoot cries "Help!" to the speck of light![10]

The table abruptly ceased tapping at five o'clock, just as dusk began to fall.

A variant on the theme of the dynamic of devotion between the stars and planets had already been revealed to the séance attendees at Marine-Terrace almost a year before, when, on December 10 and 14, 1853, and at greater length on December 16, 1853, the shade of Niccolo Machiavelli briefly addressed the group.

Machiavelli, a political philosopher and diplomat at the time of the Renaissance, was born in Florence, Italy, in 1469 and died in 1527. He is best known for his political treatise, *The Prince* (1513), which has become one of the cornerstones of modern political philosophy.

At the first two séances presided over by Machiavelli, politics was the subject. At the third, on December 16, Machiavelli introduced a new wrinkle into the concept of reincarnation.

It began with Victor Hugo's presenting a theory to the shade: "It has occurred to me to wonder if that invisible world where you now have your being does not often superimpose itself upon our visible world, and if there does not exist in your realm, in some manner, a reflection of our actions here on earth. That is, it seems to me that Socrates' judges must have sat like invisible ghosts behind Jesus's judges; that Jesus's judges, after being carried off in their turn by the Shadow of Death, must have sat behind the judges who condemned certain great Christians to death by burning at the stake. In other words, it seems to me that in the course of living their lives certain men must at certain times be possessed by their counterparts in the past—their spiritual ancestors, so to speak. What do you think?"

Machiavelli replied:

The genealogy you speculate about does in truth exist. In the afterworld there are certain groupings of souls, certain tribes of souls, so to speak. Cain—he who slew his brother Abel—is the representative of one of those groups. From his shadowy lair [in the afterworld], Cain—that first arch-criminal, that true patriarch of crime—keeps an eye on those miscreants who have followed after him, and who seem to him to wander our earth like chastised legions lost in an endless sea of remorse. Little by little, the disreputable forefathers [now in the afterworld] reflect on what they themselves did while on earth, and their reflections prompt them to improve their behavior while in heaven; and, to the extent that their behavior in heaven improves, their descendents on earth behave in less evil a fashion. Thus Judas [due to the invisible influence of Cain] is necessarily less guilty of criminality than Cain. . . . The grandsons of the Miserable Old One who committed the first crime somehow become less perverse. Oh, world, you may rejoice: Cain has begun to weep.[11]

Such was Machiavelli's account. But Auguste Vacquerie had objections, and when, on August 16, 1854, the spirit called Idea paid a visit, he brought them up.

Vacquerie wondered if Idea did not think that the presence (as we in the twenty-first century might put it) of "backseat drivers" in the evolution of mankind, as set forth by Machiavelli, did not deprive mankind of a certain degree of personal freedom and responsibility. Vacquerie's words were: "Machiavelli said there's a genealogy of crime and that, to the extent that the forefathers of evil repent and better themselves, their spiritual descendants on earth better themselves. This seems to me to make the extent of evil among the living more or less dependent on the extent of self-improvement among the dead. In such cases, the living are no longer the sole owners of their actions; they are no longer alone in their conscience and their will; they have a deceased collaborator, one from thousands of years ago, who pushes them toward good or evil according to that collaborator's predilections. How can they then be responsible human beings? What becomes of man's freedom in this case? What becomes of the God of justice?"

Idea replied:

First, the creatures of the planets of punishment are not absolutely free. In raising your objection, you speak from the point of view of someone on a world of reward. Total freedom exists only in heaven. Freedom is the mighty beating in infinity of eternity's wing. To be free is to be fortunate indeed. The degree of punishment meted out to the soul is a function of its degree of emancipation, of the degree of freedom that it enjoys. The pebble is more enslaved than the plant, the plant more than the beast, the beast more than man, man more than spirit. The punishment is greatest in the plant's roots, least in its perfumed petals. It is greatest in the beast's claws, least in the tips of its wings. Punishment begins in the stone and ceases with godhead. . . . It is God's wish that the improvement of the dead also improve the living. He doesn't want Cain's crime to keep man in chains forever; he wants the repentance of Cain to deliver man from human criminality. Divine law is gentle, and in its generosity sometimes touching. Thus it desires that every being that betters itself in death improves someone in life; thus it transforms the ditch of crime into the furrow of mercy.

Human life has two sorts of benefactors, the righteous and the wicked: the martyrs who, while on earth, bestow their suffering on it; and the executioners who, when they are dead, bestow their repentance on it. The former bleed while on earth; the latter weep while in heaven. The first sort have names like Galileo, John Hus, Savonarola, Socrates, Joan of Arc, Dante; the second group has names like Nero, Heliogabalus, Tiberius, Torquemada, Charles IX, Henry VIII, and Cesare Borgia. Calvary has two names: Jesus and Judas.

What about great writers? Was Shakespeare, in improving his works in heaven (in the manner described in our chapter on translating and channeling Shakespeare), simultaneously improving the writing of Hugo and his peers on earth? Was the experience of "channeling Shakespeare through the tapping tables" merely the only way the human mind could conceive, at least temporarily, of this process? This question leads us on to the strange doctrine of the *homo duplex,* or "double man," expounded by the Jersey Island spirits. We will take this doctrine up in the next chapter.[12]

Twenty

"YOU WILL AWAKEN ME
IN THE YEAR 2000 . . ."

In this chapter we will hear mainly from the spirit called Death, though the shade of the ancient Greek philosopher Plato will put in an appearance.

We'll begin with a short discourse by Death on whether we rejoin our deceased loved ones when we die. This discourse was tapped through the tables at the séance of Sunday, September 3, 1854, the day before the eleventh anniversary of the drowning of Léopoldine Hugo Vacquerie and Charles Vacquerie.

The session began at two o'clock in the afternoon. Present were Mme Hugo, Jules Allix, Emile Allix, and Auguste Vacquerie. Mlle Augustine Allix and Charles Hugo sat at the table.

The table stirred. "Death" made its presence known.

Auguste Vacquerie led the questioning. "On whose behalf do you come?"

On behalf of the tomb.

"Speak."

The charming couple carried off by the river [Charles and Léopoldine] *think of you. They love you. They see you. They wait for you and keep a place for you in this immense embrace called death.*

Vacquerie continued: "You say that our beloved dead await us in the world where they are now. Will they stay in that world? Or will their ascension continue? Explain how and where we will rejoin those who left this earth before us. Won't they have left their new world before we get there? If their ascension continues steadily throughout eternity, tell us how we can make up for the head start they already have."

The shade replied:

The "I" of the being who loves is the "I" of the being who is loved. Your dead are your "I's" and you are the "I's" of your dead. Your deceased are nothing other than a parcel of your life beginning elsewhere. Their graves are the walls of your dwelling place and the sides of your soul. Once you are dead, you will become them and they will remain you. There is no rejoining in heaven; there is only dissolving into one another. Paradise has just one mouth, and love is its two lips.

Mme Hugo had a question: "What you just said disturbs me. We and our dead dissolve into one another? Does that mean we will become confused with them, that they will no longer exist outside us and distinct from us? They have their own life on earth: a body we can touch, a shape we can recognize. When we meet them again, we want it to be with their personality intact. We want them to be them, not us. Tell me how we will be able to recognize them."

Death replied:

The body is not the shape of being; it is the formula of being, in the same way as language is the formula of idea. The body varies infinitely and then it vanishes; being is one and immortal. Language varies infinitely and then it vanishes; idea is one and eternal. There are worlds where ideas dwell without formulae and where beings live without bodies. The body is merely the traveling clothes of the soul. You change your clothes in the tomb; the sepulcher is the changing-room of heaven. The dead recognize one another by their souls.[1]

The séance ended prematurely. Some visitors were knocking on the door at Marine-Terrace.

⁂

Having engaged the subject of death (with Death!), we'll now address the subject of dreams and how it is that our dreams can be a conduit to the afterworld. The ancient Greek philosopher Plato (428–ca. 347 B.C.) will be the spokesperson for the spirit world.

When Plato finishes, we'll engage the momentous subject of *homo duplex*—the "double man (or woman)" that represents the dual nature of our identity, one part of which inhabits the physical world while we are awake, and the other part of which inhabits the astral reaches and/or afterworld while we're asleep.

First, though, let's hear about dreams from Plato. This séance took place on Sunday, April 29, 1855. Present were Victor Hugo, Mlle Augustine Allix, Emile Allix, and Auguste Vacquerie. Seated at the table were Charles and Mme Hugo.

An initial brief exchange on technical issues took place between Victor Hugo and the table. Then the table stood still for five minutes. Finally, it trembled, and the shade of Plato introduced itself. The new guest was invited to speak his mind.

Plato did so:

I've come to speak to you of dreams. When the living person falls asleep, a communication immediately establishes itself between his bed and his grave. Each sleeping body fixes upon its own soul as a vanishing point.* The sleeper serves as a wake-up call to the beyond; he isn't motionless, he flies through the cosmos; he isn't blind, he peers into infinite reaches; he's not deaf, he hears the pulsations of space; he's not mute, he speaks in the language of death; he isn't lying down, he's winged; he isn't stretched out, he's hovering; he hasn't fallen but rather he's been resuscitated. The sleeper is the assailant of the night; every time we fall asleep we lay siege to the mysteries of the cosmos; every bed, even the most abject, breaches the wall of the sepulcher; dreams are missiles hurled at the stars. When a mortal being falls asleep, communication is immediately established between his bed and his grave. Every sleeping body focuses on its own soul as the vanishing point on the horizon of reality.

In the day you live and at night you die; millions of suns burst through your bedroom ceiling and set about lighting up your room; your night light goes out and in its place your room is illuminated by a star; in the course of the night your lamp will consume a drop of the Milky Way; the candles of the afterworld are going to glitter around this nocturnal funeral; infinity will take your bedsheets and bury you till tomorrow in a pauper's grave of sleep; while you're still alive you'll get in touch with your mortuary self. Your flesh will feel the touch of your ashes rub against it; your limbs will feel the touch of your bones; your head will feel the touch of your skull; your skeleton, now encasing your body, will be the formidable warrior's armor of the night. O besieger of

---

*The reference is to painting, where the vanishing point is the single point in the center of the horizon toward which everything else in the painting (or drawing) recedes.

death's dark fortress; O you who are alive, set down your ivory armor before death's ebony dungeon and behold: dreams, come and tumble over the sleeper, you are tender or terrible visions; you spurt from smiling Venus or from irritated Saturn. You are archangel's kiss or spector's knife-thrust; you are loves or crimes; you're soul's ghosts; you're a rendezvous with a woman who's adored, you're the return of the cherished daughter; you're also the victim's ambush and the dagger thrust into the assassin as he sleeps, and you shake out all of the grave's winding sheets in the curtains of the terrified alcove, while in the shadowy room the giddy clock face, compass of the sleeper's ship, eternally turns its minute hand toward death.[2]

The séance ended, leaving them wondering: When we're asleep do we literally visit ourselves as we will be when we are dead? Do we visit an eternal form of ourselves, one that, being a sort of repository of the knowledge of all of our lives (and from whatever existence we have in an afterlife), gives us at least enough knowledge to get through the day?

Such questions seemed as unanswerable to the séance attendees of Jersey Island as they seem to us today.

We'll recall that, on December 29, 1853, the shade of André Chénier, just before he described his own beheading, broached the subject of the "double man" (*homo duplex*) for the first time.

He told Victor Hugo and the assorted guests: *My work will be a double one. I must create my known work and my unknown work. The first will be royalist, the second republican. One will curse the French Revolution, the other bless it. My head, in falling, grasped the idea, which my eyes saw only as an ax. Those thoughts, watered by my blood, flowered in the grave.*[3]

At a séance held on September 19, 1854, beginning at 1:30 p.m. the spirit called "Death" held forth at much greater length on the subject of *homo duplex* and associated matters. Present at the séance were Victor Hugo, François-Victor Hugo, and Auguste Vacquerie. Seated at the table were Mme Hugo and Charles Hugo.

Here is what Death said:

During their lives, all great minds create two bodies of work: their work as living beings, and their work as phantoms of the night. Into the living work they throw the living, terrestrial world; into the phantom work they pour that other, celestial world.

*The living speak to their century in the language that it under-
stands, work with what is possible, affirm the visible, effect the real,
light up the day, justify the justifiable, demonstrate proof. Engaged in
this work, they fight, they sweat, they bleed; while in this martyrdom
genius must bear with imbeciles; a flame, it must bear with shadow;
the chosen, it must bear with the crowd, and die Christlike, God's
dowry to the world, between two thieves, vilely, scorned, and wearing
a crown of thorns so heavy a donkey could graze on his forehead.*

*While the living being creates this first work, the pensive phan-
tom, in the night, in the silence of the universe, awakens within the
living human being. Oh, terror! What, says the human being, that
[daytime living]* wasn't everything? No, replies the specter: Get up!
Get on your feet! *There's a high wind blowing, dogs and foxes bark,
darkness is everywhere, nature shudders and trembles under God's
whipcord; toads, snakes, worms, nettles, stones, grains of sand await
us: Get on your feet!*

*You've only worked for man. That's fine! But man is nothing;
man isn't the bottom of the abyss, man isn't the headlong fall into
horror. The animal is the precipice, the flower is the gulf; it's the bird
that makes you dizzy, because you've had only a worm's-eye view of
the grave.*

*Wake up! Come perform your other work. Come gaze upon what
cannot be gazed upon, come contemplate the unseen, come find what
can't be found, come leap what can't be leaped, come justify what can't
be justified, come make the unreal manifest, come prove what can't be
proved.*

*You've been day; come be night; come be shadow; come be dark-
ness; come be the unknown; come be the impossible; come be mystery;
come be infinity. You've been the face; come be the skull. You've been
the body; come be the soul. You've been the living; come be the phantom. Come die, come be resurrected, come create, and come be born.*

I wish that, having witnessed your burden [as a creative genius
struggling during the day], *man could watch you taking flight and
confusedly sense your formidable wings beating in the stormy sky of
your Calvary. Living being, come be wind of night, noise of forest,
foam of wave, shadow of den; come be hurricane, come be the horrible dread of the savage darkness. If the herdsman shivers, may it
be your step that he has heard; if the sailor trembles, may it be your*

breath that he has heard. I bear you away with me; the lightning flash, our pale horse, rears up in the clouds. Come on! Enough sun. To the stars! To the stars! To the stars!

The phantom ceases to speak and the dreadful work begins. The ideas in that work no longer have a human face: the phantom-writer sees phantom-ideas; the words quake with fear; the words thrill through your every limb, the paper begins to rattle like a ship's sail in a storm, the quill pen feels its beard bristle, the inkwell becomes the abyss, the letters blaze forth in fire, the table vacillates, the ceiling trembles, the windowpane pales, the lamp gets scared. How quickly they pass, these phantom-ideas! They enter the brain, glitter, terrify, and disappear; the eye of the specter-writer catches sight of them hovering there by the light of the phosphorescent whirlwinds of the black spaces of immensity: they come from infinity and they return to infinity; they are splendid and grim and frightening; they inseminate or they thunder; they are what created Shakespeare, Aeschylus, Molière, Dante, Cervantes. Socrates was born from a phantom-idea; they are transparent and through them you can see God; they are great, they are good, they are majestic; crime, suffering, matter itself, flee before them; they are the tremendous electric current of universal progress. Their cry is: Woe unto evil! and it is a formidable hour when they pass by in the sky, taking flight toward the Sabbath of the immense mystery, affrighted and seated upon the prodigious broomstick of the iniquities and all the witches in paradise!

Charles was exhausted, and the assembled group took a break. Victor Hugo asked the table to "complete what you've begun." It continued in the same vein, and we will pass over several paragraphs. It concluded with the following:

The drama is beginning. Silence. The winding sheet is going up. I'm getting to your question. It's a delicate one. Above all, what we wish for man is that he act out of his own free will. I cannot command you in these matters. Publish [these transcripts], if you wish. The only thing I want to say is this: Be the Oedipus of your life and the Sphinx of your grave.[4]

The séance ended at 7:30 p.m.

What are we to make of all this? Is Death saying that men and women of genius—or perhaps all of us?—travel through the astral reaches when asleep so as to imbibe extradimensional experiences that, when they awaken, feed (however unconsciously) their daytime creative endeavors? And are these experiences indispensable? They would seem to be.

Perhaps the contemporary American philosopher Ken Wilber, in *Sex, Ecology, Spirituality: The Spirit of Evolution,* points us in a useful direction when he says,

> For Plotinus, Dionysius, Eckhart, and company [all visionary philosophers], these higher dimensions of existence are, above all else, *potentials* inherent or present in each and every being (since each and every being issues forth from them), and thus these higher potentials can be *realized* or consciously *actualized* for any being who can find the requisite height/depth in his or her own soul. These higher levels are *not* angels out there, or metaphysical notions merely postulated to exist somewhere, or philosophical or logical assumptions used to fill in any "gaps" in the world. They are potentials that can be *directly experienced* and *directly realized.* There is absolutely nothing *other* about them, except the otherness created by our own lack of inner awareness.[5]

Death had scheduled a second séance for the next day, Wednesday, September 20, 1854, beginning at one in the afternoon. Victor Hugo was present, as were Mme Hugo and son Charles, both seated at the table.

Death recommenced:

Spirit, do you not have secret thoughts, visions, mysterious perspectives, fears, lightning transportings away into the invisible? Does not your hope for the infinite sometimes pour itself into the unfathomable? Don't you find yourself turning abruptly, precipitously, upon God? Haven't you had constellation tempests and shipwrecks among the stars? Has your raft never collided with Saturn and touched upon the sandbars of the Milky Way? Have your two eyes never gotten so filled with millions of stars all of a sudden that your eyelids became the two shores of the firmament? Has your anchor never searched out the bottom of the night and has it never wanted to take a sounding of the abyss? Aren't you a searcher after skulls, a gravedigger of worlds, a Hamlet of suns, a stroller through the cemetery of immensity, a seizer of planets, one of heaven's digging spades? Have you never cried out, Yes! Yes! Yes! in the midst of this great grim No? Have you never stood

your ground against moonless nights and said Good! to starry nights?
Have you never sometimes thought that you were being brought before
a tribunal of speechless planets? Have you never been frightened, have
you never shivered, have you never felt your hair stand on end and be
caught up in the stars as if by dreadful pulley wheels? Have you never
reflected on all the forms that creation takes? Have you never reflected
on faces and glances, on lips and faces, and often as well on the teeth
between those lips? Are you not in love with some of these forms and
in terror of others? Aren't you just a little smitten with Venus? Are you
not extremely frightened of Saturn? And while you sense above your
head the stars speaking to you, don't you sense pebbles in your shoes
talking to you? Do you not carry on intrigues with certain brambles
on the beach? Don't you impute souls to animals? Don't you impute
souls to stones? Don't you impute souls to plants? Don't you
impute a soul to dust, a soul to ashes, a soul to the gutter, a soul to
garbage, a soul to all that the body rejects, a soul to the spit of Judas,
a soul to the tears of Magdalene, a soul to the blood of Jesus? Isn't
it somewhere there, trembling, vacillating, affrighted, between this sky
and this earth, between all the worlds so high above and all the souls
so far below, between this paradise and this hell, between these sparks
and these stones—isn't it somewhere there, and do you not ask what
the formidable tinderbox is that will make the constellations leap up
from these pebbles like sparks?[6]

Charles was exhausted. They took a long break before returning
to the tables. The séance went on for a little longer in the same vein.
Then Death was finished—for the day at least. It was five o'clock in
the evening.

We'll skip the session of September 23, 1854, at which Death, pursuing
the same themes, spoke as powerfully and eloquently as before. We'll go
on to the séance of September 29, 1854, attended only by Victor Hugo,
Mme Hugo, and Charles, with the latter two sitting at the table.

At this session, Death had an unexpected proposition for Victor
Hugo.

The shade began by regretting that great writers such as Aeschylus,
Dante, Cervantes, Shakespeare, and Molière, once dead, are dead and
gone forever. This seems obvious! But Death had something more in
mind. The problem, he explained, was that though the great works of

these creative geniuses would be available through the ages, their living voices would not, and so they would not be able to adapt their evolving creative processes for each successive generation of mankind.

Death wanted something different for the posthumous works of Victor Hugo. He wanted them to have some flexibility, some power of evolving. And so he said to the poet:

Thou: May your posthumous work be still a living thing so that at certain intervals it can talk to posterity and speak to it of unknown things that have had time to ripen in your tomb. What is impossible today is necessary tomorrow. In your Last Will and Testament, space out your posthumous works, one every ten years, one every five years. Can you not see the greatness of a tomb, which—from time to time, in periods of human crisis, when some shadow passes over the progress of mankind, when clouds blot out the ideal—suddenly opens its stone lips and speaks? People seek; your tomb finds. People doubt; your grave affirms. People deny; your tomb proves. And what does it prove? It proves what it contains; it proves, with I do not know what somber and solemn authority, all the truths that today still lie in the future. Thou, dead, you help the living. Thou, mute, you educate them. Thou, invisible, you see them.

Your work does not say, "Perhaps." It says, "Certainly." It does not resort to subterfuges; it goes straight to the point. Know that a ghost does not hide behind rhetorical devices. Ghosts are bold, shades do not blink before the light. So make for the twentieth century an affirmative work rather than one for the nineteenth century, which engenders doubt. Seal it up with you in your sepulcher, so that, at certain times decided by yourself, people will come looking for it.

Christ was resurrected only once; you can fill your grave with resurrections; you can, if my advice seems good to you, have an extraordinary death; you will say as you die: "You will awaken me in 1920; you will awaken me in 1940; you will awaken me in 1960; you will awaken me in 1980; you will awaken me in the year 2000." Your death will be a formidable rendezvous entered upon in light, and a formidable threat launched against the night. The generations will behold with huge admiration this prodigious tomb marching through a century of human life—[7]

Abruptly, the transmission broke off. Death had vanished.

———

The shade called Death returned one more time, on Sunday, October 22, 1854, at 2:30 p.m. Present were playwright and Hugo supporter Paul Meurice and his wife, Victor Hugo, and Auguste Vacquerie. Mme Hugo and Charles Hugo were seated at the table.

Victor Hugo had a question. He explained to the spirit that eventually the tapping table conversations would be published. He believed that they would be "one of the Bibles of the future"—and that, although this would not happen for years, it would certainly happen before all of Victor Hugo's posthumous works had appeared (if one were to follow the schema of the Last Will and Testament as set forth by the spirits), for example, those slated for publication in 1940, or 1960, and so forth.

But Hugo's posthumous works would be infused with all that the Jersey Island spirits had revealed to him, and therefore they would not be of great interest because they would already have been preceded by the publication of the transcripts, which would say the same things, and with more authority.

Did the Jersey spirits perhaps mean that Hugo's posthumous works should consist only of his poetry?

What should lie in Victor Hugo's tomb? The body of a prophet? Or the body of a poet?

"My reason says a poet," Victor concluded. "But I await your answer."

Death replied:

We're talking about a formidable work called Advice from God [Conseils à Dieu]. *The earth disappears; the sepulcher, that great stone bat, opens its wings of shadow in the dusk of the resurrection and in its flight beats those wings against the blazing plate-glass window of the stars; the sinister bird goes from planet to planet, and its night cry, each time it touches the edge of a constellation, becomes a song of light. It emerges bringing the dawn out of the dusk; it takes flight from hell and announces paradise; it departs as an owl and arrives as a lark; it escapes from the ancient trunk of the human tree and alights at the end of each branch where the fruit becomes a star; it leaves the hollowed-out spaces of skulls and leaps from paradise to paradise, and it nests from joy to joy, and it sits on all the globes one after the other and hatches in the sky the egg of every archangel.*

Oh, living one, here's my advice for you: Your soul's work must be your soul's journey; you must not prophesize; you must predict, you must draw predictions in the starry sky, trace your itinerary there, designate your inns with your finger, and attach the relay horses of love to your thoughts so that, invisible traveler that you are, you can mark out in advance the unknown steps on the great route made up of precipices that leads to incomprehensibility's wild hotel. Governor of immensity, you must say in those pages what are the planets that await you, and speak of their civilizations, and of their light and shadow, of their thorns and their flowers, of their places of horror or their walks of joy, of their cries or their hymns; and, from the depths of your tomb, the world must hear you say: There is in infinity a world called Saturn, and which suffers; there is in infinity a world called Mercury, and which suffers; there is in infinity a world called Mars, and which suffers. Oh, my God, what punitary stars there are! What crucified constellations! Lord, your heavens are covered with wounds; your stars are drops of blood! Your suns have become gangrenous, your moons are afflicted with the dreadful pestilence of punishment, your constellations, which have been on their knees for millions of years, have ended up cracking their skulls and fists against darkness and are no longer anything more than hellish stumps; your creations are no longer anything more than shreds of flesh, your halos are no longer anything more than rags of sunbeams, the greatest of your creations have had their heads cut off, your firmament is an immense gutter in which all corpses roll, and your splendid locomotives of light, mad with rage and taking the bit between their teeth, are drawing and quartering every inch of the astral reaches.[8]

Then, abruptly, the séance was over.

Death was gone. He would not return.

Hugo's most profound poetry (such as *The End of Satan*), written during this period on Jersey Island and a little after and deeply influenced by the spirits, wasn't published until after Hugo's death in 1885.

Except for a handful of séances, the Jersey Island transcripts were not published until 1923, and then only a small portion of them were published. Most all the extant transcripts were published in 1970. (But possibly two-fifths of the transcripts of all the Jersey Island séances have been lost.)

No translation of the transcripts was available in any language except French until the first edition of this book, entitled *Conversations with Eternity: The Forgotten Masterpiece of Victor Hugo*, appeared in 1998.

Twenty-one

THE UNITED STATES
OF EUROPE

Victor Hugo liked solidarity and he liked it in the open air. That was what he was seeing on this afternoon of July 21, 1855—Saint Victor's Day—as, wineglass in hand, he observed the festivities on the terrace at the back of his house.

Before him, the lanes and gardens of Marine-Terrace stretched down and away: white-washed, granite-faced, straight-as-a-die pathways crossing each other at right angles as they snaked through the fourteen flower beds near the bottom of the terrace and the equal number of vegetable gardens at the top.[1]

Today the terrace was filled with so many visitors that Hugo, standing with his back to the door, could observe its paths and garden plots only intermittently. Here, a proscrit's stout wife with a parasol and a baby under her arm moved aside and let him see for a moment the sparkling flower bed of red and yellow and orange nasturtiums cared for by Hennett de Kesler as tenderly as if the flowers were his children. There, a short, harried proscrit, uncomfortable in a tattered frock coat he hardly ever wore, mopped his brow with a handkerchief and stepped off the path to get a glass of wine; in so doing he revealed to Victor Hugo the vegetable garden (turnips and watermelons, mostly) of Count Sandor Teleki, tended with so much assiduity by the taciturn Hungarian that he spent whole hours on winter days grinding sandstone down to the finest bits, the better with which to fertilize the soil.[2] Two small boys, dressed in sailor suits and trundling large wooden hoops over a marigold-covered mound of grass, suddenly hid from Hugo's view Teleki's garden but unveiled for him the bank of daisies cultivated by his wife. Everywhere the scent of roses and bougainvillea mingled with the salt sea tang of the air.

Upwards of sixty political exiles (Charles reckoned forty men, married and unmarried, and twenty wives, along with a good number of children) milled around in groups and chatted. Gossip, about the Russian commander at Sebastopol, about the romantic dalliances of the hated Louis Napoleon, about the churches being burglarized in Saint Helier, echoed through the afternoon air.[3] In twos and threes the proscrits strolled down the paths admiring the pleasing geometrical shapes of the garden plots, or sat at black octagonal tables piled with wineglasses and bottles and inverted bowls containing candles waiting for the night. Jersey Island servant girls, flustered and coquettish in their servant's costumes, hurried down the lanes carrying small trays heaped with tiny sandwiches. Everywhere there was animated chatter, frequent peals of laughter, sudden shouted exclamations.

A hush fell across the terrace.

A spoon had clinked once, twice, three times, loudly, on a glass. The sound of voices and bustling and objects colliding dropped like an ocean wave dipping into a trough. Hurried whispers of, "She is going to speak!" or "Hush! This is his day!" died down across the terrace. Then there was only the almost soundless beating of a seagull's wings across the sky and the steady pounding of the surf upon the shore.

Victor's wife, Adèle, seated five feet from him (the young Adèle sat by her side, while Charles lay stretched out on the lawn beside the table), stood up from the wicker chair beside the little octagonal table. She glanced downward under the roses of her big straw hat (these occasions made her shy), then lifted her face to her husband, smiled, and picked up her wineglass.

"On the occasion of my husband's fifty-third Name Day," she said quietly, "on Saint Victor's Day,* I propose a toast to him whose wife I am proud to be."[4] She raised her glass.

They cheered. Glasses clinked all around the terrace. Victor beamed

---

*Europeans not only have birthdays but Name Days as well. Birthdays are usually celebrated just in the immediate family. Name Days, however, are widely known and celebrated. Each first name is assigned to one day of the calendar, based on religious traditions, historical events, and so on, and depending on the respective country and the culture. Victor Hugo was born on February 26, 1802, and turned fifty-three in 1855. Now, on Saint Victor's Day, July 21, he was celebrating his fifty-third Name Day.

and was about to speak when Charles scrambled to his feet, picked up his glass, and called out: "I propose a toast to all those whom the tyranny of Napoleon the Little has deported to Guiana! To the prisoners of Cayenne!" Hennett de Kesler came up quickly beside him and, holding his own glass high, shouted: "To those whom Bonaparte has deported to Africa, particularly to Lambessa!"[5]*

There were shouts, curses, cheers, clinks, and the sound of breaking glass. Two proscrits shouted in unison: "To the universal democratic socialist republic!"[6]

Victor Hugo raised his glass and joined in the cheering. It was brought to a sudden halt by General Le Flô who, standing up very tall and elegant among the exiles, banged a mug loudly several times on an empty bottle. Hugo knew Le Flô was alarmed that these anti-monarchical outpourings might offend the Jerseyans who were passing by on the street outside. The general held his wineglass high and proposed a toast to "Auguste Vacquerie, our friend who is now in France on vacation!"[7]

They all cheered lustily.

A voice far back in the crowd—they never found out who it was—shouted: "To the health of the two Victors! To Victor and François-Victor!"[8]

The cheering was deafening. After all, it was Victor Hugo's Name Day. Then the sound died down. There was an awkward pause. Charles got to his feet and, raising two wineglasses, shouted:

"I ask you to drink to *my* health!"[9]

Clinking echoed across the terrace. The cheering was louder than ever.

Charles sat down on the lawn and let his two wineglasses fall to his side. Victor saw that he was pale and dejected. He looked down at his son, appalled. No one had proposed a toast to Charles Hugo. Victor knew how hurt his elder son must be. He cast about for something to toast, something to say, that would banish from Charles and the guests all memory of what had just happened. His eye lit on the big

---

*The notorious Devil's Island penitentiary, near Cayenne, the capital of French Guiana, had been opened by Napoleon III only in 1852. Many of its earliest inmates were men taken prisoner during the coup d'état of December 2, 1851. Napoleon III also had prisoners transported to the penitentiary at the military base at Lambessa, in then-French Algeria. More than five hundred deportees were sent to these two penitentiaries as a result of the December 2 coup.

white tent that had been set up at the bottom of the terrace the night before as a place to store some Name Day festivity supplies. Above the tent flew a long red flag on which were sewn the words, "The United States of Europe."

Hugo raised his glass to toast the flag and the words written on it and then to make a beguiling speech about the United States of Europe. He raised his glass—and then he thought better of it and lowered his glass. Like Le Flô, he did not want to provoke the Jerseyans unnecessarily.

It wouldn't do to have them think that Victor Hugo wanted to turn Marine-Terrace into the county seat of the Republic of Jersey Island.

But Hugo still wanted to help his unhappy son. Charles still sat dejectedly on the lawn. Victor opened his mouth to speak—

"Papa, someone wishes to see you in the house."

He turned around. His daughter Adèle, who had gone into the house after her mother had toasted her father, stood before him. It was she who had spoken.

"By all means invite him out to the terrace," he said. "Ask him to take part in the festivities. I will see him here."

"He doesn't want to come out on the terrace. He says there are too many people here. He says he's suspicious of them. He also says he doesn't like the sun."

"Who is this strange unsociable creature?"

"Monsieur François Tapon-Fougas."

Victor stared at his daughter thoughtfully. He had met this Tapon-Fougas fellow two months ago. He remembered him as small and slightly built, in his early forties, a political exile like the rest of them. Apparently he was very rich. He was the publisher of what he intimated to Hugo was "an extremely important periodical." He had neglected to reveal its name to Victor Hugo.

"Tell M. Tapon-Fougas I will come and see him right away," said Victor. He turned to his son: "That bizarre publisher fellow whom we met at Teleki's is here. You know, the one with the game-bag and the eyes. You found him interesting. Come! Talk to this strange man with me."

Charles got to his feet. There was a glimmer of interest in his eyes. He had certainly been intrigued, in almost a morbid way, with Tapon-Fougas. He strode with his father into the house. Tapon-Fougas's eyes, on the one occasion they had met him, had gleamed with an unholy, almost an eerie, light. He had carried in front of him, strapped to his belt, an enormous leather game-bag; straps attached to the belt went up over Tapon-Fougas's shoulders and down his back and were attached to the belt on the other side. Only explosives, and a good many of them, could separate Tapon-Fougas from his game-bag.

They entered the drawing room. The owner of the game-bag—he was wearing it that afternoon—stood halfway down the room, gazing with moody suspicion at the silver statuette holding up the defective gas burner at the foot of the stairs.

"But my dear M. Tapon-Fougas," exclaimed Victor Hugo, "thank you for coming!"

The little man turned to them. He had an extremely smooth complexion and a neat, tiny black mustache. Victor was startled by his eyes, which gleamed with a light that must surely have come from some other world—a profoundly afflicted world. Tapon-Fougas stepped forward and grasped Hugo's hand. "May I congratulate you, *maître*," he said, producing a thin smile, "on the occasion of your fifty-third Name Day."

"Thank you," said Victor Hugo. "Of course you already know my daughter Adèle and my son Charles." He turned and gestured in the direction of the two, who had already taken their seats.

Tapon-Fougas acknowledged them with a perfunctory nod. Hugo urged him to sit down and took a seat himself in the big orange armchair.

Tapon-Fougas did not sit down. He stood in the middle of the floor staring gloomily at Victor Hugo for a moment. Then he burst out: "Monsieur Hugo, I have an important story to tell you—one that is important to the world!" He reached down and, unbuckling the top of the game-bag, yanked out seven copies of a periodical. Victor Hugo had no trouble reading the title, which was written in huge red letters. It was: *The Anti-Pope*.

Tapon-Fougas flung the first issue down on the floor. "See this?" he shouted, glancing around at the three of them angrily. "This first issue contained several errors deliberately put there by the printer, who was in the pay of the Jesuits. I changed printers!" He flung the second copy to the floor. "See this?" He glared at them ferociously. "This second issue also contained errors, also put there by the new printer, who had also been bribed by the Jesuits! I changed printers again!"

He flung the third, the fourth, the fifth, and the sixth numbers to the floor. "It was the same for all of these!" he roared. "Each time I changed printers, and each time the slaves of the Anti-Christ bribed the printer!" He held up the seventh issue, which was shiny and spotless and had been published just three weeks before. "Behold Number Seven!" he cried triumphantly. "I have bought my own printing house. I have become my own printer, and the spawn of the Vatican can no longer corrupt my journal."

He paused. Hugo opened his mouth to reply. Tapon-Fougas threw himself down on the long black couch and launched into a second monologue that, when it was finished, had gone on for a good ten minutes. He had fled Paris in April 1852 with the Jesuit-adoring emperor Napoleon III in hot pursuit. He had bought a house in Rome. The Jesuits had tried to murder him there; they had paid peasants to infiltrate the basement of his house and send jets of poisonous nitrogen gas up through the walls. He had fled to New York City—and there, the same story! The Jesuits had recruited pale-faced little girls from the streets—pale because they had performed these deeds on others and were half-dead from inhaling the gases—to crack open the walls of his house and send lethal jets of the nitrogen gas up between the walls to asphyxiate him. He had fled once more, this time to Jersey, where he had rented a cottage in the woods near Saint-Aubin—and the Jesuits had found him once again and were once more mining his walls with nitrogen gas! But in smaller quantities this time; they only wanted to harass him, and especially to keep him from sleeping. And this time the Jesuits were smaller—pygmy Jesuits! They had hollowed out the spaces between the walls, and night after night they monitored his every move by tramping around the walls surrounding his bedroom. He could almost—not quite—see them.

Tapon-Fougas lapsed into an intense and gloomy silence. No one dared speak. Surely, thought Hugo, this charming madman is finished and about to allow us to go back to the party. But the publisher of *The Anti-Pope* exploded into words again. "And do you know, Monsieur," he said, glaring wildly at Hugo, "that I was just stepping out of the house this morning, just on my way to see you, when the Jesuits assailed me again, and this time in the form of my landlord!" So great was his agitation that he sprang to his feet. "I was in the hallway when the door was flung open and that treacherous man was standing there, smiling and thrusting into my hands—a shrub! Yes, a potted shrub!

And then he said: 'I have come to present you with a gift, my dear sir. This plant is a token of my gratitude at your having been so kind as to pay an entire year's rent in advance.'

"'Potted plant be damned,' I screamed at him, 'I know what that plant is! I will not take it inside the house to poison me!' I grabbed him by the shoulders and gave him a good thrashing. Then I threw him out the door. He got up at once and fled, just as the 'shrub' was beginning to emit noxious gases. I bolted out of the house, flung the shrub into the woods, and mounted and rode here as fast as I could."

He peered around him with grim, defiant satisfaction. They were silent. Charles stretched out his arms and legs and lay back in his arm-chair, feigning an immense indifference that under the circumstances even he was having trouble feigning. Finally he observed languidly: "It must cost the Jesuits a pretty penny to do all this to you."

"One hundred thousand francs a day," Tapon-Fougas spat out gloomily.

"How," asked Charles quickly, "do you know the exact figure?" He went on: "Why exactly is it, my dear Tapon-Fougas, that the Jesuits spend so much money on you? You who are, while certainly a man of considerable importance, perhaps not as important as, say, my father, or perhaps Mlle George Sand—persons of eminence and influence who also hate the Jesuits, but upon whom they have lavished not a penny?"

Charles's words had fallen on deaf ears. The publisher of *The Anti-Pope* had been packing up his things, and now, with the seven issues of his periodical crammed back into the game-bag, with his eyes suddenly blank and impenetrable, he favored Charles and Adèle with the swift-est of glances, bowed curtly to Victor Hugo, turned, and wordlessly made his way across the floor and out the door.[10]

Victor, scowling but wordless, rose quickly from his orange arm-chair, strode rapidly across the drawing room, and in a moment was back out on the terrace.

How he loved the light of day! How he hated conspiracy theories!

Victor paused. An anti-conspiracy theory tract by his beloved Voltaire, one illustrated with a dreadful story, had flooded spontane-ously, almost instantaneously—almost as if it were an antidote to what he had just heard—into his brain. He stood quite still in the rays of the sun and savored the shocking details that now raced through his memory.

On May 14, 1610, in Paris, a demented thirty-two-year-old school-teacher named François Ravaillac had run out into the street to where the carriage of King Henri IV was stalled in traffic and had stabbed the king to death.

Ravaillac was saved from the furious mob by only a hair and dragged to the Conciergerie. There he was tortured for twelve days as the authorities sought to extract the names of his accomplices from him. Despite hideous tortures, he insisted there were no accomplices. Ravaillac claimed he had had a vision in which angels told him that Henri IV was about to make war on the pope. The voices had urged him to kill the king and save the Roman Catholic Church. Under the worst tortures Ravaillac did not deviate from his story. At his execution, when he was being torn apart by wild horses, he still insisted that he had acted alone, even though the bishop who was present told him he could not be granted absolution unless he gave up the names of his accomplices. Ravaillac still insisted there were none. When he died, he had been granted only "three-quarters" absolution.

Despite Ravaillac's words, the entire world had insisted, then and ever afterward, that this demented teacher must have been part of a conspiracy, that he must have had accomplices. On the flimsiest of evidence they insisted that he must have been in the pay of one or another of the good king Henri's enemies, or the king's courtiers, or the Jesuits, or Henri's mistress, or even Henri's wife.

Voltaire—whom Hugo adored, and from whose smile (along with Jesus's tears), he believed all the grace of present civilization was derived—had been the first to pierce the muddled veils of these conspiracy theories. He had written with indignation of how the most hideous accident ever to befall Europe—Henri IV's assassination—had produced the most odious of conjectures and that (in 1722, when he wrote) it was still true that no one ever talked about the murder without putting forward some rash judgment or another. Voltaire had expressed astonishment at the unfortunate facility with which those men least capable of evil loved to impute the most hideous crimes to those in power. It was because the accusers wanted to make these men pay for being so much more powerful than themselves, and because it made them look good (both to themselves and others) to be able to reveal such secrets. Tales of secret conspiracies deployed by powerful men played the same role in ordinary conversation as grand passions and great crimes played in theatrical spectacles and tragedies performed on the stage: they drew attention.

The brilliant Voltaire with his endlessly compendious mind had exhaustively investigated every one of the hundreds of theories put forth in journals or in memoirs, by commentators and historians, from 1610 to 1722. He had found not a shred of truth in any of them and had sometimes been able to trace words imputed to powerful, knowledgeable sources to the gossip of half-witted servants willing to accept money to "tell all that they knew." Examining every syllable of every word of the transcripts of Ravaillac's testimony, Voltaire asked the reader: If this man had accomplices, what did he have to gain personally from not revealing their names, especially under the most horrible tortures? It was a fact, asserted Voltaire, that criminals under like torture always ended up betraying all their accomplices. And how, asked Voltaire, could you believe that the man was lying who, out of a haze of pain and knowing more was to come, signed one of his confessions with the words:

"François Ravaillac: May Jesus always be the conqueror in my heart."[11]

Victor Hugo emerged from his furious reverie and began to advance purposefully down the central pathway of the garden. He was on his way to the big white tent at the bottom of the terrace. The exiles moved quietly and politely out of the way of his vigorous stride. He looked around at the garden plots and thought to himself: This is how it should be. The soldiers of freedom of four countries are met here this afternoon in the light of this glorious day. They do not plot in darkness. They act in light. Hugo saw that, in the slight lull that had overtaken the Name Day festivities, Teleki had gone to sprinkle sandstone on his garden plot, and Kennett de Kesler, near the bottom of the terrace, was squatting over his nasturtiums in his Sunday best and watering them out of a big red watering can.[12] This, too, was how it should be, thought Hugo: each of the multinational gardeners of Marine-Terrace toiled with his particular gifts to benefit the garden, just as each toiled with his particular gifts to benefit humanity—and all in the brilliant light of day.

Victor had arrived at the big white tent at the bottom of the terrace. Over it the long red flag with the words "The United States of Europe" sewn on it floated in the breeze coming in from the sea. Hugo had come here to retrieve from the tent and show to the proscrits something special he and Charles and François-Victor had put in the tent the night before.

Hugo reached inside the flap. He found the small container where he had placed it and brought it out. He opened it, turned his back slightly to the crowd, and lifted out of it a small red flowerpot. It was filled with rich brown earth. On top of the earth lay an acorn.

Hugo's desire was to plant this acorn in the center of the terrace tomorrow afternoon. He wished to tell the proscrits about it at these celebrations this afternoon. The acorn would symbolize the seed of the United States of Europe; they would plant it, and each year it would grow bigger and taller, until one day it became the mighty oak of the United States of Europe.

This was his conspiracy. All the proscrits on Jersey Island were his accomplices.

The acorn stood for each and every one of these brave and freedom-loving exiles; the mighty oak into which it grew would be the life lived in martyrdom of each and every one of them and the glorious fruit that it would one day bear.

Victor Hugo turned slowly beside the tent beneath the flag, trying to decide if he should, in the gardens of Marine-Terrace, on this afternoon of his fifty-third Name Day, under the light of the brilliant sun filling every corner of the terrace, announce to the assembled proscrits his plan to plant the acorn of the United States of Europe.[13]

Hugo and the exiles didn't plant the acorn the next day, nor on the day after. The seed of the United States of Europe wasn't planted until November 1870, on Guernsey Island. Napoleon III had been driven from power in September, and Victor Hugo, free at last after nineteen years of exile, was preparing to go home.

Victor Hugo presided over one more symbolic planting of the oak of the United States of Europe, when he had at last returned to Paris, six months later.

This planting of an acorn to produce a mighty oak tree—or, more accurately, its symbolism as the creation of a future United States of Europe—is the main reason why, in the early twenty-first century, with the worldwide success of Dan Brown's novel *The Da Vinci Code*, Victor Hugo came to be thought of by some as one of the grand masters of a powerful secret society known as the Priory of Sion.

᪵᪶

What exactly is the Priory of Sion?

By mid-2006 the phenomenal success of Dan Brown's 2002 novel *The Da Vinci Code*—translated into forty-four languages, sixty million copies sold worldwide—had made the name of that enigmatic organization a household phrase. The Priory of Sion is the key component of Brown's wildly popular novel in which a brilliant Harvard expert on symbols and a beautiful French police code decipherer suddenly find themselves involved willy-nilly in the search for the Holy Grail. Their almost unwilling search is confounded by two mysterious groups—the legendary Priory of Sion, a nearly 1,000-year-old secret society whose members have included Botticelli and Isaac Newton, and the conservative Catholic organization Opus Dei. Both have their reasons for wanting to put the symbologist and the cryptologist off the trail. The two survive to unlock the secret of the Grail, but not before there has been a string of grisly murders and Western religion has been threatened by chaos.

In *Truth and Fiction in* The Da Vinci Code: *A Historian Reveals What We Really Know About Jesus, Mary Magdalene, and Constantine* (2004), Dr. Bart D. Ehrman, chairman of the Department of Religious Studies at the University of North Carolina at Chapel Hill, summarizes author Dan Brown's description of the Priory of Sion.

> [It is] a secret religious group . . . which has always guarded the secret to the true nature and whereabouts of the Holy Grail [, claiming that] the Grail is not the cup of Christ but the container that held his seed—it is in fact a person, Mary Magdalene, who was Jesus's wife and lover, who became pregnant by him and bore him a daughter. After his crucifixion, Mary and her child fled to France, and there the divine ancestral line of Christ was continued down through the ages.
>
> There were secret documents kept about the existence of the bloodline of Christ. These documents celebrate the feminine principle in early Christianity and include a number of early Gospels that came to be suppressed by Christianity in the fourth century, specifically by the Emperor Constantine. Constantine destroyed the eighty-some Gospels that were vying for a position in the New Testament, elevated Jesus from being a mere mortal to being the Son of God,

and completely silenced the tradition about Mary and the divine feminine, demonizing the feminine in Christianity and destroying its true nature as a celebration of the feminine deity.

But the Priory of Sion has, for centuries, known the truth about Jesus and Mary and has long met in secret in order to celebrate their holy union and to worship the divine feminine. This secret society . . . has kept the tomb of Mary Magdalene and the hundreds of documents that told the truth of the divine feminine. . . . [It has pursued the ancient practice of goddess worship] through the ritual known as *hieros gamos*—literally "sacred marriage"—in which participants observe a male and female leader of the group engage in the sacred act of sex.[14]*

For his depiction of the priory, *Da Vinci Code* author Dan Brown drew heavily on the 1982 non-fiction bestseller *The Holy Blood and the Holy Grail* by Michael Baigent, Richard Leigh, and Henry Lincoln. Dr. Ehrman's summary has focused on *The Da Vinci Code*'s description of the alleged far-flung roots of the priory in the life of Christ; *The Holy Blood and the Holy Grail* focuses on the story from the actual founding of the organization in 1099 up to its role in modern times. The Amazon.com listing of *The Holy Blood and the Holy Grail* tells us that it is "the story of the Knights Templar, and a behind-the-scenes society called the Prieuré de Sion [Priory of Sion], and its involvement in reinstating descendants of the Merovingian bloodline [of French kings] into political power."[15] These French kings were the descendants of the children of Jesus and Mary. Baigent, Leigh, and Lincoln offer a list of twenty-one men and four women who, they claim, served as directors, or "grand masters," of the Priory of Sion through its one thousand years of existence. The list runs from obscure figures like Edouard de Bar and Blanche d'Evreux to world-famous personages such as Sandro Botticelli, Claude Debussy, Leonardo da Vinci (hence the title of Dan Brown's novel), Sir Isaac Newton—and Victor Hugo. Hugo, say the authors, was grand master from 1844 to 1885.

---

*Excerpts from pages xvii–xviii and 164 of *Truth and Fiction in* The Da Vinci Code: *A Historian Reveals What We Really Know About Jesus, Mary Magdalene, and Constantine* by Bart D. Ehrman. © 2004 by Bart D. Ehrman. Reprinted by permission of Oxford University Press, Inc.

A more recent grand master was Pierre Plantard, a relatively obscure Frenchman who died in 2000.

Christian scholars from Catholic through Evangelical have mounted a sustained attack on *The Holy Blood and the Holy Grail* and *The Da Vinci Code,* considering the latter in particular to be an out-and-out attack on Christianity. In *Cracking Da Vinci's Code* (2004), James L. Garlow and Peter Jones claim that *The Holy Blood and the Holy Grail* relies solely on documents provided by one Pierre Plantard, who was both anti-Semitic and spent time in a Paris jail for fraud in 1953. They say Plantard created the Priory of Sion out of whole cloth in the 1960s and 1970s by planting a number of fake "historical" documents in the Bibliothèque Nationale in Paris; these documents "proved" the existence of a bloodline descending from Mary Magdalene, through the kings of France, down to the present day, and including—Pierre Plantard. Garlow and Jones state that in 1993 "Plantard's name came up in light of a political scandal involving a close friend of then-French president François Mitterand. Plantard had, in one of his documented lists of the Priory of Sion, listed Roger-Patrice Pelat [Mitterand's friend] as a Grand Master. When called before the court to testify, Plantard, under oath, admitted he had made up the whole Priory scheme. The court ordered a search of Plantard's house, which revealed further documents that proclaimed Plantard to be the true king of France. The judge gave Plantard a stern warning and dismissed him as a harmless crank."[16]

In *The Sion Revelation: The Truth about the Guardians of Christ's Sacred Bloodline* (2006), authors Lynn Picknett and Clive Prince assert that Plantard's house was never searched and he never spent time in jail for fraud. At the same time, they argue convincingly that the Priory of Sion was indeed a tissue of lies concocted mostly by Plantard. They argue that the notion of a Priory of Sion was fabricated to serve as a cover organization for the existence of another, actual secret society. It's with the existence of this other, "non-Priory of Sion" society that we will be concerned at a later point in this chapter. For the moment, however, let's see if there's any basis in fact for the sensational statements made in *The Holy Blood and the Holy Grail* and *The Da Vinci Code* about the nature of Jesus Christ and the early Christian church.

Dr. Bart D. Ehrman, who has a Ph.D. from Princeton Theological Seminary and is proficient in Latin, Greek, Hebrew, Coptic, and

Syriac, begins *Truth and Fiction in* The Da Vinci Code by asserting that, contrary to what *The Da Vinci Code* says, the final composition of the New Testament was not imposed by the emperor Constantine at the Council of Nicaea in A.D. 325. Rather, says Dr. Ehrman, "the formation of the New Testament canon was . . . a long and drawn-out process that began centuries before Constantine and did not conclude until long after he was dead. So far as we know . . . the emperor was not involved in the process."[17]*

The non-canonical texts of Jesus's life (the texts that didn't make it into the New Testament) that have come down to us, along with descriptions in ancient documents of texts that haven't come down to us, do *not* emphasize the humanity of Christ (or, as believers in the Priory of Sion put it, "chronicle His life as a mortal man" and "revere him as a wholly human teacher and prophet"). Instead, says Dr. Ehrman, these non-canonical texts "tend to portray Christ as more divine" than do the books that now make up the New Testament. Moreover, only a couple of dozen non-canonical texts are known to exist—nothing near the eighty such texts *The Da Vinci Code* claims exist.[18]†

Constantine did not impose upon Council of Nicaea attendees the proposition that Jesus was the Son of God; this notion had been accepted by most of the attendees prior to the council, with only a tiny minority dissenting.[19]‡ Nor did the Council of Nicaea insist that the bishops vote on this one proposition alone. As the great majority already believed Christ was the Son of God, what the council really debated, says Dr. Ehrman, was "how to understand Christ's divinity in light of the circumstance that he was also human." The council allowed two ways of looking at this paradox: (1) God and Christ were

---

*Excerpt from page 24 of *Truth and Fiction in* The Da Vinci Code: *A Historian Reveals What We Really Know About Jesus, Mary Magdalene, and Constantine* by Bart D. Ehrman. © 2004 by Bart D. Ehrman. Reprinted by permission of Oxford University Press, Inc.

†Excerpt from pages 47–49 of *Truth and Fiction in* The Da Vinci Code: *A Historian Reveals What We Really Know About Jesus, Mary Magdalene, and Constantine* by Bart D. Ehrman. © 2004 by Bart D. Ehrman. Reprinted by permission of Oxford University Press, Inc.

‡Excerpt from page 14 of *Truth and Fiction in* The Da Vinci Code: *A Historian Reveals What We Really Know About Jesus, Mary Magdalene, and Constantine* by Bart D. Ehrman. © 2004 by Bart D. Ehrman. Reprinted by permission of Oxford University Press, Inc.

absolutely one, and (2) Christ was slightly subordinate to God, having been created by God, but so close to the beginning of things that his creation should be thought of as "before eternity."

The outcome of the Council of Nicaea vote was the adoption of the notion that God and Christ are one; this notion would soon evolve into the doctrine of the Holy Trinity, which is the cornerstone of the Roman Catholic Church. Dr. Ehrman adds that, contrary to the claims of *The Da Vinci Code,* the vote at the Council was not close but was carried by "the vast majority of the 200 or 250 bishops present."[20]*

The Da Vinci Code also maintains that Jesus Christ was married. Could this possibly have been true?

"In *none* of our early Christian sources," says Dr. Ehrman, "is there any reference to Jesus's marriage or to his wife. This is true not only of the canonical Gospels of Matthew, Mark, Luke, and John but of all our other Gospels and all of our other early Christian writings put together. There is no allusion to Jesus as married in the writings of Paul, the Gospel of Peter, the Gospel of Philip, the Gospel of Mary, the Gospel of the Nazarenes, the Gospel of the Egyptians, the Gospel of the Ebionites—and on and on. List every ancient source we have for the historical Jesus, and in none of them is there mention of Jesus being married."[21]†

In *The Da Vinci Code,* Priory of Sion apologist Leigh Teabing says that, according to the extracanonical Gospel of Philip, Jesus and Mary Magdalene were married. His proof: the Aramaic word for "companion," used in Philip to describe Jesus's relationship with Mary, actually means "spouse." But, counters Dr. Ehrman, the Gospel of Philip is written in Coptic, not in Aramaic, and the Greek loan word that is used for "companion" (*koinōnos*) "in fact means

---

*Excerpt from pages 21–23 of *Truth and Fiction in* The Da Vinci Code: *A Historian Reveals What We Really Know About Jesus, Mary Magdalene, and Constantine* by Bart D. Ehrman. © 2004 by Bart D. Ehrman. Reprinted by permission of Oxford University Press, Inc.

†Excerpt from page 153 of *Truth and Fiction in* The Da Vinci Code: *A Historian Reveals What We Really Know About Jesus, Mary Magdalene, and Constantine* by Bart D. Ehrman. © 2004 by Bart D. Ehrman. Reprinted by permission of Oxford University Press, Inc.

not 'spouse' (or 'lover') but 'companion' (it is commonly used of friends and associates)."[22]*

Scouring all the available texts, Dr. Ehrman finds no mention of anything resembling the *hieros gamos*. Referring to a passage Teabing claims describes Jesus's kissing of Mary on the lips, Ehrman tells us there are so many gaps and physical holes in the original manuscript that the text is finally totally ambiguous. Teabing asserts that Jesus's life "was recorded by thousands of followers across the land"; Dr. Ehrman responds that "we don't have any document written by a single eyewitness to the life of Jesus." The "vast majority of the population of Jesus's day was illiterate," says Ehrman, "able neither to read nor to write." Moreover, he says, Acts 4:13 suggests that two of the disciples, Peter and John, were in fact illiterate, and this was probably true of the other, lower-class, peasant-disciples. (Dr. Ehrman also reminds us that all four Gospels were written some decades after Jesus's death.)[23]†

What has Victor Hugo got to do with any of this?

If there really were a Priory of Sion, and we were recruiters looking for a grand master, we might put Victor Hugo fairly high on our list for several reasons.

Though brought up as a Catholic and respectful of Christianity, Victor Hugo did not believe Christ was divine. He believed Christ had been the mightiest figure in the history of mankind because (as Adèle notes in her diary for Valentine's Day, 1853) he had regenerated humanity "not by spilling the blood of others, but by spilling only his own blood, by achieving great things through his death."[24] But, as Adèle notes on April 28, 1853, he also believed that Christ had failed in his mission because he had not been able to root selfishness out of the human heart. Though radical socialists like Pierre Leroux were trying "to redo the failed work of Christ," no amount of social engineering could change the

---

*Excerpt from pages 142–44 of *Truth and Fiction in* The Da Vinci Code: *A Historian Reveals What We Really Know About Jesus, Mary Magdalene, and Constantine* by Bart D. Ehrman. © 2004 by Bart D. Ehrman. Reprinted by permission of Oxford University Press, Inc.

†Excerpts from pages 103, 106–7, and 178 of *Truth and Fiction in* The Da Vinci Code: *A Historian Reveals What We Really Know About Jesus, Mary Magdalene, and Constantine* by Bart D. Ehrman. © 2004 by Bart D. Ehrman. Reprinted by permission of Oxford University Press, Inc.

fact that self-interest would always be stronger than devotion for mankind. Christ's mission had been to change that. He had failed.[25]

Hugo's adoration of a kind of divine femininity, his belief in the sacredness of sexuality—aided and abetted by his reading of the *Zohar*—puts him at least near the ballpark of those entertaining Priory of Sion–like notions of female sexuality. In 1859, Hugo wrote a poem, *Le sacre de la femme* (The Crowning of Women), which contains a description of Eve's feeling a child stirring in her womb for the first time.[26] John Porter Houston believes that this image was "a deliberate criticism of the 1854 papal bull on the Immaculate Conception [declaring that not only Jesus Christ but his mother Mary was born immaculately], which outraged Hugo, for whom sensuality in nature and in divinity was a natural assumption."[27] In his 1855 poem *Dante's Vision* (not published until 1883), Hugo consigned Pius IX to one of the circles of hell; the ostensible reason for this was the pope's support for Napoleon III, but Hugo might not have gone through with the poem had it not been for the papal bull on the Immaculate Conception.[28]

To this may be added Hugo's intense and abiding interest in non-Christian theologies such as Hinduism, the Cabala, spiritism, and others, which interest, exaggerated by the spin doctors of the Napoleon III regime who wished to publicly convey the impression that Victor Hugo on Jersey Island was engaged in a kind of devil worship, would certainly (even one hundred and fifty years later) lay him open to the charge of being a grand master of the Priory of Sion.

Except that there was no Priory of Sion.

※※※

In late 1855, Victor Hugo, his family, and many of the other political exiles left Jersey Island to continue their exile on Guernsey Island.

Victor returned to Jersey only once, on June 14, 1860, to speak in Saint Helier at a special dinner and celebration designed to raise money for Garibaldi's men fighting for independence in Italy.

Had Hugo returned any time between 1862 and 1870, he would have almost certainly been greeted at the dock by a tall and awkward young man, a strange mixture of a wild-eyed fanatic, a dignified aristocrat, and a struggling arts and science teacher, named Joseph Alexander Saint-Yves, Marquis d'Alveydre (1842–1909). By the age of twenty,

Saint-Yves knew and loved the works of Victor Hugo; when Hugo died in 1885 and was escorted to the Panthéon by a rapturously grieving nation, Saint-Yves wrote a poem to the great poet, eulogizing him as the next stage in human evolution come to mankind to help us grow.

There is more. Lynn Picknett and Clive Prince tell us in *The Sion Revelation* that the Priory of Sion was a fiction created by Pierre Plantard as a front or cover organization behind which another, quite different, secret society could continue to flourish. The authors write that "inevitably we found ourselves investigating the politico-occult school of synarchy, first formulated by . . . the Frenchman who rejoiced in the name of Joseph Alexander Saint-Yves, Marquis d'Alveydre."[29]

Synarchy is the opposite of anarchy. It is a method of governance that regiments societies and fashions them into rigidly hierarchical structures. These societies are ruled by an élite. Picknett and Prince summarize Saint-Yves's views.

> Some people are *naturally* intended to lead: in other words, Saint-Yves advocated government by predestined elite. And although much of his work is about the practicality of applying synarchy to the government of society, at its core it is an essentially spiritual or mystical philosophy. The elite is spiritually attuned to the universal laws—effectively a priesthood. Synarchy is therefore a form of *theocracy*, rule by priests or priest-kings.
>
> Synarchy even suggests that this enlightened elite is in direct contact with, and receives its instructions from, the spiritual intelligences of the universe. . . . Saint-Yves himself believed he was in contact with invisible forces . . . [though] ultimately such elites are always self-selected.[30]

Late in his life Saint-Yves made sensational claims for synarchy, declaring that in archaic times a synarchical golden age reigned over a single empire comprised of all of Asia, Europe, and Africa. He declared that all later religions were a corruption of synarchical theocracy. According to Picknett and Prince, Saint-Yves "introduced the idea of Agarttha (or Agartha, as it is now), a synarchically organized land somewhere in the Himalayas." Saint-Yves came to believe that these primordial synarchical realms were underground, or at least their capitols were—and perhaps still are. He is at the origin of a line of esoteric thinking that can still be found in much "New Age" writing today.[31]

Picknett and Prince assert that Saint-Yves arrived on Jersey Island in 1862 and remained there until 1870 and that he enjoyed mixing with the political exiles on the island, particularly Victor Hugo. But we know that Hugo was not on Jersey at the time. Nor is there any record that he ever knew Saint-Yves.

However, it seems likely that Saint-Yves's ideas about synarchy began to germinate while he was on Jersey. We know that he came to believe that synarchy should be exercised over a number of nations at once as its smooth functioning could easily be disrupted by less synarchical neighbors. The best candidate for synarchy, he thought, would be a United States of Europe. We can imagine that Saint-Yves must have been impressed by the enthusiasm of the Jersey Island proscrits for a United States of Europe. He would have learned, and been very excited to learn, that Victor Hugo, perhaps the most eminent of the believers in a United States of Europe, had regularly communed with spirit intelligences at tapping-table séances.

Whether he ever discussed this with Hugo—and there is no record that he did—the founder of synarchy would have had little trouble convincing himself that the genius who wrote *Les Misérables* had been chosen by discarnate intelligences from higher realms of the universe to be part of an enlightened synarchical elite ruling a United States of Europe.

In all the vast correspondence of Victor Hugo, there is no mention of synarchy or of Saint-Yves. We know that Saint-Yves admired Hugo to the point of idolatry. Auguste Viatte writes in *Victor Hugo et les illuminés de son temps* (Victor Hugo and the Illuminati of His Time), "Later, the Marquis of Saint-Yves d'Alveydre, one of the masters of occultism between 1870 and 1900, will associate himself with the funeral of Victor Hugo by means of an ode; he will canonize him in the way Hugo would have loved; he will depict him 'in the heaven of the prophets,'

> *Comet whose fiery tail may illuminate*
> *Other stars that cradle on the Ocean of Being*
> *Another human race!*"[32]

Saint-Yves's thinking never ceased to evolve. The cavern-cities of his dreams of ancient synarchical illuminocracies acquired an internal "black sun," glimmering darkly over these underground metropoli. Perhaps Saint-Yves found the visionary image of a black sun in Victor Hugo's poetry.[33] If so, it's a good example of how an artist not of the highest order can borrow a metaphor from an artist of the highest order and allow it to overwhelm him in such a way that he wrongly begins to regard it as a literal representation of the truth. Hugo's black sun was a visionary black sun, an astral black sun—though the poet may have regarded it as having in its way a more substantive reality than any literal black sun. So it's possible that the Marquis of Saint-Yves d'Alveydre's adoration of Victor Hugo, along with his appropriation into the subterranean landscapes of his imagination of what he considered to be plain facts put forward by Hugo, may have played a role in making some people (especially Plantard) believe that Victor Hugo could have been a grand master of the Priory of Sion.

But, as Plantard himself knew, there never was a Priory of Sion.

VICTOR HUGO, JAMES MERRILL, AND WILLIAM BLAKE

THREE VISIONARIES, ONE VISION

You would not know us as men
We have only a dark shape
We once flew
We once soard

JAMES MERRILL, *THE CHANGING LIGHT*
AT SANDOVER

Every bird that flies holds the thread of the infinite in
its claw.

VICTOR HUGO, *LES MISÉRABLES*

How do you know but ev'ry Bird that cuts the airy way,
Is an immense world of delight, clos'd by your senses five?

WILLIAM BLAKE, *THE MARRIAGE OF*
HEAVEN AND HELL

The morning light, climbing high into the sky above Long Island Sound, brought out in piercingly sharp detail, as if striving to reveal their unchanging essence, every line and every curve of the pleasure boats rocking gently at anchor in the harbor at Stonington, Connecticut. It was midsummer 1955; the light flooded across the old port town; it poured through the kitchen window of the three-story house on Water Street, bathing in a pool of radiance the large white sheet of paper lying on the kitchen table between the two seated men.

One of the men was James Merrill, a small, wiry, twenty-nine-year-old poet; the other was David Jackson, a composer/writer just a few years older and a bit more heavyset. On the sheet of paper, in two curving rows, were written the letters of the alphabet. A blue-and-white upsidedown teacup was crawling awkwardly across the sheet of paper, moving from letter to letter. Each man had a finger on the teacup.

Until just a few minutes before, the moving teacup had been scrawling gibberish. Just now it had spelled out a message. That message was: *hellp o sav me.* Merrill and Jackson looked at each other in bewildered concern. They'd used this improvised Ouija board, meant to communicate with the dead, twice before, during the previous winter. Each time it had communicated messages so bizarre and nonsensical that they couldn't take them seriously.

This morning, though, was different. The two men had sensed a more purposeful energy flowing through the teacup. Then this awkward plea for help had emerged as the teacup lumbered from letter to letter.

Merrill asked the teacup to elaborate.

Suddenly a new and forceful energy seized the cup. It swerved, clung, hesitated—darted off. James Merrill asked it to tell them who was there.

Twenty years later, the poet, now enjoying an international reputation, would insert the teacup's reply into a lengthy poem along with commentary. He would write,

> *Ephraim*, came the answer. A Greek Jew
> *Born A.D. 8 at Xanthos* [in Greece] . . .
> Later a favorite of Tiberius Died
> *AD 36 on Capri.* Throttled
> By the imperial guard for having *loved*
> *The monsters nephew* [sic] *Caligula.*[1]

"Ephraim" immediately seized upon the imaginations of the two artists. That day, and in messages of increasing length over the next weeks and months, this shade of a Greek Jew told them about his other reincarnations, including one as a witty and salacious courtier at the court of Louis XVI at Versailles. He described to them the afterworld and an interdimensional system in which the souls of the dead, called "patrons," guided the souls of the living, called "representatives." The patron was a kind of guardian angel, though patrons were strictly forbidden to intervene directly in the lives of their representatives and had to operate through dreams and extremely subtle nudges; this system of heavenly patronage was open only to the roughly two million mortal "mover and shaker" souls who largely run our world.

Merrill and Jackson alternated between incredulity and delighted belief as the teacup spelled out beneath their fingers these revelations. They drew back periodically from these enchanting tales sent from a—most likely!—totally imaginary afterworld and swore to abandon their homemade conduit to the beyond. Just as regularly Ephraim, like a spirit Scheherazade telling yet one more tale to ward off execution, blazed back with a story even more exhilarating than the last.

Included among these stories was a three-layered tale of Atlantis. Merrill and Jackson were told that God had experimented with three other species before placing *Homo sapiens* on earth. First was a race of immortal flying humanoids, living in what is now China, who destroyed themselves in an atomic war.[2] Next came a race of immortal hairless centaurs—the true Atlanteans—who were immensely intelligent but, because they had forepaws instead of hands, had to artificially breed a species of immortal, erect, and six-foot-tall, humanoid bats to help them with their manual activities.

The humanoid bats rebelled against their masters and destroyed them with atomic bombs. Then the former servants built huge floating cities that, lasting a thousand years, finally crashed to the ground due to the negligence of the bats, every one of whom perished.[3] Now all three of God's immortal species were extinct. The creator brought forward *Homo sapiens*, mortal, but each representative with upwards of three hundred incarnations. Perhaps man, with death as his deadline, would learn enough not to destroy himself.

Throughout all this four powerful archangels ministered to mankind's needs. As the months turned into years at Merrill and Jackson's house in Stonington, Connecticut, these four archangels spoke to their mortal contacts with increasing frequency while a host of other spirits periodically dropped by. These encounters unfolded steadily, improbably, exaltingly, through the decades, until James Merrill, now considered America's premier poet, published the entire Ouija board saga in 1982 in a five-hundred-and-fifty-page epic poem entitled *The Changing Light at Sandover,* more than a quarter of the book consisting of direct quotations from the spirits. *The Changing Light at Sandover* garnered the National Book Critics Circle Award for Poetry in 1983.

Throughout all this time James Merrill remained hardly the type of person you would expect to find talking to a Ouija board. The future poet was born in New York City on March 3, 1926, the younger son of Charles Edward Merrill, cofounder and senior partner of the investment brokerage firm of Merrill-Lynch. Charles Merrill settled an unbreakable trust fund on his son when the boy was only five. James grew up in a milieu of great wealth and privilege. He attended the best schools in New York and New Jersey, and, after taking a leave of absence to serve in World War II, graduated from Amherst College with highest honors.

By the summer of 1955, Merrill had published two books of poetry and authored a favorably received off-off-Broadway play. He wrote and traveled extensively (he and Jackson came to own a house in Key West and an apartment in Athens, Greece, as well as the apartment in Stonington), steadily acquiring international fame as a poet. The first of his three Ouija board–based volumes of poetry, *Divine Comedies,* was published in 1976 and won the Pulitzer Prize for Poetry in 1977. The second, *Mirabell: Books of Number,* was published in 1978 and garnered a National Book Award. The final volume, *Scripts for the Pageant,* appeared in 1980. The latter two volumes, along with the poem "The Book of Ephraim," which made up the greater part of *Divine Comedies,* were published by Alfred P. Knopf in 1982 as the single-volume *The Changing Light at Sandover.* James Merrill died suddenly of an AIDS-related heart attack on February 6, 1995. He was not quite sixty-nine.

In January 1978, eight months after Merrill had won the Pulitzer Prize for Poetry, the author of this present book, then a reporter, interviewed him at his home in Stonington, Connecticut. Merrill's companion, David Jackson, was then vacationing in Key West. The reporter brought with him a friend, Judy, who had mediumistic abilities and had enjoyed a long and productive relationship with spirits on a Ouija board.

Then fifty-one years old, James Merrill was a well-put-together dynamic package of suave energy, even if the package was on the small side. His features were patrician, regular, fine, with the subtle near-invisible creases of a man who has used his mind intensely. He wore a natty brown corduroy jacket with matching trousers, a yellow silk shirt, and a friendly orange cravat. The outfit made him look elegant while convincing you he didn't take elegance seriously at all.

The brilliantly accomplished Merrill, raised in wealth and power and moving in the highest circles, might have been expected to display a certain *hauteur* toward a reporter and his medium/companion. Nothing could have been further from the truth. The distinguished poet was the soul of graciousness. From the moment he cheerily greeted his two guests on the landing of his second-floor apartment, to the moment when, bidding them good night, he released them with an extra bottle of wine into the cold Connecticut night, James Merrill took infinite pains to make the two feel at ease. He was urbane and witty and kind and thoughtful. He engaged his guests on a number of topics: teaching (he admired teachers and couldn't imagine how they did it), ideas (they made him uncomfortable, metaphor being his thing), war, peace, and much more. He cooked them a chicken dinner.

After dinner, the three sat down at Judy's Ouija board—not a homemade model but the customary piece of brown pressed wood the size and shape of a placemat with the letters of the alphabet, the numbers 1 to 0, and the words yes and no printed across it. James Merrill and Judy sat facing each other with the Ouija board between them; each rested a finger on the little three-legged heart-shaped marker called a planchette (and the descendant of the three-legged tapping table Victor Hugo knew). The reporter sat on one side and worked a tape recorder.

Judy called on her spirit guide, Sarah. The marker sprang to life. Skittering rapidly from letter to letter, it spelled out:

I emerge and I am here.

"It's a pleasure to meet you, Sarah!" exclaimed James Merrill.

The spirit (Judy knew for a certainty this was Sarah) replied, *Pray tell me, where is he who knows the way?*

James Merrill replied: "You're asking *us?*"

Yes. For it is you who lights the candle of tomorrow in the shadow of today.

"Still, I am blind to the light. The light is for others to see."

The light is warm.

"So even the blind may see?"

You feel it.

"And you don't?"

In the featherbed of dreams.

"Ah, you know about my featherbed!"

I make a nest there.

"Help my insomnia!"

James Merrill was delighted with Sarah. He asked to speak with his own first spirit guide, Ephraim. "Ephraim," he called, "are you there?"

The marker moved swiftly. *He emerges.*

"It's Ephraim," exclaimed Merrill happily. "Ah, my dear, *voilà!*"

The marker spelled out: *It's been quite a while. I have met Judy before.*

"Would you like to be more specific?"

Yesterday. Ah, yesterday, the wine of Wednesday, the vinegar of Sunday. Judy was my mistress.

"Which life, Ephraim?"

The life of dreams. Then: *I dare not say.*

"Ephraim, my dear, always the courtier!"

It was in Ancient Egypt. I abducted her. I loved, I loved, and never again. I love still. And never before. Always and never. I am he who bore Athena.

"If so, it's a very well-kept secret."

I speak in metaphor.

"Ah, well, indeed, in that case . . ."

A certain lassitude seemed to be overtaking Ephraim, as if he were suddenly weary of being a spirit guide. *We are indeed tired*, he spelled out slowly. *What have you to say to us?*

Merrill was quick to reply: "What have *you* done to be tired? We have lived in the smoggy atmosphere of daily life. What have you done, you who need no sleep, you who are higher intelligences—?"

We have spoken through ages of dreams and visions and missions and tasks. I have been your very dreams. We are powers.

There was more, a great deal of it of a personal nature. The séance ended after three-quarters of an hour.[4]

The reporter was struck by how surprised James Merrill and Judy had been at each response of the spirits; none of the answers had been the least bit expected. The marker hadn't seemed to be pushed by either of them; rather, it pulled their fingers along. Merrill was impressed by Judy's mediumistic abilities. He explained that he was not a psychic himself; that was David Jackson. Few other mediums had been able to summon up his guides; Judy had been the most successful.

What, the reporter asked James Merrill, did he make of this experience? Did he think he was speaking with spirits from the afterworld, or merely projections of his own imagination? Merrill answered that he'd maintained an attitude of perfect ambivalence toward the spirits for twenty-five years. He could neither completely accept them nor completely reject them; he didn't know what they were. But he never failed to be excited each time they came.

Merrill used the word coined by the poet W. B. Yeats, who had had similar experiences, when he said the "communicators" were either outside of us and working on our minds, which was, of course, fascinating, or they were inside of us, part of our total consciousness or unconsciousness, which was equally fascinating. Whether you were talking about a visitor from outside or about a sudden revolution of our DNA moving upward another spiral—both prospects were equally exciting. Seven years later, interviewed in 1985 by the Canadian Broadcasting Corporation on its radio documentary series *Voices and Visions: A Guided Tour of Revelations,* Merrill was to add,

> I worked very hard, in putting the poem [*The Changing Light at Sandover*] together, to try to persuade the reader that these things actually happened. Not to persuade him of the truth of the messages, but to persuade him of the actuality of the experience. I don't mind if people doubt what we were told, if people look at the page and say, "Huh, they call this revelation, you know, these are just banalities that anybody could stitch together." What does rather sadden me are the critics who think that we were pretending—that we didn't have the experience.[5]

To what extent did Merrill think that what the spirits said was true? The poet told the reporter that much of the time what they said to him seemed to be pure metaphor—though he felt sometimes that somehow they spoke to him both metaphorically and literally at the same time. The shades of the deceased bat-creatures, for example (Merrill had told the reporter about the contents of *Mirabell: Books of Number,* which hadn't yet been published), described the destruction of their floating cities as if that were an actual historical event.

Yet at the same time these bats—whose immortal souls now worked for the four archangels—also insisted they manifested from "within the atom," that they were a part of the elemental forces of nature. Merrill wondered if the account of the fall of Atlantis, which had culminated in the death of the bats, wasn't also an account of a fatal destabilizing of the atom—or perhaps of the extension of man's brain through the addition of the cortex at an early stage in his development.

Merrill insisted to the reporter, and would insist to everyone else, that the spirit guides, if they possessed an objective reality, were dependent for the expression of that reality on the memories and images and ideas that the living carry in their minds. In an interview in *The Paris Review* for Summer 1982, he would state that the powers or energies that constitute the spirits would be "invisible, inconceivable, if they'd never passed through our heads and clothed themselves out of the costume box they'd found there."[6]

The reporter asked finally if there were other writers apart from Merrill and Yeats who had had a similar experience? In response Merrill went over to a bookcase and pulled down a copy of *Chez Victor Hugo: les tables tournantes de Jersey,* edited by Gustave Simon and published in Paris in 1923.

"Victor Hugo had a similar experience," he said. "This is a collection of the transcripts. Hugo felt the spirits multiplied his creative powers by five."

That was how the reporter first learned about the Jersey Island spirit encounters of Victor Hugo. In James Merrill's answer lay the genesis of this present book.

❧❦

Victor Hugo was a hugely democratic author. He wrote for everyone and succeeded to the point that, when *Les Misérables* was published, thousands of people who couldn't read paid people who could to read the book to them.

James Merrill, whose instincts were generous, must surely have admired this. But his own poetry is dense, gemlike, intricately honed. It's hard to read, and his audience has consisted largely of his peers, of poetry lovers, and of university professors.

This basic difference notwithstanding, the information communicated to James Merrill by his spirit guides, and that communicated to Victor Hugo by his spirit guides, is strikingly similar in many ways.

It's natural to think that Merrill may have been influenced, or may have influenced what came from the Ouija board, by his reading of the transcripts of Victor Hugo's séances in *Chez Victor Hugo: les tables tournantes de Jersey*. But *Chez Victor Hugo* contains relatively few of the more controversial transcripts, and it is principally on those transcripts that the following comparison is based. (When he wrote *The Changing Light at Sandover*, Merrill hadn't read the far more complete collection of séance transcripts published in volume nine of the eighteen-volume *Complete Works of Victor Hugo*.)

In the messages conveyed to Victor Hugo there are no sentient species preceding mankind—no immortal winged men or hairless centaurs or humanoid bats.

But, in the cosmologies channeled to both poets, all nature has a soul. Victor Hugo speaks to Ocean itself; James Merrill and David Jackson speak to Mother Nature, who holds forth in the following manner (this excerpt is not complete):

> *Let me now say my soul*
> *speaks from within the greenness of a blade of grass.*
> *I take this humble station to best imagine*
> *how it was, that fourth or fifth dawn, when*
> *looking out I saw the rising sun*
> *over a faint haze of green sprouts. We peopled*
> *the virgin earth, and for a long spell ruled*
> *in a congress of slow but profound command, in league*
> *with the acid and mineral council . . .*

> *So the races of vegetable green began*
> *their sites apportioned with their attributes,*
> *and aside from some profusion & some slight*
> *extinction these have sensibly prevailed*
> *for 980,000,000 sun years. And now*
> *let me talk of the tongues & ways of communion*
>   *among us.*
> *Our "ruling" ones, the family of moss*
> *established a tactile language . . .*

In fact, Mother Nature sums up, *we are the resting place of soul.*[7]

Both the Merrillian and the Hugolian spirits declare that mankind is caught up in a reincarnational cycle that includes lives as animals, plants, and stones as well as lives as men and angels.

Merrill is told that this is his two hundred and sixty-eighth and last incarnation; Jackson is told he has lived two hundred and eighty-nine lives and has two or three more to go.[8] Reincarnation does not work the same for everybody, according to the guides. Mirabell (the shade of one of the bat-creatures) tells Merrill and Jackson (here Merrill is summarizing),

> *Soul falls into two*
> *Broad categories: run-of-the-mill*
>   *souls who*
> *Life by life, under domed thicknesses,*
> *Plod the slow road of Earth—billions of these*
> *Whom nothing quickens, whom no powers indwell*
>
> *The other soul belongs to an elite:*
> *At most two million relatively fleet*
> *Achievers . . .*

Though all souls reincarnate, the souls of the two million "movers and shakers" are recalibrated between lives. This procedure, called "cloning," takes place in the "Research Lab" ("an *emptiness packd full*") and is carried out by numberless shade-of-bat-creature laborers working under the direction of the archangels.[9] Merrill is told that between this lifetime and his last, the spirits

> *wafted him hither, added the humus of*
> *the Jew plus the gene of a chemist (& failed musician)*
> *et voilà U are not JM [James Merrill] what u might want*
>   *to be*
> *but a productive 5.5.*[10]

"5.5." is what Merrill's guides call his "talent rating," a part of his "Basic Formula." 5 is the maximum rating a soul can attain to on earth, and quantifies the capability of that soul to aid manknd; Merrill is a "partial 5."[11]

Sometimes the soul density of plants, called *shooting,* is introduced into the souls of the elite while they rest between lives. *Shooting is a cool upward thrust of / carbons. An intensity that might translate as pride;* its insertion into a soul being prepped for reincarnation triggers a particularly vital if somewhat short-lived life. The poet Edwin Muir and the horticulturist Luther Burbank were "cloned" in this fashion.[12] Sometimes the souls of the movers and shakers are reborn entirely as stones or plants or animals. But, in contrast to the universe as described by Hugo's spirits, a lifetime like this is not a punishment. It is, rather, a privilege—a *saintly elevation,* say the spirits, an opportunity to explore different realms of reality.[13] The deceased poet W. H. Auden (whose shade is now helping guide Merrill and Jackson) has taken life again as a mineral; one night the spirits excitedly report that *Our witty poet surfacing off Alaska as a vein of pure / radium has havocked a nosy radio ship: 58 in lifeboats!*[14]

What about the "run-of-the-mill souls who / Life by life, under domed thicknesses, / Plod the slow road of Earth?" Rather than being cloned in the Research Lab between lifetimes, these souls mostly "get a short pep-talk, then rejoin the race."[15] Today's population explosion has created new problems, resulting in run-of-the-mill souls being brought to the Research Lab in greater and greater number. Why? The bat-creatures laboring in the lab are running short of soul-matter and therefore

> *. . . we have in the past half century had to resort to*
> *souls of domestic animals, most recently the rat.*
> *By 2050 these too will be exhausted & then?*

Wilder strains, mountain cats and forest monkeys. So
    now u
Begin to see how without visibly interfering
We of the Lab must go about our work.[16]

The big difference between all-ensouled Nature as revealed to Merrill and that same nature as revealed to Hugo is that Merrill's guides don't describe the soul of Nature as constantly in pain. For them, earth does not consist only of prison cells. It (and other stars and planets in the universe) are not penal colonies straight out of Kafka.

The two sets of transcripts share in their differing ways a strange wrinkle regarding reincarnation. This is the idea of, as Merrill's guides put it, "safety deposits." The spirits tell Merrill that the soul-matter of deceased men and women of great distinction becomes part of a sort of celestial soul bank, from which transfusions are available to those talented mortals—especially geniuses—who might be expected to profit from it. Mirabell asserts:

Since mid 19th cent. souls of the great scribes
Have been used 1/9 on earth reincarnated, 8/9
as let us say safety deposits. We mine them. MM*
finds Plato lightweight & indeed he is nearly a shell.
But our haute cuisine is stockd with his live soul
    densities
which spice & fortify numberless earthly dishes. Proust
is deservedly enshrined. Tap him & as a statesman
at a dull banquet he converses, seems to be himself.
But part of his mind literally wanders: Out on loan.[17]

Merrill and Jackson are told that the shade of the French poet Arthur Rimbaud shared his soul-matter with that of the living British-American poet T. S. Eliot, in a sort of interdimensional Vulcan mind meld. The result: it was really Rimbaud who wrote *The Wasteland*![18]

---

*MM is Maria Demertzi Mitsotáki (1907–1974), daughter of a prime minister of Greece and close friend to Merrill and Jackson. She appears in *The Changing Light at Sandover* as a shade and one of the guides of her two friends (the same role played by the deceased W. H. Auden).

(This is not unlike the assertion of the English Romantic poet William Blake that the soul of the poet John Milton entered Blake's left foot on the day of his birth, thereby consolidating the Romantic poet's powers of writing epic poetry, which were quite literally an extension of Milton's.)[19]

A kind of analogous mind meld of distinguished deceased souls with distinguished living souls is hinted at by Victor Hugo's spirit guides. On December 16, 1853, the shade of Niccolo Machiavelli, the famed Italian Renaissance author of *The Prince,* tells the séance attendees on Jersey that, in the afterworld, *there are certain groupings of souls, certain tribes of souls, so to speak. Cain—he who slew his brother Abel—is the representative of one of these groups. From his shadowy lair* [in the afterworld], *Cain—this first arch-criminal, this true patriarch of crime—keeps an eye on those miscreants who have followed in his footsteps and who seem to him to wander the earth like chastised legions lost in an endless sea of remorse. Bit by bit the sinister forefathers* [now in the afterworld] *reflect on what they did while on earth, and in doing so they improve their behavior in heaven; and, to the extent that they improve their behavior in heaven, their descendents on earth behave in less evil a fashion.*[20]

What is the spiritual impetus that sustains the spirits in their mission to aid mankind? For that matter, what is the spiritual impetus that sustains mankind as it struggles to get through life?

The spirits of Victor Hugo and James Merrill concur that it is the quality that both call *devotion.* We saw in an earlier chapter that, on November 10, 1854, Death told the Jersey Island séance attendees that *the laws of the heavens conform to the laws of the earth; that law is the devotion of the great to the small, of the good to the bad, of the rich to the poor, of the beautiful to the ugly, of the just to the unjust—of the joyous to the joyless and the smiling to the bleeding.*[21] The Shadow of the Sepulcher echoed Death's words on December 18, 1854, declaring that *a tremendous need for devotion, that is the law of the worlds. . . . Love, love, you are the supreme solution, you are the final figure, you are God's billion and the prodigious sum total formed by all the dazzling zeroes in the starry firmament.*[22]

Merrill and Jackson's spirit guides believe no differently, even using the same word. Ephraim tells the two on October 26, 1961: *About devotion. It is I am forced to believe the main impetus. Devotion to each other, to work, to reproduction, to an ideal. It is both the mould and the clay. So we arrive at God or a devotion to all or many's ideal of the continuum. So we create the moulds of heavenly perfection & the ones above of rarer & more expert usefulness & at last devotion with the combined forces of falling & wearing water prepares a higher more finished world or heaven. These devotional powers are as a fall of waters pushed from behind over the cliff of even my experience . . . our state is exciting as we move with the current and devotion becomes an element of its own force.*[23]

What about good and evil? What do the spirit guides of the two poets say about God and the Devil?

The God of the Jersey Island spirits is, as we have seen, like the God of the *Zohar:* he has withdrawn a part of himself from himself to create the physical universe.

The God of James Merrill's spirits is also a God in retreat. The spirits call him "God Biology" or "God B," and he is the "youngest brother" of a galactic pantheon of gods. The Milky Way has been parceled out to God B, who has sent his four archangels—they are a fourfold form of himself—across space to create what will become our solar system. Over the millennia, through a process of trial and error, the archangels create our sun, the planets, and a succession of species on the earth. The three sentient species preceding mankind having destroyed themselves, God B brings forth, through the agency of the four archangels, *Homo sapiens,* whom God B had previously created but kept in reserve. Though God has denied man immortality, he gives him freedom of will. By the thirteenth century B.C., however, God B has decided mankind cannot handle such freedom, and the deity is obliged to withdraw this gift. He clones a "No Accident" clause into the souls of the religious leaders of mankind, beginning with Moses: God B controls their free will to a degree and obliges them to impose similar restrictions on their followers.

By the time the twentieth century arrives, the No Accident clause has begun to unravel. Religious leaders are losing their authority. Science and technology are providing souls outside the two million movers and shakers with too much power and spare time.[24] All this has weakened God B himself, since we humans stem from his essence.

The more we fall away from the divine, the more God B himself is diminished; mankind is pushing its creator further and further into retreat. The archangels grant Merrill and Jackson the privilege of hearing God B singing, but what the two hear is devastating. The Ouija board spells it out:

> *I've brothers hear me brothers signal me*
> *alone in my night brothers do you well*
> *I and mine hold it back brothers I and*
> *mine survive brothers hear me signal me*
> *do you well I and mine hold it back I alone in my night*
> *brothers . . .*[25]

A spirit guide who has been listening in remarks that God B is now a shipwrecked sailor *alone / keeping up his nerve on a life raft.*[26] A truth has been borne in on Merrill and Jackson that oppresses even these two airy skeptics: God cannot rescue us. We must rescue him.

Such is the predicament of God B, youngest brother of the gods of the pantheon of the galaxies, who was given the custodianship of our galaxy and created the earth and ourselves. But what about the Devil? Do wholly evil forces lurk anywhere in the universe as it is presented to Merrill and Jackson by their guides?

There seems to be a force somehow analogous to evil. It is located in the center of the earth and is called the Monitor. It really is a monitor, since it was originally a globe that was brought to this sector of the galaxy by God B's four archangels to enable his brother gods in the pantheon to keep track of the cosmos-building mission entrusted to God B. The Monitor is also an *anti-god of antimatter,* not even a *void* but rather a *solid emptiness.* To perceive it, say Merrill's spirit guides, would be as if one *should fling / a window up onto a wall of grey cement.*[27]

Since the Monitor is a minus quantity but yet a real presence, its location in the center of the earth exerts a downward sucking on the surface. This sucking force is essential; only in struggling against it can men and women achieve great works. It is also seductive; to yield to it completely is to do great evil. Hitler had given way entirely to the Monitor.

The spirit guides tell Merrill and Jackson that twentieth-century man, increasingly unconstrained by traditional moral and religious values, is gradually succumbing to the siren song of the Monitor. To be so much in its thrall can drive us to destroy ourselves; the guides as much as say that God B expects this to happen. That is why this greatly weakened deity has instructed his four archangels to prepare a fifth species, Alpha Man, in the event that mankind collapses. Alpha Man will be winged and immortal, greatly resembling the first three species. But he will *not* possess genius, genius being a faculty that flourishes only in the shadow of the Monitor and that, when it succumbs to the sucking force, visits immense evil on mankind.

There is still time for us to prevent our own collapse. But this will take an unremitting effort on the part of everybody. The guides beg Merrill to convey this message to mankind; it's why they came to visit him in the first place.[28]

Remarkably, a creation resembling the Monitor peeps through the words of the Jersey Island spirits and the poetry of Victor Hugo as inspired by those words. This Monitor-like entity also lies at the center of our earth. It is called the "black sun," and it, too, exerts a malevolent sucking influence on the surface of the earth.

The narrator of *What the Shadow's Mouth Says* tells us that the endless chain of being of metempsychosing souls ascends to the archangels *and in the heights vanishes in God,* while at the same time it descends to the center of the earth and plunges into *a hideous black sun from which radiates the night.*[29] The "shadow's mouth" that "says" is almost certainly the Shadow of the Sepulcher, and a great deal of *What the Shadow's Mouth Says* likely comes from the unrecorded words of the Jersey Island spirits (though Hugo denied this). In Balaam's Ass's first discourse, on December 27, 1853, the animal/spirit implies that the center of the earth is a hellish region blackly illuminated by a black sun.[30] In Hugo's *The End of Satan,* begun the next year, Satan, having plummeted down through interstellar space to the center of the earth (which center his fall in a sense creates), exclaims that in this region, *everywhere I go, looming up behind me, erect, the immense hydra of darkness opens its black wings.*[31]

Is the black sun the Devil?

No; in the work of Hugo, it is distinct from Satan. In the work of Merrill, it is both a black beacon monitoring God B's progress for the galactic pantheon and a sucking force against which man must necessarily struggle in order to achieve greatness.

We catch glimpses of a black sun here and there throughout world literature. It is a symbol in the pre-Buddhist religion of Tibet called *bon*. It is the luminous "black light" that rises in the north over the imaginal city of Hurqalya, in Sufism's "World of the Celestial Earth." It is present in Albrecht Durer's engraving, *Melancholia*. In his first-person novel *Aurelia*, French poet Gérard de Nerval sees it rushing across the western sky; this is synonymous with his slipping into madness. Among Victor Hugo's last words as he lay dying were: "I see a dark light!"

Jungian analyst Dr. Stanton Marlan tells us that the black sun was an aspect of the alchemical philosopher's stone in the thinking of the great psychologist/philosopher Carl Jung. In *Alchemical Studies,* Jung described it as "the light of darkness itself," a light "which illuminates its own darkness. . . . [and] turns blackness into brightness"—a light that "darkness comprehends" and which is "the central mystery of philosophical alchemy." Dr. Marlan contends that the black sun is "a kind of black hole whose gravity draws the vulnerable ego or self . . . into a doomed stasis." He speculates that the successful confrontation with the inner black sun may be the step that, in pushing the soul beyond reason and imagination, makes possible the total reintegration of the ego.[32] In confronting our inner black sun, we confront our worst self. If the confrontation is successful, we take a huge stride toward fulfillment. If the confrontation is not successful, we risk succumbing to murder, madness, or suicide; we may, so to speak, be taken over by the dark side.

The black sun plays a role in the work of the English Romantic visionary poet and engraver William Blake.

Blake perceived soul in every aspect of the world, seeing it as a perfected human form in all of nature's myriad manifestations from the smallest pebble to God. He lived his life as much in the presence of spirit forms as in the presence of human beings. The poet wrote:

> *For double the vision my Eyes do see,*
> *and a double vision is always with me.*
> *With my inward Eye 'tis an old Man grey;*
> *With my outward, a Thistle across my way.*[33]

When his "eyes did expand," he saw not only landscapes and sea-scapes flooded with sunshine but also numberless "particles of light, each in the form of a man."[34]

Blake's painting *The Body of Abel Found by Adam and Eve* (1826) can be interpreted in terms of the symbolism of the black sun. And in one of the "Memorable Fancies" in his prose poem *The Marriage of Heaven and Hell* (etched in 1793), Blake describes an encounter with the black sun.

The poet tells of being conducted by an angel to a dark "eternity" where, he is told, he will end up after death because of his blasphemous beliefs. The poet is led to a vast underground cavern dominated by a black sun. He writes,

> By degrees we beheld the infinite Abyss, fiery as the smoke of a burning city; beneath us, at an immense distance, was the sun, black but shining; round it were fiery tracks on which revolv'd vast spiders, crawling after their prey, which flew, or rather swum, in the infinite deep, in the most terrific shapes of animals sprung from corruption; & the air was full of them & seem'd composed of them: these are Devils.

A cloud of fire bursts from the depths. The cave is filled with black smoke roiling everywhere; Blake sees snarling monsters and souls streaming with blood. He is abruptly transported back to the "real" world and finds himself standing beside a little country church. The night is calm and moonlit. Blake's "astral eyes" have closed, if temporarily.[35]

How is it that the paranormal universes revealed to us by visionaries are, however outlandish they may seem, often so similar? Is there an objective reality out there? Or in there? In the final chapter of this book, we will touch upon some answers.

Twenty-three

GALILEO EXPLAINS
THE INEXPLICABLE

How would we feel if an archaeologist discovered and released to the world the text, which could be authenticated, of a biography by his father Joseph of Jesus Christ giving a complete and truthful account of the first twenty years of Jesus's life?

Or if an archaeologist exploring Mount Ararat discovered Noah's Ark and inside it the text, which could be authenticated, of the Holy Book of mankind before the Flood—the book which was the prototype of all religious texts and had given rise not only to Judaism but to every other faith as well?

We would probably feel profound awe and wonder, and eagerly look forward to scouring these texts for answers to mankind's problems.

This is how Cosimo de' Medici, ruler of Florence, Italy, in the fifteenth century, and Marsilio Ficino, one of the most influential humanist philosophers of the early Italian Renaissance, felt when an aging monk brought a certain Greek manuscript from Macedonia to the court of Cosimo in 1462.

The manuscript was the near-complete text of the *Corpus Hermeticum,* a book thought to date from the time of Moses and to contain the writings of the Egyptian god Hermes, also called Thoth. The ancient Egyptians believed that Hermes had invented writing; the *Corpus Hermeticum* ("the Works of Hermes") was thought to contain a synopsis, written by Hermes, of all the by-then-forgotten arts and sciences of ancient Egypt.

Ficino (1433–1499), an astrologer and reviver of Neoplatonism whose Florentine Academy had an enormous impact on the development of European philosophy, was then translating the works of Plato into Latin on the orders of Cosimo (1389–1464), himself a great patron of the arts. The ruler ordered Ficino to put aside Plato and begin translating the *Corpus Hermeticum*. The old man was ailing and wanted to read the *Corpus* before he died. In fact, Cosimo de' Medici died just before Ficino completed the translation in 1464.

A century and a half later, in 1614, an analysis of the *Corpus Hermeticum* by French philologist and theologian Isaac Casaubon (1559–1614) demonstrated that the texts originated between A.D. 200–300, thereby overturning the general opinion in Europe that they dated from the time of Moses.

Nevertheless the *Corpus Hermeticum*, first translated into Latin by Ficino, has never lost its power to beguile. And indeed so strange, original, and powerful are its contents that it's hard not to imagine that it comes from some aboriginal time when man still remembered what it was like to be a god. Following is an example:

> Unless you make yourself equal to God, you cannot understand God: for the like is not intelligible save to the like. Make yourself grow to a greatness beyond measure, by a bound free yourself from the body; raise yourself above all time, become Eternity; then you will understand God. Believe that nothing is impossible for you, think yourself immortal and capable of understanding all, all arts, all sciences, the nature of every living being. Mount higher than the highest height; descend lower than the lowest depth. Draw into yourself all sensations of everything created. . . . If you embrace in your thought all things at once, times, places, substances, qualities, quantities, you may understand God.[1]

One Renaissance thinker who fell under the spell of the *Corpus Hermeticum* was the great heretical Dominican monk Bruno Giordano, burned at the stake in February 1500 for insisting on the plurality of worlds and because he had set himself up to be, not a Christian priest, but an ancient Egyptian mage writing in the vein of the great god Thoth. We have already met Bruno, in our chapter on Balaam's Ass. For the Italian seer, Balaam's Ass is a metaphor for a messenger who is too pure to understand the message he is delivering; the Jersey Island spirits imply that Balaam's Ass, the spirit who holds forth on reincarnation theory, is itself a spotless, noninvolved conduit of God's word.

Bruno's last Italian moral dialogue, *The Heroic Frenzies* (1585) is (as well as being much else) a kind of subtle and complex elaboration on the basic concept of the *Corpus Hermeticum* as expressed in the selection cited above. Dr. Ramon Mendoza tells us that Bruno "firmly believed that human beings, because they have a soul united to the divinity in virtue of its intellectual capacities which 'transforms itself in god as if it itself were god,' needed to strive for the highest worth and dignity (*dignitas*) achievable by them." To do this, we have to transcend ourselves. But such transcendence "can only be achieved by a frenzied drive towards the true, the good and the beautiful." Man does not need a God to justify his actions; "he justifies himself through his own actualized transcendence."[2]

It sounds very much as if the man engaged in the quest for heroic frenzy had, like the student of the *Corpus Hermeticum,* to make himself "grow to a greatness beyond measure" and thereby "understand God."[3]

What does this have to do with Victor Hugo and the tapping-table spirits of Marine-Terrace?

Hugo knew something of the works of Giordano Bruno, if not through his German mentor Rabbi Alexander Weill, then through philosopher/socialist/journalist Pierre Leroux, who shared his exile on Jersey—or perhaps through his great friend and rival, the poet-politician Alphonse de Lamartine. Perhaps some memory of Bruno's *The Heroic Frenzies* lurked at the back of Hugo's mind to add spice to the cosmic brew when, on Sunday, December 10, 1854, beginning at nine p.m., the shade of Galileo Galilei (1564–1642) came to the tapping tables.

Galileo Galilei was the Italian scientist (then called a "natural philosopher") who formulated the basic laws of falling bodies, which he verified by careful measurements. Galileo constructed a telescope to study lunar craters and discovered four moons revolving around Jupiter. Espousing the Copernican cause, he spent the last nine years of his life under house arrest for refusing to tell the Inquisition that the earth did not move.

Present at the séance that night were Victor Hugo, François-Victor Hugo, Mlle Adèle Hugo, Auguste Vacquerie, and Théophile Guérin. Seated at the table were Mme Hugo and Charles Hugo.

The presence at the table introduced itself without prompting as *Galileo* and declared, *I've come to respond to Victor Hugo's objection about the scientific inexactitude of the cosmology of the tables. Let him formulate that objection.*

Hugo lost no time in reformulating his objection: "Obviously, what we humans call constellations are fictitious groupings, put together from stars that appear to be more or less the same size." Hugo went on to explain that our construction of the constellations was purely arbitrary, really just an optical illusion. But what, he wanted to know, were the real constellations? Their names were likely from a celestial language, not a human one; but surely humans could be taught to understand that celestial language. What then were the names of the actual constellations?

Galileo's answer began as follows:

My answer is in two parts. Firstly: If the table had to speak celestial language, not human language, you wouldn't understand a word. In celestial language, man is not called man, nor beast beast, nor plant plant, nor pebble pebble, nor earth earth, nor air air, nor water water, nor fire fire. Heaven is not called heaven, star is not called star, constellation is not called constellation and God is not called God.

Where there is no body, there are no words. Words are fashioned from physical reality; ideas are constructed from those words. But infinity is anonymous. Eternity doesn't have a birth certificate. Time and space are frightened unknowns careening through infinity. Space cannot throw a glance and time does not have feet; the first is a shadow that falls across a gulf, the second is a gulf that falls across a shadow. Time and space: two masks, two appearances, two visions, two dreams, two impossibilities, two eyes wide open with horror, two paws bloodied by the punishment they've given, two formidable jaws rising out of the unfathomable depths.

But time and space do not have a face. Or, it is a face that does not speak, a face that does not hear, a face that does not formulate. God speaking is God language, God language is God mouth, God mouth is God body, God body is God man, God man is God beast, God beast is God plant, God plant is God pebble. Can you imagine it? God pebble! He who is not even God star!

No, there is no celestial language. There is no alphabet of the uncreated, there is no grammar of heaven. You don't learn Divine like you learn Hebrew. Celestial is not a dialect of Terrestrial. Infinity is not an unknown type of Chinese. Angels are not Professors of Divine Language, substitute lecturers in the Faculty of Infinity . . .

No; everything is nameless, everything is sunlight and unknowing, everything is sunbeam and mask, everything is sun and roving. Infinity is a family of wanderers, space has no passport, and heaven has no specifics. Eternity has no genealogy, creation has no Christian name, God is neither fire nor place. All that which is uncreated is unnamed, the speech of celestial language is bedazzlement, to express oneself is to be resplendent, clarity of speech is luminosity. The sublime consists in being instantly overwhelmed; to speak the celestial language is to blaze forth in flames; the speaking-forth of heaven is the lighting up of the sky with stars; the shutting-up of heaven is the closing of the lips of darkness; and each letter of this stupendous vocabulary is a conflagration through which blows the breath of night's dark mouth. The dictionary of infinity is filled with the punctuation of stars, and what would you say, puny man, if, to speak to you in the language that you want, this little table, instead of syllables, words and sentences, suddenly hurled millions of stars in your ear, launched Jupiter, Aldebaran, and Saturn in your face, and spread out on your page the immense ink blot of the starry night while scribbling down corrections with furious comets?[4]

Galileo was finished for the time being. He promised to return on Sunday.

The shade of the great scientist indeed returned, on Sunday, December 17, 1854, at quarter of ten in the evening. Present at the séance were Théophile Guérin and Victor Hugo, with Mme Hugo and Charles Hugo sitting at the table.

Galileo announced his presence. Hugo asked him if he would complete his answer of last time by explaining the nature of the real constellations as distinct from the unreal constellations fabricated by mankind.

The shade replied: *That is your other mistake. Listen: I've talked about how the tables are forced to use your language to make themselves understood by you. Now, your language is merely a set of conventions; your language is a smoke screen issuing from your mouth and covering the stars over with clouds.*

Does that mean you humans are wrong about everything? No!

In feeling out the heavens, your hands sometimes touch the radiant knobs of the doorways of the divine. All man's falsehoods are filled with all God's truths; in the absolute there is no error; the relative is not the relative; lies are no more lies than discoveries are not discoveries. The astronomer Herschel finds out nothing new about God; true astronomers are no more truthful than false astronomers; all human telescopes are more or less resumed in a single one; this isn't the translation of what I'm saying, nor is it a mistranslation.

You say to me: I want the real heaven and not an imaginary heaven; I want the real firmament, real constellations, real suns; I want the total immensity of God, without a break, without a gap; I want the abyss without emptiness; bring me infinity; bring me mystery; I demand a map to Jesus's tomb, the itinerary of the resurrection; may they show me the incommensurable, sound the unsoundable out for me, open the seals of heaven for me. I want to go through the premises of the stars with a search warrant. Human constellations, let's see your papers. Big Dipper, identify yourself. Capricorn, you're lying. Aquarius, you're lying; you're a suspicious character. Firmament, you're under suspicion, I want to search your pockets, no more subterfuges. Lock all the doors; let no star escape! Handcuff God; I've got to question Him! And now, dark night, come before the court. And now, radiant day, answer. And now, accused suns, rise in your seats. I am president of the nighttime court of the assizes; I have a jury of ghosts; I declare the court to be in session. Silence in the gallery of the stars!

Let the witness Galileo enter!

I enter, and I say: O you who live, do I know heaven? Have I traveled over its immensity, not having traveled over eternity? How can you expect me to tell you about the tenants and the borders of infinity when it is not tenantable and has no borders? No one has ever been privy to the confidences of that immense being who is in the defendant's chair, namely, mystery itself. That being has no intimate friends who can confide its nature to you; it alone knows its secret. Not a single star will speak up. The conspirators of the shadows will all shut up, and the secret society of the stars will cover for God. Truth will swear no oaths, the absolute will not allow itself to be intimidated, and no examining magistrate will put paradise on the stand. No clerk of this court will draw up a list of constellations, no attorney will leaf through God's file, and before the crowd in this courtroom no sentences shall be pronounced, such as, the suns are acquitted, the constellations are convicted, the Big Dipper is declared liquidated, the complaint against Jupiter is dropped, and Aldebaran will be released and allowed to resume its motions through the skies. As for creation, we'll keep our eye on it and sentence infinity to monitor the lofty thoughts of mankind for a hundred million years.

I, Galileo, declare that I don't know the contents of infinity; I don't know where it begins and where it ends; I don't know what comes before, after, in the middle, to the right, to the left, east, west, south or north of infinity; I don't know its inside or outside; I see heavenly bodies, heavenly bodies, heavenly bodies; I see stars, stars, stars; I see constellations, constellations, constellations; I see sunbeams mixed with cloud-bedecked splendors and great blazings-forth of flame, bedazzlement lost in contemplation, contemplation plunged into bedazzlement; I'm caught up in the prodigious turning of the golden-hubbed wheel of heaven. Where is it going? I have no idea.

Night is the beaten track of the stars. I look up at the night and all I see are the millions of wheels of all the wagons of the conquering forces of the eternal, launched at top speed toward a goal that is invisible. I am an ignoramus of the unknown. I don't know the first heavenly body any better than I know the last. I defy you to find anybody who can say any more about the night than I can: It's a coalmine filled with shadows and with veins full of stars; you can only hollow out a shadow with a shadow, just as you can only polish a diamond with a diamond; from time to time the quarry of black marble gives the sculptor a vision of what the completed statue will look like; and God, what heaven is like. That's it. The firmament is a colossal riddle to which there are millions of keys; one star negates another, the heavenly bodies all deny and affirm each other, and no one knows if these millions of gold ducats that radiate out their light belong to the realms of the negative or the realms of the positive.[5]

Thus the séance ended, at 1:20 a.m.

Victor Hugo was not satisfied with this answer. On Monday, December 18, 1854, he, his wife, and their son Charles, the latter two sitting at the table, begged the spirits to be more specific.

Not Galileo, but the Shadow of the Sepulcher, made his presence known. Here is what he said:

I've come to bring you, not one of the keys to heaven, which must remain closed to human science, but one of the keys to God the whole power of whom is to fling open the gates to the loftiest progress of which the human spirit is capable. The firmament is full of abrupt and somber doors; it's an eternal din of brass hinges and splendid nails and flaming bars and luminous pincers. But God has no door-bolts; his way of shutting himself up is to exist without limits; his wall is the unlimited; his horizon is the impenetrable; you don't enter into him, because in him everything is majestically free to move to the beat of its own soul. You could take endless trips in his bottomless being; you could lose yourselves in this God, in this Word, in this inextricable network of flashing roads, in this virgin forest of effulgence.

God is the great wall; God is he who above all is accessible; he escapes into the inaccessible, and he gives himself to the accessible. He does not steal away, he does not isolate himself, he does not flee. He is all alone everywhere; millions of worlds comprise this enormous, solitary being; crowds of creations make up this immense anchorite; the multitudes of the heavens constitute the prodigious cavern that he is; the throngs of heavenly bodies and the populations of suns are the unity and soul of this tranquil monk who tosses on our world his rough, homespun, hair shirt made of clouds. Universal freedom has created this incommensurable prisoner. God is secretly in on this mystery. God is the prison master who is moved to pity by every slave but is a slave himself. He is nothing but misery; he is nothing but pain; he is nothing but pity. God is infinity's mighty teardrop. I come then to tell you God's thoughts regarding this firmament you want to know more about. And so, first, I ask you: Why just more? Why not everything? Since you're asking anyway, why ask for so little? You're not very demanding! What difference does a crumb of the sky make more or less to you? What a mediocre appetite for infinity is that which asks for an additional portion of stars and complains to its jailer about its ration of heavenly bodies! That's some mighty will you've got! That's a really awe-inspiring revolt! Some fear-inspiring riot!

. . . Do you want the optical point of view of [the astronomer] Herschel? Do you want the mirage of the planet to your left instead of the will-o'-the-wisp of the planet to your right? Do you desire, not the absolute, but a different relativity from your own; not the truth, but a different falsehood from your own; not the true meaning, but a different counter-meaning?

Are you fond of smoke, are you a fog gourmand, are you starved for shadow? You think you're asking for a bigger piece of reality, but you're asking for a bigger pile of lies; you want a greater variety of cloud, but not the full light of day. You want to be able to make a bundle of light out of a heap of shadows; and, finding that your world doesn't see clearly enough into heaven, you complain at not having been notified of three or four more planets, and you write self-pityingly: If only I were blind enough not to know how much more there is to know! Whereupon, like petulant street urchins, you throw rocks at the streetlights of God.

You know what I would do if I were in your place? I'd ask for all or nothing; I'd insist on immensity; I'd read the riot act to infinity, I'd raise my barricade to the top floor of the sky, I'd finish the revolution, I'd want to know everything, touch everything, take everything; I wouldn't let the sky off the hook about paradise; I wouldn't let it hide hell from me; I'd even put myself in the abyss; I'd make my brain the engulfer of God; I'd give myself a formidable mouthful of infinity: I'd be an immense and terrible Gargantua* of stars, a colossal Polyphemus† of constellations, of whirlwinds, of thunders; I'd drink the milk-basin of the Milky Way; I'd swallow comets; I'd lunch on dawn; I'd dine on day, and I'd sup on night. I'd invite myself, splendid table-companion that I am, to the banquet of all the glories, and I'd salute God as: My host! I'd work up a magnificent hunger, an enormous thirst, and I'd race through the drunken spaces between the spheres singing the fearsome drinking song of eternity, joyous, radiant, sublime, hands full of bunches of grapes made of stars and my face purple with suns! I wouldn't leave a star unturned, and at the end of the banquet I'd pass out under the table of the heavens radiant with light!

But you, you're more modest. You ask the world for alms, you merely beg from God, you stretch out your hand as you say to him: a little star, please! I'm getting to the question that preoccupies you. Your scientists are going to laugh, you tell me, at our astronomy; they'll holler: What is the meaning of these meaningless constellations? They'll be taking our optical illusions seriously! There don't have to be any connections between the stars we've used to make up

---

*A giant in Rabelais's book *Gargantua*.
†A one-eyed giant in *The Odyssey*.

the grouping of the Big Dipper, the grouping of Capricorn, and so on and so on. There are incalculable distances between these worlds whose roles you mix together in the sky! You impute to stars actions in common that those stars are not aware of! You joke about grouping stars together that are millions of leagues apart and have never spoken to one another. What a joke! Is the sky the hand of a juggler on which heavenly bodies leap about and perform tour-de-forces? *Is your astronomy a conjurer's table on which sufficiently gifted magicians make distances go away? No constellations, no sky, no God. . . .*

O scientists, beyond your calculations there is unity. Unity is the sum total of God. There is no figure one thousand, no figure one hundred, no figure ten, no figure two; God only counts to one. The sky is one immense constellation. There are not even two groupings of heavenly bodies; there is only one. There aren't millions of leagues, there aren't millions of feet, there are no distances under the sky; there is only nearness, only one family, only one people, only one world.

All these little constellations are false groupings relatively speaking and true groupings absolutely speaking; the Big Dipper and Aquarius and Orion are couplings tailor-made for you to gaze at and that don't disturb the harmony of the spheres; all these heavenly bodies see each other, and know each other, and attract each other, and love each other; they seek one another out and they find each other; they understand each other and they enliven each other; among them are those who communicate between themselves, those who marry, those who beget children, those who are entombed; there are no solitary heavenly bodies, no orphaned heavenly bodies, no widowed stars, no lost suns; not a single corner of the night is in mourning; not a single day is abandoned; there is not a single sphere that is not all by itself the hub of the heavens! The entire vault of the sky is filled with a single heavenly body that is ever-expanding; all the others are merely the seeds of this celestial flower. An immense need for devotion, that is the law of the worlds; night is a democracy of stars; the firmament is a symbolic republic that mixes together heavenly bodies of every rank and makes manifest brotherhood and sisterhood by . . .

Victor Hugo interrupted, referring to a line of his poetry, "I said: 'The future is the hymen of men on earth / And of the stars in the heavens.'"

. . . by the divine effulgence. The heavenly-body palace helps the

heavenly-body workshop, the heavenly-body workshop helps the heavenly-body garret, the heavenly-body garret helps the heavenly-body cellar, the heavenly-body cellar helps the heavenly-body prison; the infinitely small is the younger brother of the infinitely large; the genius star is the older brother of the idiot star; Hercules-suns always lie close to cradle-suns; the faces of happy worlds are forever peering about by the side of unhappy worlds; punitary stars are always weeping by the side of stars of reward; stars of reward are always smiling by the side of punitary stars. Consolation is the form that reward takes. There is always a heavenly-body dove near a heavenly-body grave. There is always a sun that is dressing wounds near a sun that is bleeding. Immensity is the love song of eternity. Love, love: You are the supreme solution, you are the final figure, you are God's billion and the prodigious sum total formed by every dazzling zero in the starry firmament. You are the supreme calculation, the sepulcher's treasure, the heritage of the dead. You are packed full of resurrection, and you turn the celestial wine-vaults into places of sublime celebration.[6]

The table stopped tapping. The séance, which had begun at half past three in the afternoon, had gone on until seven o'clock in the evening. Had Victor Hugo's questions been answered? On Tuesday, December 19, 1854, he wrote the following note, which has been preserved in the transcripts:

> I persist in making no objection. All this is enormous. Still, I don't confuse enormousness with infinity. God alone is infinite. It seems to me that what was personally addressed to me confirms my earlier note. The great biblical reproaches are there, but under a different form: According to the lights of my conscience, I do not believe that I have deserved them.
>
> As far as all the rest is concerned: I don't believe I'm mistaken in my thinking; but I don't believe that the world of the sublime, which speaks to us in such magnificent language, is mistaken either. It does as it must with respect to us: It leaves us in doubt. The table ended up by practically jeering at me. It asked me, "What difference does a crumb of infinity matter to you more or less?" I will insist no further. I believe in my heart that I'm right; but I silently bow my head before the sublime being who spoke to me yesterday, and who ended with such lofty, and such gentle, words.[7]

Twenty-four
JOSHUA BRINGS DOWN
MORE WALLS

In the following passage from *The Toilers of the Sea,* Victor Hugo holds forth on the interconnectedness of all things. (Schwabe and Slough, to whom Hugo refers, are nineteenth-century astronomers.)

From October 10, 1781, to March 25, 1782, while the fifty-fifth star in Hercules was in process of extinction, the ocean was convulsed with storms. Schwabe vouches for the solar event, Slough for the stellar. Why not? An ant weighs upon the earth; a star can well weigh upon the universe. Who knows to what extent we depend upon the variations of the *Gamma* star of Antinoüs, on *Delta* of Cepheus, and on *Alpha* of the Dragon? Who knows the dimensions of cosmic influence? The length of emanations? Do we not in some measure feel, in the repercussions upon our own planetary system, all those distant yet enormous presences—Sirius, Mira Ceti, Argo at times attaining nearly the intensity of Canopus, and Hevelius's oscillations of Hydra?[1]

Ten years earlier, in *Les Misérables,* published in 1862, Hugo discoursed with equal power but more poetically on the mysterious, seeming interconnectedness, of all parts of the universe. In part 4 (*Saint-Denis*), book 3, chapter 3, the narrator writes,

No thinker would dare to say that the perfume of the hawthorn is useless to the constellations. Who could ever calculate the path of a molecule? How do we know that the creations of worlds are not determined by falling grains of sand? Who can understand the

reciprocal ebb and flow of the infinitely great and infinitely small.
. . . There are marvelous relations between beings and things; in this
inexhaustible whole, from sun to grub, there is no scorn; each needs
the other. Light does not carry terrestrial perfumes into the azure
depths without knowing what it does with them; night distributes
the stellar essence to the sleeping plants. Every bird that flies has the
thread of the infinite in its claw.[2]

Victor Hugo had nurtured such beliefs for most of his life. So
he could hardly have felt uncomfortable when, in the table-tapping
séances of December 28 and 29, 1854, these ideas (and others like
them) found brilliant and bewildering expression in the words of—or
so the tapping tables declared—the shade of the same Israelite warrior
Joshua who had brought down the walls of Jericho with trumpets and
made the sun stop in its tracks. The December 28 session was attended
only by Victor, Mme Hugo, and Charles Hugo, the latter two seated at
the table while Victor Hugo recorded the proceedings. The table was
a brand-new one, borrowed from the Allixes; the regular table had
become permanently warped by the violent shaking to which the spirit
world regularly subjected it.

What Joshua was to say that night would be integrally connected
to all that the spirits had said before. But it would be complex. Let us
summarize in advance the main thrust of his argument.

Every discrete entity in the universe—atom, plant, angel, even created objects, like scissors, guillotines and mirrors—has a soul.
Every discrete entity in a man or woman's body has a soul—every
atom, cell, organ, every part of every organ.
Every discrete entity in a man's body participates in a reincarnational cycle: that which is nearest to a stone (the bones?) evolves
into a stone and beyond; that which is nearest to a plant (the
lungs?) evolves into a plant, and beyond; and so forth.
Every discrete part of the body was, is, and becomes a part of
everything else in the time-space continuum, and if that space-
time continuum were to be cleansed from our senses for just an
instant and we could see creation *sub specie aeternitatis*—from
the viewpoint of eternity—we would see that everything is
everything else; that is, that everything is one.

Such is the nature of this unity that if God were to annihilate the entire universe except for the smallest discrete entity that can possibly exist, then the entire universe could and would re-merge from that single discrete entity.

These concepts seem to lie at the heart of what the shade of Joshua told the séance participants on the night of December 28, 1854—though his words were inevitably clothed in the somber images of imprisonment and suffering that came to characterize so many of the spirits' utterances. (The word "I" [*moi*], appearing often in the transcript of this séance, seems not to refer to the first person singular but rather to designate a single discrete entity.)

Here is what the shade of Joshua said:

Man is not a simple I. He is a complex I.

In his epidermis there are millions of beings who are millions of souls. In his flesh there are millions of beings who are millions of souls. In his bones there are millions of beings who are millions of souls. In his blood there are millions of beings who are millions of souls. In his hair there are millions of beings who are millions of souls. In his nails there are millions of beings who are millions of souls. Every breath exhaled from his mouth is a whiff of souls; every glance from his eye is an outward radiation of souls.

The biggest nest of all is in the brain. There every fiber is a soul that thinks; an idea takes shape only because of the slow and painful work of every prisoner soul laboring under the vault of the human skull. A brain is a solitary confinement cell; an idea is an escape from that cell. Every limb of a man's body is a prison corridor. His head is a solitary confinement cell. Man is a prisoner who also serves as a prison. He is an infinite I filled with imperceptible I's; he is a world unto himself.

He is a hell to the tips of his nails and a hell to the roots of his hair; his veins are rivers filled with drowned bodies; his bones are hitching posts hung with horses' collars; his hairs are the cords of an invisible whip whose grim throngs are used by the wind to lash convicts imprisoned in the man's skull.

Man is filled with criminals about to be executed; he is the instrument of those executions even as he is the one about to be executed. He is both the hanged man and the noose, both crucified savior and cross.

At this point Joshua seems to pass over to the subject of man's astral body, which also swarms with I's.

He is a man drawn and quartered, whose four limbs draw and quarter the world and whose arms and legs are like four furious horses bearing bloodied souls away to the unknown. Man rises in the evening in the world of shadows, and all nature beholds him with great dread; heaven says, It is Christ; Earth says, It is Calvary. Man bears on his head a gigantic crow that is eternally in flight and whose huge wing man glimpses only at night. Gaze into this abyss:

Man is an I peopled with I's who do not know him and whom he does not know. Each I is in its turn filled with other I's, and so on to infinity. The I of the man dwells in complete wholeness, and each I interior to the man is equally entirely whole. Man knows nothing of his being. He cannot know what lives, what dies, and what is born within him. Man is nothing but the principal soul of the human body; within him are the souls of other men, the souls of animals, the souls of plants, the souls of stones. There is more: There are souls of stars. Man is the world; man is the sky; man is the infinite; man is eternal; man is the seed of creation tossed to the four winds and scudding through the great gulfs of God.

The merest I is an infinite atom containing within it the template of all other I's. Beast contains all the I's of man. Plant contains all the I's of beast. Pebble contains all the I's of plant. The heavenly spheres contain all the I's of man, beast, and plant. They contain all the I's of man, beast, plant, and pebble. The sky contains all the I's of all the spheres. God contains all the I's of all the heavens; but here the horizon is only beginning to open out.

You'll see; you'll see; you'll see. Oh, all-powerfulness of God! He has made the world into something that cannot be lost; he has placed the seed of every being in every other being; he has made every fruit the pit, and every pit the fruit; he has enclosed man in beast and beast in man, plant in pebble, and pebble in plant; he has placed the star in the sky and the sky in the star, and he has placed himself in all and all in himself, in such a way that if it were to happen one day that a whirlwind, a flood, or a hurricane destroyed men, beasts, plants, and stones, if it were to come to pass that a comet devoured the stars and, annihilating itself, left nothing more of creation than a single grain of sand, God would smile and, taking the grain of sand in his hands, would toss it up into space and shout, "Emerge, millions of worlds!"[3]

These enigmatic—even impenetrable!—declarations sound curiously modern in certain ways.

There are certain contemporary cosmologies, often viewed with skepticism by scientists who believe they point more to metaphor than to empirical fact, that remind us of the cosmos described by the shade of Joshua. One such cosmology is quantum holography.

Michael Talbot writes in *The Holographic Universe,*

> Unlike normal photographs, every small fragment of a piece of holographic film contains all the information recorded in the whole. . . . This was precisely the feature that got [neurophysiologist Karl] Pribram so excited . . . it seemed equally possible for every part of the brain to contain all the information necessary to recall a whole memory . . .[4]
>
> As soon as physicist [David] Bohm began to reflect on the hologram he saw that it . . . provided a new way of understanding order. Like the ink drop in its dispersed state, the interference patterns recorded on a piece of holographic film also appear disordered to the naked eye. Both possess orders that are hidden or *enfolded.* . . . The more Bohm thought about it, the more he became convinced that the universe actually employed holographic principles in its operations, *was itself a kind of giant, flowing hologram . . .*

Bohm believes that the quanta making up the universe may be holographic. He dreams of someday being able to harness the "quantum holographic" aspect of the universe.[5]

Did the historical Israelite warrior Joshua know how to manipulate the interconnectedness of all things, including sun, earth, stone, and sound?

Such speculation seems outlandish, to say the least. But before we close our minds let's listen to what Joshua had to say at the séance of December 29, 1854—the second, and final, "Joshua" séance. The session began at 10:15 p.m. In attendance were Victor Hugo, Jules Allix, Augustine Allix, and Auguste Vacquerie, with Mme Hugo and Charles Hugo sitting at the table.

For the first few minutes nothing happened. Then the table began to vibrate. Joshua announced his presence.

Victor Hugo asked: "Do you want to continue from yesterday, or should we ask you questions?"

The spirit replied: *Some questions.*

Hugo asked: "People attribute to you the impossible miracle of making the sun stand still in the sky. How should we understand this? What have you to say on the subject yourself?"

We come here not so much to verify facts as to illuminate ideas; however, since you as a man of ideas ask me about this, I am going to answer you. The sun is the life of nature; night is its death. The day is a being who lives for twelve hours and drags behind him a corpse that is dead for twelve hours. Eliminate night and you will have a being that is alive for twenty-four hours. I have been prophet, I have been light, I have eliminated night. I have been the idea of the sun that stops its beams from shining upon suffering. I said to my soul, You shall go no farther; I stopped the star from shining on worms, on caterpillars, on rags, on wounds; I stopped the clock from ticking and the hour of light from illuminating the clock face of night; I stopped noon from shining on midnight.

Maybe it was because he was bewildered—or maybe because he had a topic of more immediate interest on his mind—but Victor Hugo now changed the subject by asking the shade of Joshua if he were the same spirit who had come to them the year before, and who had predicted the overthrow of Napoleon III for 1855.

The tapping table replied:

You're wasting time asking me if I know Bonaparte. From the way you talk about him, Bonaparte is a bad fellow. Bad people do not come within my purview. I read words that are, not words that have been erased.

The shade returned to what was apparently the main theme of his lecture:

Let's talk about the stars. Man will find everything, he will eliminate everything and all the distances of God from himself. There is nothing but distance. Night is only distance from day, evil distance from good, pain distance from happiness, earth distance from sky. Man has already eliminated the distance of man from man with democracy, the distance of country from country with a railway, the distance of pain from well-being with chloroform, the distance of darkness from daylight with electricity, the distance of life from death *with science, the distance of air from earth with the balloon, the distance of sea from earth with the steamboat, the distance of fire from coal with the Volta pile,* the distance of pearls from women with the diving bell, the distance of stone from house with the worker in quarries, the distance of iron from tool with the blacksmith, the distance of lead from idea with the printing house,† the distance of gold from falsehood with paper money, the distance of cradle from grave with the mother, the distance of grave from cradle with the father, the distance of man from beast with the dog, the distance of beast from plant with the garden, the distance of plant from stone with the swallow's nest . . . the distance of seed from wheat field with the sower, the distance of winter from spring with the ploughman, the distance of spring from summer with the farmer, the distance of summer from autumn with the harvester, the distance of autumn from winter with the grape gatherer, the distance of snow from heat with the radiator, the distance of matter from idea with art, the distance of plastic beauty from moral splendor with the Parthenon, the distance of pain from the crown of thorns with Calvary . . . the distance of yes from no with perhaps, the distance of strength from love with the promise kept, the distance of two arms from the cross with the two arms of Jesus Christ, the distance of two arms from Jesus Christ with the knees of Mary Magdalene, the distance of the cosmos from eternity with prayer, the distance of the thunderbolt from the abyss with the lightning bolt captured by the lightning rod, the distance of Nero from the gladiator with the martyr, the distance of mystery from doubt with faith, the distance of faith from mystery with doubt, the distance of the infinitely small from the infinitely large with the eternally fallen to its knees.*

He has eliminated every distance that comprises a hand's length, a foot's length, an eye's length—and he wants to stop there! He doesn't want to be able to leap the distance from one star to another! He

---

*In 1800, Alessandro Volta (1745–1827) invented the voltaic pile, an early electric battery, which produced a steady electric current.

†This statement seems to mean the following: Movable type is made from lead. So lead made possible the invention of movable type. Movable type made possible the invention of the printing press. The printing press made possible the universal dissemination of ideas. So the invention of the printing press eliminated the distance between lead and idea; lead leads directly to ideas.

wants to be attached to this planet forever, like an animal is attached to its harness. He doesn't want to be able to look at the sky in any other way than attached to his leash, and he wants to be restricted solely to that nocturnal glance! He wants to be the center of the universe! He wants to put his stamp on darkness! He wants to bark at the stars! He doesn't want to take a bite out of the starry worlds. Where are you, you million leagues that can stop mankind? Show us your empty zeros, numbers without sense; merely a mad chain, show us those links. You are nothing but clouds, you millions of leagues, and man is a torch with all the boldness of a torch. Watch out, heavenly distances: Man hungers for the stars, man is the mighty traveler, man is the great devourer of the impossible, man is the mighty igniter of realities; if you don't want him to do these things, he will force you to accede; he will take you, abysses, in the hollow of his hand; he will boot you out, you, mastiff made of nothing but night; he will pile you up, faggots of cloud, vine-shoots of fog, coal made of evanescent emptiness, and he will set fire to these shadows with the colossal spark of his spirit, so that the very stars will shout out: Let us go and watch the conflagration.[6]

The table abruptly stopped moving. It was one o'clock in the morning.

Whatever was Joshua talking about? He seemed to be saying that distance is merely an illusion. He seemed to be implying that it is through the constant repetition in our minds (as if we were chanting a mantra or telling prayer beads) of the infinite varieties of distance that actually create these distances, and that if we were somehow able to move beyond this, we would be able to access within us the laws of the universe in such a way that distance would no longer exist.

Unfortunately, there is no record of what the participants thought about this profoundly enigmatic second séance of Joshua's. Its concepts do tend to put us dwellers in the twentieth-first century in mind of the concept of non-locality that lies at the heart of the modern cosmology called quantum holography.

Following is a final quote from Michael Talbot:

An even more surprising feature of the quantum potential was its implications for the nature of location. At the level of our everyday lives things have very specific locations, but [physicist David] Bohm's interpretation of quantum physics indicated that at the subatomic level, the level in which the quantum potential operated, location ceased to exist. All points in space became equal to all other points in space, and it was meaningless to speak of anything as being separate from anything else. Physicists call this property "non-locality."[7]

We seem to have arrived at the border between science and mysticism. Let's clear the air by shifting to what is unequivocally just religion and hearing what the shade of Jesus Christ had to say, nineteen centuries after his crucifixion, about the religion he himself had created and about other religions as well.

Twenty-five
JESUS CHRIST REVISES
HIS THINKING

When the spirit calling itself Death told Victor Hugo on October 22, 1854, that the tapping-table transcripts should be published as a book entitled *Advice from God,* Hugo asked what was for him an important question:

"What ought to be written on my tombstone? Prophet? Or poet?"

Hugo had begun to believe his destiny was to found a new religion. Denis Saurat sums up what the poet thought would be the two central tenets of this new religion:

"The idea that there are individual and conscious souls everywhere, even in stones;

"The conception of a universal pardon that leaves no soul without redemption; that this happens is not only possible but inevitable."[1]

Three months later, on Sunday, February 11, 1855, at 9:30 p.m., none other than Jesus Christ himself appeared at the tapping tables to give Victor Hugo some hints as to what his destiny might be.

Christ had come to the tapping tables twice before, on September 15, 1853, and on February 27, 1854. Each time his words had been brief. On the first occasion he had merely said, *Christ announces the resurrection,*[2] and on the second, *I have the key [to freedom from imprisonment].* (On that second night, in response to the request of Judas's shade to *give me the key,* he had replied, *There it is, Judas.* And, on that second night, both times that Jesus spoke, the table shook.)[3]

However, at the séance of February 11, 1855, Christ had a great deal to say. In attendance were Augustine Allix, Jules Allix, François-Victor

296

Hugo, and Auguste Vacquerie. Mme Hugo and Charles Hugo sat at the table.

After a brief exchange of commonplaces, the founder of Christianity began a lengthy disquisition. He asserted that mankind's destiny has been to be successively governed by three great religions, the first two of which now belong to the past. Those first two religions are Druidism and Christianity. Druidism had erred by sacrificing mankind to the supernatural—by using cruel and violent means to teach him about eternity. (Throughout, Christ seems to be speaking only about the Western world.)

Here are Christ's words:

Druidism is mankind's first religion. It is the first explosion of soul into body. The Druids radiate the soul out across the debris of bloody matter. They break the body with blows made out of heaven. They assassinate mankind with blows made out of God. They kill the child with blows of prayer. They crush old men with blows of the grave. They turn the soul's splendor into the liberator of all and the murderer of all. Druidism's soul is an angel with hatchet wings. Druidism fills forest, stream, animal, stone with flecks of blood and reflections of stars. It gets the word out about eternity by inflicting injuries and of immortality by filling up tombs. It tears suns out of men's bodies by torture. It teaches humanity about infinity by torturing its body; it tears men's flesh with pincers made of the two sides of the firmament. To teach mankind about eternity, it pours melted sunbeams into his veins, draws and quarters him with the four winds, beheads him with the golden cutting-edge of the moon and throws his head into that charnel house of enormous darkness that is the heavens. Druidism is the soul's crime against man. It is eternity, immensity, heaven, stars, lightning, thunder, bandits.

Christianity represented a step upward. However, it was still a barbarous religion in that it made God a cruel God, one who avenged Himself on mankind by providing us with an eternity of suffering in hell.

Christianity represents a step forward in terms of life on earth but a step backward in terms of life in heaven. It teaches love in the name of charity and hatred in the name of hell. Man is everything; animal, plant, and stone are nothing. Christianity says: The soul is immortal and punishment is eternal. Christianity heals the sick and tortures the guilty. It exalts human sacrifice to a place in the firmament, makes the grave the answer to our questions, rewards physical suffering with a place in the immaterial world, and turns the stars into infamous firebrands in a funeral pyre made of darkness.

Pardon me, my God, but Christianity is vengeful, Christianity steals things away from us, Christianity punishes unremittingly. Christianity dies on the cross and inflicts torture in the lofty heights of heaven. It turns night into death's somber will. It talks gloom to the sin, matter to the soul. It is the fall into the body, not the flight of the soul. Druidism pleads with the living body; Christianity martyrs the corpse. Christianity wants a heaven in flames; Druidism wants an earth soaked in blood. Christianity is, like all things human, progress and evil. It is the door of light locked by the night. The key is in front of the door; the passerby opens the door and thinks he is in the presence of God. But the passerby is mistaken. God is the one who's not there. God is He who is eternally in flight.[4]

Christ returned a week later, on Sunday, February 18, 1855, at 9:45 p.m., to pursue the same theme. Present were Augustine Allix, Jules Allix, and Auguste Vacquerie. Sitting at the table were Mme Victor Hugo and Charles Hugo.

The table was silent for about ten minutes. Then it began to move. Christ announced his presence. Victor Hugo asked the shade to begin.

His words were:

Christianity is the body happy on earth (because of the abolition of druidic human sacrifice) but tortured on high. Christianity is the soul happy on earth but made to suffer above; the essence of Druidism is human sacrifice while the essence of Christianity is divine sacrifice.

Christianity is made up of two things: love and hate. It makes mankind better and God worse. It is the possessor of a cradle full of kisses and a grave full of wounds; it cures the living but burns the dead at the stake; it blesses the adulteress while it consigns her corpse to hell; it resurrects Lazarus even as it burns his ashes; the lips of Christianity are made of honey, but its tongue is made of fire; what has begun as a sunbeam ends up as flames. Christianity makes an Eden of earth and a hell of heaven; it makes flowers that charm and stars that horrify; it enlightens woman while it sets Venus on fire; it makes dawn white-hot, day white-hot, and the sunset white-hot; it is the great savior and the great executioner; it is the glance that weeps for the earth and the glance that sends flames rising up to heaven; it is the sublime weeper and the formidable avenger; it dresses the wounds of life and opens the wounds of eternity; it inserts softness into matter and terror into idealism; it pours balm on man and boiling oil on suns.

Druidism made hell on earth, while Christianity makes it in heaven; Druidism takes iron, stone, lead, brass and tortures the living soul with the material, while Christianity tortures the resurrected body with the ethereal. Christianity uses as its tools the lily of the ether and the roses of the sky; it gives to the dawn the fingers of a tormenter; it suffocates the dead beneath the pillow of the tomb; its hell has millions of furnaces, millions of fires of live coals, millions of funeral pyres; it goes from north to noon and immensity to eternity; it swirls up dust, it flashes, it thunders, it exhausts birds as it crushes souls; it has the Milky Way as underground passage, the Southern Cross as crossroads, Saturn as muddy hole in the road, Mars as a precipice, anger as an inn, and in that inn's hearth eternal flames for a fireplace. Druidism gazes at forests, hills, plains, and says to them: let us torture.

Druidism hides its victims in the dens of animals. Christianity exposes them to infinity; Druidism hides itself in the woods, Christianity hovers in space; Druidism lives beneath the ever-somber oak; Christianity resurrects pain beneath the ever-radiant blue of the sky; Druidism makes tree branches bristle with horror. Christianity makes the beams of heavenly bodies shiver with fright; the dolmens of the druids are drenched in blood; the autos-da-fé of the Christians are drenched in sulphur. Jesus Christ sees God only in the purple of fire; religions are great hammer blows delivered to mankind's skull, each spark putting out a star and lighting up a hell.[5]

Almost three weeks later, on Thursday, March 8, 1855, at quarter of ten in the evening, Jesus returned a third time. Present at the séance were, again, Mlle Allix, Jules Allix, and Victor Hugo, while Mme Hugo and Charles Hugo again sat at the table.

In this third talk, Christ advocated a universal pardon—a pardon for everything in the universe. The third religion was the "true religion" because it corrected that huge error of Christianity, the creation of hell. It was also the true religion in that it declared that every entity, down to the smallest stone, possessed a soul.

Here is what Christ said:

The Gospel had this about it that was wonderful: it made men brothers, women sisters, and every child a twin. It put forth mighty words, such as: Love one another. Do not do unto others as you would not have done unto yourself. Love your neighbor as yourself. A prophet is not without honor except in his own country and in his own house. The first shall be last. Suffer the little children to come unto me. Let he who is without sin cast the first stone. Verily I say unto you that one among you will betray me. Eat and drink. This is my flesh, this is my blood. And Christianity produced this mighty cry, which throughout all eternity shall issue from the exalted mouths of those who confront the savage sky: Eli, Eli, Lamma Sabactani. ("My God, my God, why hast Thou forsaken me?")

The Gospel took man out of the shadows and elevated him to the heights. It chased the moneylenders out of the temple and returned weights made of stars to the scales of the divine. It wrung out rags, making pity ooze from them in great drops. It turned a deaf-mute God into a living God who heard and spoke. It restored sight to suns struck blind by two thousand years of darkness. It remade man, and it made woman. It had a mother's compassion and a father's compassion and a child's compassion. Its eye was the first to see mother as more than a breast. It wept the largest tear that ever nourished child at mother's breast. It drained the biggest cup of sorrow that ever rose in pain through tree trunk. Finally it cracked the formidable mystery of nature with hammerlike blows, and, standing on Golgotha, bleeding, sublime, forced the four winds of the night to fail to notice [Christ's] four gaping wounds of love crucified in the vastness of things. The Gospel made the grave a merciful place for repentance, but—and here is its great error—a merciless place for the wicked.

The great concern of religion should be not so much the just as the unjust, not so much the good man as the wicked, not so much he who repents as he who feels remorse. Mankind's monsters are love's true flock. True religion is an immense taming of wild beasts, not an immense funeral pyre of the skins of lions; it is an enormous tenderness for ferocious beings, for foul deeds, for sufferers deformed by their own bestiality, for the hated of the earth, for the cursed of this life. It loves the despised; it rescues the lost; it gilds brass pillars.

It says to animals: Animals, rise up unto death, which rises up to mankind. Grow with all your body. It says to plants: Plants, rise up unto death, which rises up to animals. Grow with all your fall. It says to stones: Stones, rise up unto death, which rises up to plants. Grow with all your dust. It cries out: Rottenness, excrement, vileness—go sow! Flower—go give forth light! Monstrosities, deformities, terrors—go blaze into resplendent power! God is the huge vase of perfumes from which the feet of created beings are washed eternally; it pours forgiveness forth from all its pores; it exhausts itself in loving; it labors mightily at absolution. The Gospel of the past said: the damned. The Gospel of the future says: the forgiven.[6]

A week later—on March 15, 1855, at half past nine in the evening—Christ was back again. This time he described the coming of the third, new, true religion, the religion that declared the forgiveness of all things and the ensoulment of all things in the universe, and the religion of which Victor Hugo was the prophet. Hugo was present at this séance; Mme Hugo and Charles Hugo were at the table. Victor Hugo asked the spirit to "continue with the great things you have told us."

Here are his words:

Druidism had said: believe. Christianity had said: believe. Their words brought generations to their knees; but one day, all of a sudden, in the temple, someone unknown entered dressed in rags, hair standing on end, feet bare, hands blackened, head held high, and gripping with one hand the powerful staff that helps us travel to the future. This man was the human spirit in search of alms . . .

He was also Victor Hugo, that is, humankind in its most brilliant aspect, a visionary poet at the cutting edge of unknown, fearful, and wonderful realities. The man in the temple was:

. . . the traveler of twilights, the stroller in shadows, the walker of chasms; he was the shepherd of lions and the shepherd of tigers; he was the seer of the lair; he was the wise man, the brave man, the man who traverses millions of leagues of infinity; he was the being who doesn't believe but he who thinks; he was the mighty questioner of God.

This new prophet, Hugo, came from a long tradition of artists and prophets.

He had several names: his forehead was called Moses, his expression Socrates, his mouth Luther, his wounds Galileo, and his scars Voltaire. He emerged from four deserts, those of Aeschylus, Dante,

Shakespeare, and Molière; and in his torn sandals were the thorns of every Calvary and the pebbles of every prophet who has ever been exiled to the desert.

The French Revolution paved the way for the coming of this new prophet in that it destroyed once and for all the idea that autocratic monarchs must rule mankind; it enabled the people to create their own ideals. And so the prophet says:

"Wake up, slaves. Wake up, you who cannot speak. Onward, ghosts. Onward, specters. To the gallop, you statues!" The crowds get up, the black horsemen sit up in bed; you hear the year 1789 whinnying; the people only have to make a single bound and idealism will be in the saddle.[7]

Thursday, March 22, 1855, at quarter of ten in the evening, was the last coming of Christ for which there is a published transcript. Victor Hugo was present; Mme Hugo and Charles Hugo were at the table.

Christ's words were:

He [the new prophet] leaves, and with a slash of spurs to the horse's side leaps over chasms; he hurls himself from the dungeons of feudal days to the roofs of modern-day suburbs; from Bastille to city; from lord to serf, from king to commoner, from priest to philosopher—from philosopher to atheist, from atheist to God. [His horse] kills the stableman, knocks over the stable, and, if the horse falls, his four iron shoes spark lightning bolts whose thunder shakes the world; this centaur [horse] holds within himself all past and future, all truth and falsehood . . . he bears humanity away to freedom, freedom away to equality, equality away to fraternity; where will this fugitive from the shadows stop? This taker-between-the-teeth of the bit of eternity and infinity? What is there to stop him? What can his final step be?[8]

Suddenly the table was still. The séance was ended. As far as we know, Jesus Christ did not return to Marine-Terrace.

From all that the spirits have told us up to this point, we can surmise that the prophet's last step will be the revelation to humanity of God's forgiveness of all beings, good or evil, and of His ensoulment of all beings, from the lowliest pebble to the loftiest angel. What we don't know is how the unknown beggar riding on the steed of revolution will achieve this—or how Victor Hugo was to achieve it.

By way of comparison: What were the pronouncements of the Jesus

Christ of James Merrill and David Jackson in *The Changing Light at Sandover,* published in 1982? "Christ" speaks only once in the more than five hundred pages of this epic poem. But he, too, declares that the Christianity he created is dead and that something new must emerge.

> *Jesus:*
> *Father God! Yahweh? Ah lords, my brothers, shalom!*
> *(His voice is hollow. Like the Buddha, he*
> *Acts out his own exhausted energy.)*
> *What a dead sound, my name, in half the World's*
>   *pulpits.*
> *We, as my princely brother [the Buddha] says,*
> *spin down our words.*
> *Like God's own planets in one last nova burst and*
> *Gravity stills & our power loses its pull.*
> *He [the Buddha] & I came to deliver laws, mine for man*
> *To shape himself in God's image, Buddha's for man*
> *To become God. Words, words. But our message,*
>   *brothers!*
> *I beg of you, intercede.* Before the wine returns*
> *Wholly to water let my father make me flesh*
> *That I may a second time walk earth and implore*
> *Wretched man to mend, repair while he can.*
> *Amen.*[9]

---

*Here Jesus speaks to the four archangels, Gabriel in particular.

THE JERSEY SPIRITS

REALITY AND LEGACY

On October 15, 1855, Charles Hugo, eldest son of Victor Hugo, plump and flabby at age twenty-nine, pushed a creaking wheelbarrow piled high with driftwood and rocks and seaweed and seashells along a Jersey Island road.

Charles was wearing a peaked peasant's cap and an orange shirt and red checkered pants. This wasn't because he wanted to express solidarity with the workers or because he wanted to say that he was an artist and bohemian and therefore exempt from the rules. It was because he was unhappy with himself and wished, with this garish and ill-fitting costume, to proclaim his unhappiness to the world and especially to his father.

The flotsam and jetsam swaying in the wheelbarrow were for the grotto he was building in the greenhouse. Lifting huge stones, heaving angular pieces of driftwood into the wheelbarrow, pushing the whole heavy and ill-balanced load along the rocky roads of Jersey—this was also a good way of dealing with his rage against his father. He and his mother and his brother and his sister were on Jersey Island on account of Victor Hugo. Only the father had been exiled; the sons, the daughter, and the wife were free to return to the mainland whenever they wished.

The family had accompanied Victor Hugo into exile as a gesture of solidarity. He had demanded it, and they had obeyed. But how they chafed against the paternal yoke! They could take long trips off the island, and they did; but Charles did not want to be here *at all*. But how could he possibly leave his father? Victor Hugo had been, and still was, the most famous writer in the world; now, because of his fearless and intransigent stand against not only Napoleon III but also every other form of tyranny, he was also the most famous political exile in the world. How could you not show solidarity with that? How could Charles Hugo ever leave his father permanently?

Charles had been a successful journalist in Paris. He still wanted to be a writer. But he had always labored in the towering shadow of his father. He had always been timid about showing his work to the Olympian poet whose eldest son he was, even about discussing it with him, and the proximity of them all to one another in the house on Jersey Island had somehow made all this worse.

Charles's mood had not been helped by the horrific row he had just engaged in with a Jersey native. On his way home from his scavenging expedition over beach and field he had passed a beguilingly shaped rock the size of a pineapple lying in the road; he had picked it up and heaved it into his wheelbarrow. The door of the house across from him had been flung open and a man, appearing suddenly and looking cross, had shouted: "Where are you taking that rock? It's mine!"

Charles had yelled back: "The rocks lying in the road outside your house aren't yours!"

"Yes, they are!" the man had shouted back.

There had ensued an argument of the most astonishing ill will. Charles had to surrender the rock. The Jerseyman had then demanded all the rocks in his wheelbarrow. Charles, hopping mad, had delivered his refusal in a storm of invective. He had taken off down the road, wheelbarrow clattering and bouncing in front of him, as the man, waving his fist in the air, had yelled profanities after him.[1] Charles was still angry when he passed the front door of Marine-Terrace on his way to the greenhouse in back.

Victor Hugo suddenly came out on the veranda.

"Charles," he called, "for God's sake, come up here and see what your greyhound Lux has done!"

Charles set the wheelbarrow down. He mounted the veranda steps slowly, still fuming and scarcely looking at his father. Victor ushered him through the doorway and pointed to a pool of urine lying on the floor by the umbrella stand. Lux, resting nearby, scratched himself happily.

"This mess," said his father, "is the work of Lux. We have witnesses."

"And did you thank Lux?" asked Charles. He got down on the floor and, tousling the dog's head, made a show of sniffing the urine. "Ah!" he exclaimed. "It's like perfume. Like rosewater, the purest of waters! Lux's urine, Papa, makes exquisite embalming fluid. I send some to M. Guérlain the undertaker every week."

His father grimaced. "It stinks to high heaven," he pronounced. "It will infect the whole house. It is Lux herself who should be sent to the undertaker, not her pee." And then Victor turned and strode away.

Lux afforded Charles one of his few pleasures on Jersey Island. He unequivocally adored her. Now, forgetting his problems, he drew Lux into his lap and, stroking the greyhound's slender quivering little body, contemplated with admiration her fine little pink muzzle, her handsome little greyhound paws—[2]

A deep voice shattered the silence: "The snails! What about the snails?"

Charles looked up slowly. He recognized the voice. The tall, impossibly slender figure of Jules Allix was looming over him. Allix brought his head down until his face was inches away from Charles's. He screwed his black-rimmed monocle into his eye and stared intently into Charles's eyes.

"I wish," boomed Allix, "to speak to the snails at the séance tonight."

Charles got to his feet surlily. "Séance tonight?" he murmured with irritation. "What makes you think there will even *be* a séance tonight?"

Then Charles stopped. He was not unafraid of Jules Allix. Allix had been banished to Jersey Island in 1853 for eight years for his role in the attempt to throw a bomb into the Paris Hippodrome and assassinate Napoleon III.[3] Jules had defended himself with such insane utterances at the trial that the judges had first wanted to send him to the asylum at Charenton; then, as a compromise, they decided to banish him to Jersey. Allix had a reputation for eccentricity and violence that made most people try to avoid him. Charles wished he could, but this was out of the question: Jules's sister, the fairly well-known singer Augustine Allix, with whom Allix lived in a house in Saint Helier (she had come to Jersey solely to share her brother's exile with him),[4] was Charles's on-again, off-again mistress.[5] Reflecting on all this, Charles softened his tone. "Yes," he said cordially. "There will be a séance tonight. I will see you there."

He tried to squeeze through the door past Allix. His mistress's brother barred the way. Jules seized Charles's shoulder. "Do not forget the snails," he boomed menacingly. Behind the black-rimmed monocle, his eye seemed to go strangely blank.

"How could I forget?" asked Charles. "Yes. The snails. Tonight!" He pushed his way past Allix and out onto the veranda. Charles leaped down the stairs, seized his wheelbarrow, and began to push it furiously toward the greenhouse.

Allix's damned telepathic snails! Four years earlier, in Paris, Jules had been involved with a half-mad occultist named Jacques Toussaint Benoit in an ill-advised project that had made the two of them the laughingstock of the Parisian upper crust for several months. Benoit had gotten it into his head that two snails that have mated always remain in permanent communication, no matter how far apart they are. Benoit had come up with the idea of placing a box of twenty-six snails in every major city in the world. Each snail represented a letter of the alphabet, and all the snails that represented that letter had previously mated with each other. It followed that if you were in Paris and touched snail E, then snail E in Peking or Rio de Janeiro would respond. You could spell out a message by pressing one snail after another, and, since the astral fluid of the snails was independent of space and time, the message would be received instantaneously in the destination city.

It seemed to Charles, now trundling his overloaded wheelbarrow down the center aisle of the greenhouse, that Benoit had glossed over a great deal. If you wanted to be sure that you had a pair of snails that had mated, then surely you would have had to see them mate—or, better still, arrange the mating yourself. And, assuming for the sake of argument that snails were monogamous (though there was no reason to believe this), you would then be restricted to a single destination city . . .

Charles had arrived at the grotto and had begun to heave flotsam and jetsam into the rocky, cavernous center of the sprawling decoration he was cobbling together in the greenhouse. With each load that he flung he expunged from his consciousness one more absurd detail of the story of Benoit's telepathic snails. Allix, though by no means stupid, and a trained engineer, had enthusiastically thrown his support behind Benoit's project. In late 1851 the occultist gave a demonstration in a room in Paris with one set of snails on one wall and another set of snails on the opposite wall. Jules was the assistant. The experiment was a total failure. Moreover, Benoit was caught fraudulently manipulating the receptor snails. This diminished not one whit Allix's enthusiasm, but other passions, such as assassinating Louis Napoleon, soon took its place, at least temporarily.[6]

Charles had finished hurling into the grotto with angry abandon all the rocks and driftwood and other debris in the wheelbarrow. He turned to enter the house by the back door and saw that his mother had come into the greenhouse silently and was standing beside him.

Mme Hugo wore a fall coat, but she shivered slightly in the cool breeze that passed through the greenhouse. "Charles," she said, "please sit between Adèle and Jules Allix at dinner. You know that she finds him strange, even menacing. He has just told me that he intends to talk to her tonight about his six propositions concerning the nature of matter and energy. This will certainly not make her less uneasy."

"All right," sighed Charles. "I will sit between them."

"Don't tease your father tonight. He's very tired."

"Is he coming to the séance?"

"Perhaps. Perhaps not. The doctor has advised him to cut down on his activities."

With a final glance at Charles, his mother turned and made her way back to the door. Charles followed. He knew she wouldn't be attending tonight herself. Delphine de Girardin, who had launched the séances so admirably, had died of cancer and hadn't come back to the tables to continue the conversation from the other side. This had weakened Mme Hugo's faith in the spirits. The faith of them all had been weakened by the fact that, at the beginning, the spirits had predicted Napoleon III would be overthrown in two years. It was now over two years later, and the emperor was still firmly in control.

They entered the hallway. Charles went upstairs to change for dinner. Poking about in his room for what to wear, he found his mind returning to the séances.

For a long time now, Charles had not enjoyed being a medium.

The sudden explosion of the talking tables into his life two years before, his swift emergence as the presumptive "medium" or "master of the fluid," had not made him happy. He was humbled by the experience of being a medium. He did not even acknowledge that he *was* the medium, not to the séance participants and hardly even to himself. Sometimes he knew beforehand what the tables would say—sometimes, but not often, and never more than a phrase or two. It seemed to him that the spirits did not need his intelligence at all, but rather needed to shunt him aside so that they could come through. He had the impression that the table leg would not—could not!—move until he, Charles, had, in some incomprehensible manner, rendered himself invisible or in some way allowed the spirits to render him invisible.

This was not an experience that he liked. Increasingly, it made him feel bereft of talent. Increasingly, he resented it.

Increasingly, he resented his father's role in all of this. It was because Victor wanted the tapping tables to keep talking that he persisted in telling Charles that he was a seer, a prophet in the desert, a Saint John of Patmos—a Saint Charles of Jersey! But this was not so! Charles was *not* a seer! He did not in fact know *who* he was, and he had begun to long for the intrusion of the spirits to end so that he could find out.

Now Charles expelled these thoughts from his mind. He was descending the staircase to dinner. He entered the dining room. Only the family, and Jules Allix, were seated at the table; François-Victor had decided not to have dinner that evening but was keeping his family company by sitting in the embrasure of the large front window and reading Shakespeare.

Charles seated himself. The new cook, Olive, served them veal. A glass of rum stood by every setting. The family ate silently, gloomily, as if wrapped in a kind of exhaustion.

Victor devoured his cutlet and then looked across the table at Charles. "Charles," he said, "when you arrived back at the house this afternoon in your strange working-man's uniform, you were pushing a wheelbarrow filled mainly with stones. Why?"

His father didn't know he was building a grotto in the greenhouse? "Because I wish to become a stonemason," Charles said, petulantly and to provoke his father.

"A man of your intelligence and education does not need to become a stonemason. If you want to work, you should write. But you don't have to work. You have enough money."

"Jersey Island bores me exceedingly," said Charles. "A beginning writer must be in a big center, such as London, or Brussels, or Paris, where there is a wide range of activities for him to observe."

"Nonsense. If a writer is really a writer, his work gets done no matter where he is."

"But a man of genius must study humanity close up. He can do so only in a big city."

"No. Look at Voltaire. He spent much of his life at his estate in Ferney. He did not go anywhere. But he dominated the world."

"But I am not Voltaire!"

Victor sat back in his chair. A pained expression crossed his face. "Charles," he said almost imploringly, "not once in three years have we agreed on anything. Not once have you ever admitted that I was right about anything. I am consoled only by the thought that my daughter agrees with me. Adèle is my little listener. She is not saying anything right now, but I'm sure she agrees with me about this."

Charles was taken aback. His father seemed to be genuinely hurt. But the conversation had made Charles angrier. He knew Adèle agreed with their father no more than he did. But Adèle, being a woman—being Victor's daughter—did not even have the right to speak out, and in fact she never did. Charles turned to his sister: "Adèle, are you writing all this down? You should be. Is it true that Papa and I have never ever agreed about anything?"

She lowered her eyes. "It's true," she said. "Never. It's even comical."

Their father beamed. "Ah! Innocence has spoken. Never! You see, Charles, I'm right."

"But, Papa," Charles stammered, "surely it is helpful for you, surely it is a good thing, that you and I should disagree about everything. That way, you are not surrounded by adoring yes-people—"[7]

Charles stopped. A moan of unspeakable misery was welling up from beneath the table. It grew steadily in volume. It proclaimed the horror of everything, the hopelessness of everything, the end of everything. It was a whining moan that was startling, almost unbelievable, in its sheer, unalloyed and appalling unpleasantness.

The family knew what this sound was. They heard it almost every mealtime. It was a sound they all hated, with the exception of Victor Hugo. It emanated from Carton, Victor's black alley cat, a stray female, who—Charles Hugo would swear to this—was the ugliest, the most monstrous feline that had ever lived, with twisted paws, hair sticking out like porcupine quills, and the shameful brazenly soliciting eyes of a Place Pigalle prostitute.

But Victor Hugo adored Carton. At every meal, when she began to moan like this, he would take a roll from his plate and break it up into crumbs and throw the crumbs under the table. He began to do so now.

Suddenly the moaning stopped. They all looked at each other in surprise. Carton usually went on for much longer.

François-Victor stirred in the embrasure of the window. "But what is that *smell*?" he demanded querulously.

Mme Hugo stood up. "Victor," she exclaimed, "that creature has done its business beneath the table. Kindly get it and its business out of here!"

They held their noses. Victor, confused and embarrassed, proceeded to the task. In a moment he was headed toward the door with Carton. Charles stood up and yelled after his father: "Papa! Even the *thought* of Carton stinks to high heaven! Even the *thought* of her will infect the entire house!"

The door slammed. There was silence.

François-Victor slowly unwound himself from the embrasure, stood up, and turned to face his brother.

"Charles," he said firmly, "must you and Papa fight even over the respective merits of your animals? Must you eternally wage war using even your beloved pets as weapons?"

Charles stared at his brother. François-Victor never rebuked anybody and Charles suddenly felt ashamed. He said to himself: My brother is correct.

It had been true for some time that if by chance an anonymous piece of canine or feline business was deposited in the house without either of the animals' being caught *in flagrante delicto*, Victor would declare with absolute certainty that this was the handiwork of Lux, while Charles would insist with equal conviction that it bore the mark of Carton.

The two would inspect the fur of their respective pets, then get down on their hands and knees and carefully examine the hairs around the dropping for purposes of comparison. Charles, hailing Lux as a saint of cleanliness, would declare that Carton was the culprit and should be thrashed, while Victor, singing the praises of Carton as a paragon of virtue, would proclaim that Lux was the malefactor and should be horsewhipped. The maids would be called in to carefully scrutinize the evidence and give their opinion. The upshot was that neither Lux nor Carton ever got punished, and so they would, very soon, in some way or another, bestow their blessings somewhere else in the house.[8]

Victor returned to the dining room. Charles was silent. They were all silent. Dinner ended. They briefly discussed the séance for that evening. It seemed no one wanted to come. Allix, yes; but even he had to go back to the house he shared with his sister Augustine to pick up something first. Victor wasn't sure if he would attend or not. Charles knew Auguste Vacquerie was coming, though even Vacquerie did not care much for the séances these days, having persuaded himself that the spirits were merely themselves, the participants, somehow "highly magnified." If Charles had not been certain Auguste was coming, he would have decided not to come himself, thereby effectively canceling the séance.

But there was Allix to think of.

Charles sat gloomily ruminating in his chair. After a while, the dining room—indeed, most of the house—was empty. Darkness had fallen. Charles got up and lit the candles in the kitchen and around the room. He took the rum bottle—it was still one-third full—and his glass and went over to the orange armchair beside the tapping tables. He poured himself a drink and sat down.

The tables had been prepared for the séance. The little three-legged pedestal table sat on top of the big square table. Charles, seated in the armchair, reached out and set the rum bottle down beside the little table on top of the big one. He sat back. He was thinking about Jules Allix.

Jules had only begun to come to the séances in early June. Charles had increasingly caught glimpses, out of the corner of his eye—in the penumbra of the séances, so to speak—of the snail enthusiast's tall, dark, and impossibly lean figure leaning forward attentively. Allix would arrive late; he would leave early; he would never ask questions; he would sit as far away from the tables as he could; and always he would scrutinize Charles implacably, stealthily, through the black-rimmed monocle that was screwed into his eye.

This pattern had never varied. But yesterday afternoon something different had happened. Allix had been visiting with Mme Hugo, sitting on the long blue couch in the drawing room. He had lapsed into silence—and then, when Mme Hugo had spoken to him, he hadn't replied.

He did not speak for four hours. He sat mute and immobile on the blue couch for that whole time, as if asleep, though his eyes were wide open. And then, all of a sudden, he had come awake. "What happened?" Mme Hugo asked, concerned. "I have seen such things tonight," he muttered, with a touch of horror in his voice. Then he was gone.[9]

Now it was a day later, and Charles, sitting in the orange armchair in the darkened dining room, his elbow resting on the large square table, his forearm propped against the little three-legged table, muttered to himself, "Allix must have seen his snails." Then he closed his eyes and fell asleep.

It seemed only a second later that he was awakened.

"Charles, you drunken seer, it is I." It was Auguste Vacquerie, whispering. Charles opened his eyes. Vacquerie was bending over him, shaking his shoulder.

Charles's right arm was still crooked against the little three-legged table. He straightened it out, sat up, and groggily rubbed his eyes. "What time is it?" he asked.

Auguste sat down in his preferred place two chairs away. "Nine o'clock," he said. "Séance time. Nobody here?"

"No," said Charles. He looked around. "Allix said he would come."

"You mean we will be all alone with that lunatic?"

Just then a shadowy figure with the vague silhouette of a tilting scarecrow detached itself with the utmost slowness from the darkness at the end of the kitchen. It began to move forward, unsteadily, almost at a crawl, as if it were unaccustomed to darkness, to light—to everything. It began to take on a human form as it slouched past the flickering light of the candles on the kitchen table. It approached them and spoke in a sepulchral, haunted voice:

"It is I. I am come. Jules Allix."

Ever afterward, Auguste would wonder if Allix had heard his remark about lunatics. Now Allix advanced slowly, wordlessly, toward them, his black frock coat gleaming dully in the in the uncertain light of the candles. He did not seem as tall as before. His face was haggard.

He approached to within five feet of Charles and stopped. His arms dangled down by his sides. In one hand he held his black-rimmed monocle.

In the other hand he held a pistol, which he now raised and pointed at Charles.

Charles got to his feet. "How are you, Jules?" he asked in a mild voice.

"I am God," said Allix, in a deep abrasive voice that permitted no argument.

He aimed his pistol at Charles's breast. "And you, sir, are the Devil."

Charles gazed at him thoughtfully.

Allix swiveled and pointed the pistol at Vacquerie. "And you, sir— you are the Devil, too."[10]

Auguste unwound his long gray-suited frame from the chair he was sitting in and got slowly to his feet. His face was pale. He was trembling slightly.

Allix turned back to Charles and pointed the gun at him again. "And you, sir—you—."

He seemed to forget himself. He lowered the pistol and remarked (it seemed like an afterthought), "And now, let us talk to the snails."

"Of course," said Charles evenly.

Charles had been afraid, but now he was not afraid. A towering rage had replaced his fear. He reached to his right and with a single motion picked up the little three-legged table and hurled it at Allix. It struck the enthusiast of telepathic snails squarely in the stomach. He doubled over with a gasp, dropping his pistol and his black-rimmed monocle.

Allix collapsed to the floor slowly, in a pile, like a puppet whose strings have been cut. Auguste, who had scrambled over two chairs, stood above him staring down mutely.

Allix rolled over on his stomach. Convulsions shook his body from head to toe. He panted in quick dry rasping pants.

Abruptly he swivelled around and faced the kitchen door. He began to pull himself across the floor on his elbows. With amazing rapidity, Jules, his long, incredibly thin body twisting from side to side, pulled himself across the dining room floor and across the kitchen floor. He seized the knob of the back door and pulled himself up to a sitting position. The door swung open abruptly and he jettisioned himself into the darkness of the night like some wretched piece of garbage. The door swung shut.

In his departure he left behind him a scene that the dining room at Marine-Terrace had never witnessed before and would never witness again. First, Charles had watched in consternation as the long, dark, trembling figure crawled away across the floor. Then, face suddenly contorted with anger, he aimed his booted foot at the little three-legged table that was lying on the floor where it had fallen beside Allix. He kicked the table hard. He kicked it again, and again, and again, until finally it had shattered into a dozen pieces.

He paused, breathing hard.

"Charles," a voice came softly from across the room.

Charles and Vacquerie looked up. Victor Hugo stood framed in the doorway to the hall.

"Charles," his father said softly. "What are you doing? This is an odd sort of séance."

"Papa!" Charles shouted, "to the devil with these leprous séances! There shall be no more séances! *You* use me, the *gods* use me, the spirits use me—but no more!" He thundered at his father, "What am I? Nothing? Who am I? God's telegraph? No! I am Charles Hugo. I am a Hugo, too! No, it's over! It's all, *all,* over!"

He stopped.

"Yes, my son," said Victor Hugo calmly. "Yes, my Charles, it is over."

Charles, feeling calmer now than he had in several years, hardly heard his father. He was on his way out the door.

Neither Charles nor Victor Hugo nor Auguste Vacquerie ever spoke about this evening again, not to each other, and not to anybody else.

It was the last of the seances.

At eight o'clock the next morning a frightened little girl arrived at the Hugo household to tell them: "Mlle Allix asks that someone come to her house quickly. She thinks her brother has gone crazy." Mme Hugo sent Charles and Auguste running. Auguste came back to report that Jules was completely insane. That morning his sister Augustine had found him lying stretched out on his stomach trying to infuse a watch with magnetism so he could mentally make its hands point to twelve noon. Allix shook perpetually and wouldn't stop writing in his hand.

After a few days he was taken to an asylum.[11] He remained there for several weeks.

It took Charles several years to recover from his experience of being a medium on Jersey Island. His confidence, which had been so badly eroded in his early youth by the presence of his father, had been almost destroyed by the equally powerful presence of the spirits. On Guernsey Island, he wrote a novel called *Le cochon de Saint-Antoine* (Saint Anthony's Pig), the subject of which was the Universal Spirit and the heroine of which was a drop of water. Published in 1857, it was not well received. But Charles had slowly begun to remember who he was. He left Guernsey for Paris at the end of 1864, unable to sacrifice himself any longer to his father's prophetic mission. In the French capital he became a prolific and successful journalist. He married in March 1865 and had two children.

Six years later, on March 13, 1871, Charles Hugo died of a massive heart attack. He was just forty-four years old.

Was it worth it?

If Charles sacrificed himself on Jersey Island so that the spirits could speak, was it worth it for Victor Hugo?

Was it worth it for the world?

In *La religion esotérique de Victor Hugo,* Denis Saurat asserts that while on Jersey Island Victor Hugo transcended ordinary human experience.

Saurat believes that, sometime in 1855, the conscious "I" of Hugo ceased to exist as an entity unto itself and became identifiable with the world and with God. Saurat declares that when Hugo says "I" in this state, it is "no longer Hugo speaking, but the world, but God, who is speaking."[12]

He writes of the years 1853–1855 in the poet's life:

> It is difficult to describe the extraordinary state Hugo lived in during that period, the horrendous tension that lasted for several years and gradually went away only because the poet ended up establishing himself in that permanent ecstasy, in that constant communication, with the beyond.
>
> But this made him a man completely different from ordinary human beings. Beyond any doubt, what saved him from madness

was his extraordinary physical strength. Neither his body nor his soul were derailed by the enormous pressures that weighed upon him. On the contrary, his powerful organism ended up absorbing the psychic forces set free within; the equilibrium that the poet had never lost but that demanded the deployment of all his energies was actually easier to maintain now; and, after a period of several years of frenetic inspiration, Victor Hugo passed gradually into the "normal" state of a prophet.

It is certain that after this transformation he and average humanity no longer saw eye to eye. We have, then, wrongly interpreted the psychology of Hugo when we talk about his "pride." Was it an expression of pride for Saint Theresa to believe that she was—feel that she was—within God? No; God had seized her up. In the same way had Hugo's God seized him up. We will see that sometimes Victor Hugo in his capacity as suffering human being was sorry this had happened. He would have preferred to remain a normal human being.[13]

In *Victor Hugo et le spiritisme* (Victor Hugo and Spiritism), published in 1981, French surgeon Jean de Mutigny takes an entirely different tack. He believes Hugo was temporarily insane while he was on Jersey Island. He claims the poet was suffering from a rare mental disease known as "fantastical paraphrenia" (*la paraphrénie fantastique*). Dr. de Mutigny lists the symptoms as follows:

- Often the illness appears in the person's thirties and is characterized by worry, anxiety, paranoia, and a generalized sense of the hostility of the world;
- In later years, exorbitant fantasies and full-blown megalomania (i.e., delusions of grandeur) emerge—a sense that the person is here on a vitally important cosmic mission;
- Paranoia and a sense of persecution persist; though there are periods of remission, the sufferer is plagued by these feelings.

De Mutigny backs up his diagnosis with the following remarks:

- There was a high incidence of schizophrenia in the Hugo family, including Victor's brother Eugène and his daughter Adèle;

- As a political figure, Hugo often displayed a pathological hostility toward his opponents;
- In some of the poetic and literary personae he created while in exile, Hugo showed a tendency toward solitariness;
- His handwriting changed radically from 1853 onward, indicating radical psychological change;
- Hugo's residence on Guernsey Island, Hauteville House, was a "veritable house of the paranoid. It was a combination church, sacristy, funeral chapel, pagoda and cave of Ali Baba."[14]

Most commentators explain the table-tapping communications in the same way as American Hugo scholar John Porter Houston in *Victor Hugo:* "[Clearly,] his unconscious . . . was being projected through his rather passive elder son, whose whole life was overshadowed and made difficult by the towering figure of his father."[15] Others, de Mutigny among them, claim that the unconscious mind of Charles Hugo also fed into the communications; they assert that Charles, while creative and intelligent, was only able to express his gifts through the personae of the tapping-table spirits, all of this quite unconsciously.[16]

De Mutigny believes that Victor Hugo, when writing out clean copies of the transcripts, often added words of his own, using the mediumistic process known as automatic writing. He believes that Hugo did this unconsciously, that at such times he was in the grip of a delirium caused by fantastical paraphrenia. De Mutigny makes a good case for this. He takes as an example the séance of December 17, 1854, at which Galileo appeared. The French surgeon-author notes that the séance took place between a quarter of ten in the evening and 1:20 a.m., that is, for a total of two hundred and fifteen minutes, or roughly thirteen thousand seconds, and that the transcript of the séance contains four thousand letters.

De Mutigny then calculates that it takes an average of ten taps to identify a letter. (He arrives at this conclusion on the basis that the letter *a* requires one tap and the letter *z* requires twenty-six taps.) The surgeon-author concludes that Galileo would have had to communicate at the astonishing rate of three taps per second without even taking into consideration the pauses between the letters and the breaks taken during the séance.

"With the best will in the world," declares Dr. de Mutigny, "it is totally impossible, over two and one-half years, to decipher messages evening and morning at the rate of three taps a second. It was thus totally impossible for Victor Hugo, despite his genius, to be capable of such record keeping."[17] This is why de Mutigny concludes that some of the transcript contents must have been added by Victor Hugo in bouts of post-séance fantastical paraphrenia-induced automatic writing.

About Dr. de Mutigny's conclusions, two things may be said. The first is that, during the séances, the spirits may not have finished every sentence. Often, in channeling sessions, a word or two is dictated and then it becomes clear to the channel or the participants what thought is being expressed, so that the "spirit," prompted or not, does not finish the sentence but goes on to the next thought, and so on and so forth. Thus séances can, in actuality, take much less time than a transcript might suggest.

Second, Victor Hugo may well have added to the transcripts but not necessarily through automatic writing while in a state of delirium. Hugo was a controlling man who meddled into everything where writing was concerned. He often added to his daughter Adèle's diary, correcting what she had written, giving her writing lessons, and telling her outright what to write. He did this whenever and wherever he could, and he may well have done it with the séance transcripts.

This is not to say, however, that he changed in any way the essence of the séance contents as they were dictated by the "spirits."

⫸⫷

So what was Victor Hugo, then: ascended master or madman? If it's a sign of their ultimate sanity that visionaries faithfully, coherently, and effectively practice what they preach, without harming others, and indeed often helping others, then Victor Hugo was a sane man.

As we've seen, the poet conceived of his prophetic mission as being one of revealing to humankind that God forgives all things, both good and evil, and that the stuff of souls is part of every discrete entity in the physical universe, including every stone, plant, and animal as well as every human being. Hugo tried during his lifetime to be totally forgiving of and loving to all persons (Napoleon III may be seen as an exception!) and to treat all representatives of the animal, vegetable, and mineral kingdoms with great love and respect.

We see this in his poetry of the time as well as in his actions. In 1854 he wrote in *Les Contemplations, III, xxvii* (published in 1856): "I love the spider and I love the nettle . . . ;"[18] Claudius Grillet tells us that "after 1853, at every crossroads of his life and thought, and under a thousand diverse forms, we find the same prescriptions: 'Do not mistreat animals! Peace to plants!'"[19] Auguste Vacquerie wrote in his journal in 1856,

> Victor Hugo only likes standing flowers. He outlaws bouquets and regards cut flowers as persons in agony. We've never seen him snip a flower, not even for the most attractive of female visitors. . . . He explains to his grandchildren that flowers live and breathe like us, are living persons, and that there shouldn't be too many in one room.[20]

In 1854, in *What the Shadow's Mouth Says*, Hugo wrote,

> *A sense of horror makes the bird's feathers shiver.*
> *All is pain. Flowers suffer beneath the scissor,*
> *And close in upon themselves like an eyelid closes;*
> *The tint on a woman's cheek is the blood of roses.*
> *The debutante at the dance, corsaged and whirling to the*
>   *melody*
> *Breathes in, with unwitting smile, a bouquet made of*
>   *agony.*
> *Weep for ugliness and weep for ignominy.*[21]

In *Les Contemplations, V, xxii*, the narrator pities crabs.

> *I paid the fisherman who passed by on the strand*
> *And took that horrible beast in my hand*
>
> *It opened a hideous mouth; a black claw*
> *Shot from its shell, my hand was pawed*
> *. . . the crab bit me*
> *I told it: Live! Be blessed, poor soul damned to hell*
> *And I threw it back into the sea's deep swell . . .*[22]

As has already been mentioned, Hugo exhorted his entire family to feel love and respect for all the domains of nature. Grillet wrote, "On any given day on Jersey you might have been able to see his daughter Adèle hastening toward the beach to return to the ocean a lobster she was having difficulty defending herself against."[23]

Auguste Vacquerie, a skeptic at first, was eventually entirely won over to Victor Hugo's conviction that nature is suffused throughout with consciousness. Vacquerie wrote in *Profils et grimaces* (Profiles and Grimaces) in 1873,

> Could it be that the oak and stone have souls? I believe they do. . . . The souls of vegetables and minerals exist in harsher conditions than the souls of others. We have speech; animals have mobility. But they, the [stones, are] immobile and mute. Take pity on them! . . . . At present, I would no sooner tear a petal from a camelia than I would tear a wing from a fly or an eyelash from an infant. The young ladies who pluck the petals from marguerites to see if somebody loves them passionately make the same impression on me as do the dreadful priestesses who cut the throats of their victims, then try to divine from their dying convulsions answers to questions, and I would not touch their cruel hands [the young ladies']. . . . I wouldn't harm a match. I pity rusty nails. . . . When an execution takes place, it's the guillotine's blade that is condemned.[24]

On Guernsey Island, Hugo insisted that no effort be made to clear snakes and toads from the garden of Hauteville House where the family lived. The property was very soon infested with the creatures. The cook came home one day with two live ducks and was preparing to slaughter them when Victor Hugo suddenly arrived on the scene. He declared he would make the whole family go to bed without dinner rather than have animal blood spilled on his property. He won the day: the ducks were given their complete freedom of the garden. Claudius Grillet writes that, from that day on, the ducks "survived ostentatiously. Glossy, glorious, garrulous, they were cherished by their master, no more so than the toads, of course—but almost. We read in . . . [Victor Hugo's *Notebooks*], dated December 16, 1860: 'I let the ducks run free in the garden, for their Sunday.'"[25]

Victor Hugo was at least a century ahead of his time with these beliefs and practices. In the mid-twentieth century, researchers acknowledged the reality of animal consciousness, animal intelligence, and animal linguistic ability and began research in these areas. Toward the end of the century, analogous investigations were being carried out with regard to plants, especially trees. New, often startling discoveries are made almost every day.

There's a more important reason for supposing that Victor Hugo was not temporarily insane during his stay on Jersey Island in 1853–1855. Most critics agree that, during the same period that he was talking to the tapping-table spirits, Victor Hugo was composing his greatest poetry.

Those critics would add that this wasn't because of the spirits but rather despite them—or they would say, perhaps, that the poet's "encounter with the spirits" was some kind of epiphenomenal side effect of the vast new explosion of poetry that was emerging within him.

In *Victor Hugo,* John Porter Houston takes a slightly different position. While not imputing an otherworldly origin to the spirits, he suggests that the tapping-table experiences gave a perhaps indispensable impetus to Victor Hugo's poetry of the time. He writes: "It is clear that, despite much empty verbiage and despite Hugo's refusal to take anything from the spirits verbatim for his own work, the shades served to encourage him in certain directions and to confirm much that was in his conscious mind. The whole episode has more than a merely anecdotal interest; the history and publication of some of Hugo's most important works may have been influenced by the séances." Exactly what poetry was written during this period? Dr. Houston states, "Perhaps before the revelations of the table had had their effect, Hugo began a long poem of great scope in its account of terrestrial history and divine design . . . *La fin de Satan* [*The End of Satan*], as it came later to be called." Separately, *What the Shadow's Mouth Says,* completed in 1854, established that God does not judge us and He does not intervene (two themes of occult theologies); in *The End of Satan,* God forgives Satan himself—not a theme with much appeal for fire and brimstone Christians. On Jersey, Hugo began work on an even more controversial epic poem, *God,* a work even more informed by esoteric philosophies. Key sections of it were not published until after Hugo's death; and certain parts still have yet to be published.[26]

In *Selected Poems of Victor Hugo: A Bilingual Edition*, translators E. H. and A. M. Blackmore add to Dr. Porter's account:

> In 1869–70, Hugo returned to this project, making some minor revisions and adding . . . a short dedicatory piece. In its final structure this conforms to a familiar Hugolian pattern. . . . On 12 August 1870 [Hugo] left a note to his literary executors, stating that *Dieu* [*God*] proper (the nine numbered sections) "could be published as it stands" and the prologue was "very far advanced, and almost finished." After his death, the whole poem (with dedication and prologue) was edited by Paul Meurice and published in 1891.[27]*

To describe at any length these little-known masterpieces is beyond the scope of this book. The reader is referred to the superb translations of the Blackmores.

※※

What are we to make of the tapping-table spirits and their outlandish, fantastical, and often frankly unbelievable statements? Were these spirits the creations (however unconscious?) of Charles Hugo? Did they owe their existence (unconsciously?) to Victor Hugo's endlessly teeming genius? Were they actual spirits? Have we to do with some strange synergetic mixture of the first two? Of all three?

Investigators of the nature of channeling usually explain that, if spirits do indeed speak to us from the beyond, they are necessarily highly limited in what they can say. Deborah Blum tackles this complex subject in *Ghost Hunters: William James and the Search for Scientific Proof of Life after Death,* and it is one that James Merrill, author of *The Changing Light at Sandover,* not infrequently addressed in his writings and interviews.

Blum's *Ghost Hunters* is the story of the nineteenth-century founders of the British Society for Psychical Research and the American Society for Psychical Research. These distinguished scientists

---

and philosophers felt constrained to launch a scientific investigation into the "unexplainable" incidences of clairvoyance and ghostly visitations that were increasingly taking place. Their most famous representative is Harvard University psychologist-philosopher William James. Science has never really accepted the findings of these savants, not even those of James, but the savants themselves were hard put to dismiss some of the phenomena they witnessed, even while they could not completely accept them.

The investigators were fortunate in coming across the remarkable American medium Mrs. Leonora Piper. In February 1892, Mrs. Piper apparently began to channel a student of philosophy named George Pellew who had died just five months before. One of the attending investigators, Dr. Richard Hodgson, had known Pellew personally. Hodgson quickly came to the conclusion—reversing the skepticism he had felt earlier about mediumship—that this really was George Pellew (or "G. P."—as the spirit called itself).[28]

One thing in particular puzzled Hodgson. When another A.S.P.R. investigator, Dr. Henry Sidgwick, questioned "G. P." about philosophy, the spirit's answers showed little understanding of the field. Hodgson wondered how this could be, since George Pellew had been a highly competent philosopher when alive. This question made Hodgson reflect, in author Deborah Blum's words, on

> . . . one of the most interesting and compelling aspects of spirit communication, the difficulty of communicating through a medium. It called to mind . . . the way that one mind may alter information received from another. As Hodgson pointed out, Mrs. Piper knew nothing of philosophy. She was unlikely to understand it or relay its finer points with any grace. Her ability was to receive these flickers of communication but she wasn't necessarily a competent interpreter. "If Professor Sidgwick were compelled to discourse philosophy through Mrs. Piper's organism, the result would be a very different thing from his lectures at Cambridge," he emphasized.

As Hodgson considered the issue, he'd come to believe that some things might be easier for spirits to communicate than others. Emotional connections—with their pure, personal power—might survive fairly intact through the translating mechanism of the medium. Intellect and sophisticated knowledge would be unlikely to fare so well, especially if the translator were uneducated or if the medium lacked the language and training to understand what was being said in the first place.

He reminded Sidgwick of all the obstacles that must be overcome for any spirit communication, even of the most primitive type, to occur. If one considered the difficulty of communication between two living people in the same room—the way one person interprets or misinterprets another's thoughts during a conversation—how much more difficult to conduct that conversation with someone speaking from another dimension, using the awkward device of an entranced medium to relay messages?[29]

Others, including the recipients of channeled material, have begun to reflect on this question. In an interview in *The Paris Review* for Summer 1982, American poet James Merrill, whose *The Changing Light at Sandover* (1982) was based on Ouija board experiences (see chapter 22) explained how the "spirits" must necessarily have to clothe themselves in the words, images, and experiences of those through whom they spoke. Merrill asserted that the spirits "would be invisible, inconceivable, if they'd never passed through our heads and clothed themselves out of the costume box they found there. How they appear depends on us, on the imaginer, and would have to vary wildly from culture to culture, or even temperament to temperament. . . . A process that Einstein would entertain as a formula might be described by an African witch doctor as a crocodile."

Merrill carefully explained that he was not dismissing the spirits. "The powers they represent are real," he said, "as, say, gravity is 'real.'" But he speculated that, in whatever realm the powers/spirits dwell, human language itself "doesn't exist, except perhaps as vast mathematical or chemical formulas which we then personify, or tame if you like, through the imagination."[30]

In an interview with the critic Helen Vendler in 1994, the year before his death, Merrill reiterated that he thought the reality of the "channeled entities" lay in their being personifications. "There are forces in the world that it is convenient for us to personify," he explained. The gods and goddesses of Homer's *Iliad* were an example from ancient times, while in the modern era, "the new angels ought to be things like electricity and gravity; they too would lend themselves to personification."[31]

As they pursue these questions, Deborah Blum and James Merrill both quote statements allegedly from the spirits describing from the spirits' point of view the difficulties inherent in these sorts of communication. Frederick W. H. Myers, author of *Human Personality and Its Survival of Bodily Death* (1903), was one of the British Society of Psychical Research investigators. After his death in January 1901, the ostensible spirit of the deceased Myers spoke through the medium Alice Kipling Fleming. Blum tells us that, according to the transcripts, the spirit of Myers "seethed with frustration" at the difficulty of communicating. She quotes "him":

"'Yet another attempt to run the blockade—to strive to get a message through—how can I make your hand docile enough—how can I convince them?

"'The nearest simile I can find to express the difficulties of sending a message is that I appear to be standing behind a sheet of frosted glass—which blurs sight and deadens sound—dictating feebly—to a reluctant and somewhat obtuse secretary.'"[32]

In *The Changing Light at Sandover,* Merrill's guides describe other difficulties inherent in the communication process as far as the spirits are concerned. The channeled "Ephraim" writes:

The patron [spirit guide] *is often dumb with apprehension. . . .* [He] *is nervous lest he expose too much. . . . His representative* [guidee] *sits looming up;* [we guides feel his] *hope and despair, the memory and the pain. O, my dears, we are often weaker than our representatives!*[33]

The spirit of Matt, David Jackson's recently deceased father, is punished with intense cold when he says too much. Before this happens he raps out hurriedly: *a cold place O God O God:* then he disappears. Later on, when his son David asks him what happened, the spirit replies: *The reprimand can be severe.* A little later on, when "Matt'" starts to say something he shouldn't again, his son's hand grazes the board and is held there as if by glue; this time the spirits are directing a warning at the mediums.[34]

Ephraim and others make it clear to Merrill and Jackson that they are very sorry not to be allowed to intervene or to provide proof that they are who they say they are:

> *With what regret that we can never say: Careful, dear*
>   *friends,*
> *Do not take that false step! Or in any way protect you*

*Who are our loved ones. Would that we could lead you
    to that lost
Vermeer, that manuscript of Mozart, or leave you simply
A little glowing medal struck in heaven saying: TRUE.*[35]

Of course, it may be argued that the spirit world does not exist and that none of these observations about the difficulties of communication comes from the spirit world, but rather they come from the medium (and/or the participants) who is somehow unwittingly putting these observations together him- or herself. But, even if this is true, these statements do suggest that, if spirit communication does exist, its modalities must be extraordinarily complex, elusive, and arbitrary—so much so that, finally, if we can indeed communicate with the spirits, we can't hope to learn very much from them.

The most important reservation we should have, perhaps, is the one spelled out by James Merrill when he says the spirits would be invisible and inconceivable if they didn't pass through our heads and clothe themselves out of the costume box they found there—in other words, that if the spirits exist, their communications with us are necessarily heavily colored by our subjective, personal universe. To take just one example of how heavy that coloring can be: James Merrill and David Jackson were gay, and perhaps that is why there are so many immortal races—the winged people of China, the centaurs, the bat-creature servants of the centaurs, the "A-species" that may supersede us—in *The Changing Light at Sandover.* Immortal races do not need to produce offspring—which is what the couple of James Merrill and David Jackson could not do.

Today there is a great deal of literature ostensibly channeled from "aliens" that describes the nature of our Milky Way galaxy. In many cases, where the human channel is an Evangelical Christian, our galaxy with all its billions of stars and, quite likely, even greater number of planets, is described as supporting only one intelligent species—us. Whether or not this is in conformance with actual galactic history, it is certainly in conformance with fundamentalist Christian doctrine.

Our universe as described by the Jersey Island spirits, and in Victor Hugo's poem *What the Shadow's Mouth Says,* sounds like a paranoid nightmare. Can planet Earth really be the most evil planet in the universe, a prison for the most evil souls who are serving out heavy reincarnational time in stones, plants, animals, and humans? Probably not; but the séances, and that poem, *do* accurately reflect Victor Hugo's huge guilt, his huge terror, and his profound sense (not at all imaginary!) of imprisonment in the years 1853–1855. (We should also, perhaps, try to summon the courage to consider whether—given that our species produced the Nazi Holocaust as far on in our history as the mid-twentieth century—we are not in fact an unusually flawed species.)

As has been suggested in chapter 22, there may lie beneath the skin and muscle and nerve—the reflection of our subjectivities—of channeled utterances a skeleton of objective truth. However wildly the details differ, the channeled worlds of Hugo and Merrill—and William Blake—reveal at their core startling similarities: black suns, the travail of reincarnation, man's chronic failure to overcome himself, and more.

It is in the direction of the examination of this core data, and not in the compulsive consideration of all the strange and occult outlying details, that the future path of the study of channeling should perhaps lie.

❧※❧

Victor Hugo as madman. Victor Hugo as saint and seer.

What about Victor Hugo simply as a man?

Let's conclude our discussion with the words of Paul Stapfer, who, as a young French professor on Guernsey Island, frequently visited the Hugo household over a three-year period in the late 1860s.

When Victor Hugo died on May 22, 1885, Stapfer had not seen him for many years. He was now a full Professor of French Literature at the Faculty of Arts at Bordeaux University in Bordeaux, France. Stapfer writes in *Victor Hugo à Guernsey: Souvenirs personnels* (Victor Hugo on Guernsey: Personal Memories) that, on May 27, 1885, the day of Hugo's state funeral, he mounted the podium for his lecture, spoke to the students for several minutes about the death of this very great man, and then canceled the class.

Later in the day, in the privacy of his study at home, Stapfer thought with a new clarity about all that Victor Hugo had meant to him. He penned the following words, with which he concludes *Victor Hugo à Guernsey,* and with which we will conclude this book:

When I thought of how badly I had responded to the immense honor, to the inestimable privilege that had been mine for over three years, of having talks with such a man, I deeply regretted how superficial I had been. I was ashamed of having sometimes opposed the resistance of my personality to the precious words which I should have drunk in as avidly as the earth sucks up the dew from the sky and absorbs it. I was sorry for the mad and insolent pretentiousness I had displayed in making myself the judge of this poet, when I should have contented myself with being merely his modest secretary and taking down every word he said. I felt the huge impertinence of my careless manners, the scandalous nature of my laughter and my irreverent gaiety. The bold independence of my criticisms, asserted so proudly, now struck me with bitter force as mere foolishness and blind ingratitude. There came to me the poignant vision of the exquisite and tireless great-heartedness that that grand old man had shown toward my mere youth, a youth with nothing special about it, without experience, without titles, without works, without strong ideas, without knowledge of any depth or solidity.

Amid all this remorse troubling my conscience, I recalled with a melancholy thrill the seductive gentleness of the enchanted isle of Guernsey with its mild climate, and the hours of unforgettable literary ecstasy that I had passed at Hauteville House.

As I remember all this now, my heart gives way to the weight of memories. Tears fill my eyes and run down my face. Sobs choke me.

I cannot continue . . .[36]

Appendix

FIRST ACT OF A PLAY SAID TO BE CHANNELED FROM WILLIAM SHAKESPEARE

Marine-Terrace, April 27, 30,
May 2, 3, 5, 12, 28, 1854[1]

ABOUT THE PLAY

An unsigned article in *The Times Literary Supplement* [London] No. 3,295, for April 22, 1965 ("Hugo Turns the Tables"), summarized the channeled play as follows:

> The play opens with a wager between Heaven and Hell. Hell himself shall be pardoned if he can turn the most evil of men into a good man. The figure chosen is Louis XV, who, in his old age, has abducted the peasant maiden Nihila on her wedding day. In the room to which she has been taken, the furniture, the walls and ceiling, the lilies and roses, speak, and so does the cross upon Nihila's bosom. In the last scene, the King has already died and been entombed among his predecessors at St. Denis. The surrounding bones, the worms, the earth, the coffin nails and the royal corpse speak (in verse, whereas the earlier scenes have been in prose). It is a coffin nail which informs the King that, if he will undertake to save the unhappy peasant couple, he can be restored to life for a while.[2]

Hugo attended none of the seven seances (the first one divided into

330

two parts) during which this material was ostensibly dictated by the spirit of William Shakespeare. In *Victor Hugo: Oeuvres Complètes*, Jean Massin writes,

> Shakespeare had, on April 27 [1854], begun to dictate the "drama" that Vacquerie had asked him to. . . . Learning about this from a transcript on April 29, Hugo, who hadn't attended the séance, noted: "The analogies between the beginning of this scene and the idea behind something I did on November 23, 1853, entitled, 'Two Voices in the Starry Sky: Zenith, Nadir,' oblige me to absent myself—and I deeply regret it—from all participation in the séance . . . during [the dictation of] this drama, and only for this drama. I note that the analogy (and this only with regard to the beginning, which I wrote not knowing what was to follow) lies in the idea and in several of its details."[3] A note in Adèle Hugo's diary for April 30, 1854, explains Hugo's decision: "I don't want to read or to know about this play of Shakespeare's. I have a fear of meeting myself in those spirits."[4]

ACT ONE

A starry night. A serene night. The stars are twinkling. Their twinkling seems to be the murmuring of mysterious words. All at once, something strange happens to two of the stars: they become enormous, and, as if the audience's opera glasses had been changed into magical telescopes, everyone can hear the following words issue from these two monstrous globes:

STAR AT NADIR (*to Star at Zenith*). Good morning, Paradise.

STAR AT ZENITH. Be on your way, Hell.

STAR AT NADIR. Don't get angry if you want people to keep thinking you're one of the lucky ones.

STAR AT ZENITH. Go to Paradise.

HELL. I'm quite fine here. God makes his light to shine on everyone; he doesn't belong to anyone in particular. I'm one side of the coin and you're the other. I'm stamped with the effigy of punishment; you're stamped with the effigy of mercy.

PARADISE (*not hearing Hell*). O radiance! O splendor! O light!

HELL. O shadows!

PARADISE. God smiles!

HELL. God is menacing!

PARADISE. How happy mankind is! No more evil! No more blood! No more tears! Mankind is an immense flower whose roots are bathed in light and who has as many petals as the mouth of God has kisses. Infinity and eternity are as soft to him as swaddling clothes. He sleeps in God's arms, a smile on his lips and at peace with the world. He awakens joyfully in the morning and falls asleep rapturously at night. This colossal God of abyss, of storm and of wind turns into a father who is infatuated with his children and who seems so tender, so devoted, so gentle that men call him: Mother! Creation retracts its claws and becomes only caresses.

The elements grow calm; air, water, earth, fire, the four ancient enemies of man, surround him with love and happiness. The air is no longer filled with storms nor the water with shipwrecks, fires no longer burst into conflagrations and there are no more graves in the earth; the furious hydras and dragons that tumble about in the waves and flames are transfigured into celestial forms; gnashings of teeth are transformed into smiles, tears become dewdrops, and emptiness is metamorphosed into fullness; and I see Giant Chaos and Ghost Nothingness fleeing into darkness and aloneness, both of them gloomy, garrulous, grumbling, muttering curses, and very frightened. The rosebush no longer has thorns and feels a soul budding within it; the thorn has become a rosebud, and unhappiness, creeping from sphere to sphere like a kind of hideous insect, has sensed its thousand monstrous paws being transformed into two wings; atonement's chrysalis has released joy's butterfly into the clear blue sky. O thistle, now you're a flower; and you, O scorpion, you're a bird; O toad—a swan! O swan, you've become a woman! Woman, you're an angel now! Nature is filled with mystery, with shadow, with the moon's reflection, with silent pools, with underbrush and clearing, rocks, forests, chasms— with tumult, with deep and secret actions, with swarmings and birthings. O veiled nature, masked nature, hidden nature—now you are naked! Falsehood, now you're truth! Volcano, you've become a mountain peak! Lairs, you've become hearths! Shadow, you're explosions of light! You, death, are life! And in the eye-sockets, suddenly ablaze with light, of skulls resurrected for all eternity, you, O grave-worms, have become heavenly beams of illumination!

HELL. Paradise, you lie. Everything weeps and everything bleeds; there is only crime and suffering; the human heart is a night that contains not millions of stars but only two moons: the suspect moon and the blind moon. Traitor moon and miser moon! Judas star and Job star! The human bird has wings with claws, the human nest is a heap of dung, the human sky is a den of shadows. Horror is everywhere. Remorse is the red cloud where the sun sets and the sun's chariot is a cart full of corpses. Infinity is a hangman's mask, eternity is a heavy weight striking and shattering man's feeble faculty of reason with its implacable oscillation, and the pendulum-bob of its heavy weight, resounding in the human skull, fills it, then submerges it, in its ebb and flow like the tide of an ocean of sobs. Because every hour, every minute, every second is a cry of pain, and the clock hand, going round the world, always points to a nighttime hour. Gaze, Paradise, at the darkness in me! What desolation! What disgrace, what shame! Man, beast, flower, stone—all are wicked fellows. The four elements are miserable creatures. Air makes vultures devour doves, water makes big fish devour little, fire makes volcanoes eat up grasslands, earth makes wolves devour sheep. Inanimate objects commit acts more disgraceful than those of men: Brambles yearn to prick, plants long to tremble beneath a storm, roads yearn to go astray, rivers long to drown, roof tiles yearn to fall in. Doors seek out dungeons, the pitch-black bottom of the mine shaft calls out for the astrologer, the Manchicheel apple tree [a West Indian tree whose fruit, resembling apples, is poisonous] hungers for the traveler, sword yearns for blood, copper bowl yearns for the verdigris of suicides [verdigris is a coating that appears on copper; along with sick persons who are being bled, the bowl longs for suicides to bleed into it], gold dreams of prostitution. In dreams the fir-tree beholds itself transformed into the broken mast of a vessel in distress. Stones see themselves as castle dungeons. Oaks see themselves as gibbets. The sponge, hidden at the bottom of the sea where Jesus fished with the apostles, broods on Calvary's bile [the sponge longs for Christ to be crucified so that it can sponge his wounds]. The hemlock, hidden at the bottom of the garden where Socrates strolls with his disciples, glowers at him angrily, and the poisons of the Locust laboratory dream of Nero [this may be a reference to the group of apothecaries who manufactured poisons that were used by the Roman emperor Nero against his enemies]. Nature is horrible. Gloomy mandrakes, pale helleborins, ghastly poppies chat with hideous mushrooms, and these plants of the night conspire against man. One says, I'm a narcotic. Another says, I'm venom; let's shut up! Monstrous! Monstrous! Monstrous! And pestilence, fevers, sickness, epidemics, and choleras pass by like wings beating in a sky filled with crime. Mankind tumbles about in this hell, not to get better, but to make himself worse. Every one of his actions is a breach of honor. You might say that crime is one of man's muscles. Man is a walking crime. When he comes to a halt, that's a crime. His rising in the morning is crime. His going to bed is crime. When he's a child he kills birds. When he's a man he oppresses women; when he's an old man he strangles ideas at birth. His cradle is an owl's nest, with night sitting on the egg of day or death sitting on the egg of life. Mankind's wet-nurse has two teats: want and ignorance. The newborn child is wrapped in the swaddling clothes of darkness. It suckles on love with hate, it suckles on faith with irony. It suckles on the bad with the good, and, in biting God, it suckles on life. Half of human society is selfishness; the other half is envy. Mankind's summit is degradation, his base is blood. The monstrous reptile wreathed around the temple column hisses at the starry ceiling. The poets sing of kings, and when Mme Pompadour [Louis XV's mistress] has finished kissing Louis XV's ulcers, Voltaire comes to peddle a smile with those kisses [by writing about them]. Science thinks it finds remedies, but it finds evils. Columbus thinks he's found America, but he's found sickness. Franklin thinks he's discovered the lightning rod, but he's aroused the thunderbolt's indignation. Fulton thinks he's discovered steam, but he's discovered explosions. Guttenberg thinks he's discovered printing, but he's discovered revolution and civil war. Evil comes out of good. The hand that writes a useful thought doesn't know how to realize it. Catechisms mimic gospels, and with its alms the Church makes counterfeit money, which it lends to Satan. O, formidable claw of crime! It holds the world's skull in its grip, and it keeps the skull from seeing and hearing by plunging two claws into its eyes and two into its ears. So, Paradise, you're right: Let's flee, let's flee! Let's flee! The sky is too luminous for me; come, my breaches of honor, come, my horrors, come, my basenesses, come, my depravities! And, since heaven's glory doesn't want us, leave it, and let us seek to roll eternally through space and be its sun, its black firmament of infamy!

PARADISE. Not eternally!

HELL. What?

PARADISE. Forgiveness is the supreme word. The shadow cast by God's hand is a punishment, but His gesture is always a blessing.

HELL. O Paradise, could I possibly be forgiven? Is it possible that my crimes that roar in the darkness should at some point be permitted to lick the feet of the Lord? Is it possible that my damned souls should one day be enveloped in God's smile? Is it possible that the tips of Satan's pincers could become the lips of angels' mouths? No, you're wrong. Shadow is shadow. Night is the monstrous gaze of the blinded eye; dawn is the loving gaze of the radiant eye. Darkness is that which is sentenced, that which is damned, that which is forgotten; the blackness of the sky is the wall of the dungeon within which you will sense through all eternity the groping of punished stars. O Paradise! I don't believe you; but for no other reason than to hear you speak to me of forgiveness, I, who am envious, I, who am wicked—I have huge tears in my eyes. The nadir of the heavens pardoned by the zenith, filth forgiven by light, soiled feet washed by the pure hands of winged seraphims, the gutter kissed by the bird—no, none of that is possible.

PARADISE. Yes, it is.

HELL. How? Quick, tell me! Oh! To be forgiven! Eternity put out of commission! To share God! Quick, speak! O my gentle brother!

PARADISE. There is a way.

HELL. Quick, tell me.

PARADISE. You are covered in criminals. Take the guiltiest, the most perverse, the most disgraceful, and make a just person of him. If you, Hell, succeed in making an angel out of a demon without the help of Paradise, you will be forgiven.

HELL. O joy! My gentle brother, how can I ever thank you?

PARADISE. By making an angel.

Just then day breaks. The last stars blink out and the talking stars grow pale in the whiteness of the dawn. They haven't stopped talking, but their voices, like those of two chatterers who move apart, no longer reach the audience's ears. The two stars suddenly vanish and the sun appears. The backdrop falls to reveal:

A village near Versailles. A charming countryside. To the right, an inn with the sign: To Louis the Well-Loved. *To the left, a peasant house, radiant with flowers as if during a festival. In back, a thatched cottage and a church. It's evening. Two men enter in cloaks and gold-embroidered hats, with swords sticking out of their cloaks. They have powdered hair.*

FIRST MAN. You're quite sure she's worth the trouble of taking to bed? You're not bothering me for nothing?

SECOND MAN. She's a charmer, Sire.

FIRST MAN. How old is she?

SECOND MAN. The age when birds leave the nest and when young ladies look for one. A rosy little springtime, a pretty morning filled with light.

FIRST MAN. How old is that?

SECOND MAN. Fifteen.

FIRST MAN (*yawning*). That's old enough. Love's eternal; it's always the same age. Fifteen! Why not fifteen? Decidedly, all the male-factors who did wicked things before me were fools lacking in imagination. I have a great craving to gather rosebuds and fruit that's in bloom. I feel a thirst for human sap; I'd like to quaff a tall glass of virginity in one gulp and get blind drunk on the stuff of innocence.

SECOND MAN. I hear wedding music.

FIRST MAN. What wedding?

SECOND MAN. The one your little friend is having, Sire.

FIRST MAN. Hold on, that adds a little spice to things. I'll be able to shatter the youth of two people at one blow. Husband and wife in a single brimming glass! Drinking a virgin is the drunken orgy of a lifetime; drinking a husband along with it is like going on a drinking spree with death itself. I've suddenly got an appetite for life like a grave that's been fasting for a year.

SECOND MAN. Some people are coming. Let's go inside.

They disappear into the inn. Peasants arrive, the men singing and dancing, the women in a holiday mood and dressed in their Sunday finest. Bagpipes play. The youngest man knocks on the door of the house while the others form a circle behind him.

JEROME (*calling*). Nihila! Nihila!
NIHILA (*opening door*). I'm here.

The young man takes her by the arm as a dance air begins. The dance finished, Nihila sits down on a bench in front of the cottage door and sings:

NIHILA (*singing*). For my wedding bouquet, as is today's custom, Mr.
　　Worker, what have you picked for me?
A PEASANT (*advancing in time to the music and singing*). I searched
　　for the rose
　　All around here
　　Not one had blossomed
　　I picked a marigold.

He deposits a marigold on Nihila's knees, who rejects it. He is sent away by the dancers, who thump him on the back in time to the music.

NIHILA (*singing*). For my wedding bouquet, as is today's custom,
　　Mr. Schoolmaster, what have you picked for me?
A PEASANT (*singing*). I searched for the rose
　　To make you a gift
　　Not one had blossomed
　　I gathered the thistle.

He deposits a thistle. The same scenario as for Mr. Worker takes place.

NIHILA. For my wedding bouquet, as is today's custom,
　　Mr. Village Priest, what have you gathered?
A PEASANT (*singing*). I searched for the rose
　　In the midst of the meadows
　　Not one had blossomed
　　I gathered some cypress.

He offers a branch of cypress. Same scenario.

NIHILA. For my wedding bouquet, as is today's custom,
    Mr. Spouse, what have you gathered?
JEROME (*singing*). I searched for the rose
    Like everyone here
    Just one had blossomed
    This single one here.
NIHILA. In my wedding bed, as is today's custom,
    Mr. Spouse, come and pluck it.

Jerome kneels before Nihila. The other peasants withdraw discreetly, leaving them alone. There is a long silence. Dusk has fallen. The two lovers gaze at each other, ravished. Nihila is still seated. Jerome is still on his knees.

JEROME. I love you.
NIHILA. I love you.
JEROME. I want to be happy! I would like to always be alone with you. I feel very changed! I see with different eyes. I breathe with a different mouth. I'm trembling. I'm hot and I'm cold. My Nihila, you are my everything. Yes, I'm trembling. Here, touch my hands. So what am I afraid of? I don't know. I have the feeling that we're not alone.
NIHILA. Yes.
JEROME. I want you to be very happy. I'll do anything you want.
NIHILA. We'll keep hens.
JEROME. Yes.
NIHILA. Two cows, a white one and a black one. I'll make you drink the cream off the top and I'll give the rest to the beggars who come by.
JEROME. Yes.
NIHILA. We'll have a goat so we can have little goats. I love little goats! They're as joyful as birds. They're always jumping against your legs and knocking you over, and it's so much fun to watch their horns grow.
JEROME. Yes.
NIHILA. We'll have a pair of canaries, but I don't want to put them in a cage; caged birds are a sad sort of joy. I'll tame them.
JEROME. Yes.
NIHILA. You'll need a horse for your plow, but one that's been broken in so I can ride on it. We'll have to work hard, sleep hard, pray

hard. Every morning you'll go to the village with your vegetables, and on days when there's a fair you'll buy me gingerbread. We'll be as happy as little sparrows flying through the air. I'll take care of your clothes. I'll mend your trousers. Men get so many holes in their pants!

JEROME. Tell me that you love me.

NIHILA. I don't know why you're asking me that today of all days. Since the day I came into the world, you've been the only father I've known, the only brother I've known, the only mother I've known. I love you with all my heart. I'm not like those fortunate women who love all sorts of people, who love left and right, who love their father and their mother. I'm not one of those lucky persons; I love what's straight in front of me, and I can give happiness to one only. You see, Jerome, there's no one else can love like orphans can. So many persons have been absent from their lives that the one they end up loving becomes an altar to the sacred memory of those dead, an altar the orphan is always kneeling in front of. An orphan's heart is a cemetery where love sprinkles perfume on the graves. Look, see that flower? It has five petals that are about to fall off [she plucks the petals]. This petal is the forefather; this one is the father, and this one is the mother; this is the son, and this is the daughter. And this stem is you, my Jerome [she puts the petals in her mouth]. I've got a mouth full of kisses for the dead. My love for the dead is my prayer. My love for them is on my mind every morning and every evening. I love them as if I were in church. I live as if I were sitting on a prayer stool. The day I married you, we got married on a grave [of all my beloved dead].

JEROME. I can't describe how much I love you, but I know that I would give up all the love I ever felt for my father and mother rather than lose a particle of the love I feel for you. I'm your other half. I feel like I'm attached to you by a horse's bridle. I'm your dog, your servant, your guardian; I'm the shadow cast by your light. I'd sleep on your doorstep every night if I could be sure I'd see you stepping on me. I believe your feet would do me good by walking on me. To me you're one of the birds of God. I love you, I love you, I love you! Let me weep; you at least owe me that. Tears of joy purify the heart. I wish I could always weep like this. Men's sorrows come from the fact that they don't weep from their souls and that their heart is never swollen enough with love! O, my little creature, run your hands over my eyes. What soft skin she has!

NIHILA. Your skin is as rough as anything. It doesn't matter; give me your silly paws so I can eat them like cakes. Listen, Jerome: promise me you'll always have work-roughened hands and I promise you I'll kiss them every night to soften them.

JEROME. My little dream, it's late, let's go in and sleep.

NIHILA. Not yet. I have a surprise for you and for surprises you don't need the full light of day.

JEROME. I have a surprise for you, too.

NIHILA. Okay, you first.

JEROME. No, after you.

NIHILA. No, you start.

JEROME. It's a little thing that's not worth much.

NIHILA. Let's see it.

JEROME. I don't dare show you.

NIHILA (*getting impatient*). Would you kindly give it to me this moment?!

JEROME. It's not much.

NIHILA. How foolish this fellow is!

JEROME. Okay, you give me your gift while I'm giving you mine.

NIHILA. No, I want to see yours first.

JEROME. Here it is.

NIHILA. O, what a pretty little cross! I'll put it around my neck. O my! That's not gold, is it?

JEROME. Yes, it is.

NIHILA. Pure gold?

JEROME. Yes.

NIHILA. No, that can't be gold.

JEROME. What does it matter?

NIHILA. It's made of silver.

JEROME. Give it to me.

NIHILA. That's not a cross.

JEROME. Give it to me.

NIHILA. It's a ring.

JEROME. Give me.

NIHILA. I'm sure his fingers are too thick. Even though I got the biggest ring.

JEROME. You naughty little creature, my fingers aren't that thick.

NIHILA. Show me.

JEROME. See?

NIHILA. Where's your little finger?

JEROME. This one.

NIHILA. Looks like a knitting lady's bobbin.

JEROME. Put the ring on it.

NIHILA. There! Push your finger inside. O, it'll never be able to get in. My goodness, I give up. Ah! Finally. The ring is on your finger. Some thumb you've got!

JEROME. I want this ring to become my flesh and bone. I feel like there's a piece of your soul in this piece of jewelry. The most precious metal isn't gold; what makes jewelry a divine metal is the essence of soul mixed in with the gold. The good Lord's gifts are made of love.

NIHILA. Let's stay a little longer. Night is half the heart's joys. Souls are the reflections of stars. Tonight there's a star inside me.

JEROME. Yes, Venus.

NIHILA. Let's both pray (*they kneel*). O my God, I pray for you make us very happy and that you should make my Jerome most faithful. Heap upon us all the riches of joy, of hope and of love, and give us the daily bread we need. Give us strength, and enable us to console others who are weak. Allow nothing around us to suffer, neither flowers, nor birds, nor beasts, nor men, and may nothing in our garden ever complain about heaven. Take a little happiness from heaven and give it to our poor little marriage. Heaven is very able to give alms to unhappy beggars who wait at heaven's door. Give health to the poor and courage to the sick. Finally, O God, send us one of your angels. We'll make him very happy, and we'll always talk to him about you so he won't forget heaven. My God, you are our father. Bless us, bless us, bless us.

For some minutes several individuals have been spying on the two lovers. Two of them approach, and just as Nihila finishes her prayer a gag is stuffed in her mouth and one is stuffed in Jerome's. The others come forward and tie up the newlyweds despite their resistance and carry them off. A moment later the noise of a carriage is heard, quickly becoming lost in the distance.

A sumptuous room. Boule furnishings. Mirrors, flowerboxes

loaded with flowers, pictures, sofas. There is a bed in the back, set into an alcove; hangings hide the alcove, as they do the doors in the room. There is gilt everywhere and a painted ceiling depicting angels and clouds. On the fireplace mantle is a representation of the god Jupiter, in the form of a swan, raping the mortal woman Leda. There are lit candelabras and a rock-garden clock. When the curtain rises, the room is empty.

CLOCK. Midnight.

ALCOVE. My hour has come.

LILY. Alas!

CANDELABRA. It's dark as night in here! The darkness of this disgraceful room is harder to disperse than the darkness of the other rooms. You'd think it was night twice over here, that this was a place where being a torch was a particularly tough trade to follow.

CEILING. What would you say, Torch, if you were forced like me to look like the sky? There are times when I'd just like to collapse. Maybe you suffer, Torch, but at least you don't tell lies; I tell lies. You light up crimes, but you can be indignant about them; as for me, I see them but all I can do is smile down on them. You are light; you're the real thing; I'm just an imitation blue sky with fake clouds and phony angels. I'd like to strike down the malefactors; I'd like to punish them . . . but I can't. You can. I can't hurl lightning bolts at them, but you can turn the room into a blazing inferno.

TORCH. I think about it every night.

ALCOVE. It's Sodom here! Sodom! Sodom!

CLOCK. Is the king coming tonight?

ALCOVE. Yes.

ROSEBUD. He's a bit old for lovemaking.

ALCOVE. The lovemaking of old men spatters more filth on young women than the splashing of all the gutters in the world— especially when the old man is a king. O, the poor soiled flowers! I've seen so many of them fall into the royal gutter at my feet.

FLOWERPOT. I'm a cradle for flowers.

ALCOVE. I'm a grave for virgins.

CLOCK. Be patient.

ALCOVE. What time is it in Louis XV's life?

CLOCK. A quarter to death.

ROSEBUD. When is he going to die?

CLOCK. In three years.

CEILING. I'm furious! I've got three more years of telling lies and pretending I'm the sky!

THE TORCHES. Three more years of bringing light to this den of darkness!

ALL THE FURNISHINGS AT ONCE. It's all the bed's fault.

BED. Oh, come off it! You flowers are free to fade, you torches are free to go out, the ceiling is free to fall down, the clock is free to stop; all of you who partake of life here are free to die. You annoy me! I'm ashamed of you! You won't let me be as blind and deaf as I'd like to be. Get out of here, all you furnishings who still have some life in you!

LEDA (*speaking from the mantelpiece*). Alcove, I blame you, too! You're love, but I was virginity. Your neatly creased sheets are naught but funeral shrouds covering the whiteness of souls. Your snowy sheets are made of mud. Your gauzes and laces are filmy wings that only move and flutter on the bodies of fallen goddesses and fallen angels. Alcove, be damned! In the name of virgins, Love be damned. In the name of guilelessness, Voluptuousness be damned! Kisses: in the name of the pure and limpid souls that, hidden in the shade, live deep and simple lives, you be damned! [Referring now to Jupiter, the god who raped her in the form of a swan] Swan be damned, in the name of lakes!

[*Variant:* Night bird be damned; be damned, Royal Love. Be damned, Divine Love. It hurts so much! I was the virgin, and I've become the prostitute for having believed you, Love, for having believed you, Jupiter, for having believed you, Beautiful White Bird (the Swan). I was a clear and unruffled soul; I've become troubled; I was diaphanous; I've become dark. I was a light; I've become a stain. I was a lake; I've become a gutter for having loved a swan.]

MASKED DOOR. Be quiet. Someone's coming. (*Several lackeys enter and deposit the unconscious body of Nihila on the bed.*)

LIVERIED SERVANTS. How horrible!

The lackeys retire, leaving Nihila alone.

NIHILA (*waking up and looking around with staring eyes*). Where am I? Jerome! Where am I? He's not here. (*She gets up.*) What's this mean? What's this room? I'm not dreaming! I mustn't be afraid. I'm a brave girl. That's it! I remember: I was with Jerome in the field outside our place. I was praying to God with him. I felt a hand on my mouth, and then . . . nothing. It's awful not to see Jerome! (*She begins to weep.*) It's my fault; he wanted to go back in. Robbers must have noticed us. Poor little house! You and I spent so much time together. Who lives here? It must be a very wicked person, to take poor little girls who have no money and lead them into all this gold! My God! My God! I'm still frightened! Jerome! Jerome!

WALL (*to door*). Open up; let her escape.

DOOR. I'm not the key.

WALL (*to key*). Okay, you, key, open up for that poor girl.

KEY. I'm not a hand.

WALL (*to Nihila, who doesn't hear*). Alas! My poor dear child, you see that I did everything I could to save you. But it isn't in my power; we are merely men's instruments. We have enough life in us to feel things, but not enough to act. We see, but we are forbidden to bring light to others; we speak, but no one can hear us. We are commanded to suffer but not allowed to console. We are most unfortunate; there you have it. Take our case to heaven for us. You are the fortunate one: You're only a prisoner who'd like to flee; I'm a hiding place who wants to hide. You see, my little one, the essence of Paradise is freedom; we escape suffering by embracing suffering. Atonement is an immense rope plunged into an abyss; the rope's knots are stars; the captives of crime clamber up that starry rope out of the darkness into light.

KEY. Look: the jailer's hand is lying on me; I'm turning in the lock.

DOOR. I'm opening.

LILY. I'm closing.

THE ENTIRE ROOM. Help!

Enter the King. His face is withered. His robes gleam brilliantly. He's an old man, already stooped, wearing the Cross of St. Louis on his ceremonial sash.

KING. Well, my child, how do you like this room? Is it to your taste? Everything here is yours. I am your prisoner.

NIHILA. What have you done with my husband?

KING. What do you think of this bed, this rug, these silks, these mirrors? Do you think your cottage is worth the value of this room? Reply, beautiful bird: Is this nest worthy of your feathers? You're trembling. Calm yourself! I'm not some awful bird-catcher. I won't cut off your wings; I'll gild them.

NIHILA. What have you done with my husband?

KING. I am replacing him for tonight, if it pleases you. Your Jerome is a rustic who would have soiled you; I'll make you so radiant you'll dazzle the sun. A fine union that would have been! Jerome, your husband! That pebble, marry a pearl! I intend to marry you to a crown!

NIHILA. Who are you?

KING. I'm riches, I'm power, I'm the world, I'm heaven. My name? Your happiness is my name. They call me Nihila's smile. I'm called Nihila's fortune. I have a whole family of Nihila's: Nihila's bracelets, Nihila's lace, Nihila's palace. I'm the magician of your hours and, as they take flight one by one from the clock face, I'll turn them into minutes. I'm the magician of the minutes of your life; I'll turn them into seconds. I stop the clock's hand at your youth and keep you from growing older by using pleasure to hold you in the heart's eternal blossoming. I make the roses, and turn them into the rouge on women's faces. Since I am gold myself, I make the sunbeams. I don't stop the sun in its tracks like that imbecile Joshua did. I do one better: I make it disappear.

[*Variant:* Life, happiness—I'll give you anything you want. Would you like a palace, gardens, Versailles's statues? You know Versailles, of course. I'll give them to you. Do you want silk robes, jewels, finery more splendid than fairy tales have ever dreamed of? I'll give them to you. Do you want a bed of brocade so prodigious the sun will want to write its name upon it? Do you want to ride through the streets pulled by eight horses? Do you want to be so beautiful that the admiration of the universe itself will kneel before you? Would you like me to make your two little feet so powerful that they will be able to climb right up to the throne of Louis XV?]

NIHILA. Tell me your name, Sir, so I can tell God.

KING. It's not about telling God. It's about kissing me.

NIHILA. I'd rather kill myself than be unfaithful to Jerome. He's the only one I love; I'll never kiss anyone but him. My first kiss will be for Jerome—and my second, and my third, and my millionth. I'd rather die than rob him of his well-being. One single kiss given to another would feel like a lie to me. Look, sir, rather than tell me what you're telling me, you'd be better off letting me leave and telling me where Jerome is.

KING. All I want is a kiss.

NIHILA. Never.

KING. A plague on you! What a fortress! I declare to you, my little one, that I don't like to be kept waiting and I'm not in the habit of dancing attendance in front of my bed. Let's go! That kiss—or I'm calling my men. (*He seizes Nihila.*)

NIHILA. Ah! You're the king of France!

He wants to kiss Nihila. She struggles. Her collar opens, revealing the cross Jerome gave her. At that instant the exhausted candles gutter out. We hear only muffled cries.

CROSS (*in the darkness*). See you soon, Sire. (*The curtain falls.*)

The cellars of Saint-Denis. The tombs of the kings of France fade off into the darkness. At the front of the scene lies the tomb of a king who's just been buried.

BONES.* We were the powerful arms of a France usurped.
    I was the bludgeon and you were the sword.
    We bore flags with us.
    We wrongly weighted the scales with human values
    Thus making God incline toward hatred's side.

WORMS. No, you were only bones.

BONES. I was Tolbiac and you Pavie.†
    I was the death of a people and you its life.
    We were giants.
    This claw was bloody; these hands ferocious;

---

*These are the bones of the rulers who, though with cruelty, have fought in the defense of France.

†The Battle of Tolbiac was fought between the Alamanni (pre-Germans) and the Franks under Clovis I in 496, according to tradition. The Franks were victorious. The Battle of Pavie was fought in Northern Italy in 1525. The French lost and their leader, François I, was taken prisoner.

We were heroes; we were colossi.

WORMS. You were nothing.

ONE OF THE SKULLS. Always kneeling before the amulets

    I filled black gibbets with a world of skeletons.

    People feared my balcony.

    O worms, your grim teeth hollow me out at every turn.

    Whence come you, hangmen? Whence come you, vermin?

WORMS. The bones of Montfaucon.*

ANOTHER SKULL. Cowardly king, I betrayed my country into ruins.

    I saw my people fall beneath the shadows

    Of trees in my park.

    With an English bonfire I reddened France's sky.

    Whence come you, worms? Whence come you, suffering?†

WORMS. The bones of Joan of Arc.‡

ANOTHER SKULL. O death, when will this torment end that breaks my
    heart?

    At least a million worms swarm on my corpse.

    O enemy sepulcher!

    Piece by piece my poor king's flesh is rotting off.

    Who launched you, hideous worms, into my grave?

WORMS. Saint Barthélemy.§

---

*Montfaucon, a broad hill now a part of the tenth district of Paris, was used as a place of execution in the Middle Ages. Sixty-four criminals could be hanged at once. This was the sea of gallows immortalized by the poet François Villon (circa 1431–1465) in *The Ballad of the Hanged*: "Our flesh, once too well nourished, rots now, torn by beaks, devoured," etc. These executions were sanctified by the Church; hence the line, "Always kneeling before the amulets." Montfaucon was so grotesque a collection of weird structures—it included a giant pot used to boil counterfeiters alive—that one section resembled a giant balcony; hence the line, "People feared my balcony."

†These lines may refer to the crushing victory of Henry V of England over the French at the Battle of Agincourt in 1415, which victory apparently was facilitated by French treachery.

‡As commander of the French forces at the Siege of Orleans in 1428–1429, Joan of Arc defeated the English and began to erase the effects of the Battle of Agincourt. It was due to Joan that the English were eventually driven back across the Channel.

§This is a reference to the massacre of French Protestants, beginning on Saint Barthélemy's Day, August 24, 1572, and continuing on into October, that was ordered by France's rulers. An estimated three thousand Protestants met their death in Paris alone, with seventy thousand more being murdered in the rest of France.

ANOTHER SKULL. As gallant as Henry, as brave as Xaintrailles,
> I raised up France and built Versailles.
> I was the king dressed in vermilion.
> Now I am like a flower devoured by leprosy;
> Who was it, gnawing worms, made you squirm in the sockets of
> my eyes?*

WORMS. Sire, your sun.†

EARTH (*speaking to all the kings*). O kings! At some time soon,
> beneath the feet of haying machines
> You'll be reborn as weeds and poisonous plants.
> Your crimes were pitiless.
> You'll be reborn as thistles on hilly slopes.
> It's you who'll be the crowns of thorns
> Upon the heads of crucified gods.
> Scoundrels, you'll be the essence of scoundrel
> You'll be the hemlock on the lips of Socrates.
> Tyrants, victors, soldiers,
> Poison and nettles will spring out of your heads
> And beasts will graze upon you in the darkness
> And Judases will pluck you.
> In the crumbling battlements of your castle turrets you'll be
> Mosses whose ears are boxed by wings of winds,
> You will be crumpled blades of grass,
> Each of you, O kings whose names we speak with terror,
> For having trampled on mankind's vast brow
> Will be reborn under the feet of man.

AIRHOLE (*through which the starry sky can be seen*). Be hopeful,
> damned souls, and forget who you are.
> Deliverance gleams through the planets,
> At horizons' edges;
> And those stars that seem like jewels in the sky

---

*A reference to Louis XIV (1638–1715), here said to be gallant as Henri IV (the
French king who reigned from 1589 to 1610, and who was called *le galant vert*—"the
gallant dressed in green") and as brave as Poton de Xaintrailles (1390–1461), Joan of
Arc's lieutenant at the Siege of Orleans and later a Marshal of France.

†Louis XIV was called the Sun King. Ironically, it is Earth that speaks to him, since
he is condemned to be reborn as grass or weed under the feet of men for his ignomini-
ous crimes.

Are the holes of every lock of every prison, through which
The light of heaven beams.

All the tombs that had been open, close. Louis XV's tomb, which had stayed closed, opens. We see the king's corpse. He is supine, his hands crossed on his chest. Four coffin nails grow slowly longer and pierce his hands and his feet. The corpse lets out a terrible cry.

FIRST NAIL. I am the iron nail; I arrive at where you've come to.
  Be reborn, monster! I'm the penknife of Damiens.*
  I deliver you to the dark punishment of metal,
  I assassinate you merely to make you live.
  You will be metal.
SECOND NAIL. Wicked one, I will make you worse yet.
  Be cursed by iron and by gold be punished!
  You'll be reborn money in infamous places
  You it will be who purchases women's virtue.
  You'll suffer, tyrant, the evils that once gave you pleasure
  And keep, as a coin, the monstrous name of Louis†
  You'll frequent orgies in filthy gambling houses
  And I stamp your soul with your effigy.
  You'll be gold.
THIRD NAIL. Damned one, I am granite.
  I am the fatal nail that's hammered into him who's punished.
  In this world filled with obscure penitences,
  I'm at the root of your horrific gallows.
  O kings, my duty's to torment your bones
  And make sure your gibbets' dead are in your tombs.
  Because the gallows, that tree that's hammered from the stuff of
    crimes,
  Strangled your victims with the dark flower of its knot,
  I now must make you feel, as you lie here,
  Its roots—another knot—on your hangmen's necks.
  I am the one who feels the skeletons shudder.
  I am the pillory, I the solitary confinement

---

*Robert Damiens was hanged, drawn, and quartered in 1757 for stabbing Louis XV with a penknife. Louis XV was not harmed.
†The "louis" was a French gold coin.

Despot, you'll be (it is decreed by God),
Stone in a convict-wall serving in a convict's cell.
Chained you'll live, within the darkness of bastilles,
And you, vice, and you, mud and despoiler of woman,
To redeem your life, that enormous treason,
Living you were a gutter and dead you are a prison.

FOURTH NAIL. I am a human fingernail. Miserable ghost,
You're going to make up for everything.

CORPSE. And will I become a man again?

FOURTH NAIL. Yes, I promise.

CORPSE. So there's a way I can take form again?

FOURTH NAIL. Yes, there is.

CORPSE. How do I do it?

FOURTH NAIL. Do good.
Damned one, your life's an enormous abyss
Where, like an endless waterfall, the water of crime has flowed.
But you can lift up the corner of your shroud.

CORPSE. Explain.

FOURTH NAIL. Everything you've forfeited comes together in one thing.

CORPSE. What's that?

FOURTH NAIL. Thanks to you, a happy couple bled and suffered. Two
rejoicing children fell into your gulf: Jerome and Nihila.

CORPSE. My eyes are blinded. What can I do?

FOURTH NAIL. They are lost.

CORPSE. What can I do?

FOURTH NAIL. Save them.

Here the channeled transmission ends.

NOTES

INTRODUCTION: "VICTOR THE GRANDIOSE"

1. Gobron, *History and Philosophy of Caodaism*, 20.
2. Ibid., 35–36.
3. Ibid., 50.
4. Ibid., 23, 27.
5. Ibid., 61–67, 89.
6. Ibid., 207.
7. Ibid., 89.
8. Robb, *Victor Hugo: A Biography*, 5–10.
9. Ibid., 9–12.
10. Ibid., 21–23.
11. Ibid., 29–41.
12. Ibid., 44, 48–63.
13. Ibid., 75–77.
14. Ibid., 123–24.
15. Ibid., 91–92, 93.
16. *American Heritage Dictionary of the English Language,* 1st ed., s.v. "Romanticism."
17. Robb, *Victor Hugo: A Biography,* 64–67.
18. Ibid., 100–101.
19. Ibid., 89.
20. Ibid., 91.
21. Ibid., 96–98.
22. Ibid., 119–20.
23. Ibid., 145–53.
24. Ibid., 162–68.
25. Ibid., 156.
26. Ibid., 158.
27. Ibid., 179–85.
28. Ibid., 237–39.
29. Ibid., 246–50.
30. Ibid., 263–67.

31. Ibid., 280–81.
32. Ibid., 281–82.
33. Ibid., 288.
34. Ibid., 305–18.
35. Ibid., 320–23.
36. Ibid., 325–29.
37. Ibid., 331.
38. Ibid., 444.
39. Ibid., 420.
40. Ibid., 536–37.
41. Ibid., 518.
42. Ibid., 522–26.
43. *Correspondence*, ed. C. Daubray, 4 vols.: IV, 2, quoted in Graham Robb, *Victor Hugo: A Biography* (New York and London: W. W. Norton, 1998), 477.

CHAPTER I. JERSEY ISLAND

1. Vacquerie, *Les Miettes de l'histoire, Second edition, 362–63.*
2. (Mlle) Adèle Hugo, *Le journal d'Adèle Hugo, Journal IV,* 221–22.
3. (Mlle) Adèle Hugo, *Journal I,* 248–49.
4. Vacquerie, *Les Miettes de l'histoire,* 59–61.
5. Victor Hugo, *The Toilers of the Sea,* 3.
6. (Mlle) Adèle Hugo, *Journal I,* 248.
7. Levaillant, *La crise mystique de Victor Hugo (1843–1856),* 72.
8. (Mlle) Adèle Hugo, *Journal I,* 249–50.
9. Victor Hugo, *Toilers,* 309.
10. (Mlle) Adèle Hugo, *Journal I,* 247.
11. Victor Hugo, *Toilers,* 21.
12. Vacquerie, *Les Miettes de l'histoire,* 365–66.
13. (Mlle) Adèle Hugo, *Journal II,* 54–55.
14. Ibid., 60–65.
15. Levaillant, *La crise mystique de Victor Hugo (1843–1856),* 28.
16. Maurois, *Olympio: The Life of Victor Hugo,* 236.
17. Levaillant, *La crise mystique de Victor Hugo,* 26–27.
18. Viatte, *Victor Hugo et les illuminés de son temps,* 117.

CHAPTER II. LÉOPOLDINE BECKONS

1. Viatte, *Illuminés,* 22.
2. Stapfer, *Victor Hugo à Guernsey: Souvenirs personnels,* 148.
3. Viatte, *Illuminés,* 114–15.
4. (Mlle) Adèle Hugo, *Journal II,* 101.
5. Viatte, *Illuminés,* 29.
6. Grasset, *The Marvels Beyond Science,* 12–13.
7. Matlock, "Ghostly Politics," 54.
8. Mutigny, *Victor Hugo et le spiritisme,* 21.
9. Matlock, "Ghostly Politics," 54.

10. Levaillant, *La crise mystique de Victor Hugo,* 75.
11. Mutigny, *Victor Hugo et le spiritisme,* 24.
12. Victor Hugo, *Oeuvres Complètes,* vol. 9, 1185–88.

CHAPTER III. CHANNELING THE ENEMY

1. Gooch, *The Second Empire,* 61.
2. Rheinhardt, *Napoleon and Eugenie: The Tragicomedy of an Empire,* 90.
3. Ibid., 170–71.
4. Gooch, *The Second Empire,* 61.
5. Victor Hugo, *Oeuvres Complètes,* vol. 8, 424.
6. Rheinhardt, *Napoleon and Eugenie,* 77–78.
7. Ibid., 192–93.
8. Victor Hugo, *Oeuvres Complètes,* vol. 9, 1189–99.

CHAPTER IV. WHEN THE SPIRITS SPOKE HUNGARIAN

1. Iranyi and Chassin, *Histoire Politique de la révolution de Hongrie 1847–1848. Second Part: La Guerre,* 605–9.
2. Deak, *The Lawful Revolution: Joseph Kossuth and the Hungarians, 1848–1849,* 334–35.
3. Ibid.
4. (Mlle) Adèle Hugo, *Journal IV,* 358.
5. Victor Hugo, *Oeuvres Complètes,* vol. 9, 1203–4.
6. Ibid., 1214–17.
7. Lazar, "Les émigres Hongrois dans les Îles de la Manche." *Le Bulletin de la Société Jersiaise,* 178.
8. (Mlle) Adèle Hugo, *Journal III,* 261.

CHAPTER V. THE SHADOW OF THE SEPULCHER

1. Victor Hugo, *Oeuvres Complètes,* vol. 9, 1199–1201.
2. Vacquerie, *Les Miettes de l'histoire,* 386–87.
3. Levaillant, *La crise mystique de Victor Hugo,* 77.
4. Ibid., 96.
5. Victor Hugo, *Oeuvres Complètes,* vol. 9, 1206.
6. Ibid., 1238–39.
7. (Mlle) Adèle Hugo, *Journal II,* 279.
8. Ibid., 283.
9. (Mlle) Adèle Hugo, *Journal III,* 109.
10. Victor Hugo, *Oeuvres Complètes,* vol. 9, 1231–32.

CHAPTER VI. HANNIBAL STORMS THE TAPPING TABLES

1. (Mlle) Adèle Hugo, *Journal I,* 34–45.
2. Ibid., 114–16.
3. Starr, *A History of the Ancient World,* 483–88.
4. Victor Hugo, *Oeuvres Complètes,* vol. 9, 1242–45.
5. Flaubert, *Salammbô,* 288.

CHAPTER VII. GOD'S CONVICT

1. Pakenham, *Meetings with Remarkable Trees,* 27.
2. Tompkins and Bird, *The Secret Life of Plants,* 131.
3. Nollman, *The Man Who Talks to Whales: The Art of Interspecies Communications,* 97–98.
4. Hill, "Stones." *Man Myth & Magic: An Illustrated Encyclopedia of the Supernatural,* no. 97, 2706–8.
5. Stapfer, *Victor Hugo à Guernsey: Souvenirs personnels,* 140–41.
6. Ibid., 143–45.
7. Ibid., 226–27.
8. (Mlle) Adèle Hugo, *Journal II,* 20.
9. Viatte, *Illuminés,* 190.
10. Walker, "Reincarnation," *Man Myth & Magic: An Illustrated Encyclopedia of the Supernatural,* no. 84, 2347.
11. Grillet, *Spirite,* 50–51.
12. Viatte, *Illuminés,* 186.
13. Ibid., 186–87.
14. Ibid., 193.
15. Lamartine, *Oeuvres poétiques completes,* 795–1108.
16. Victor Hugo, *Oeuvres Complètes,* vol. 12, 16–17.
17. Viatte, *Illuminés,* 186.
18. Ibid., 192.
19. Victor Hugo, *Oeuvres Complètes,* vol. 9, 383.
20. Ibid., 1268.
21. Victor Hugo, *Oeuvres Complètes,* vol. 10, 453.
22. Blackmore, *Selected Poems of Victor Hugo: A Bilingual Edition,* 342–45.
23. Yates, *Giordano Bruno and the Hermetic Tradition,* 295–97.
24. Victor Hugo, *Oeuvres Complètes,* vol. 9, 1266–69.

CHAPTER VIII. ANDRÉ CHÉNIER LOSES HIS HEAD BUT ENDS UP KEEPING IT

1. Victor Hugo, *Oeuvres Complètes,* vol. 3, 695–96.
2. Vargas Llosa, *The Temptation of the Possible: Victor Hugo and* Les Misérables, 125–26.
3. Ibid., 126–27.
4. Richardson, *Victor Hugo,* 36.
5. (Mlle) Adèle Hugo, *Journal II,* 439–40.
6. Scarfe, *André Chénier: His Life and Work 1762–1794,* 22–364.
7. Chénier, *Oeuvres complètes. Première édition intégrale,* 193–95.
8. Scarfe, *André Chénier,* 356.
9. Ibid., 1.
10. Grillet, *Spirite,* 29–30.
11. Chénier, *Oeuvres completes. Première édition intégrale,* 195.
12. Victor Hugo, *Oeuvres Complètes,* vol. 9, 1249.
13. Ibid., 1257–59.
14. Ibid., 1375–76.

15. Grillet, *Spirite,* 213.
16. Victor Hugo, *Oeuvres Complètes,* vol. 9, 1251–54.
17. Ibid., 1269–70.
18. Ibid., 1433.
19. Victor Hugo, *Oeuvres Complètes,* vol. 3, 711.
20. Guerlac, *Impersonal Sublime,* 64.
21. Victor Hugo, *Oeuvres Complètes,* vol. 9, 1275–76.
22. Ibid., 1277–78.

CHAPTER IX. WILLIAM SHAKESPEARE, CHANNELED AND TRANSLATED

1. Guille, *François-Victor Hugo et son oeuvre,* 94.
2. (Mlle) Adèle Hugo, *Journal III,* 173–74.
3. Ibid., 205–6.
4. Ibid., 203; 212–13.
5. Guille, *François-Victor Hugo et son oeuvre,* 78.
6. Stapfer, *Victor Hugo à Guernsey: Souvenirs personnels,* 148.
7. Guille, *François-Victor Hugo et son oeuvre,* 81–87.
8. Victor Hugo, *Oeuvres Complètes,* vol. 12, 159.
9. Victor Hugo, *Oeuvres Complètes,* vol. 9, 1224.
10. Ibid., 1280–81.
11. Ibid., 1282.

CHAPTER X. METEMPSYCHOSIS SPEAKS

1. Maurois, *Olympio: The Life of Victor Hugo,* 230–31.
2. Auguste Vacquerie, *Profils et grimaces. Nouvelle edition,* 396.
3. Ibid., 398–99.
4. Victor Hugo, *Oeuvres Complètes,* vol. 9, 379.
5. Grillet, *Spirite,* 47–48.
6. Baudouin, *Psychanalyse de Victor Hugo,* 193–96.
7. Victor Hugo, *Oeuvres Complètes,* vol. 9, 1364–65.

CHAPTER XI. VICTOR HUGO AND THE *ZOHAR*

1. Saurat, *La religion ésotérique de Victor Hugo,* 22.
2. Ibid., 23.
3. Ibid., 22.
4. Ibid.
5. Ibid., 19–21.
6. Ibid., 301–4.
7. Ibid., 24–32.
8. Ibid., 28–29.
9. Houston, *Victor Hugo. Revised édition,* 27.
10. Saurat, *La religion ésotérique,* 71.
11. Ibid., 24.
12. Ibid.
13. Ibid.

14. Ibid., 79–81.
15. Yates, *Bruno*, 92.
16. Victor Hugo, *Oeuvres Complètes,* vol. 9, 1087.

CHAPTER XII. MARTIN LUTHER ON DOUBT

1. (Mlle) Adèle Hugo, *Journal II,* 339.
2. (Mlle) Adèle Hugo, *Journal III,* 92.
3. Ibid., 107–8.
4. Saurat, *La religion ésotérique,* 46–47.
5. Ibid., 47.
6. Victor Hugo, *Oeuvres Complètes,* vol. 9, 1298–99.
7. Saurat, *La religion ésotérique,* 47–48.
8. Victor Hugo, *Oeuvres Complètes,* vol. 9, 1299.
9. Ibid., 1282.
10. Ibid., 1299–1300.
11. Ibid., 1414–16.

CHAPTER XIII. OTHER VOICES, OTHER ROOMS

1. (Mlle) Adèle Hugo, *Journal III,* 19–20.
2. Ibid., 33–34.
3. Ibid., 20–21.
4. Dow, *Adèle Hugo: La Misérable,* 76.
5. Victor Hugo, *Oeuvres Complètes,* vol. 9, 1399–1401.
6. Dow, *Adèle Hugo: La Misérable,* 70–73; 182–84.
7. Truffaut, *L'Histoire d'Adèle H.,* VHS movie.

CHAPTER XIV. THE SECRET LIFE OF ANIMALS

1. (Mlle) Adèle Hugo, *Journal III,* 290–92.
2. Ibid., 416–17.
3. Victor Hugo, *Oeuvres Complètes,* vol. 9, 1359–61.
4. Ibid., 1404–6.
5. (Mlle) Adèle Hugo, *Journal III,* 329.
6. Victor Hugo, *Oeuvres Complètes,* vol. 9, 1418–20.

CHAPTER XV. ROARINGS OF OCEAN AND COMET

1. (Mlle) Adèle Hugo, *Journal IV,* 54–57.
2. Victor Hugo, *Oeuvres Complètes,* vol. 9, 1353–54.
3. Ibid., 1354–56.
4. Ibid., 1357–58.
5. (Mlle) Adèle Hugo, *Journal III,* 233–34.
6. (Mlle) Adèle Hugo, *Journal IV,* 152.
7. Victor Hugo, *Toilers,* 23.
8. Victor Hugo, *Oeuvres Complètes,* vol. 9, 1384–86.
9. Ibid., 1387–89.
10. Ibid., 1348–49.

CHAPTER XVI. THE LADY IN WHITE

1. (Mlle) Adèle Hugo, *Journal III*, 153.
2. (Mlle) Adèle Hugo, *Journal IV*, 37–38.
3. Levaillant, *La crise mystique de Victor Hugo*, 125.
4. Stevens, *Victor Hugo in Jersey*, 36.
5. Levaillant, *La crise mystique de Victor Hugo*, 125.
6. (Mlle) Adèle Hugo, *Journal III*, 153.
7. Ibid., 153–54.
8. Ibid., 154.
9. Ibid., 154–55.
10. Victor Hugo, *Oeuvres Complètes*, vol. 9, 1330.
11. (Mlle) Adèle Hugo, *Journal III*, 95.
12. Victor Hugo, *Oeuvres Complètes*, vol. 9, 1330.
13. Ibid., 1344–45.
14. (Mlle) Adèle Hugo, *Journal III*, 155.
15. Victor Hugo, *Oeuvres Complètes*, vol. 9, 1337.
16. (Mlle) Adèle Hugo, *Journal III*, 155.
17. Victor Hugo, *Oeuvres Complètes*, vol. 9, 1338–39.
18. Ibid., 341–44.
19. Levaillant, *La crise mystique de Victor Hugo*, 130.
20. Ibid., 136.
21. Ibid., 131.
22. Victor Hugo, *Oeuvres Complètes*, vol. 9, 1339–40.
23. Levaillant, *La crise mystique de Victor Hugo*, 135.
24. Victor Hugo, *Oeuvres Complètes*, vol. 9, 1402–4.
25. (Mlle) Adèle Hugo, *Journal III*, 275–76.
26. Victor Hugo, *Oeuvres Complètes*, vol. 9, 1456–58.
27. Victor Hugo, *Oeuvres Complètes*, vol. 10, 1521–22.

CHAPTER XVII. THE LION OF ANDROCLES

1. (Mlle) Adèle Hugo, *Journal III*, 328–29; Victor Hugo, *Oeuvres Complètes*, vol. 9, 1500.
2. Victor Hugo, *Oeuvres Complètes*, vol. 9, 1279.
3. Ibid., 1322.
4. Ibid., 1328.
5. Ibid., 1337–38.
6. Grillet, *Victor Hugo spirite*, 64–65.
7. Blackmore, *Selected Poems of Victor Hugo*, 356–63.
8. Victor Hugo, *Oeuvres Complètes*, vol. 9, 1343–44.
9. Victor Hugo, *Oeuvres Complètes*, vol. 10, 459.
10. Grillet, *Victor Hugo spirite*, 64–75.
11. Victor Hugo, *Oeuvres Complètes*, vol. 9, 1424.
12. Ibid., 371.

CHAPTER XVIII. ASTRAL VOYAGE TO THE PLANET MERCURY

1. Richard Westfall, *Never at Rest: A Biography of Isaac Newton*, 359–61.
2. Pearson, *Voltaire Almighty*, 220–21.
3. Charles Hugo, *Le Cochon de Saint-Antoine*, preface; Victor Hugo, *Oeuvres Complètes*, vol. 10, vol. 11, 1795–1803.
4. Kardec, *The Spirits' Book*, 126.
5. Grasset, *The Marvels Beyond Science*, 12–15.
6. Victor Hugo, *Oeuvres Complètes*, vol. 9, 1233–34.
7. Ibid., 157–59.
8. Ibid., 1422–23.

CHAPTER XIX. PLANETS OF PUNISHMENT AND WORLDS OF REWARD

1. Victor Hugo, *Toilers*, 84–85.
2. Ibid., 333.
3. Victor Hugo, *Oeuvres Complètes*, vol. 12, 30.
4. Ibid., 1171.
5. Saurat, *La religion ésotérique*, 28.
6. Victor Hugo, *Oeuvres Complètes*, vol. 9, 170.
7. Ibid., 200.
8. Ibid., 1442–43.
9. Ibid., 1448–50.
10. Ibid., 1442–43.
11. Ibid., 1262.
12. Ibid., 1425–26.

CHAPTER XX. "YOU WILL AWAKEN ME IN THE YEAR 2000 . . ."

1. Victor Hugo, *Oeuvres Complètes*, vol. 9, 1429–30.
2. Ibid., 1465–66.
3. Ibid., 1270.
4. Ibid., 1433–34.
5. Wilber, *Sex, Ecology, Spirituality: The Spirit of Evolution*, 422.
6. Victor Hugo, *Oeuvres Complètes*, vol. 9, 1435–36.
7. Ibid., 1439–40.
8. Ibid., 1440–42.

CHAPTER XXI. THE UNITED STATES OF EUROPE

1. (Mme) Adèle Hugo, "Lettres," 325.
2. (Mlle) Adèle Hugo, *Journal IV*, 290.
3. Ibid., 288.
4. Ibid., 289.
5. Ibid.
6. Ibid.
7. Ibid.
8. Ibid.
9. Ibid.

10. Ibid., 232–37.
11. Voltaire, *Dissertation*.
12. (Mlle) Adèle Hugo, *Journal IV*, 289.
13. Victor Hugo, *Oeuvres Complètes*, vol. 10, 736–39.
14. Ehrman, *Truth and Fiction in* The Da Vinci Code, xvii–xviii, 164.
15. Amazon.com, "Buller, Jodie."
16. Garlow and Jones, *Cracking Da Vinci's Code*, 112–13.
17. Ehrman, *Truth and Fiction in* The Da Vinci Code, 24.
18. Ibid., 47–49.
19. Ibid., 14.
20. Ibid., 21–23.
21. Ibid., 153.
22. Ibid., 142–44.
23. Ibid., 103, 106–7, 178.
24. (Mlle) Adèle Hugo, *Journal II*, 32.
25. Ibid., 66–67.
26. Victor Hugo, *Oeuvres Complètes*, vol. 10, 435–40.
27. Houston, 110.
28. Victor Hugo, *Oeuvres Complètes*, vol. 8, 817–34.
29. Picknett and Prince, *The Sion Revelation*, 338.
30. Ibid., 339.
31. Ibid., 346–49.
32. Viatte, *Illuminés*, 266–67.
33. Victor Hugo, *Oeuvres Complètes*, vol. 9, 376.

CHAPTER XXII. VICTOR HUGO, JAMES MERRILL, AND WILLIAM BLAKE

1. Merrill, *Sandover*, 8.
2. Ibid., 458–59.
3. Ibid., 167–71.
4. Personal Communication. January 28, 1978.
5. Martin, *Voices and Visions*, CBC-Radio.
6. Merrill, *Recitative*, 68.
7. Merrill, *Sandover*, 388–89.
8. Ibid., 143.
9. Ibid., 139–40.
10. Ibid., 145.
11. Ibid., 143.
12. Ibid., 151.
13. Ibid., 309.
14. Ibid., 511.
15. Ibid., 139.
16. Ibid., 145–46.
17. Ibid., 189.
18. Ibid., 217, 219.
19. Frye, *Fearful Symmetry*, 337–38.

20. Victor Hugo, *Oeuvres Complètes*, vol. 9, 1262.
21. Ibid., 1442.
22. Ibid., 1449–50.
23. Merrill, *Sandover*, 59–60.
24. Ibid., 360.
25. Ibid., 362.
26. Ibid., 461.
27. Ibid., 396.
28. Ibid., 439–40.
29. Ibid., 461.
30. Victor Hugo, *Oeuvres Complètes*, vol. 9, 376.
31. Houston, *Victor Hugo. Revised édition*, 69.
32. Marlan, *From the Black Sun*, 12–13.
33. Keynes, *Poetry and Prose of William Blake*, 860 (Poem in letter to Butts, Nov. 22, 1802).
34. Ibid., 846 (Poem in letter to Butts, Oct. 2, 1800).
35. Ibid., 188–89 (*Marriage of Heaven and Hell*).

CHAPTER XXIII. GALILEO EXPLAINS THE INEXPLICABLE

1. Cited in Yates, *Bruno*, 32.
2. Mendoza, "Metempsychosis and Monism in Bruno's nova filosofia," 282–83.
3. Cited in Yates, *Bruno*, 32.
4. Victor Hugo, *Oeuvres Complètes*, vol. 9, 1444–45.
5. Ibid., 1445–46.
6. Ibid., 1447–50.
7. Ibid., 1450.

CHAPTER XXIV. JOSHUA BRINGS DOWN MORE WALLS

1. Victor Hugo, *Toilers*, 366.
2. Victor Hugo, *Les Misérables*, 886.
3. Victor Hugo, *Oeuvres Complètes*, vol. 9, 1450–51.
4. Talbot, *Holographic Universe*, 16–17.
5. Ibid., 46.
6. Victor Hugo, *Oeuvres Complètes*, vol. 9, 1452–53.
7. Talbot, *Holographic Universe*, 41.

CHAPTER XXV. JESUS CHRIST REVISES HIS THINKING

1. Saurat, *La religion ésotérique*, 36.
2. Victor Hugo, *Oeuvres Complètes*, vol. 9, 1217.
3. Ibid., 1334–35.
4. Ibid., 1454–55.
5. Ibid., 1455–56.
6. Ibid., 1459–60.
7. Ibid., 1460–61.
8. Ibid., 1461–62.
9. Merrill, *Sandover*, 443–44.

CHAPTER XXVI. THE JERSEY SPIRITS

1. (Mlle) Adèle Hugo, *Journal IV,* 342–44.
2. Ibid., 250–51.
3. (Mlle) Adèle Hugo, *Journal III,* 151.
4. (Mme) Adèle Hugo, "Lettres," 255.
5. (Mlle) Adèle Hugo, *Journal IV,* 236.
6. Victor and Victor, "Eau de vie et songes et liqueur de rêves: Éloge de Jules Allix."
7. (Mlle) Adèle Hugo, *Journal IV,* 68–71.
8. Ibid., 250–52.
9. (Mme) Adèle Hugo, "Lettres," 326.
10. Victor Hugo, *Oeuvres Complètes,* vol. 9, 1584.
11. (Mme) Adèle Hugo, "Lettres," 326.
12. Saurat, *La religion ésotérique,* 158.
13. Ibid., 158–62.
14. De Mutigny, *Victor Hugo et le spiritisme,* 81–87.
15. Houston, *Victor Hugo. Revised édition,* 64.
16. De Mutigny, *Victor Hugo et le spiritisme,* 79–81.
17. Ibid., 80.
18. Victor Hugo, *Oeuvres Complètes,* vol. 9, 193.
19. Grillet, *Spirite,* 79.
20. Lesclide, *Propos de table de Victor Hugo,* 278.
21. Victor Hugo, *Oeuvres Complètes,* vol. 9, 385.
22. Ibid., 286.
23. Grillet, *Spirite,* 83.
24. Vacquerie, *Profils,* 401–3.
25. Grillet, *Spirite,* 82.
26. Houston, *Victor Hugo. Revised edition,* 65–74.
27. Blackmore, *Selected Poems of Victor Hugo,* 464.
28. Blum, *Ghost Hunters,* 185–87.
29. Ibid., 217–21.
30. Merrill, "The Art of Poetry," 196–97.
31. Merrill, *Voices,* VHS movie.
32. Blum, *Ghost Hunters,* 285.
33. Merrill, *Sandover,* 59.
34. Ibid., 107.
35. Ibid., 258.
36. Stapfer, *Victor Hugo à Guernsey: Souvenirs personnels,* 245–47.

APPENDIX

1. Victor Hugo, *Oeuvres Complètes,* vol. 9, 1363–93.
2. *Times Literary Supplement* 3, 295, "Hugo Turns the Tables," 308.
3. Victor Hugo, *Oeuvres Complètes,* vol. 9, 1172.
4. (Mlle) Adèle Hugo, *Journal III,* 192–93.

BIBLIOGRAPHY

Abry, E., C. Audic, and P. Crouzet. *Histoire Illustrée de la littérature française.* Paris: Henri Didier, 1922.

Appelbaum, Stanley, ed. *Introduction to French Poetry: A Dual-Language Book.* New York: Dover, 1991.

Baigent, Michael, Richard Leigh, and Henry Lincoln. *Holy Blood, Holy Grail.* London: Jonathan Cape, 1982.

Baudouin, Charles. *Psychanalyse de Victor Hugo.* Geneva: Mont Blanc, 1943.

Ben Abed Ben Khader, Aïcha, and David Soren, eds. *Carthage: A Mosaic of Ancient Tunisia.* New York: Norton (The American Museum of Natural History), 1987.

Blackmore, E. H., and A. M. Blackmore. *Selected Poems of Victor Hugo: A Bilingual Edition.* Chicago: The University of Chicago Press, 2004.

Blum, Deborah. *Ghost Hunters: William James and the Search for Scientific Proof of Life after Death.* New York: Penguin, 2006.

Brown, Dan. *The Da Vinci Code. Special Illustrated Edition.* New York: Doubleday, 2004.

Buller, Jodie. "*Holy Blood, Holy Grail* Review." This review can be found on Amazon.com, on the page advertising the book.

Chambers, John. "The Channeled Myths of James Merrill." *The Anomalist,* no. 5 (Summer 1997): 41–58.

Chénier, André. *Oeuvres complètes. Première édition intégrale.* Edited by Gérard Walter. Paris: Gallimard, 1958.

Daubray, C., ed. *Correspondence.* 4 vols. Quoted in Robb, 1998.

de Mutigny, Jean. *Victor Hugo et le spiritisme.* Paris: Nathan, 1981.

Deak, Istvan. *The Lawful Revolution: Joseph Kossuth and the Hungarians, 1848–1849.* New York: Columbia University Press, 1979.

Dow, Leslie Smith. *Adèle Hugo: La Misérable.* Fredericton, New Brunswick: Goose Lane Editions, 1993.

Ebon, Martin. *They Knew the Unknown.* New York: World, 1971.

Ehrman, Bart D. *Truth and Fiction in* The Da Vinci Code: *A Historian Reveals What We Really Know About Jesus, Mary Magdalene, and Constantine.* Oxford: Oxford University Press, 2004.

Flaubert, Gustave. *Salammbô*. Paris: Le Livre de Poche, 1970.

Frye, Northrop. *Fearful Symmetry: A Study of William Blake*. 2nd ed. Boston: Beacon Press, 1962.

Garlow, James L., and Peter Jones. *Cracking Da Vinci's Code*. Colorado Springs, Colo.: Cook Communications Ministries, 2004.

Gaudon, Jean. *Ce que disent les tables parlantes: Victor Hugo à Jersey*. Paris: Pauvert, 1963.

Georgel, Pierre, ed. *Drawings by Victor Hugo*. London: Victoria and Albert Museum, 1974.

Gobron, Gabriel. *History and Philosophy of Caodaism*. Saigon: Tu-Hai Publishing House, 1950.

Gooch, G. P. *The Second Empire*. London: Longmans, 1960.

Goodstein, Laurie. "It's Not Just a Movie, It's a Revelation (About the Audience)." *New York Times*, May 21, 2006, national edition, sec. 4:3.

Grasset, Joseph. *The Marvels Beyond Science*. London: Funk & Wagnalls, 1910.

Griffin, David Ray. "Why Critical Reflection on the Paranormal Is So Important—and So Difficult." *Critical Reflections on the Paranormal*. Edited by Michael Stoeber and Hugo Meynell. Albany: State University of New York, 1996.

Grillet, Claudius. *La bible dans Victor Hugo*. Paris: Emmanuel Vitte, 1910.

———. *Victor Hugo spirite*. Paris: Emmanuel Vitte, 1929.

Guerlac, Suzanne. *The Impersonal Sublime: Hugo, Baudelaire, Lautréamont*. Palo Alto: Stanford University Press, 1990.

———. "Phantom Rights: Conversations across the Abyss (Hugo, Blanchot)." *Diacritics* vol. 30, no. 3 (Fall 2000): 73–89.

Guille, Frances Vernor. *François-Victor Hugo et son oeuvre*. Paris: Nizet, 1950.

Guillemin, Henri. *L'Engloutie: Adèle, fille de Victor Hugo 1830–1915*. Paris: Éditions de Seuil, 1985.

Hill, Douglas. "Stones." *Man Myth & Magic: An Illustrated Encyclopedia of the Supernatural* 97 (1971): 2706–2708.

Houston, John Porter. *Victor Hugo. Revised edition*. Boston: Twayne, 1988.

Hugo, Adèle (Mlle Hugo). *Le journal d'Adèle Hugo*. Edited by Frances Vernor Guille. 4 vols. I: 1852; II: 1853; III: 1854; IV: 1855. Paris: Lettres Modernes Minard, 1968, 1971, 1984, 2000.

Hugo, Adèle (Mme Hugo). *Victor Hugo raconté par un témoin de sa vie*. 2 vols. Paris: Librairie International, 1863.

Hugo, Victor. *Les Misérables*. Translated by Lee Fahnestock and Norman MacAfee. New York: Signet Classic, 1987.

———. *Oeuvres complètes. Édition chronologique*. General editor Jean Massin. 18 vols. Paris: Club Français du Livres, 1967–71.

———. *Toilers of the Sea*. Translated by Isabel F. Hapgood. New York: Signet Classic, 2000.

Iranyi, Daniel, and Charles-Louis Chassin. *Histoire Politique de la révolution de Hongrie 1847–1848. Second Part: La Guerre*. Paris: Pagnerre, 1860.

Ireson, J. C. *Victor Hugo: A Companion to His Poetry*. Oxford, U.K.: Clarendon Press, 1997.

Jean, Raymond. *La dernière nuit d'André Chénier*. Paris: Michel Albin, 1998.

Kardec, Allan. *The Spirits' Book*. Las Vegas: Brotherhood of Life Publishing, 1989.

Keynes, Geoffrey, ed. *Poetry and Prose of William Blake, Complete in One Volume*. London: The Nonesuch Library, 1956.

Laing, R. D. *The Politics of Experience*. New York: Ballantine, 1967.

Lamartine, Alphonse de. *Oeuvres poétiques complètes*. Edited by M. F. Guyard. Paris: Gallimard, 1963.

Lazar, André. "Les émigres Hongrois dans les Îles de la Manche." *Le Bulletin de la Société Jersiaise* (1978): 176–80.

Leroux, Pierre. *La grève de Samarez*. 2 vols. Paris: Editions Klincksieck, 1979.

Lesclide, Richard. *Propos de table de Victor Hugo*. Paris: Dentu, 1885.

Levaillant, Maurice. *La crise mystique de Victor Hugo (1843–1856)*. Paris: Librairie José Corti, 1954.

Maison de Victor Hugo. An exhibition catalog. Paris: Ville de Paris, 1934.

Marlan, Stanton. *The Black Sun: The Alchemy of Art and Darkness*. College Station: Texas A & M University Press, 2005.

———. "From the Black Sun to the Philosopher's Stone." *Alchemy: A Journal of Archetype and Culture: Theory and Practice* 74 (Spring): 1–30.

Martin, Heather. *Voices and Visions: A Guided Tour of Revelation*. 2 vols. Toronto: Canadian Broadcasting Corporation-Radio, 1985.

Matlock, Jann. "Ghostly Politics." *Diacritics* vol. 30, no. 1 (Fall 2000): 53–71.

Maurois, André. *Olympio: The Life of Victor Hugo*. New York: Harper, 1956.

Mendoza, Ramon G. "Metempsychosis and Monism in Bruno's nova filosofia." *Giordano Bruno: Philosopher of the Renaissance*. Edited by Hilary Gatti. Burlington, Vt.: Ashgate, 2003: 273–97.

Merrill, James. *The Changing Light at Sandover*. New York: Knopf, 1982.

———. "The Art of Poetry XXXI." *The Paris Review*, no. 84 (Summer 1982): 184–219.

———. *James Merrill: Voices from Sandover*. VHS. Princeton, N.J.: Films for the Humanities & Sciences, 1994.

———. *Recitative*. Edited by J. D. McClatchy. San Francisco: North Point Press, 1986.

Moffett, Judith. *James Merrill: An Introduction to the Poetry*. New York: Columbia University Press, 1984.

Nietzsche, Friedrich. *The Birth of Tragedy and the Genealogy of Morals*. New York: Doubleday, 1956.

Nollman, Jim. *The Man Who Talks to Whales: The Art of Interspecies Communications*. Boulder, Colo.: Sentient, 2002.

Pakenham, Thomas. *Meetings with Remarkable Trees*. New York: Random House, 1996.

Pearson, Roger. *Voltaire Almighty: A Life in Pursuit of Freedom*. New York: Bloomsbury, 2005.

Picknett, Lynn, and Clive Prince. *The Sion Revelation: The Truth about the Guardians of Christ's Sacred Bloodline*. New York: Simon & Schuster, 2006.

Publishers' Weekly. "*The Da Vinci Code* Review." To view, go to Amazon.com and search on *The Da Vinci Code*; it will be found in the reviews.

Reynaud, Jean. *Terre et ciel.* Paris: Furne, 1854.

Rheinhardt, E. A. *Napoleon and Eugenie: The Tragicomedy of an Empire.* New York: Knopf, 1931.

Richardson, Joanna. *Victor Hugo.* New York: St. Martin's, 1976.

Robb, Graham. *Victor Hugo: A Biography.* New York: Norton, 1998.

Saurat, Denis. *La religion ésotérique de Victor Hugo.* Paris: La Colombe, 1948.

Scarfe, Francis. *André Chénier: His Life and Work 1762–1794.* Oxford: Clarendon Press, 1965.

Selected Poems of Victor Hugo: A Bilingual Edition. Translated by E. H. and A. M. Blackmore. Chicago: University of Chicago Press, 2004.

Shaw, George Bernard. *Androcles and the Lion: An Old Fable Renovated.* London: Penguin, 1946.

Simon, Gustave, ed. *Chez Victor Hugo: Les tables tournantes de Jersey.* Paris: Conard, 1923.

Stapfer, Paul. *Victor Hugo à Guernsey: Souvenirs personnels.* Paris: Société Française d'Imprimerie et de Librairie, 1905.

Starr, Chester G. *A History of the Ancient World.* Oxford: Oxford University Press, 1991.

Stevens, Philip. *Victor Hugo in Jersey.* Chichester, Sussex: Phillimore, 1985.

Stoekl, Allan. "Hugo's *Le dernier jour d'un condamné*: The End as Contamination." *Diacritics* vol. 30, no. 1 (Fall 2000): 40–51.

Stuart, Nancy Rubin. *The Reluctant Spiritualist: The Life of Maggie Fox.* New York: Harcourt, 2005.

Talbot, Michael. *The Holographic Universe.* New York: HarperCollins, 1991.

Times Literary Supplement [London] 3,295. "Hugo Turns the Tables." April 22, 1965: 308.

Tompkins, Peter, and Christopher Bird. *The Secret Life of Plants.* New York: Harper & Row, 1973.

Truffault, François, director. *L'histoire d'Adèle H.* Paris, 1975. Feature film.

Vacquerie, Auguste. *Les miettes de l'histoire. Second édition.* Paris: Pagnerre, 1863.

———. *Profils et grimaces. Nouvelle édition.* Paris: Pagnerre, 1864.

Vargas Llosa, Mario. *The Temptation of the Possible: Victor Hugo and Les Misérables.* Princeton, N.J.: Princeton University Press, 2007.

Viatte, Auguste. *Les sources occultes du romantisme. Tome premier: Le préromantisme. Tome second: La génération de l'Empire.* 2 vols. Paris: Librairie Honoré Champion, 1969.

———. *Victor Hugo et les illuminés de son temps.* Geneva: Slatkine Reprints, 2003.

Victor, Paul, and Mick Victor. "Eau de vie et songes et liqueur de rêves: Éloge de Jules Allix." Nov. 27, 2006 at 23:06. *Les Éloges*: #167: rss. www.paul-et-mick.com/index.php?2006/11/27/167-eloge-de-jules-allix. Accessed Feb. 17, 2007.

Voltaire. *Oeuvres Complètes: La Henriade: Dissertation sur la mort de Henri IV.* www.voltaire-integral.com/Html/08/24_Dissertation.html.

Walker, Benjamin. "Reincarnation." *Man Myth & Magic: An Illustrated Encyclopedia of the Supernatural* 84 (1971): 2346–50.

Weisberg, Barbara. *Talking to the Dead: Kate and Maggie Fox and the Rise of Spiritualism.* New York: HarperCollins, 2004.

Westfall, Richard S. *Never at Rest: A Biography of Isaac Newton.* Cambridge, U.K.: Cambridge University Press, 1980.

Wilber, Ken. *Sex, Ecology, Spirituality: The Spirit of Evolution.* 2nd ed., rev. Boston: Shambhala, 2000.

Yates, Frances A. *Giordano Bruno and the Hermetic Tradition.* Chicago: University of Chicago Press, 1964.

———. *The Rosicrucian Enlightenment.* London: Routledge, 1972.

INDEX